HART CRANE
&
ALLEN TATE

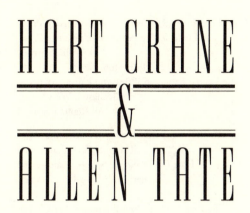

HART CRANE & ALLEN TATE

JANUS-FACED

MODERNISM

by Langdon Hammer

PRINCETON UNIVERSITY PRESS

PRINCETON, NEW JERSEY · MCMXCIII

Library of Congress Cataloging-in-Publication Data
Hammer, Langdon, 1958–
Hart Crane and Allen Tate : Janus-faced
modernism / Langdon Hammer.
p. cm.
Includes bibliographical references and index.
ISBN 0-691-06877-1
1. Crane, Hart, 1899–1932—Friends and
associates. 2. Tate, Allen, 1899–1977—Friends
and associates. 3. American poetry—20th
century—History and criticism. 4. Authorship—
Collaboration——History—20th century.
5. Poets, American—20th century——Biography.
6. Modernism (Literature)—United States. I. Title.
PR3505.R272Z6717 1993
811'.5209—dc20 92-27146

This book has been composed in Postscript Janson

Princeton University Press books are printed on
acid-free paper and meet the guidelines for
permanence and durability of the Committee on
Production Guidelines for Book Longevity
of the Council on Library Resources

Printed in the United States of America

1 2 3 4 5 6 7 8 9 10

For Jill

Contents

Preface

REGARD THE CAPTURE HERE, O JANUS-FACED.

—Hart Crane, "Recitative"[1]

This book has two poets at its center, Hart Crane and Allen Tate. Its subtitle, *Janus-Faced Modernism*, describes that double focus; it images the opposition between Crane and Tate as well as their connectedness. The subtitle also refers to the historical process in which both poets participate—the making of modernist literary culture in America, a process in which opposing energies contend and cooperate, working to undo traditional authority and to reconstruct it in new forms. The book's design reflects the relation between my particular focus and my general argument. The two central sections concern Tate and Crane, respectively, each poet being the subject of three chapters, while the two framing sections locate the story of their relations in the history of modernist poetry, from T. S. Eliot's arrival in London in 1914 to the publication of Robert Lowell's *Life Studies* in 1959. The history I construct around Crane and Tate concerns the struggle to define for poetry a place and purpose in twentieth-century American society. It is an account of poetry's ambiguous progress toward institutional sanction and professional organization, a story in which sexual identities, poetic traditions, and literary occupations are in question and at stake.

Crane and Tate were friends. They became acquainted in 1922 when they published poetry side by side in the *Double Dealer*,[2] and Crane wrote to Tate, "because your poem seemed so much in line with the kind of thing I am wanting to do."[3] Bonded by a shared sense of what it was they wanted "to do" in poetry, Crane and Tate were typical of a Jazz Age cluster of young authors, loosely conscious of themselves as a "generation," who claimed cultural authority by asserting a special aesthetic self-consciousness, an expertise in culture as such. When he first wrote to

ix

Tate, Crane was calling him to membership in that generation, a community formed across regions, outside of existing institutions, without official sponsors or accreditation, on the basis of its members' mutual dedication to the formal, self-reflexive properties and possibilities of art. As Raymond Williams puts it, "The artists and writers and thinkers of this phase [of modernism] found the only community available to them: a community of the medium; of their own practices."[4] Little magazines expressed and promoted the interests of this nascent community "of the medium"; in their pages its members learned to recognize each other and themselves. To return to those magazines today is to encounter a modernism bearing little resemblance to the literary period represented in textbooks: it is unstable, various, and unsorted; the names of contributors are misspelled; there are ads for shoe polish and candy and Great Books; and it all feels precarious—liable at any moment to close up shop and disappear, as little magazines very frequently did.

The future of that self-observing, self-authorizing, still largely unfunded literary culture is the issue in "Recitative," a lyric Crane wrote in 1924. It begins with this riddling address:

> Regard the capture here, O Janus-faced,
> As double as the hands that twist this glass.
> Such eyes at search or rest you cannot see;
> Reciting pain or glee, how can you bear!
>
> Twin shadowed halves: the breaking second holds
> In each the skin alone, and so it is
> I crust a plate of vibrant mercury
> Borne cleft to you, and brother in the half.

(Crane, Poems, 25)

As he often did with new work, Crane sent "Recitative" to Tate; when Tate wrote back perplexed, Crane gave this gloss: "Imagine the poet, say, on a platform speaking it. The audience is one half of Humanity, Man (in the sense of Blake) and the poet the other. ALSO, the poet sees himself in the audience as in a mirror. ALSO, the audience sees itself in the poet. . . . In another sense, the poet is *talking to himself*" (Crane, *Letters*, 176). In another sense, Crane could have added, *I am talking to you*. For Crane's letters repeatedly cast Tate in the roles of reader and confidant, interpreter and brother, as they summoned him to a union of "twin shadowed halves." The friendship in his early letters to Tate is a type of the mutually sustaining bond between men Crane projected in his poems, from his appeal to the "religious gunman" in "For the Marriage of Faustus and Helen" to his handclasp with Whitman in "Cape Hatteras." In each case, a scene of intimate communication between male peers prefigures the forging of a nonhierarchical, fully democratic community, which is the special promise of American modernity in Crane's work. In "Recitative," the poet's nightlong communion with his "brother in the half"—which could be a tryst as well as a vigil—culminates in a redemptive moment when "darkness, like an ape's face, falls away, / And gradually white buildings answer day." With this city in sight, Crane ends, in the manner of Whitman, by inviting his reader to set forth in step beside him: "And let us walk through time with equal pride" (Crane, *Poems*, 25).

Tate was eager to accept that invitation, however perplexed he may have been about the meanings of a poem like "Recitative." When he received Crane's first letter, Tate was a member of the Fugitives, a group of gentlemanly poets and intellectuals based in Nashville. The Fugitives have a central place in some studies of modern literature in the South; but it is really the later careers of Tate and three of his colleagues—John Crowe Ransom, Robert Penn Warren, and, to an extent, Donald Davidson—that make the group important. In the early 1920s, Tate viewed the other Fugitives as old-fashioned and amateurish, trapped in the middle-class manners of Nashville, as in many ways they were. By contrast, Tate saw Crane as the representative of a new, cosmopolitan avant-garde; in Tate's eyes, Crane stood for a modernism that challenged the traditional, identity-defining authority of religion, family, and region, and that approved the artist's freedom to respond to the demands and potential of the aesthetic medium itself. Under the banner of literary autonomy, Tate affronted his fellow Fugitives with arguments on behalf of experimental art, and he took the side of "the Moderns" against "the Tradition."

Throughout his career Tate remained an influential advocate and interpreter of modern literature, but the terms of his advocacy changed dramatically. The change can be seen in Tate's use of the word "modern" itself. In the 1920s, Tate joked with Davidson about his own "ultramodernism," and he wrote with conviction, as late as 1927, in "defense of modernism." But Tate would later look back on the late 1920s as a period when, moving toward the conservative anticapitalist politics of the Southern Agrarian movement, he and other former Fugitives were "rebelling against modernism."[5] In the latter case, "modernism" means something like "modernization"; the word has passed from Tate's literary to his political discourse, and it has become strongly pejorative in transit. At the same time, Tate has also revised his definition of the modern artists he

admired: rather than an avant-garde, they represent a *remnant* community, dedicated to the marginal but enduring values of premodern cultures. Or so Pound and Eliot, Yeats and Joyce (the latter disguised as "a
provincial Irishman"), enter Tate's later accounts of modernist literature,
each of them understood as a spokesman for "organic" form in both society and art. "Theirs is the right kind of modernism," Tate decided, "which
by opposing everything modern is reactionary."[6]

As he moved toward a modernism that opposes "everything modern,"
Tate turned away from Crane, and Crane turned away from Tate. Tate
came to see Crane as a romantic poet whose mystical claims to personal
"vision" seemed naive and reckless beside the learned skepticism of Eliot;
reduced to a cautionary lesson, Crane's work stood for a poetic ambition
that high modernist art had renounced. For his part, Crane no longer saw
Tate as an ally or "brother"; rather, Tate spoke for a developing intellectual consensus, a fashionable "pessimism" associated with *The Waste Land*,
from which Crane felt personally and programmatically excluded. Tate
had rejected the Whitmanian appeal to comradeship and "equal pride" in
"Recitative"; turning on Crane, Tate had turned against the liberating
promise of modernity.

These shifting alliances were charged with a particular sexual drama.
For Crane, the making whole of a divided self in "Recitative" was in part
a fantasy of homosexual identity freed from secrecy and shame, from the
burden of a double life "cleft" by desire for the same sex. Crane saw in
modernist texts a literature capable of including homosexual authors and
homosexual meanings: the future imagined in "Recitative" is "white," because its veiled sexual meanings, with the collaboration of readers like
Tate, will be fully and freely shared. When Tate declined to take part in
the future Crane envisioned, he withdrew as well from the sexual valences
of his friend's appeal. In effect, Tate's unfolding resistance to Crane allied
"the right kind of modernism" with an embattled heterosexual masculinity. At the same time, Crane's isolation as the "wrong" kind of modernist
converged with his isolation as a homosexual man. Pledged to prohibited
desires in art as in life, Crane wrote *The Bridge* in exile and defiance, acknowledging the hostility of the audience he addressed.

We might conclude that the sexual identities of these poets, straight and
gay, determined their ways of locating themselves in poetry, their literary
preferences and goals. In one sense, this is perfectly true: Crane's identification with Whitman was so much a part of his identification as a homosexual that Tate found himself unable to share in Crane's literary tastes
without being implicated in his sexual ones as well. But it is also true that

the positions these poets chose *in poetry* defined what it meant for them, as poets, to be gay and straight.[7] I want to emphasize how much was undecided when Crane and Tate first encountered each other, and, in that sense, how much was at stake.

The opposing roles Crane and Tate went on to create I will call those of "the genius" and "the poet-critic." They signify in literary, sexual, political, religious, and ethical registers; they also indicate professional identities shaped by new avenues of publication and employment. Eliot was central to every phase of these developments, a mediating figure through and against whom Crane and Tate defined themselves. Crane, resisting Eliot, approved the self-authorizing powers of "the individual talent" at the cost of standing outside the developing institutions and styles of high modernist art. Crane became a kind of outlaw. By contrast, Tate identified himself with "tradition," and adapted Eliot's stance to a career sustained by reviewing, literary criticism, and the teaching of poetry, including classes in "creative writing." As a poet and New Critic, Tate brought modernism into the American university.

The argument between Crane and Tate over Eliot came to a climax in 1926 when Crane was living in the country in Patterson, New York, with Tate and Caroline Gordon, the fiction writer, who had married Tate in 1925. The arrangement led to a bitter quarrel, both literary and domestic; and Tate and Gordon, who had invited Crane to join them, commanded him to leave. The collapse of their complex, ill-fated ménage was a pivotal moment in the lives and work of both poets; it is an emblematic event I return to repeatedly in this book, narrating it from the perspectives of Tate, Gordon, and Crane, in turn. The Patterson farmhouse is the scene of the rupture that drove Crane and Tate apart; at the same time, Gordon won a place for her fiction writing when she took over Crane's vacated rooms for her work. Gordon, I shall argue, first gained authority as a fiction writer by deferring to the expertise of "the poet-critic," her husband; and yet, in her late fiction, written after she became a Roman Catholic, Gordon identified with Crane, "the genius," against Tate.

The fundamental differences between Crane and Tate have meant that different readerships have valued them; in fact, they have seldom been discussed together, and never at length.[8] Of the two poets, Tate is the less familiar now. Although he lived to pronounce judgment on Crane's work, after 1960 Tate's reputation was obscured by Crane's, as the power of the New Criticism's canon of modern poetry waned and readers deliberately sought alternatives to it. As a result, where Tate is still discussed today, it is primarily as a Southern writer. Acknowledging the pertinence of that perspective, I will place Tate in another context, and use his career as a way into the American reception of high modernist writing. Tate was the critic who introduced the first volumes of poetry of both Hart Crane and Robert Lowell, a distinction that suggests his significance for thinking about the development of American poetry across midcentury, the customary boundary between modern and postmodern periods. If the scale and derivativeness of his poetry make Tate a minor poet, the range and representativeness of his literary career make Tate a minor poet of major interest.

The ambition and originality of Crane's poetry have never been in doubt, for either its admirers or its detractors. But these qualities have made Crane's work seem anomalous, hard to place in the field of modernist poetry. Tate's criticism is so crucial to Crane's reception that Crane scholars have always had to take it into account; but they typically do so in order to *extricate* Crane from Tate. Putting Crane and Tate together, I insist that Crane's pursuit of a major, culturally central poetry be read against and in relation to Tate's polemical refusal to sanction it. When he began *The Bridge*, Crane hoped his work would transcend "History and fact, location, etc." (Crane, Letters, 124); I will return his work to at least certain facts and locations—some of the contexts from which Crane's will to transcend context arises. I want to make modernism more important for a reading of Crane, and Crane more important for a reading of modernism.

Predominantly, this book draws on formalist analysis and biography: intertextuality and prosody are prominent; so are careerism, cruising, and madness. Whatever general argument can be made for these interpretive modes ("methods" sounds too scientific), there are good reasons for using them—and using them together—in this particular case. Reading lives and texts conjointly, I analyze the separation of "the literary" and "the personal" that modernist poetry constructs, and constructs by means of charged negotiations, lived and linguistic, of the kind investigated here. For Tate and Crane, that separation had both repressive and enabling effects; its centrality to their work and to modernism generally is suggested by Lowell's effort in *Life Studies* to get outside modernism precisely by making the personal literary. The life/work binary endures in confessional poetry's drive to override it—a fact which implies that, although it is possible and desirable to talk about a period shift between 1920 and 1960, the postmodern is made out of the modern.

In general, I am less concerned with where modernism came from than with where it went. That focus reflects the position of Crane and Tate in literary history. Examine a copy of the first edition of *White Buildings*, and the face you will find on the back cover is not Crane's but Ezra Pound's, for the back of the book jacket is an advertisement for Pound's *Personae*. The rooms Tate and Robert Penn Warren lived in as undergraduates at Vanderbilt were decorated, by Warren, with murals representing scenes from *The Waste Land*. Pound and Eliot were part of the world in which Crane and Tate learned to think and write. How would it feel to wake up in Nashville in 1923 to hand-colored, wall-sized pictures of "the rat creeping softly through the vegetation, and the typist putting a record on the gramophone"?[9] That situation made Tate and Crane postmodernists, like ourselves; it forced them, as much as Lowell or any American poet after him, to decide what it means to write "after modernism."

Their answers were in many ways unhappy. Crane's writing terminated in suicide. "Suicide," Walter Benjamin remarked, "is *the* achievement of modernism in the realm of the passions."[10] Tate lived forty-five years longer than his friend, and became an internationally recognized "man of letters"; yet Tate's willing submission to imaginative limits, enforced by privately torturous writing blocks, truncated his poetic production too. Still, it is possible to feel that Crane's leap to death and Tate's poetic droughts both affirm modernism's utopian potential. The silence these poets came to share can be heard as a refusal of the speech available to them, preserving, although in a negative form, the high purposes that called them to poetry.

Acknowledgments

This book is addressed and indebted to friends, several of whom I would like to mention here. To John Hollander, whose imagination, energy, and time sustained this project from the start, I am especially grateful. John Guillory was a shrewd and sympathetic reader, and a guide. Jeff Nunokawa teased and delighted and taught me during every phase of my work. Richard Halpern's good faith and intelligence set high standards for my own. Alfred Corn urged me on to the end of this manuscript with his eagerness to read it. I benefited from the responses of Harold Bloom and Marie Borroff to a draft of the whole; James Longenbach was an enthusiastic and insightful reader for Princeton University Press. I also learned and borrowed from the comments of friends who read particular chapters: Charles Berger, David Bromwich, Jonathan Freedman, Penelope Laurans, Susan Schultz, Heather White, and Elizabeth Wilson. For their encouragement and their examples, I am grateful to Richard Brodhead, Nathaniel Clark, Elizabeth Heckendorn Cook, Yannis Drossinos, Joseph Gordon, Wayne Koestenbaum, Vera Kutzinski, R.W.B. Lewis, J. D. McClatchy, Alan Trachtenberg, Candace Waid, and Jennifer Wicke. Meetings of the Marx Study Group delayed this book— and improved it. James Najarian checked facts, read proof, and made me think harder. Joan Hunter was a tactful and expert copy editor. Alan Golding and Veronica Makowsky both shared their writing with me and read mine with discernment. Brom Weber and Nancy Tate Wood answered queries. Thomas Underwood, Tate's biographer, helped in small ways and large. William Slater Brown talked with me about Tate, Gordon, and Crane on a July afternoon in 1990; and he gave me the portrait of Crane by William Lescaze that is so central to this book.

Becoming authors, the modernists I discuss left their families behind, or tried to. I want to bring mine forward now: Helen and Francis Selleck, Mary and Warren Campbell, Alice and Raul Léon. Cheri Pies cheered me. Forrester Campbell Hammer, who waited to be born until this page was written, will want to find his name on it. I write Jill Campbell's name here with special pride and pleasure. Her assistance has been intellectual, practical, spiritual, and continual.

The research for this book was begun with the support of the Whiting Foundation; the writing was completed with the aid of a Morse Fellowship from Yale University. The Frederick W. Hilles Fund sponsored manuscript preparation.

Parts of Chapters Five and Six were published in *Western Humanities Review*; an earlier version of Chapter Eight appeared in the *Yale Review*. I thank the editors of these journals for permission to reprint.

I am grateful to the following individuals for their help with my research and for permission to quote from material held in their collections: Don C. Skemer of Princeton University Library, Kenneth A. Lohf of Columbia University Library, Patricia C. Willis of the Beinecke Rare Book and Manuscript Library at Yale University, Rodney G. Dennis of the Houghton Library of Harvard University, and Marce Wolfe of the Jean and Alexander Heard Library at Vanderbilt University.

Previously unpublished material by Robert Fitzgerald, copyright © by Penelope Laurans Fitzgerald, is used by permission of Penelope Laurans Fitzgerald, literary executor for the estate of Robert Fitzgerald. Previously unpublished material by Allen Tate, copyright © by Helen H. Tate, is used by permission of Helen H. Tate, literary executor for the estate of Allen Tate. Previously unpublished material by Hart Crane, copyright © by David Mann, is used by permission of David Mann, literary executor for the estate of Hart Crane. The lines from *The Poems of Hart Crane*, edited by Marc Simon, are used by permission of Liveright Publishing Corporation © copyright 1986 by Marc Simon. Material from *Collected Poems 1909–1962* by T. S. Eliot and *Selected Poems* by Robert Lowell is reprinted by permission of Faber and Faber Ltd. Material from *Selected Poems* by Robert Lowell and *Collected Poems* by Allen Tate is reprinted by permission of Farrar, Straus & Giroux, Inc. Excerpts from *Collected Poems 1909–1962* by T. S. Eliot, copyright 1936 by Harcourt Brace Jovanovich, Inc., copyright © 1964, 1963 by T. S. Eliot, are reprinted by permission of the publisher.

I.

JANUS-FACED MODERNISM

ONE **Toward the Institute of Literary Autonomy and Tradition**

I MUST LEARN TO TALK ENGLISH.
—T. S. Eliot in 1914[1]

Until the recent and intensive reorganization of the field, "modernism" had for many years maintained a surprisingly stable and coherent meaning in American literary criticism. Lionel Trilling's remarks on the "adversary culture" of modernism come out of that consensus and reflect on it: "Any historian of the literature of the modern age will take virtually for granted the adversarial intention, the actually subversive intention, that characterizes modern writing—he will perceive its clear purpose of detaching the reader from the habits of thought and feeling that the larger culture imposes, of giving him a ground and a vantage from which to judge and condemn, and perhaps revise, the culture that produced him."[2] Whether the subversive intentions at issue were "philosophical" or formal and linguistic in nature, the modernist author Trilling evokes was a type of the sovereign individual, normatively white and male, a hero-artist defending his autonomy against the encroachments of "the larger culture." His story was "the legend of the free creative spirit at war with the bourgeoisie" (Trilling, *Beyond Culture*, xv).

Although it persists, this paradigm has been strongly challenged by scholars working in feminist criticism and African-American studies. The challenge has been partly archival. In the course of publishing and discussing formerly devalued modern writing, especially work by blacks and women, these critics have proposed new taxonomies of the modern, in effect redefining the conventional modernist canon as merely one grouping among many (and renaming it "masculinist," "male," or sometimes "Western"). The expansion of the field of modern writing not only denies to *The Waste Land* and *Ulysses* the splendid isolation they once enjoyed; it argues that the prestige of such works was asserted at the expense of other kinds of writing and experience. This argument holds that modernism's canonical texts are anxiously structured—like psyches—to uphold the privileges of white male elites. When modernism warns of chaos and decline, "What really seems under threat," Houston A. Baker, Jr., writes, "are not towers of civilization but rather an assumed supremacy of boorishly racist, indisputably sexist, and unbelievably wealthy Anglo-Saxon males."[3] Other revisionary discussions focus on the rival claims of "feminine," "popular," or "sentimental" writing. In their panoramic study of the period, Sandra M. Gilbert and Susan Gubar ask, "Which figure comes first, the neurasthenic man of letters or the imaginative female romancer?"[4] The question is rhetorical: the nervous man who wrote "Prufrock Among the Women" (as Eliot once thought to call his "Love Song") exemplifies "a modernism constructed not just against the grain of Victorian male precursors, not just in the shadow of a shattered God, but as an integral part of a complex response to *female* precursors and contemporaries. Indeed, it is possible to hypothesize that a reaction-formation against the rise of literary women became not just a theme in modernist writing but a motive for modernism" (Gilbert and Gubar, *No Man's Land*, Vol. 1, 156).

Andreas Huyssen advances a related hypothesis in his brief but ramifying essay, "Mass Culture as Woman: Modernism's Other." Modernism came into being, Huyssen proposes, "through a conscious strategy of exclusion, an anxiety of contamination by its other: an increasingly consuming and engulfing mass culture," which male modernists typically saw as "feminine."[5] The opposition between these two forms of cultural production is visible, according to Huyssen, in the vexed bond between the male author and the female heroine of one of modernism's founding fictions: "Madame Bovary, c'est moi," Flaubert teasingly confessed. But the novelist's imaginary femininity—his identification with the female consumer of mass-produced romance—is really only a preliminary moment in the process of his authorial self-definition. In the end, "woman (Madame Bovary) is positioned as reader of inferior literature—subjective, emotional and passive—while man (Flaubert) emerges as writer of genuine, authentic literature—objective, ironic, and in control of his aesthetic means," able even to confess his longing for the popular pleasures it has been his business as a high-art novelist to renounce (Huyssen, *After the Great Divide*, 46). In other cases, Emma Bovary's dreamworld of mass-produced fantasies becomes for the male modernist a nightmare in which the threats posed by woman and the masses converge in "a fear of nature out of control, a fear of the unconscious, of sexuality, of the loss of identity and stable ego boundaries in the mass."[6] "Seen in relation to this kind of paranoid view of mass culture and the masses," Huyssen concludes, in language strikingly close to Gilbert and Gubar's, modernism "begins to look more and more like a reaction formation, rather than like the heroic feat steeled in the fires of the modern experience" (Huyssen, *After the Great Divide*, 52 and 53).

The modernism one encounters in the criticism of Huyssen, or Baker, or Gilbert and Gubar is a vigorous demystification of "the men of 1914" (Wyndham Lewis's metaphor for modernism as battle);[7] it rejects a reading of modernism that Trilling thought beyond debate. But even as it overturns the old paradigm, and brings forward new texts (and contexts) for inspection, the new paradigm leaves certain features of high modernism's self-representation intact. The conceptual primacy of "reaction" in both paradigms illustrates my point. The political stance of the "reactionary" was proudly assumed by modernist poets such as Yeats, Pound, and Eliot; they claimed for their art a foundation in the culture of the past that isolated it from the degradations of democratic politics and middle-class manners. To call their modernism a "reaction formation" is to redefine significantly the motives of the "adversarial" position, and to refuse its ideal of aesthetic autonomy. But to interpret those poets in this way is also to accept too readily their claims to speak with and on behalf of traditional authority. I want to put those claims in question here. In particular, in the chapter that follows, I intend to argue that reactionary modernists did not defend an old cultural order, but that they struggled to legitimate a new one; and to this end they struggled both alongside and against other modern authors, other readings of the modern.

My evidence will come from the working lives of three American poets—T. S. Eliot, Hart Crane, and Allen Tate—each of whom found a different place for poetry in the economy of early twentieth-century capitalism. A banker by day and an author by night, the young Eliot separated economic self-interest and art in such a way as to maintain his commitment to both. Crane refused that arrangement, seeking in poetry a magical alternative to Eliot's separation of spheres. Tate preserved that separation—at the same time that he discovered, as an English professor, a way to make poetry paying work. Together, Crane and Tate created for themselves the competing roles of the outlaw and the cultural official, the genius and the poet-critic, roles that reflect the contradictions of modern poetry's status as a profession. I will fill out these claims through anecdotal case histories of Eliot, Crane, and Tate, in turn. First, though, I need to say something more about new and old modernisms.

Especially valuable in the work of recent critics, I find, is the insistence that modernism's claim to "a ground on which to judge and condemn ... the culture that produced [it]," as Trilling puts it, is itself relational, dependent on the Other from which modernism tries to set itself apart. That structure is central to this book. "The right kind of modernism," as I call the attitudes and practices Tate endorsed, arose in direct opposition to "everything modern," including a mass culture that Tate associated, often quite explicitly, with the threats of madness and castration. Tate's reactionary stance was, in its first and determining form, a mode of literary antiromanticism, crucially shaped by Tate's repudiation of the romantic vision he had at one time hoped to share with Crane. That act of repudiation clearly separated Tate from Crane, assigning to Tate the more "advanced," postromantic position of technical and ethical superiority. The same "act" (really a pattern of actions) can also be read as one man's homophobic rejection of another. I would say that it decisively crystallizes for modern American poetry the interlocking positions of the heterosexual and the homosexual male poet. The relation between those two positions, in Tate's imagination, is another version of the bond between Flaubert and Emma Bovary; and the paranoid view of mass culture Huyssen describes can be glimpsed in Tate's experience of another sort of paranoia: that is, the anxiety of contamination by the sexual Other called "male homosexual panic."[8]

The new model of modernism as a "reaction formation" is deeply resonant, then, for a reading of Tate, in particular. But the case of this self-professed reactionary suggests some of the explanatory limits of that model as well. For example, when Tate rejected Crane's romanticism, he created for himself a poetic identity that, for all its "reactionary" content, permitted Tate to make his way in a rapidly changing marketplace and eventually to become a model for the university-based, formalist poet of the postwar period. From a practical point of view, "reaction" was the pivotal move in a developing career: it enabled Tate to *get somewhere* (intellectually, professionally) rather than to remain where he was. The distinction is important because it reminds us that the reactionary stance of modernists like Tate needs to be located in an emergent, not an established, literary culture. In Huyssen's analysis, one feels that modernism was already there, in place, positioned precisely in such a way as to react. That is clearly the case for Baker. In Gilbert and Gubar's account, modernist antifeminism is read as a rearguard action (disguised as an avant-garde one) meant to reclaim male prerogatives from female usurpers. The historical model Gilbert and Gubar employ, derived from Eliot, aligns the female author with the individual talent—the principle of innovation and change—and the male modernist with tradition—an immobile structure that can only be " 'modified by the introduction of the new (the really new) work of art'—and, as Woolf remarked [in *A Room of One's Own*], that 'really new work' was women's work" (Gilbert and Gubar, *No Man's Land*, Vol. 1, 162).

I think one ought to be more skeptical of Eliot's claims to inherit a traditional authority, aristocratic and patriarchal in nature. Eliotic modernism and its New Critical permutations did indeed establish a powerful (and a powerfully *nostalgic*) style of white-male authority, but they did so in the context of a distinctively new cultural system, and to this extent Eliot's "tradition" did not previously exist. It is, rather, a special instance of a general modern activity: the construction of new pasts to legitimate new claimants to culture.[9] Eliot's appeal to "tradition" is aligned not only with the tradition building of other modern authors (the literary "renaissances" in Harlem and Chicago, Van Wyck Brooks's search for a "Usable Past"), but also with the administration of tradition in schools, where the "classics" of English literature had only recently become subjects of study. In this institutional setting, as Richard Ohmann observes, "English literature carried with it the prestige of the leisured class for whom it had long been a 'natural' accomplishment"; it represented "the birthright of the old elite" made available to—and adjusted to the self-image of—a new elite, middle class in its origins.[10] Modernist exponents of tradition such as Eliot and Tate took part in this transfer of social power, as the New Criticism's success in the university after 1940 attests. In so doing, they forged an aesthetic ideology for the *coming* organization of intellectual life and not (as they are frequently felt to have done) a defense of that which was passing away.

The old model of modernism as an "adversary culture" has something to offer here. For Trilling, reflecting on the history of modernism from his vantage point in the postwar university, "the adversary culture" had a definite shape: modernism was the "program" (in some ways, perhaps, the religion) of an ascendant social formation, growing in size and coherence, and recognizable "as a class." "As such," Trilling explained, "it of course has its internal conflicts and contradictions, but also its common interests and presuppositions and a considerable efficiency of organization, even of an institutional kind" (Trilling, *Beyond Culture*, xiii). It is customary for Marxist critics like Ohmann to call this social group "the professional-managerial class"; neoconservatives and "post-Marxists" prefer a formulation more mystical (and more modernist): "the New Class." Both of these formulations, like Trilling's "adversary culture," point to the emergence of "a new *cultural* bourgeoisie whose capital is not its money but its control over valuable cultures,"[11] a specifically "cultural capital" defined as the special knowledge, competences, and techniques elaborated centrally (but not exclusively) in the modern university. Modernist reactionaries, seen in this light, do not constitute "a beleaguered gentry."[12] Their class position is comparable to that of other professionals, and their shared "program," with its "internal conflicts and contradictions," is a particular form of professionalism.

One of those internal contradictions seemed to Trilling especially pertinent. "As with any other class, the relation [the adversary culture] has to the autonomy of its members makes a relevant question, and the more, of course, by reason of the part that is played in the history of its ideology by the ideal of autonomy. There is reason to believe that the relation is ambiguous" (Trilling, *Beyond Culture*, xvi). Highly ambiguous, in fact: "the adversary culture" liberates the individual from the controls of "the larger culture," but it requires that individual to submit to controls of its own, which include, paradoxically, "the ideal of autonomy." For Trilling, this contradiction intensifies when "the adversary culture" becomes more "populous" and when the subversive double question posed by modernism—"Is it true? Is it true for me?"—is replaced by another such question: "Is it true? Is it true for us?" "This is a good question too," Trilling allows. "It has its particular social virtues, but it does not yield the same results as the first question, and it may even make it harder for anyone to ask the first question" (Trilling, *Beyond Culture*, xvi). As Trilling's historical sketch implies, the will of "the adversary culture" to "aggrandize and perpetuate itself" as a class circumscribes the possibilities for personal autonomy. The collective form of "the adversary culture" is in conflict with the individualism it advocates.

Trilling's insight points to a contradiction Magali Sarfatti Larson finds characteristic of the modern professions generally. In Larson's analysis, which is sociological and economic rather than psychological and aesthetic, professions are organized for the collective pursuit of "individualistic ends." Trilling shows how this double structure limits individuality; Larson, from a Marxist perspective, shows how it limits collectivity. According to Larson, the process of profession formation typically involves two distinct but interlocking "movements." "One movement," she explains, "attacks the privileges of exclusive groups of traditional professionals and their de facto or institutionalized monopolies," opening existing markets to new claimants and the practice of new methods; "simultaneously, the other movement attempts to regulate competition by reconstructing monopoly," in effect checking "the democratization potential inherent in the expansion of professional markets."[13] There are two drives at work here, one inclusive and one exclusive, one democratizing and one elitist. Their interaction results in dialectical progress toward "the setting up of a *partial* community" (Larson, *The Rise of Professionalism*, 55).

Modernism, I mean to argue, tends in the same direction. I call it "Janus-faced" because it is ambiguous, not only ethically and politically, but historically so, being both old and new, peering both backward and forward in time. It is forward-looking in its manifold forms because it attacks the genteel monopoly on culture: by multiplying avenues of publication, allowing diverse personal and group affiliations, expanding rules of competence by experiment, enabling new kinds of self-representation, affirming individual autonomy, and establishing by all of these means (in Trilling's words) "a ground and a vantage from which to judge and condemn, and perhaps revise . . . the larger culture." But modernism looks backward too, because it institutes and enforces its own monopolies of cultural prestige, reasserts hierarchies of sexual and racial difference, and reconstructs traditional authority in restrictive ways. It is tempting to find the democratizing drive entirely in one kind of modernism and the elitist in another—or, as in the case of the present study, to see one poet as the bearer of modernism's liberating promise, another as the agent of its discipline. But these twin tendencies characterize all modernisms, to the extent that they take part in the "collective mobility project" Larson describes. Crane was right to see in Eliot's work a potentially liberating poetics, a way of writing that could be placed in the service of his utopian vision of human community. Yet Crane's work systematically insists on its own elite status. Modernism's democratizing and elitist drives are equally present in Crane's sense of himself as the privileged, individual possessor of a collective vision.[14]

The double nature of Crane's self-image also reflects the structure of professionalism's ideology of "merit." On the one hand, *anyone* can have it; on the other hand, only *some* do. By choosing to proceed without official sanctions, Crane became the modernist type of the autodidact—the intellectual amateur. This role was fundamental to the visionary powers Crane exercised: his poems could not have been written from another position. But Crane thereby committed himself—as he attempted to sustain the value of his enterprise—to alternating states of "megalomania" and agonized self-doubt. Critics of Crane's poetry analyze the manic-depressive cycles of his creativity in psychological terms. But the vertiginous alternation of moods in *The Bridge* is also a harrowing enactment of the contradictions of "merit." Eliot mastered those contradictions through a fantasy of institutional legitimation. The tradition is always behind Eliot as "cultural capital," a fund to which the perpetually bankrupt Crane did not have access. And, of course, the form of Eliot's solution was useful for others in a way that Crane's could not be. That is, Eliot's power to project "tradition" *as an imaginary institution* made it an important tool for those engaged in the construction of a real one. This actual institution—a "partial community" of the kind Larson describes—is the postwar university, the center of a system of literary patronage designed to evaluate and reward superior individual performance. That system is the horizon of this book; borrowing a phrase from John Crowe Ransom, I will call it "the Institute of Literary Autonomy and Tradition."[15]

It should be remembered that, however important he was to the academic reception of modernism, Eliot himself was not an academic. Indeed, Eliot only became an influential presence in the American university by leaving it—by giving up the study of philosophy at Harvard and the professorial life that awaited him to live and work in London. Of course, Eliot did not give up his erudition; he found another use for it. "It is not a permanent necessity that poets should be interested in philosophy," Eliot reflected in "The Metaphysical Poets";[16] and yet, after Eliot, such an interest became advisable. For Eliot made scholarship fundamental to the writing of modern poetry: by converting his education into expertise, Eliot became (as Pound liked to say of them both) "that rare thing among modern poets, a scholar."[17] Eliot's identity as scholar-poet was obviously the model for the poet-critic Tate became. How Eliot created that identity in the course of his professional dealings in London is the question I want to take up next.

In 1917, Vivien Eliot represented her husband's routine to his mother in the following way: "The incessant, never ending grind, day and evening—and always *too* much to do, so that he is always behind hand, never up to date—therefore always tormented—and if *forced* to rest or stop a minute it only torments him the more to feel that inexorable pile of work piling up against him" (*Letters of T. S. Eliot*, 185). Vivien Eliot, it may be objected, was excessively sensitive to the torments of everyday life. But she merely gives voice to the reader's own sense of the daily round transmitted in Eliot's letters. In 1917 Eliot was a full-time employee of Lloyd's Bank, a public lecturer on Victorian literature, a teacher of a course in Modern English Literature, assistant editor of the *Egoist*, a contributor to the *Monist* and the *New Statesman*, and, somehow, the author of a book of poetry called *Prufrock and Other Observations*. The "inexorable pile of work piling up" indeed! I emphasize the rigors of this schedule to make it clear that

Eliot's writing did not issue from leisure. Rather, the Eliot one meets in the first volume of his letters is the very type of the young professional, an anxious man working fanatically, at all hours, on all fronts, to get ahead. Which, in a remarkably short time, he did. The publication in 1988 of Eliot's letters was an event comparable in kind to the appearance of *The Waste Land* drafts and manuscripts in 1971. For each book disclosed the labor, the first intentions and second thoughts, necessary to the construction of a familiar modernist monument—except that the "monument" in question in Eliot's letters is not a text but the prototypical twentieth-century man of letters, the one who wrote *The Waste Land* and founded and edited the *Criterion*.

Louis Menand, who has written on the subject of Eliot and professionalism, begins his discussion with a letter Pound wrote to Eliot's father (at Eliot's instigation) in order to justify Eliot's plan to live and work in London. For Pound, Eliot's choice to begin his career in England rather than America implied the choice of a specific kind—or really a specific *level*—of literary occupation. To choose London, Pound felt, was to choose "the fine thing and the rare thing," since "Only here is there a disciplinary body of fine taste" capable of fostering and appreciating what is "fine" and "rare" (*Letters of T. S. Eliot*, 102). As Menand remarks, Pound did not defend Eliot's challenge to his father by appealing to the special demands of his genius. Pound instead proceeded on "institutional" grounds, asserting (in Menand's paraphrase) "that Eliot's work is important because it carries on in a useful and time-honored way the traditions of an ancient vocation"[18]—specifically, traditions that are maintained in England, source of English letters. Pound has it two ways, in short. For the autonomy of the son is upheld, and the father is asked to accept his desertion, but on condition that the son will submit to another kind of "disciplinary body," the patriarchal authority vested in tradition. So, too, the impractical choice of a free-lance literary career in London is defended in terms of deferred, but for the same reason ultimately higher, rewards. As Pound cannily saw, "a literary man's income depends very much on how rigidly he insists on doing exactly what he himself wants to do" (*Letters of T. S. Eliot*, 103).[19]

"Pound's letter to Henry Eliot suggests an obvious irony," Menand concludes. "The manner in which the modern artist tried to keep his ideological distance from the businessman, to guard the autonomy of his work, was also one of the ways in which the artist and the businessman were both, in spite of their self-conceptions, bound together" (Menand, *Discovering Modernism*, 100–101).[20] Eliot himself was fully aware of that linkage. He saw at once that disinterestedness was in his own best interest, and he learned how to cultivate it, despite "that inexorable pile of work piling up." Coolly and correctly, Eliot told his brother in 1919 (the year "Tradition and the Individual Talent" appeared in the *Egoist*): "I probably have more influence and power and distinction *outside* of the journalistic struggle and having no material stake in it" (*Letters of T. S. Eliot*, 283). "I am known to be disinterested," Eliot told his mother at the same time. "I know a great many people, but there are many more who would like to know me, and I can remain isolated and detached" (*Letters of T. S. Eliot*, 280). To remove oneself from the market, Eliot saw, was a powerful way to establish oneself in it.

As Jonathan Freedman argues, this career strategy of Eliot's extends a professionalist logic apparent in a literary movement that Eliot always took pains to stand apart from: British Aestheticism. "For what is the aesthete," Freedman asks, "but the consummate professional: the possessor of a 'monopoly of knowledge' about the provenance and extent of this mysterious entity, 'the aesthetic' . . . ?"[21] Oscar Wilde is the vexed type of the professional tastemaker, the consumer who is himself consumed by a restless and ambivalent popular audience. Eliot, like Wilde, propounds the authority of his own taste, but he disdains Wilde's audience, and he draws power from that stance: Eliot influences many by influencing the few. In Eliot's case, the postures of the connoisseur and the academic, the snob and the scholar, converge, giving personal taste a quasi-official authority, an institutional aura. That aura importantly depends on Eliot's claims to superior *technique*. Technique and taste suggest opposite values—reason and feeling, expertise and intuition. Yet they come together seamlessly in the youthful Eliot's prescription for a valuable criticism: "The closer one keeps to the Artist's discussion of his technique the better, I think, and the only kind of art worth talking about is the art one happens to like" (*Letters of T. S. Eliot*, 87). For Eliot, this stress on technique (vaguely ethical in character) responds to the compromised masculinity of a figure such as Wilde by removing taste from the sphere of consumption—the feminizing, promiscuous position Wilde took up—and placing it in the service of a conventionally masculine cult of production. This move allows Eliot to preserve the self-authorizing potential of taste while foregrounding *work* and making taste "useful" (i.e., productive, which, in this case, also means safely "male" and heterosexual). Conversely, once it has been linked to taste, technique is freed from its association with the *merely* useful, the mechanical and utilitarian.

Henry James preceded Eliot in these revisionary operations, as Freedman makes clear. It was James who first "took the stance of fastidious artistic dedication cultivated by the aesthete and detached it from what seemed to their contemporaries the aesthete's hedonism and artistic inefficiency; he remodelled the figure of the aesthete" into the technician on whom Eliot and Pound patterned themselves (Freedman, *Professions of Taste*, xxv). James's importance for these younger authors came from his self-consciously professional conception of literature as an elite but fully *acquirable* skill. Richard H. Brodhead explains James's "fantasy of vocational upgrading" concisely: "The novel becomes, in James's thinking, an arena of mastery—work susceptible to a special high grade of performance, that derives not from happy knack but from disciplined training in a special skill."[22] Two features of this Jamesian fantasy should be highlighted. First, James sees fiction writing as a process of refinement whereby the material of everyday life is recast under "the meaning-producing pressures of formal activity" (Brodhead, *The School of Hawthorne*, 115). Second, James views the capacity to write refined fiction as itself the outcome of a process of refinement. In this sense, James's progressive acquisition (and demonstration) of aesthetic mastery is comparable to the credentialization procedures typical of other professional careers.

Both of these processes—the act of fiction writing and the refinement of that act over the course of a career—are processes of *elevation*. For as he learns how to lift the raw materials of writing out of their local and contingent circumstances, and make of them something "fine" and "rare" and enduring, the Jamesian artist is also uplifted, and placed in the timeless realm of true art. It is "the supreme reward of an artist," Pound wrote in appreciation of James, "that the momentum of his art . . . should heave him out of himself, out of his personal limitations, out of the tangles of heredity and of environment, out of the bias of early training, of early predilections, whether of Florence, A.D. 1300, or of Back Bay of 1872, and leave him simply the great true recorder."[23] As this formulation suggests, Pound and Eliot read James's expatriation as a transformative renunciation, one which removed James from "the tangles of heredity and of environment" and admitted him to the sodality of great artists, including those such as Dante. Whether or not this matches James's understanding of his expatriation, it reflects Eliot's and Pound's understanding of theirs. By lifting themselves out of native entanglements, Eliot and Pound enacted the transcendence of time and place they sought in art, and entered the ranks of a fantasmatic elite. To Whitman's democratic proposition

that "to have great poets there must be great audiences too," Pound replied: "It is true that the great artist has always a great audience, even in
his lifetime; but it is not the *vulgo* but the spirits of irony and of destiny
and of humor, sitting with him."[24]

Pound's distinction between two types of audience, "the *vulgo*" and "the
spirits of irony," implies a distinction between two types of language. One
is vulgar, a language of utility, and it belongs in the marketplace; the other
is spiritual, a self-reflexive language, which is pure because it is turned
away from the market ("for itself"). This opposition is the linguistic sign
of the modernism/mass culture binary, and it points to the gendered distinction Gilbert and Gubar draw between ordinary and literary language,
"the common *materna lingua* and the 'civilized' *patrius sermo*" (Gilbert and
Gubar, *No Man's Land*, Vol. 1, 252). It can be glimpsed, I think, in Eliot's
quip after arriving in England and surveying his prospects: "I must learn
to talk English" (*Letters of T. S. Eliot*, 58). This is not a joke about British-
American mutual miscomprehension. It is Eliot's acknowledgment that
getting along in England will be like learning a language; that is, learning
to use it colloquially and shrewdly and self-interestedly, as any American
would want to; learning to "talk" it.[25] The trick is that the language Eliot
must learn is one he already knows: what he must do is change his *relation*
to—his ways of using—that language. "English," that is, stands in the
same relation to "American," Eliot's language of birth, as an "elaborated"
speech code stands in relation to the "restricted" code on which it is
based.[26] Whether Eliot was really an English or an American poet is not
an important question. Modernism meant *de-naturalization* for Eliot: only
a series of intimate estrangements—from his place of origin, his family, his
"native" language, his early self—could have made Eliot the particular
poet he was. In this respect, Eliot never changed nationality; he gave up
nationality in order to enter an international community, a community
unified not by its use of a specific language, but by its relation to language
as such.

Alvin Gouldner's theory of the New Class describes the relation to language I have in mind. For Gouldner, the New Class is first of all "a speech
community"—a linguistic environment—"characterized by speech that is
relatively more *situation-free*, more context or field 'independent' " than
ordinary language use (Gouldner, *The Future of Intellectuals*, 28). The suggestive but cumbersome name Gouldner gives that community is "the culture of critical discourse." The relative autonomy of its speech (which promotes "a *cosmopolitanism* that distances persons from local cultures") is a
function of its reflexivity: its preference for utterances that refer to them-

selves, to other utterances, and to rules of utterance generally. Jamesian formalism is a literary instance of this model; it is language that subjects life to "the meaning-producing pressures" of its own operations (its "formal activity"). To use language in this manner is to apprehend it *as* something to be used: as an instrument of social power, a medium to be mastered, a *techne*.[27] An elitism, specifically an elitism of performance, rooted in the school system, is essential to this relation to words. But there is a democratizing element in it as well. As Gouldner puts it, "The grammar of critical discourse claims the right to sit in judgment over the actions and claims of any social class and all power elites," in effect contesting the authority of money and birth. For the New Class presumes, on the basis of its special, "self-grounded" language skills, that "the established social hierarchy is only a semblance and that the deeper, more important distinction is between those who speak and understand truly and those who do not" (Gouldner, *The Future of Intellectuals*, 59).

Eliot was an agent of this invisible society, a deputy of the deep order of true understanding and right speech. But his challenge to "the established social hierarchy" was disguised by his complete assimilation to it— his mastery of "English," in all senses. Eliot's assimilation was facilitated and symbolized by his employment by Lloyd's Bank. At first a stopgap measure, the position in foreign currency quickly turned into the poet's livelihood and a source of considerable pride. There is every evidence that Eliot liked his work. But even if he had not, banking served Eliot, and it served his writing in particular. Banking made money that literature did not; it was compensatory, a supplement. But the bank also enabled Eliot, in his capacity as a man of letters, *not to make money*, and so to conserve the special value literature did have, which came from its disinterestedness (in Eliot's case, from scholarly isolation and detachment). Eliot's Bond Street suits confirmed his membership in English society at the same time, then, that they signified his refusal to compromise the highness of his literary calling. Eliot's costume asserted his standing in *both* "the established social hierarchy" and the invisible one Gouldner describes.

Eliot's ability to advance in both hierarchies at once reflected his unfailing comprehension of the power of prestige. Pondering an offer to become the assistant editor under John Middleton Murry at the *Atheneum*, Eliot listed the advantages in a letter to his mother: "1. Social Prestige. /2. Probably more leisure. / 3. More money at once" (*Letters of T. S. Eliot*, 276). One notes the order. One also notes Eliot's sense that prestige can be counted, like leisure time or money. Eliot combined the avarice of the social climber who *lacks* prestige with the candor and nonchalance of the

aristocrat who *already possesses it*. This tension reflects Eliot's claim to career advancement on the basis of merit—a status possessed "naturally," as
if by birth. Eliot refused the *Atheneum* offer for several reasons ("disadvan-
tages" that he also listed for his mother). Most important was the fact that
his employment at Lloyd's promised to preserve Eliot from discreditation
in "the journalistic struggle," an arena in which Eliot might very well appear (as other authors regularly did) self-interested. Eliot instead asserted
his individuality as a man of letters by identifying himself as "a company
man." The paradox disappears, or becomes more familiar, when we recognize that Eliot was not choosing between alliance and detachment, but
between two forms of alliance, one of which distinguished Eliot by isolat-
ing him from his literary peers. In this respect, the poet's fidelity to the
bank and his confidence in the reward that would follow from it suggest
a lived metaphor for the individual talent's relation with tradition.

Certainly Eliot's decision not to join the *Atheneum* accords with his
general wariness of the public literary associations open to him. He arrived in London later than Pound, and he kept his distance on the "Alliances" and manifestos Pound promoted. "*I* think you ought to emphasise
your isolation," Eliot advised Wyndham Lewis in 1921 (*Letters of T. S.
Eliot*, 446); that had been Eliot's own strategy all along. But the power of
Eliot's isolation was predicated not on absolute individuality but on his
membership (usually implied, not asserted) in the superior collective
called "tradition." Tradition was in Eliot's mind a league of the worthy,
not a "business association" (such as Amy Lowell once thought of forming
to halt the mass reproduction of Imagist verse).[28] Its elite society was accessible to individual talent, in certain cases, but never to group movements and their insurrectionary rhetoric. Modeled, in fact, on elite society
in its emergent modern form, tradition presented itself to Eliot as an aristocracy of merit.

Eliot's founding of the *Criterion* reflected his view of aesthetic value.
Indeed, as a magazine of the best modern literature, substantially funded
by a titled aristocrat, the *Criterion* materialized Eliot's fantasied alliance of
aristocracy and merit. "If we look for a mark of modernism's coming of
age," Michael H. Levenson suggests, "the founding of the *Criterion* in
1922 may prove a better instance than *The Waste Land*, better even than
Ulysses, because it exemplifies the institutionalization of the movement,
the accession to cultural legitimacy" (Levenson, *A Genealogy of Modernism*,
213). In contrast to the avant-garde, Bohemian *Little Review*, which came
out of an earlier cultural moment, the *Criterion* was self-consciously conservative, not to say stuffy. As Eliot put it, "My theory is that the best of
the most advanced writing of our time (which of course means a very small

number of writers) will really appear to better advantage among the really respectable and serious writers of the older type" (*Letters of T. S. Eliot*, 573). A theory of aesthetic value appears here in the form of an innovative marketing device. Eliot's image of the magazine called for "a good small format and paper, neat but no extravagance and not arty" (*Letters of T. S. Eliot*, 507). This format, avoiding cheap appeals, was meant to confirm the aristocratic bearing announced in Eliot's choice of name. But the magazine's sponsoring aristocrat, Lady Rothermere, found Eliot's product alarmingly dull. "Of course," Pound told his friend, "if she says it looks like a corpse, she's right, mon POSSUM, do you expect her to see what is scarce discernable to the naked eye, that it is *supposed* to be PLAYIN' POSSUM" (*Letters of T. S. Eliot*, 589). As Lady Rothermere's displeasure implies, Eliot's aristocratic stance exposes its parvenu aspect not in a penchant for excess—the usual way—but in an asceticism that hints at the work ethic behind it. The institutional look and feel of the *Criterion* are bureaucratic, not aristocratic, in character, and it points ahead to the institutionally sponsored quarterlies of the 1940s: the *Southern*, *Sewanee*, and *Kenyon* reviews.

When Eliot expressed his concern that he would lose Lady Rothermere's funding, or forfeit editorial control to her, Pound responded with sputtering lucidity: "Chrisssstttttt cant you see that *you are* the Criterion" (*Letters of T. S. Eliot*, 590). Pound was right: it was Eliot's special achievement to have made *himself* the price-setting instrument he sought in the *Criterion*; he needed the *Criterion* far less than it needed him. Pound, the showman and entrepreneur, was less mystified than Eliot about the individualism at the heart of professional collectivity.[29] Yet Eliot's deep personal investment in corporate authority, which his detractors have seen as a sign of incipient fascism, in fact preserved Eliot, politically and psychologically, from Pound's later excesses. Eliot could not validate individual virtù apart from collective regulation. The simultaneous progress of one man toward international acclaim and the Nobel Prize and the other toward incarceration, accusations of treason, and St. Elizabeths Hospital, unfolds a basic tension in modern American poetry in a fascinating way. Focused on another pair of poets, the present study will tell another version of that story. In the remaining pages of this first chapter, I want to place Crane and then Tate in a cultural situation which, it was clear to both poets, Eliot had already mastered.

Eliot thrived by separating his economic and his literary productivity: two independent spheres of activity, two different parts of the bourgeois male's day. This was essentially Wallace Stevens's procedure, too.[30] Crane, in contrast to those Harvard men, could not embrace this division of everyday life. Stevens's elegant adage, "Money is a kind of poetry,"[31] and its implicit corollary, "Poetry is a kind of money," were simply unacceptable to him. Crane wanted poetry to *be* money, to do away with money, to make money superfluous—to be manna; and his life recurrently illustrated the truth (for him) that one cannot make *both* money and poetry at the same time.

That dilemma was continuously present to Crane in the form of the family crisis that dominated his adulthood. The divorce of Crane's parents gave concrete form to the gendered opposition between the economic and the aesthetic in American life, making Crane's own "curse of sundered parentage" (as he called it in *The Bridge*) an emblem of the cultural disjunction from which modern poetry issued. As John Irwin has proposed, "Inasmuch as Crane had cast himself [in *The Bridge*] in the role of the prototypical twentieth-century American poet..., he had come to view his successful overbearing father—the millionaire candy manufacturer who invented the Life Saver and who considered his son's poetic career as a rejection of his own life's work in creating the patrimony of a family business—and his disabling, possessive mother, with her virulent midwestern blend of bourgeois Christian Science mysticism and Chatauqua artiness, as the prototypical parents of the modern American poet...."[32] C. A. Crane did not oppose his son's writing of poetry; but he felt that poetry should be written in leisure, since it could not be counted on for the paying work needed to support a family. Rejecting this definition of his responsibilities, Crane declined the place prepared for him, as son, in the reproduction of the family. That is, Crane refused to be "like" C. A. in his defining sexual and economic roles, to the extent that, for Crane, being like his father would mean *not* being like his mother, Grace. When, after his parents' separation, the seventeen-year-old Crane left his home in Cleveland, Ohio, for New York City, he accepted his mother's suggestion that he replace "Harold" with "Hart," his middle name and her patronymic.[33] Symbolically, the name Crane chose for his poethood honored both "sides of the house." Poetry would free Crane from having to choose between the mutually exclusive, asymmetrical alternatives represented by his parents—male and female, logic and emotion, business and art.

Early on, Crane's attempts to overcome those oppositions had a comical aspect. To read Crane's letters to his parents and his grandmother is, indeed, to encounter a young man as wayward and clumsy as Eliot was expert and focused, from the point of view of making money and augmenting prestige. In 1919, at the same time that Eliot was writing to his mother about the offer at the *Atheneum*, Crane wrote to his mother about a position at another magazine: "The editors of The Little Review have offered to let me take over the advertising and subscription department of the magazine on a commission basis. If once started up well along this line, the w[o]rk would prove to be reasonably remunerative for me. . . . There is no reason why The Little Review could not be developed into as paying a periodical as The New Republic, The Nation, or The Dial" (*Letters of Crane and His Family*, 126). Crane's plan to market modernism—he sees himself in this and other letters as a sort of Horatio Alger of avant-garde art—is exactly the opposite of the strategy Eliot employed. At first, things looked promising. A week after taking the job Crane had gained "a subordinate," thus doubling the size of his "department." With "several years experience," Crane's colleague proved "a wonder." "We expect to hawl in several years contracts next week of no less than $480. each," Crane explained to his mother. "We are after about all the great establishments on Fifth Ave., and I am learning a few things going about" (*Letters of Crane and His Family*, 131–32). Two weeks later, however, the "advertising man" had "gone on a spree or else left us completely"; Crane responded to the loss of his helper by raising his dream income to "$4,000 per year" (*Letters of Crane and His Family*, 133–34). Before Crane ceased to test his "capacities" in this manner, he had succeeded in procuring only two advertisements, one from the Crane candy company for "Mary Garden Chocolates," the other from a friend for his aesthetic services: "Stanislaw Portapovich—Maître de Danse."

Crane's entrance into the work force was not facilitated by education, elite or otherwise. When he left home, his parents, or at least his father, expected Crane to study for examinations that, once the equivalent of entrance requirements had been met, would allow him to enter Columbia College. Crane engaged tutors, with impressive French names, to that end. But he quickly gave them up, along with any talk of college. The seventeen-year-old Crane felt that he could educate himself—credentialize himself, even—according to his desires and needs. "I intend this week to begin my studying,—Latin, German, and philosophy, right here in my room," Crane reported to his father. Those subjects (which he never did study) promised "to balance my emotional nature, and lead me to more exact expression." Called on, he felt, to control his "overpowering" emotions, Crane planned "to build up" (like muscles) "the logical side" of his intelligence: this, he assured his father, was "the only manly, worthy, sensible thing to do" (*Letters of Crane and His Family*, 21–22). Crane's father, ever the literalist, suggested military school (*Letters of Crane and His Fam-*

ily, 28). As that response hints, Crane's avoidance of school was also a way of avoiding the normative curriculum of heterosexual male development. Indeed, Crane's choice of sexual pleasures was consistent with his general resistance to the cultural injunction to "grow up," an imperative Crane resisted on the grounds that he was *already* grown, and able to determine his own imperatives. That resistance accounts for Crane's poetic reputation for both precocity and "immaturity." In his aesthetic confrontation with Eliot, as we will see, it informed Crane's conviction that Western civilization was not in decline, and that he himself was not "belated." In art as in life, the refusal to "act his age" expressed Crane's faith in his power to authorize himself.

Or, to find authorization in others like himself, outside of existing institutions. That is the model of comradely relations we have already seen in "Recitative." The reconciliation in that poem of "twin shadowed halves" promises a unity of mind that is different in kind from the one Crane describes in the letter to his father about the correct "balance" of mental faculties. The latter relation, structured like Eliot's unified sensibility, is hierarchical, since balance is attained only when logic controls emotion. The gender markers in Crane's letter make it clear that this "balance" is modeled on a male-dominated heterosexual union, like that of his parents. "Recitative," by contrast, projects an elective relation between peers, for which his own homosexuality was Crane's implied paradigm. "Homosexual production takes place according to a mode of non-limitative horizontal relations," Guy Hocquenghem suggests, "heterosexual reproduction according to one of hierarchical succession."[34] For Crane, male homosexuality indicates a "horizontal" order of desire validated not by the father (as in the patriarchal tradition Eliot posits) but by a brother or "second self." It disrupts the vertical, monogamic order of heterosexual reproduction, traditionally conceived, and projects in its place a self-authorizing community of equals.

For a time, Greenwich Village seemed to offer Crane such a community.[35] The Village was Crane's college. The education he gained there did not impose the usual distinction between formal aesthetic training and everyday life: Crane studied both writing and sex "right here in my room." The literary friends that Crane made in the Village were not homosexual; in many ways they were homophobic, as Crane learned quickly enough. But the modernist rhetoric of experiment and revolt they shared gave him a language in which to articulate alternatives to the sexual and economic disciplines of patriarchy. For the most part, the young middle-class whites who lived in the Village when Crane did had come to the city from elsewhere; it was a place for the displaced, where the traditional markers of social status—money and birth—mattered less than the insignia of "personal character" and life-style.[36] From the point of view of Crane and his peers, Greenwich Village was a community of private life, isolated from economic activity, in which personal autonomy could be cultivated. This spirit of separatism challenged "the established social hierarchy," and it unified otherwise widely divergent groups and practices. In 1917 *both* John Sloan and Marcel Duchamp—leaders of the Ashcan School and the avant-garde, respectively—were among the artists who "climbed into Washington Square arch" and, "at midnight, to the accompaniment of toy pistols, . . . declared Greenwich Village 'a Free Republic, Independent of Uptown.' "[37]

But of course the Village was not independent of Uptown. The Village revolt was made possible by the same economic forces that created "Madison Avenue," and it gave voice to the emerging imperatives of consumer society as insistently as the advertising industry itself. Freedom, self-expression, "paganism," the New Woman, youth—the "anti-Puritan" values of the Village were also the basis of a consumption ethic fostered by business in response to vastly accelerated production. "In the death of patriarchy," Stuart Ewen dryly remarks, "both libertarians and business had a stake."[38] Crane recognized the new intimacy between creativity and profit; he did not see that these terms were held together by being held apart. When he set out brightly as the advertising manager of the *Little Review*, Crane believed that the application of some simple business sense could make modernist writing turn a profit. Disappointed in that hope, Crane took another approach: he would find a place for his imaginative skills in the world of business; he would put art to work for advertising, rather than advertising for art. Crane moved in this direction in 1921 when, having returned home to Ohio, he took a copywriting class at Western Reserve University in Cleveland. Crane was hired by an established Cleveland firm, but he chose to move into the office of a direct-mail advertiser—unwisely, since his new employer dismissed him when business slowed down. Disgusted, Crane again left Cleveland for New York, where, at length, he got the break he had wished for: a job in the statistical department of J. Walter Thompson. "*To those who know*," Crane informed his mother, "it is a very flattering connection" (*Letters of Crane and His Family*, 168).

Quite so. The J. Walter Thompson Company was already, in 1923, one of the largest and most prestigious firms in the world. Thompson's skyscraper views thrilled Crane, confirming his sudden social elevation.

Crane got the job partly on the strength of a letter from Waldo Frank, the visionary social critic and fiction writer; and this helped Crane feel he was entering a fully cultured establishment, a business that recognized and rewarded employees with special intelligence, feeling, and taste. "They employ a lot of real writers as copy writers at Thompson's and have an entirely different feeling about art & business than you encounter any place west of N. Y.," Crane wrote home to his mother. "In fact its a feather in your cap if you know a little more than you're 'supposed to' here" (*Letters of Crane and His Family*, 175). But Crane's rise in the corporate hierarchy would be neither quick nor assured, despite the feather in his cap. In the 1920s, New York advertising executives increasingly came from colleges, and Ivy League colleges in particular: the "self-made" man had as much difficulty in business as in art. Furthermore, when Crane did move from statistics to copy (with no increase in salary), he found that "creativity" was a controversial asset. "Advertising agencies . . . had unfortunately been infiltrated by 'unappreciated poets and unstaged dramatists,'" Roland Marchand explains, summarizing an industrywide debate. "Critics of the passion for self-expression reminded their colleagues that an advertisement was 'not a personal thing' but was best produced by group effort"; and these "appeals to pride in a narrowly defined craftsmanship usually carried implications of dedication to a career of sacrifice."[39] For which Crane had no desire. Five months after joining Thompson's, Crane quit. He talked vaguely of traveling to Cuba or working on board a ship. In a "run-down state," Crane retired to Woodstock, New York, to live and write in the company of two friends, Slater Brown and Edward Nagle.

The woods and the sea: these places held out for Crane a vision of communal life on the model of, but superior to, the one he knew in the Village; they promised Crane a complete unity of work and leisure, freedom from heterosexual arrangements, and the possibility of writing poetry. Eliot separated business and art by conducting them both, each in its place. Fitting poetry into the existing social order, Eliot placed poetry on the side of that order, in the center of the city. In contrast, by refusing to write only "after hours," Crane rejected civility, and placed poetry in the wilderness (often in the urban wilderness of the subways and docks). In this way, as in others, Crane challenged Eliot's restriction of poetry's "scope": he was willing to let poetry take over his day, to give himself to it *wholly*. (This is the aspect of his career that made Crane—as a man, rather than a poet—such a powerful figure for Lowell, as we will see.) And yet, of course, poetry did not provide the utopian alternative to the offices of J. Walter Thompson that Crane sought. That poetry was riven by the same tensions that structured other professions is clear from the fact that, like the copywriter, the modernist poet was called to a cult of sacrifice and craft—an "extinction of personality" on behalf of the group. In poetry Crane would be subject to another version of the professional discipline he fled from in advertising. That is the lesson he gained from Tate. In turn, Crane gave Tate an image of poetic possibilities Tate would sacrifice in exchange for professional authority.

We have now seen two answers to the question of how a modern American poet might make a living. In their different responses to the opposition between business and art, Eliot and Crane seem to me exemplary. But also idiosyncratic: Lloyd's did not employ many poets; the *Little Review* needed not even one advertising manager. Tate is another matter. As a poet-critic, he became a poet universities paid *for being a poet*—despite the suspicions with which colleagues and administrators viewed him, despite the insecurity and marginality of some of the positions he held. In this respect, Tate lived, eventually, the kind of life that a great number of American poets have lived in the second half of this century. I say "eventually" because Tate did not become an English professor quickly or easily. Accordingly, rather than concentrate, as with Crane and Eliot, on key decisions early in a writing life, I want to consider the progress of Tate's career as a whole. Fugitive Poet, Southern Agrarian, New Critic—the sharp definition of Tate's successive literary roles make them seem more discontinuous than they were. In fact, those three roles reveal a highly consistent intention: they are all ways of defining the literary intellectual in and through a professional collective.

In a sense, Tate was just as much of an autodidact as Crane—a fact that accounts for some of the vehemence with which Tate sought to distinguish himself from Crane, after 1926. The same should be said of R. P. Blackmur, one of Crane's most moralizing readers, who, like Crane, lacked a college diploma. Tate did have a B.A. from Vanderbilt, but no higher degree, and of course he had no official accreditation in the writing of verse. Tate's poetic reputation depended (as it still does) on his membership in the Fugitive group. Although Tate met Ransom and Davidson and Warren through Vanderbilt, and they are frequently referred to as "the Vanderbilt Fugitives," the group had no formal institutional affiliation. It was first organized, rather, as a Saturday night meeting of Southern gentlemen who wished to discuss philosophy after dinner—a style of gathering that was rooted in the kind of literary "society" once found throughout genteel America. Tate's embarrassment about the old-fashioned, amateurish aspects of the Fugitive group is marked in the sharply self-deprecating letters he wrote to Crane, a peer whose intimate knowledge of modernist art made him seem much more advanced. In contrast to Crane's Village friends, Tate presented his fellow Fugitives as backward and provincial, trapped in bourgeois Nashville. As Tate tersely put it, "Existence here amounts to intellectual castration."[40]

Within the group itself, Tate fought for standards. "GUTS are the sine qua non of art," Tate told Davidson, enraged by the group's decision to publish in the *Fugitive* a poem by one of its several less accomplished members. "Art is a grim dominion," he continued, "and personalities have no place in it" (*Davidson and Tate*, 66). Tate's macho investment in impersonality implies the intensity of the pressure he felt to separate himself from the emotional, "feminine," and amateur. These threats come together in the young Tate's anxious relation to the South—and to his mother, Eleanor Parke Custis Varnell, who had taught her son to revere their antebellum Virginia ancestry. As an expression of (among other things) a shared commitment to impersonal art, the Fugitives first published their poems under pseudonyms. But the repressed personal circumstances of Tate's creativity returned in the name he chose. "Henry Feathertop" is a Hawthorne character in *Mosses from an Old Manse*, a scarecrow-man whom Mother Rigby, a "cunning and potent" witch, stuffs with straw and dresses in the garb of her dead husband. As Veronica A. Makowsky, Caroline Gordon's biographer, has noticed, Tate's "choice of pseudonym seems to hold his mother responsible for his anxieties about his identity and existence,"[41] especially Tate's fear that his love of the Old South was unmanning.

The inaugural editorial statement of the *Fugitive* declared its authors to be in flight from "the high-caste Brahmins of the Old South."[42] Tate put this policy into action with his own form of expatriation when he went to live in New York City, at first as Crane's guest, in 1924. Tate was driven forward by his ideal of a cosmopolitan community of art, a metropolitan elite of the kind Pound imagined in his writing on Henry James. Tate began to think and write extensively about the South after the *Fugitive* published its final number in 1925. But it was not until 1929 that he wrote to Warren and Davidson with a "tactical program" to promote a "Southern movement" (*Davidson and Tate*, 229), inaugurating the Agrarian phase of his career. Coincidentally, Davidson had just sent Tate the prospectus for "a collection of views on the South" that would become the book of Agrarian essays called *I'll Take My Stand* (*Davidson and Tate*, 227). *I'll Take My Stand*, much more than "a collection of views," presented itself as a unified defense of the South's "minority right to live its own kind of life" in opposition to Northern technology, capital, and state power.[43] If the Fugitives set out to escape the Old South, the Agrarians were passionately engaged in defining and, to the best of their abilities, reclaiming it.

Yet the "Southern movement" was first of all a *literary* project, a publishing venture, which reunited the most serious literary artists of the Fugitive group. This fact is important because it suggests that the reactionary political aims of the new group, always hazy in articulation, were subordinate to, or indeed in the service of, professional ones. The Agrarians, unlike the Fugitives, were not based in one place; they banded together first of all to produce a book, and the differing impulses and interests among them rapidly carried them in different directions. Davidson, who later held that Agrarianism had failed, was moved by regional fervor and a racist political vision—enthusiasms that led him, in the 1950s, to write on behalf of business-led opposition to the federal enforcement of civil rights legislation in the South.[44] Tate, who later looked back on Agrarianism with satisfaction, had other purposes in mind, as his "tactical program" makes evident. In 1929, Tate envisioned Agrarianism as "an academy of Southern *positive* reactionaries made up at first of people of our own group" who would begin their work by writing "a philosophical constitution," a systematic statement of group beliefs (*Davidson and Tate*, 229). Theory came before practice, the general before the particular. So it is not surprising that Tate, writing to Davidson from France, where he had taken a Guggenheim Fellowship to write a biography of Jefferson Davis, believed that the Southern movement should be based "less upon the actual old South than upon its prototype—the historical social and religious scheme of Europe." The elite members of the Fugitives, reunited as Agrarians, would help Tate to establish the cosmopolitan intellectual culture he had left them to join. "We must be the last Europeans—there being no Europeans in Europe at present" (*Davidson and Tate*, 230).

The differences between Tate's and Davidson's Agrarianism emerged clearly enough in a fight over the name of the symposium. Davidson and Ransom favored "I'll Take My Stand," a phrase from the Confederate marching song "Dixie"; Tate opposed it urgently. "It is an emotional appeal to ill-defined beliefs," he wrote in protest; "it is a *special plea*. The essays in this book justify themselves *rationally* by an appeal to principle" (*Davidson and Tate*, 406). Tate was anxious lest the Agrarians antagonize "the general, particularly the 'foreign,' reader"; nor did he wish to play to nativist "sympathies": his emphasis was on reason, not emotion; the cosmopolitan, not the local. Both the internecine form of the argument and its intellectual content, then, were reminiscent of Tate's objections to the publication of "personal" poetry in the *Fugitive*. As a Fugitive, Tate valued impersonality and craft; as an Agrarian, he sought philosophical rationality—justification "by an appeal to principle," not to blood. In both roles, Tate affirmed the universalist values Gouldner calls "the grammar of critical discourse."

These aspects of Tate's Agrarianism suggest that even at the height of his idealization of the planter aristocracy, Tate spoke on behalf of the New Class, not the Old South. When Tate and the other Agrarians quarreled with proponents of state-administered farming, it was not, therefore, a conflict between "two different types of intellectuals—one traditional: clerical, humanistic, petit bourgeois; the other technical: bureaucratic, scientific, professional—belonging to two different social formations";[45] it was a conflict between two forms of professional organization in a single class. The distinction matters when we try to assess the relation of Agrarianism to the New Criticism, for Tate and Ransom in particular. The transition from the middle phase of their careers to the later did not mean, for either man, giving up or selling out: it was an *extension* of the logic of their earlier association, by which they obtained institutional power. For Ransom, it was a calculated and strategic choice to put his energy into aesthetic, rather than social, theory. "The signal for this shift came in late 1936," Daniel Joseph Singal relates, "in a pair of heartfelt letters to Tate setting forth a plan for an '*American Academy of Letters*' (to be called the 'Institute of Literary Autonomy and Tradition'), which would devote itself to upholding high 'objective' standards in literature" (Singal, *The War Within*, 218). Although it was national and literary, rather than regional and political in definition, Ransom's "academy" is a version of the academy Tate proposed, in 1929, to Davidson. As general intellectuals, the Agrarians struggled to establish a public role for poets; as specialists, the New Critics succeeded in establishing such a role. The right place for Tate's "academy" turned out to be academia.

"If," Gerald Graff writes in his history of English studies in America, "there was a single career whose personal trajectory perfectly coincided with the institutional fortunes of criticism, it was that of John Crowe Ransom."[46] "Coincided with" may be too cautious: reading Graff's book one is impressed by the singular force of Ransom's actions and example at a pivotal moment in the development of "The Profession" (as English professors today grandly and ambivalently refer to their guild). Ransom's decision in 1937 to accept a lucrative professorship at Kenyon College took him away from the South and from Vanderbilt, where he had taught English for almost twenty years. Symbolically, the move marked the end of Ransom's regionalism and validated the controversial mode of criticism Ransom practiced. But the move was not only symbolically important; it gave Ransom substantial institutional resources with which to disseminate the New Criticism (a term Ransom himself made famous). These resources included the *Kenyon Review* and, after 1948, with the aid of the Rockefeller Foundation, the Kenyon School of English, an institute for graduate students and junior faculty. Ransom became an educator of educators. He was working in the same direction in his criticism. The essays in *The World's Body*, published in 1938, consisted not in criticism, Ransom wrote, but in "preparations for criticism."[47] They were the kind of philosophical reflections on principle Tate wanted; today they would be called "theory." In those essays, above all in the mystical image in the book's title, Ransom preserved, as literary values, the social values of his Agrarianism. But then Ransom's farmers, whom he called "the most important bloc of free spirits to have survived the modern economy,"[48] always had more in common with characters in the poetry of Robert Frost, or with Ransom's own "Antique Harvesters," than with rural Tennesseans. It is not that Ransom did not care about the farming people he spoke for in his Agrarian period, but that he cared about them in ways poetry had taught him to. Ransom had seen the tiller as a poet. Henceforth he would see the poet as a tiller, as the exponent of a traditional craft through which he maintained his freedom from the modern economy.

The irony of this development is that the poet-tiller's craft, his link to traditional society and a defense against the modern economy, was also the *expertise* which won for him a place in that economy; it was the specialized, disinterested knowledge on which he would stake his authority as a teacher and critic in a professional market of services. Craft meant technique—not only prosody, but a formal apprehension of structures, linguistic and narrative, that could only come from long and intensive study of tradition. In the final chapter, I will discuss Tate's supervision of Robert Lowell's education in poetry, which took place out of school, on Tate's lawn. The procedures of Tate's personal tutorial looked back to the workshop practices of the Fugitives and ahead to the teaching of "creative writing" in college (which Tate initiated at Princeton in 1939). But before American poets taught writing workshops, they wrote critical essays on Donne. Noting that many of the New Critics were also poets, Graff remarks that, at least in these cases, poetry was criticism's way into the university, a form of knowledge through which New Critics like Tate established their authority without advanced degrees, against the resistance of historical scholars (Graff, *Professing Literature*, 153). This is true, but it could also be turned around, since criticism was *poetry's* way into the university too. The hyphenated form poet-critic expressed an addition, a further development: it indicated a poet with the capacity not only to write poems but to reflect on them, to write about them, and to teach them. The poet-critic was not merely another innocent poet, one given to idealizations of a romantic nature; he was clear-eyed, modern, and scientific. Yet he was not a scientist either, an abstract intelligence trained only to take things apart. Ransom believed that poetry and criticism, properly conducted, both seek knowledge of "whole objects." True poetry, like the criticism that studies it, is "a technical act" granting access to "the untechnical homely fullness of the world" (Ransom, *The World's Body*, xi).

Eliot learned to talk English; Tate and Ransom learned to teach it; and in so doing they gave institutional form to Henry James's "fantasy of vocational upgrading." (James was of course the New Criticism's paradigmatic prose writer. When Caroline Gordon set out to prove herself as a novelist, it was perforce "the Master" she emulated, as we will find.) The Jamesian revision of British Aestheticism that Freedman analyzes is completed, then, by Tate and Ransom: they make a dedication to art-for-art's-sake paying work, a fully professional occupation. When Tate proposed his Agrarian academy to Davidson, he believed that *"Organization and discipline are indispensable"* (*Davidson and Tate*, 231). These values were preserved even after Tate had given up the cause. They pointed to a traditionalist art, a scientific criticism, and an institutionalized literary collective Ransom called, only half-jokingly, "Criticism, Inc., or Criticism, Ltd." (Ransom, *The World's Body*, 329). Tate could never have used that phrase without distaste. He was always more hostile to science than Ransom, and more suspicious of bureaucracy; Tate remained an outsider in the university, and unlike Ransom, he was always more of a poet than a critic. But for the same reasons, Tate insisted even more stringently than Ransom on the priority of technique in poetry. In criticism, Tate came to value text-specific, craft-centered observations over the "techniques" of the New Criticism itself.[49] In the end, Tate's narrowing sense of the limits of poetry takes his thinking to a pass where the poet can only speak through, and the critic about, the formal properties of poetry.

Tate's fierce antiromanticism set this high aestheticism apart from the bad aestheticism of the fin de siècle. Ransom was more clinical. For Ransom, "the poetry written by romantics, in a common sense of that term," was pathologically motivated: its idealizations were "the act of a sick mind," displaying "a poor adaptation to reality; a sub-normal equipment in animal courage; flight and escapism; furtive libido" (Ransom, *The World's Body*, ix). These comments (delivered, again, only half-jokingly) call up the dread and contempt Tate felt, in his Fugitive phase, for the personal. The misogyny they imply is made explicit in Ransom's remarkable essay on Edna St. Vincent Millay, "The Poet as Woman." Ransom praises Millay as "the best of the poets who are 'popular,' and loved by Circles and Leagues of young ladies," while he also explains that such a talent naturally "horrifies . . . a little" the male critic. The combination of "attachment and antipathy" Millay stirs in Ransom leads him to reflect on the problem of sexual difference generally: "The minds of man and woman grow apart, and how shall we express the difference? In this way, I think: man, at best, is an intellectualized woman. Or, man distinguishes himself from woman by intellect, but he should keep it feminized" (Ransom, *The World's Body*, 77). At a glance, Ransom's formulations may seem uninteresting—only a slight variation on Freud's tendency to see woman as a man who lacks something. And Ransom's "intellect" is indeed phallic: it is what men have to show for themselves that women do not. But Ransom's more intriguing claim is that the intellectual man is, "at best," a phallic woman. Ransom wants to retain a primary, imaginary femininity as the ground of poetic value; he *needs* to retain it, in fact, because the feminine position is essential exactly to his claim to be *more* than a scientist or businessman. It is the ground of his claim to spiritual and even political authority. He wants to be Millay, then—but also something more: more mature, more intellectual, more professional. In short, Ransom wants to be a critic as well as a poet. His essay is another version of Flaubert's "Madame Bovary, c'est moi."

Ransom's effort to distinguish men and women on the strength of the former's "intellect," and yet to insist that the intellect should be kept "feminized," demonstrates how imperfectly he had resolved the conflict between business and art. For Ransom and Tate, the value of the aesthetic depended for its defense on the articulation of an ideal male type: the whole or complete man. This aim was very close to the aspiration Crane expresses in, for example, "Recitative." But the unity of mind Tate and Ransom projected was based on the heterosexual paradigm Crane described, at seventeen, for his father's approval—a passage which, in his review of Crane's letters, Tate singled out to assert the clarity and dignity of Crane's early position, the height from which he fell when he was "confirmed in his homosexuality" (Tate, *Essays of Four Decades*, 325). Tate preserved himself from dissolution, he believed, by the force of logic and technique, but in such a way as to emphasize force. As Roy Harvey Pearce

acutely puts it, "The craft [in Tate's poems] is characterized by a tighten-
ing of the prosodic reins so great as to evoke for the reader an almost
unmediated hysteria. The poet cannot afford to let go."[50] The next part of
this book will study that hysteria, which I take to be an important symptom—in some ways, an achievement—of the adversary culture. The contradictory nature of the new, whole man the New Critics spoke for will be
apparent in the fact that Tate pursued psychological and spiritual "unity"
by breaking with Crane. Let me begin to put those different models of the
modern poet back together now by returning to the point at which they
permanently came apart: the winter of 1926, when, in different rooms of
the same house, Crane drafted "Atlantis" and Tate began "Ode to the
Confederate Dead."

II.

TATE: THE RIGHT KIND OF MODERNISM

TWO | *The Realism of* The Waste Land

In late December 1925, Hart Crane came to live with Allen
Tate and Caroline Gordon, who were renting part of an isolated farmhouse in Patterson, New York.[2] To both poets, worn down by the demands of improvised jobs in Manhattan, the arrangement looked like a
companionable pastoral. As he set to work on new poems, Tate could earn
a small income—and perhaps a wider reputation—from the writing of reviews; and Crane, the surprised recipient of a one-thousand-dollar gift
from the patron-banker Otto Kahn, could begin in earnest the epic poem
he had planned since 1923. But their partnership would quickly prove impossible, as the two friends found themselves caught up in less than
friendly competition. And that competition came down to an argument
over the poetry of T. S. Eliot.

During the first weeks of his stay, Crane drafted the main body of "Atlantis" or what he then was calling the "Finale" (although it was in fact the
first full section to be written) of *The Bridge*[3]—the epic poem Crane envisioned as a counter to Eliot's "pessimism." Tate, already skeptical about
The Bridge's "new cultural synthesis of values" (Crane, *Letters*, 223), replied by deepening his ties to Eliot. That winter Tate sent twelve poems
and an essay to Eliot. Eliot wrote back expressing interest in both the poetry and the prose, holding out the possibility of publication in the *Criterion*.[4] "I wish I had a lyric or so to circulate, like Allen," Crane responded.
"He suddenly sprouted last week and has been going ever since. A letter
from Eliot indicates that the Criterion may take some of his poems."[5]
Tate's sudden productivity, which Crane linked to Eliot's personal en-

33

couragement, may have included the beginnings of the intensely Eliotic "Ode to the Confederate Dead."[6] There is no doubt that, by the end of March, Tate was at work reviewing Eliot's *Poems: 1909–1925*. Tate's essay, which appeared in the *New Republic* in June, called Eliot the preeminent living poet and implicitly challenged Crane's promised recovery of the epic mode. In Tate's view, Eliot's poems definitively marked the end of "the traditional inspiration."[7] With *The Bridge* then "in feverish embryo," Crane complained about the emerging modernist consensus Tate's review had given voice to. "*Is* the last statement sentimentally made by Eliot [Crane was citing the last lines of *The Hollow Men*: 'This is the way the world ends'], is this acceptable or not as the poetic determinism of our age?! I, of course, can say no, to myself, and believe it. But in the face of such a stern conviction of death on the part of the only group of people whose verbal sophistication is likely to take an interest in a style such as mine—what can I expect?" (Crane, *Letters*, 236). As urgent as they are resigned, Crane's questions came with the recognition that Tate had taken Eliot's side against him.

Meanwhile, domestic misalliance parodied the literary debate. Gordon, who had her second novel, as well as the cooking and cleaning, to see to, was overburdened. (Tate made breakfast; Crane, when he did any work, did the dishes.) Gordon and Tate had seen their invitation to Crane partly as an act of charity, and Kahn's gift had dramatically altered Crane's circumstances. "Hart arrived in the country in African chief's costume and eating caviar," Tate remembered later. "The Tates were downstairs eating turnips and Crane was upstairs eating caviar."[8] Crane's extravagance aggravated Gordon in particular, who may have felt his intrusion as a specifically sexual threat to her marriage with Tate. As she cooled toward him, Crane commissioned the cooking and washing facilities of the owner of the house, Mrs. Addie Turner, thereby setting up an alternative household (a ménage that Gordon, with Crane's homosexuality and Mrs. Turner's dotage in mind, called "material for a Eugene O'Neill play."[9] Concerning Mrs. Turner, Ann Waldron furnishes this interesting information: "People called her a widow, but her husband, Blind Jim, had been in the insane asylum for five years. He fancied he was a girl and wore beads around his neck and flirted with a fan" [Waldron, *Close Connections*, 47–48]). Matters rapidly deteriorated. Crane thought that the Tates had turned mean-spirited and morose; Tate thought that Crane was irresponsible and imperious; and Gordon bemoaned the presence of "a romantic in the house" (Gordon and Wood, *Southern Mandarins*, 22). In January Tate had called Crane "one of the finest men alive—if possible, finer than his poetry" (*Davidson and Tate*, 157). By the third week of April the Tates let Crane know (in writing, since they were no longer speaking) that he would have to go.

In letters to his mother and friends Crane railed against both Tate and Gordon, but Crane was angriest with Gordon; she had led the way, he felt, in forcing him out.[10] Veronica Makowsky remarks that, if Crane's account can be credited, "Caroline may have been demonstrating her territorial rights over Allen to the homosexual Crane"; clearly, in Crane's version of events, "Allen seems somewhat passive, the warred over, rather than the warrior" (Makowsky, *Caroline Gordon*, 67). But even if Gordon attacked Crane to assert her exclusive possession of Tate, she was acting in the interest of her "passive" husband too.[11] For the domestic farce that Tate, Gordon, and Crane played out that April resolved the literary argument in which the two poets were locked by driving Crane from the field. We will investigate Gordon's and Crane's different perspectives on these events later on. At this point I want to emphasize only that Tate's decisive alignment with Eliot coincided, in a precise and very practical sense, with the Tates' eviction of Crane. The implication, I think, is that Tate consolidated his ties with Eliot by severing, however temporarily, his ties with Crane.

This economy of personal and literary relations is worth contemplating because, until 1926, Tate had seen no reason to choose between the two poets. Indeed, when Crane and Tate first exchanged letters in 1922, Tate was moved to recognize *both* Crane and Eliot as "his models" (Crane, *Letters*, 102). When Tate took up the cause of "the Moderns" against Ransom, Davidson, and other members of the Fugitive group, he invoked both Eliot and Crane to support his position.[12] Even as late as 1925 Tate found in Crane's visionary lyricism a persuasive example of the unity of sensibility that Eliot esteemed, and that Tate called "the kind of poetry that integrates emotion with intellect" (*Davidson and Tate*, 142). Yet Tate would later judge *The Bridge* a failure precisely because the poem demonstrated a disintegration of the mental faculties: a judgment that converted all of Crane's poetry into an object lesson in Eliot's dissociation of sensibility. "Far from 'refuting' Eliot," Tate eventually summarized, "[Crane's] whole career is a vindication of Eliot's major premise—that the integrity of the individual consciousness has broken down" (Tate, *Essays of Four Decades*, 321).

The simple permanence of that judgment, which Tate never substantially altered, which R. P. Blackmur, Yvor Winters, and other critics upheld, and which Crane's suicide could be seen to strangely confirm, gives it the intractable feeling of fact. So much so, indeed, that Crane's admirers usually have had to work to prove that (as Lee Edelman conveniently puts it) "the poetry was *not* incoherent, was *not* confused, was *not* seriously obscure."[13] Edelman's observation specifically refers to the tasks of Crane scholarship during the tenure of the New Criticism. It is by no means certain, though, that the situation has entirely changed; at least, when a critic such as Harold Bloom cites a passage from "Atlantis" beside another from *The Waste Land*, with a commentary on Crane's transcendence of Eliot's model, some form of the same argument is clearly still going on.[14] I would suggest in fact that the fairly recent rise of Crane's reputation is coordinated with the equally recent *devaluation* of Eliot's. This systematic alteration of critical taste is consistent with the tendency of poststructuralist interpreters to sustain, even as they revalue, conceptual oppositions central to the New Criticism: symbol and allegory, speech and writing, unity and difference.[15]

I want to suspend the competition between Crane and Eliot long enough to describe, in the context of Tate's career, the logic of their conflict. Accordingly, I will not be concerned with espousing or rejecting but with examining Tate's obviously tendentious censure of Crane. Why, I am wondering, did Tate change his mind about Crane? How could Tate have been, by his own lights, so entirely wrong? This chapter will approach these questions by examining the historical conditions that, according to Tate, the failure of *The Bridge* both indicated and obeyed. For poets and critics such as Tate, *The Waste Land* itself established those conditions.

In May 1926, shortly after Crane left Patterson to continue writing *The Bridge* in Cuba, Donald Davidson wrote to Tate asking for his evaluation of the preliminary drafts of (as Tate described it) "a Tennessee Faust" (*Davidson and Tate*, 166). Even if Davidson's poem, later entitled *The Tall Men*, resembles *The Bridge* only at a distance, the epic scale these poems share allowed Tate to resume with Davidson the conversation he had broken off just three weeks before with Crane. For although Tate replied that he "couldn't predict" "the possible success . . . of such a poem in the grand style," his letter is actually a tensely argued statement of the reasons why a modern epic—whether Davidson's or Crane's—could not possibly succeed. It was not, Tate was certain, a matter of the individual talent.

> I am convinced that Milton himself could not write a Paradise Lost now.
> Minds are less important for literature than cultures; our minds are as good
> as they ever were, but our culture is dissolving. Plotinus was as profound as
> Plato, but not so good a philosopher. Arnold was more intelligent than
> Shelley, but not so good a poet. Something happened to us in Arnold's time.
> You can't escape it even in Tennessee! (*Davidson and Tate*, 166)

What he gives with one hand, Tate takes away with the other, as the insistence on the perfect continuity of mind in one clause ("our minds are as good as they ever were") is countered by the observation that "our culture is dissolving" in the next: even Milton could not write *Paradise Lost* in 1926, lacking the stable inheritance of dogma, ritual, and belief, the unitary culture, that had once made epic possible. For Tate, the dissolution of the culture is imagined as the loss of an informed, aristocratic audience and the heroic genres fashioned in its image—a process of disintegration ending in the impasse Tate defines here as the modern poet's lack of an adequately "important" theme, ready to hand. "You can't put your epic of Tennessee into the minds of Tennesseans," Tate explained. "The precondition of your writing is that it must (in an equivalent of spiritual intensity) be already there" (*Davidson and Tate*, 167).[16]

The definition of an epic theme as that which cannot be invented, only inherited, locates the possibility of epic beyond the scope of any individual's conscious intention. You can't put epic into culture, Tate is arguing, any more than you can set out to construct the grammar that must be "there," already in place, before anyone begins to speak. The point is close to Matthew Arnold's contention that the production of "great literature" requires, for "its data, its materials," the kind of "current of ideas" that once flowed through "the Greece of Pindar and Sophocles" and "the England of Shakespeare."[17] But we can gauge the distance between Tate and Arnold by the strength of Tate's conviction that consensus, once collapsed, cannot be *deliberately* restored. For Arnold believed that criticism could still reconstruct the public language and social authority that British Romantic poetry, confronted with the eclipse of religion, had tried and failed to generate from private feeling. Tate's assessment of Arnold as *both* "more intelligent" and less successful than Shelley approves Arnold's statement of the problem but rejects his solution: *neither* criticism nor poetry can expect to derive from its own activity the "data" which that activity itself demands. As a critic, then, Arnold accurately describes the problem that, in Tate's view, as a poet he exemplifies.

Tate's term "culture" should therefore be distinguished from "the best that has been thought and said." Instead, Tate means the aggregate of myth and custom that the anthropologist studies, and he understands the making of a given culture not as the conscious project of specific persons and groups (Arnold's humane "aliens," for example), but rather as the occult emanation of a homogeneous "people." "If anthropology has destroyed the credibility of myths," Tate would later write, explaining the failure of Crane's "religious impulse" in *The Bridge*, "it has shown us how they rise: their growth is mysterious from the people as a whole. It is probable that no one man ever put myth into history" (Tate, *Essays of Four Decades*, 317–18). Of course, this formula might just as well be turned around, since Tate supposes that the emergence of a science that is capable of describing our *need* of myths depends, precisely, upon their inaccessibility. Arnold is a lesser poet than Shelley, in this respect, precisely *because*—and not although—he is the "more intelligent." The critical intelligence presents itself to Tate, following Max Weber, under the sign of demystification; it is aligned with science rather than religion, and it is opposed to the mythopoeic thinking that "Shelley" stands for in Tate's letter. This mode of thinking Tate imagines (with nostalgia, not scorn) as fundamentally *naive* or precritical, still in touch with the common grammar of belief.

The movement toward demystification, which coincides with the mind's progressive estrangement from "the people as a whole," may be lamentable (Arnold really *isn't*, in Tate's judgment, as "good" as Shelley), but it is also irreversible. That either Crane or Davidson should believe otherwise can only indicate the regressive force of self-deception—a failure on their parts to recognize the historical fact of cultural belatedness. When he first announced his intention to write *The Bridge*, Crane believed himself potentially "quite fit to become a suitable *Pindar* for the dawn of the machine age, so called" (Crane, *Letters*, 129). "We are Alexandrians," Tate wrote in a review of Spengler, which was published the same week he wrote to Davidson, "for our sole remaining activity in letters is morphological research into the past."[18] Alexandrianism, in this sense, evokes that moment of decay when tradition can no longer be extended, merely venerated.

Yet Tate's terminal sense of vocation should be measured against his rapid success in the role he set out for himself. I suggested in Chapter One that "reaction" was for Tate a pivotal move in a developing career. That move can be isolated with some precision. In 1926 Tate began his most celebrated and possibly his most ambitious poem, "Ode to the Confederate Dead"; he would soon visit Civil War battle sites in preparation for a biography of Stonewall Jackson, which was published alongside his first volume of poems, *Mr. Pope and Other Poems*, in 1928. In 1928 Tate also received a Guggenheim Fellowship toward work on another biography, this time of Jefferson Davis,[19] which permitted Tate and Gordon to spend the following year in France. Between 1926 and 1928, then, Tate discovered his mature style, a substantial audience, and adequate financial support (in the form of a new, prestigous grant). Tate's ideas about the "dissolution" of Western culture led directly to the material consolidation of his career; his letter to Davidson, lamenting the lack of a theme, had actu-

ally provided one. Although disinherited of his themes by history, the modern poet could still seize the theme of history itself.

And yet in the letter to Davidson, Tate is strikingly casual about actual events. "Something happened to us," he declares, moving from Plotinus and Plato to Arnold and Shelley in a breath. There is no word here of industrial capitalism, secularization, or positivist science—the massive social agencies behind the dissolution of the culture, according to Tate's somewhat later accounts. So, too, the measured distinctions between authors that Tate would no doubt enter in a published essay have been dismissed here in the excited, offhand cinching of an argument. And that argument, it turns out, has less to do with the mind's relation to the culture than with the relation of Tate and his contemporaries to T. S. Eliot. The letter concludes with the following postscript:

> Why has Eliot's The Waste Land held people against their will? Because it exhibits the present state of European culture and tells us what we hate to believe—that our traditional forms are dead. It struck a spiritual accord in every sensitive mind; some minds gave in, others combatted it: the one attitude was as significant as the other. (*Davidson and Tate*, 167)

These sentences seem to me highly suggestive, not least of all because they restate, in the register of modern literary history, the passage of cultural commentary I quoted earlier. "You can't escape it even in Tennessee!" Tate told Davidson about the dissolution of the culture, and Tate was just as clear about the options: it was not simply prudent, it was necessary, to submit to the conditions of the culture, and this meant, in practice, giving up the ambition to write a poem "in the grand style." Tate makes the same point in the postscript to this letter, but with this signal difference: here it is *The Waste Land* that is inescapable, that forces the mind into positions of submission and combat, and "tells us what we hate to believe—that our traditional forms are dead." Of course, there is not any doubt about what Tate means to say here—that *The Waste Land* merely reveals, as one piece of evidence among others, the state of the culture in which it was made—but the peculiarly arresting power Tate attributes to the poem enforces a much larger claim: it is the privilege of *The Waste Land* not only to obey, but to compel others to obey, the conditions of its making. The contest between mind and culture passes into literary history as the contest, already decided, between Eliot's poem and the minds of its readers.

Tate's interpretation of *The Waste Land* as a text radically opposed to the will of its readers begins to disclose the structure of that modernism so turned back upon its origins as to oppose "everything modern."

Before we examine the logic of that reading, and assess its consequences for Tate's evaluation of *The Bridge*, it will be helpful to glance at an earlier and quite different commentary on Eliot's work.

In 1922 the *Fugitive* ran an editorial entitled "Whose Ox." The essay introduced a young poet (Tate had only entered Vanderbilt in 1918) who was unsure whether to defy or defer to the precepts of his older colleagues in the Fugitive group. "Yes, we *are* experimentalists," Tate admits at the start of this position piece, "but perhaps not too bold. Whom and what shall our souls believe?"[20] On the face of it, there is a very definite answer in view, since Tate sets out here (rather boldly, after all) to defend the legitimacy of *The Waste Land*'s "aberrant versification." Tate does so by placing Eliot's practice in the context of "the contemporary revolt" against "the tyranny of representation," citing the precedent of other innovators:

> It is patent . . . that the art of Duncan Grant and of Picasso has no objective validity and *represents* nothing; but perhaps the world as it is doesn't afford accurate correlatives of all the emotional complexes and attitudes; and so the painter and, it may be, the poet are justified in not only rearranging . . . but remaking, remoulding, in a subjective order, the stuff they must necessarily work with—the material world.

Tate's writing leads out of lament for the imaginative limits of "the world as it is" toward an affirmation of the artist's desire and autonomy—an evocation of art's capacity to remake "in a subjective order . . . the material world." The energy of Tate's rhetoric comes from the enthusiasm of Crane's letters—the two poets had been writing to each other for about six months—but Tate's ideas specifically derive from the issues of the *Little Review* and *Secession* that Crane had, as Tate's tutor in modern art, included in his correspondence (*Davidson and Tate*, 20). Gorham Munson, to whom Crane forwarded some of Tate's poems, had started *Secession* to showcase the "new rebels . . . those writers who are preoccupied with researches for new forms."[21] Stirred by the antagonistic stance of "This Youngest Generation" (as Malcolm Cowley called them) and attracted by their claim to the making of "new forms," Tate challenged his older Fugitive colleagues. When Tate showed *Secession* to Davidson, he already knew that Davidson would be offended by the magazine's "Post-Dadaist" pranks. "I can see the back of your neck bristling now," Tate wrote after Davidson's dismayed response. "In many ways I feel the same way, checked only by an opposite tendency to sympathize with almost anything revolutionary, sensible or not, and at the same time to derogate conservatism of all kinds" (*Davidson and Tate*, 20).

"Whose Ox" was intended to carry this provocation into print. Yet, after the sentences just quoted above, Tate backs away from any clear assertion of revolutionary sympathies. His tentative approach, first aggressive, then qualified, enacts a characteristic turn of mind. That is, as soon as Tate seems to endorse a "remaking" and "remoulding" that threatens "the older, if not more authentic, tradition," a tradition that relies on the "objective validity" of "seeing life whole," he stops short, conceding simply that "the older forms are not yet sapped." What emerges at this stage of Tate's thinking is a strict opposition between the subjective, nonrepresentational art of "the Moderns" and the objective mimesis of "the Tradition." But Tate's allegiance is not so much divided as ambivalent; he has simply not yet found a way to guarantee the authenticity of modernism without actively usurping that of tradition. When he returns, at the end of the essay, to the question with which he began, Tate disclaims the polemical motives at work with a sigh: "But which tradition can the American honestly accept? A fair, if stale question. We bow ourselves out, observing that to be young is very heaven!"

Despite that disclaimer, the controversy this essay promoted forced Tate and his Fugitive colleagues into increasingly hostile positions. Here, for example, is Stanley Johnson's riposte: "Is it not time for one who is neither poet nor modern to suggest again that these young poets have prepared for themselves a freedom which looks tragically like slavery, a courage which smacks of cowardice, and in their creedless night have committed themselves to a creed of spiritual anarchy?"[22] Ransom's reply, more articulate but just as anxious, came in a review of *The Waste Land* in the *New York Evening Post*'s literary supplement that condemned Eliot for incoherence and (to Tate's personal aggravation) immaturity. The essay makes it clear that a matter of discipline, touching on Ransom's authority in the Fugitive group, was at stake: "*The Waste Land* is one of the most insubordinate poems in the language, and perhaps it is the most unequal."[23] Tate could not let Ransom's reproof pass. Instead, he wrote a letter to the editor defending Eliot and attacking his former teacher's "superannuated theories of consciousness."[24] Ransom, seriously wounded and determined to get even, exposed the aspect of Oedipal struggle in Tate's charges by mentioning in his reply that Tate had until quite recently been his student. "I take it," Ransom wrote, publicly putting Tate in his place, "his letter is but a proper token of his final emancipation, composed upon the occasion of his accession to the ripe age of twenty-three."[25]

By the spring of 1926, however, equivocation and antagonism had both disappeared from Tate's advocacy of Eliot. Indeed, in his letter to Davidson, Tate no longer allows the modern poet the possibility of choosing sides: *The Waste Land* has simply "held people against their will." Tate has stopped arguing Eliot's case, that is, and submitted the success of *The Waste Land* as an accomplished, even self-evident fact. At the same time, though, we need to remark a change in the claims Tate is making for the poem. For now Eliot's poem reports the death of "our traditional forms," and *not* the coming of an art beyond representation. From the point of view of *The Waste Land*'s reception, the difference between these two claims is the difference between necessity and choice, the incontrovertible and the merely controversial. From the point of view of the poem's poetics, it is the difference between realist and expressionist, "objective" and "subjective" art. Tate has gone so far in fact as to invest the metaphor of "the waste land" with a collective and historical, rather than a personal and psychological, reference, and thereby fixed Eliot's landscape in a specific location. It is as if Tate had finally recognized that "There *was* a Waste Land, . . . and its boundaries included his own country as well the England in which T. S. Eliot was living" (Rubin, *Wary Fugitives*, 100).

In the high court of literary authority, these are the preliminary motions required for the designation of *The Waste Land* as the canonical expression of its era—of something like, in Eliot's well-known phrase, "the mind of Europe"—and not of its author. In effect, Tate's later interpretation strategically exculpates Eliot from the charge of iconoclasm that his earlier reading deliberately invites. For Tate's claim that *The Waste Land* accurately "exhibits" the death of "our traditional forms" successfully conceals its author's previously scandalous role in the revision, or even the rejection, of those forms. In Tate's case, the celebrated impersonality of Eliot's poetry depends upon precisely this imposition of representational content—depends, we may say, upon the recognition of *The Waste Land*'s realism.[26]

And that is a remarkable turn of thought. In 1922, when Tate wrote "Whose Ox," the disparity between the content of the poet's subjectivity and the available forms of "the world as it is" legitimized an otherwise forbiddingly abstract art. It was the extraordinary distance between art and life, the absence of "accurate correlatives," that made literary autonomy a desirable and practical goal. By 1926, however, that distance has been closed by the objective truth of modernist form. Authenticity has decisively passed to the modernist camp, and yet Tate has not had to reject the criterion of "objective validity," formerly the exclusive property of (in Tate's words) "the Tradition." The "objective" content of *The Waste Land*—what the poem "tells us"—is that objective truth, as it was disseminated in the unitary forms of tradition, is no longer accessible. But this message does not authorize desire and autonomy; it presents itself, rather, as a historical limit: as Tate insisted to Davidson, "we must be subjective" (*Davidson and Tate*, 166). The "aberrant versification" of *The Waste Land*, once it has been detached from the visionary project of "remaking . . . the material world," reinforces the claims of "the world as it is." As a result, Tate's image of the author of *The Waste Land* is also altered. Eliot is no longer the shadowy, possibly disreputable agent of "the contemporary revolt." Tate sees Eliot now (and he is teaching Davidson to see him) as the unassailable cultural authority he would remain for so many British and American poets and critics, teachers and students, in the middle decades of this century. Far from a merely personal poet, this is the Eliot who, in the words of I. A. Richards, had expressed "the plight of a whole generation."[27]

The mutation in modernist ideology I have just been tracing points to a complex realignment whereby modernism links itself to tradition and differentiates itself from mass culture. For Tate, these operations result in the apparent contradiction that Eliot embodies: a poet whose talent is comparable to that of the epic poets of the past, but who is unable to write major poetry as tradition conceives it because he is isolated from "the people as a whole." The split between "mind" and "culture" expressed in this condition defines modernity for Tate. It also explains perhaps the most distinctive feature of a modernist text such as *The Waste Land*: its highly specialized, notoriously "difficult" use of language. In another letter to Davidson, Tate analyzes the phenomenon of modernist "difficulty" in this manner:

> [The modern poet] must not only make, he must sell his article, which is nearly impossible. If Eliot had cared to explain the reason why modern poetry is difficult (it *isn't* intrinsically) he would doubtless have written something like [the following]: an audience with one set of emotions, the poets, in advance, with another set, and this means nothing else than a currency of two different languages. (*Davidson and Tate*, 140)

The separation of poet and audience—what Tate calls "a currency of two different languages"—places a double burden on the modern poet. He (and the role Tate is writing about is expressly male) must make *and sell* "his article"; he must be a critic *as well as* a poet. This doubling of literary tasks Tate sees as the sign of the curtailment of poetry's traditional scope, a limitation of a fundamental kind. For the emergence of the poet-critic—

the role epitomized for Tate by Eliot—coincides precisely with poetry's removal from everyday life. Criticism as Tate defines it here is a supplemental and compensatory form of writing, a practice of "translation" made necessary by that gap; and the imperative to write it intensifies in direct proportion to the difficulty of writing major poetry.

Yet the double identity of the poet-critic might be more accurately described not as a contraction, but as an expansion, of the poet's traditional powers. The point becomes clear when we see the phenomenon Tate is describing in the context of the emergence of art as an autonomous institution. Pierre Bourdieu, discussing what he calls "the aesthetic disposition," suggests a way to do so when he links the self-reflexive features of modern art to the drive toward self-regulation on the part of modernist artists such as Eliot. "The pure intention of the artist is that of a producer who aims to be autonomous, that is, entirely the master of his product," and this intention culminates in "a field [of artistic activity] capable of imposing its own norms on both the production and the consumption of its products."[28] What Tate views as an obligation, then, Bourdieu would urge us to recognize as an opportunity. To impose one's own "norms" of evaluation is to establish a market for artistic goods controlled at least in part by artists; and as such, it is a central *goal* of modern art, not an obstacle to it. The development of a critical apparatus for valuing modernist poetry functions in the same way; that is, by maintaining, rather than overcoming, the distance between the language of modernism and that of everyday life. Far from "popularizing" modern poetry, a poet-critic such as Eliot actively sequesters it, assuring its status as an elite, self-reflexive dialect.

The linguistic difference marked as "difficulty" in modern poetry signifies, therefore, a social difference Tate is at pains to preserve. When Tate tells Davidson that "our minds are as good as they ever were, but our culture is dissolving," Tate's "but" conceals a relation between the two statements that might better be expressed as "because." For it is only in estrangement from "the people as a whole" that Tate's modern poet can affirm his solidarity with the major poets of tradition—a fantasmatic elite whose removal from the present is essential to their privilege. The circumscription of modern poetry's possibilities, represented as the inaccessibility of epic, thus introduces an image of the literary mind surprisingly unqualified by history. That is, if our minds were not as "good as they ever were"—but were more or less good, as the contingencies of historical experience decide—it would surely be *possible* to write epic. The curious determination that Milton could not write epic were he to stand in Tate's place points to the presence of the complementary fantasy that Tate, because *he* cannot write an epic, stands in Milton's.

On the axis of literary history, as John Guillory has demonstrated, this model of the modern poet is advanced through Eliot's deceptive valorization of the *minor* stance: it is the renunciation of the possibility of becoming a major poet that allows Eliot's own poetry to enter (through the side door, as it were) the "ideal order" of literature's "existing monuments." "The idealization of the very order of the monuments," Guillory explains, commenting on "Tradition and the Individual Talent,"

> means that what the new poet threatens is disorder; he must present himself
> to his predecessors with a demeanor of conformity if he is to have any
> chance of altering them or being admitted to their company. Few writers of
> our century seem more oppressed than Eliot by the feeling that the canon
> is by its very nature closed and that it can be reopened only by the most
> elaborate and even covert of strategies. I read the famous doctrine of imper-
> sonality as one such strategy, a sacrifice demanded upon the threshold of the
> temple. The "continual self-sacrifice," or "extinction of personality," is a
> preliminary stance on the way to a more subversive posture of *ironic* mod-
> esty, a posture which both contains and expresses quite a violent revisionist
> impulse.[29]

In Tate's case, this act of renunciation, which conforms to the individual talent's submission to tradition and the concomitant repression of "quite a violent revisionist impulse," specifically takes shape in Tate's abandonment of the "revolutionary" rhetoric with which he opposed "the tyranny of representation." In "Whose Ox," we remember, the abstract art of "the Moderns" threatened the survival of "the older forms"; in 1926, Tate tells Davidson that "our traditional forms are dead"; but Tate doesn't say that modernism has killed them: rather, the threat to tradition has been located *outside* literature in the historical forces of the poet's nontraditional society.

Two consequences follow. First, Tate's polemical energies can now be directed outside literature as well, as they would be when Tate re-joined the former Fugitives Davidson, Ransom, and Warren in *I'll Take My Stand*. (It is worth noting that, despite certain tactical disagreements, conformity in politics closed off matters of *literary* dispute among "the brethern." At the same time, Tate's personal relations with Eliot warmed—if that is the right way to describe their resolutely formal friendship. Their letters in 1929 and 1930 scarcely mention modern poetry, but have a lot to say about the evils of humanism. Tate's essay "Humanism and Natural-

ism," which Eliot supported, appeared in the *Criterion* in July 1929 under
the proto–New Critical title, "The Fallacy of Humanism".) The second
consequence closely follows from the first: Tate's defense of literary modernism can now be *depolemicized*. This is what is going on in the 1926 letter
to Davidson, when Tate's repudiation of "the contemporary revolt" allows
him to represent Eliot in a position of overwhelming but neutral, indeed
"impersonal," authority, ready to accommodate even reverence for the
traditional forms that, less than three years before, Eliot's own experimental practice threatened to displace. Yet the violence of Tate's earlier struggle has not disappeared. It is, if anything, intensified when it re-emerges
in the mental warfare of *The Waste Land*'s reception: "It struck a spiritual
accord in every sensitive mind; some minds gave in, others combatted it:
the one attitude was as significant as the other" (*Davidson and Tate*, 167).

       What sort of accord induces either combat or submission? It
seems that Eliot's reader is certain to be defeated either way, but that is
not entirely the case. At least, when we ask whether Tate was among those
minds who "gave in" to Eliot or among those who "combatted" him, the
answer is obviously the former. But he does not *sound* defeated here; nor
does he speak from an inferior position. Rather, Tate is far enough from
the fray to see it whole: he is authoritative, dispassionate, in charge—very
much, in other words, as he imagines Eliot to be. Submission, then, would
seem to confer an empowering identification with Eliot in the role of the
master,[30] and this identification provides Tate with an elevated perspective
on the convulsions transforming the literary situation at large: the combat
and submission of other minds. The scenario is again that of the individual
talent sacrificing itself, as Guillory has it, "on the threshold of the temple,"
but in this instance it is Eliot himself who occupies the place of "the Tradition." Surely this act of identification accounts for the influx of authority
that marks this and the other texts by Tate we will consider from the mid-
1920s.

    But let us be careful to appreciate the role of other minds in this sce-
nario, because, as Tate correctly perceives, "the one attitude was as significant as the other." We can clarify this mutuality by retracing the steps
we have just taken. The matter of choosing between "the Moderns" and
"the Tradition," which Tate found in 1922 to be "a fair, if stale question,"
returns in this letter to Davidson, only now choice has been reduced to
compulsion, to the reflexive assumption of either one of two attitudes that
an accord with Eliot apparently exacts. The first attitude, that of simply
"giving in," simultaneously invests Eliot with an overwhelming authority

and permits access to that authority by way of identification, something Tate depicts as intellectual assent or "spiritual accord." Yet an accord of this sort can only remain a relation of force with no more inherent authority than any other contingent persuasion—unless, of course, the consequences of the second attitude, open combat, can be made to demonstrate the necessity, or inescapability, of the first. Therefore, in this scenario, the status of the first attitude or stance—its value, prestige, and authority—wholly depends upon the fate of the second: combat *must fail* in order to ensure the necessity of submission.

In the postscript I have been discussing, Tate explicitly comments on Ransom's resistance to *The Waste Land*. Tate's postscript continues: "The one attitude was as significant as the other. I remember Ransom fought it, and then went on proving its thesis in every poem he wrote: 'All the wars have dwindled since Troy fell.' They verily have" (*Davidson and Tate*, 167). The line of verse Tate cites as proof of Eliot's "thesis" comes at the end of Ransom's "Blackberry Winter." Here are the third and fourth quatrains of that poem:

> Bestarred is the Daughter of Heaven's house, and cold,
> He has seen her often, she sat all night on the hill,
> Unseemly the pale youth clambered toward her, till
> Untimely the peacock screamed, and he wakened old.
>
> The breath of a girl is music of fall and swell.
> Trumpets convolve in the warrior's chambered ear,
> But he has listened; none is resounding here
> So much the wars have dwindled since Troy fell.[31]

It would be difficult to argue that Ransom's measured swell and fall were in any sense intended to *combat* the reduction of epic to lyric. In fact, in the distinctively Alexandrian genre of the epyllion, Ransom fairly celebrates the sudden superannuation of his hero—a suitably pale and starry-eyed youth whose "Unseemly" exploit the elegant, neoclassical decorum of these quatrains wryly chastens and contains. It is in this sense an approving fable of that moment when, surprised by the peacock-scream of "the Tradition," Tate himself renounced his youthful quest and "wakened old." For Ransom's resistance to *The Waste Land* was always grounded in a defense of tradition. It was Tate who felt inclined "to sympathize with almost anything revolutionary . . . and at the same time to derogate conservatism of all kinds." To the extent that "Blackberry Winter" provides a motto for Tate's interpretation of *The Waste Land*, then, it is Eliot's poem, not Ransom's, that has been brought into line with "the older forms"; and it is Eliot, not Ransom, who, in Tate's mind, has gone over to the other man's side. Ransom, who never took up the revolutionary standard of modernism, would turn out to be right all along.

In fact, though, it was never Ransom, but Crane, who occupied the position of transgression in Tate's imagination, and the scenario of submission and combat we have just reviewed has everything to do with Crane. For, in schematic form, Tate's postscript is a retelling of the past five months in Patterson—that period when Tate's submission to tradition took a concrete form in his personal correspondence with Eliot, and the sacrifice which that act of submission required was enacted in Tate's eviction of Crane. Tate's refusal to continue to share his home with Crane is in this way consistent with Tate's repudiation of the revolutionary stance of "Whose Ox": the one gesture was as crucial to Tate's alignment with Eliot as the other was to his compact with tradition. What should be clear to us now is that the success of *The Waste Land*, which I have been calling Tate's recognition of the poem's "realism," did not determine—so much as it depended on—the failure of *The Bridge*. Crane's defeat, of which Tate was convinced even before Crane had begun *The Bridge*, provided Tate with proof of the impossibility of combating Eliot, and thus of the historical *necessity* of Eliot's position. Which is to say that Tate's designation of "the right kind of modernism" required the designation of the wrong kind as well.

Meanwhile, when Tate's initial distinction between "the Moderns" and "the Tradition" collapses into a distinction between two kinds of *modernism*, right and wrong, Eliot's and Crane's, a further distinction emerges between two kinds of *tradition*: romanticism and classicism. As we will see in the next chapter, this opposition within tradition is crucial to Tate's account of the different paths he and Crane chose.

THREE Genius and the Rational Order of Criticism

POETRY IS NOT A TURNING LOOSE OF EMOTION, BUT AN
ESCAPE FROM EMOTION; IT IS NOT THE EXPRESSION OF PER-
SONALITY, BUT AN ESCAPE FROM PERSONALITY. BUT, OF
COURSE, ONLY THOSE WHO HAVE PERSONALITY AND EMO-
TIONS KNOW WHAT IT MEANS TO WANT TO ESCAPE FROM
THESE THINGS.

—T. S. Eliot, "Tradition and the Individual Talent"[1]

In the autumn of 1925, Waldo Frank persuaded Horace
Liveright to publish Crane's *White Buildings*, with the assurance that his
firm's best-known author, Eugene O'Neill, would provide a brief, lauda-
tory introduction—a favor that O'Neill, who admired Crane's poetry but
could not exactly say why, promised, then hesitated, then declined to sup-
ply.[2] O'Neill's hesitation occupied more than six months. During this
period Crane had begun *The Bridge* in Patterson, broken with Tate, and
retreated to his mother's property on the Isle of Pines, Cuba, where, unsure of the fate of his first book and blocked in the writing of his second,
Crane echoed Tate's objections to *The Bridge* in a letter to Frank: "The
form of my poem rises out of a past that so overwhelms the present with
its worth and vision that I'm at a loss to explain my delusion that there
exist any real links between that past and a future destiny worthy of it"
(Crane, *Letters*, 261).

Crane wrote that letter on June 20, 1926. By July 24, when he sent
Frank "To Brooklyn Bridge," Crane had entered the two-month period of
extraordinary poetic creation during which over half of *The Bridge* was
either begun or completed. By late July, Crane had finally received a contract for *White Buildings*—and it was Tate who, when he learned that
O'Neill had backed out of his promise and that Crane's volume was therefore in jeopardy, had volunteered to write the introduction himself (and to

49

see it published under O'Neill's name, had that been necessary). Elated, Crane wrote in pride and vindication to his mother: "My umbrage toward Allen is erased by the fidelity of his action, and I'm glad to have so discriminating an estimate as he will write of me" (Crane, *Letters*, 270). To Tate (in the first communication since their quarrel in April), Crane wrote: "It was very refreshing (in the deeper sense of this abused word) to be told of the extremity of your interest (may I say generosity or *friendship* without too much transgressing appropriate boundaries?)." Crane signed his name "with love."[3]

Tate's "estimate" of *White Buildings*, which was indeed discriminating, thus proved Tate's fidelity and won back Crane's love. Having put himself forward in place of O'Neill,[4] Tate once again assumed the role of Crane's advocate, friend, and sponsor—a role Tate had angrily renounced, only three months before, when he demanded that Crane leave Patterson. Now the two men would be bound together—literally, conspicuously, permanently—in the pages of *White Buildings*. But even as the introduction reunited them, Tate's ambivalent reading of Crane's work took up and advanced the argument that had driven them apart. Indeed, when Tate chose to connect himself with Crane again, it was no longer as Crane's disciple: new "boundaries" had been erected. For alongside his praise for the ambition (that is, the "important intention") of *White Buildings*, Tate did not shrink from an enumeration of the volume's "faults," which included its pervasive conceptual and rhetorical "obscurity." These faults, Tate allowed, were signs of an "intensely personalized" vision, but they could not be dismissed as merely idiosyncratic. Rather, "difficulty" and "obscurity" were the characteristic features of a particular kind of poetry—the romantic poetry of "genius" and "revolt"—in which the valuing of personal vision over tradition led to the hermetic and divided sensibility that Eliot had diagnosed. The literary history of dissociation, or at least Tate's rapid sketch of it, will be examined below. It is enough for now to register Tate's admonitory implication that, if Crane continued to follow the examples of Blake and Shelley, Whitman and Poe, the path would lead to the premature disintegration of his work.

From this point there are not many steps to Tate's eventual claim that Crane's work solicits our attention as an instance of instructive failure, an exemplary error. As Yvor Winters would later put it, adapting Tate's rhetoric of praise and blame to an equally astringent but rather more eccentric antiromanticism:

> Crane . . . had the absolute seriousness which goes with genius and sanctity; one might describe him as a saint of the wrong religion. He didn't have the

critical intelligence to see what was wrong with his doctrine, but he had the courage of his convictions, the virtue of integrity, and he deserves our respect. He has the value of a thorough-going demonstration.[5]

But not yet dedicated to the didactic reading of Crane's life and work that he came to share with Winters, Tate wrote the introduction to *White Buildings* poised between identification and repudiation, shadowed by the tones of elegiac feeling that more obviously color Tate's subsequent writing about Crane. Of course, in the case of a late essay like "Crane: The Poet as Hero," that sense of elegy clearly refers to Crane's suicide. I want to suggest that that same feeling refers, in Tate's preface, to a different order of event: Tate's disavowal of his identity as a romantic poet. This disavowal, charged with homophobia and regret, is the pivot in Tate's literary development—the renunciation on which his professional self-definition as a poet-critic is based. In this chapter, I plan to trace that development during the 1920s as it took shape in Tate's letters, essays, and poems. Among these, my primary coordinates will be two sonnets. Tate wrote the first in 1923, the second in 1927; both define Tate's poetic identity in relation to Crane's. The question they raise is how Tate got from the first, which treats Crane as a mystic, to the second, which treats Crane as a madman.

Let me begin with a closer look at Tate's introduction to *White Buildings*. Although this short essay effectively announces a turning point in Tate's career, the announcement is embedded in an account of a turning point in *Crane's* career, and this account is in turn embedded in a story—one that should be quite familiar to us—about the rise of modern poetry. Quickly summarized, that story goes like this: by stressing observation and experiment, discarding "the worn-out poetic phrase," and insisting on "structural economy," Imagism produced the first authentic modern poetry in English; but these were all acts of reduction, lacking "imaginative coordination," and they refined the modern poet's methods at the cost of confining them to "the dry presentation of *petites sensations*."[6] If Tate seems to assign an excessive importance to Imagism, keep in mind that it serves an expedient function here: it is put in place to be knocked down.[7] Thus Crane went to school in Imagism, we learn, but he "suddenly and profoundly broke . . . with its decorative and fragmentary world." Seeking, rather, "direct affirmation of a complete world," Crane rejected the registration of discreet images in favor of the totalizing operations of imagination—a contrast between analytic and synthetic activities that affords Tate the following scheme: "A series of Imagistic poems is a series of worlds. The poems of Hart Crane are facets of a single vision; they refer to a central imagination, a single evaluating power, which is at once the motive of the poetry and the form of its realization" (Tate, "Introduction to *White Buildings*," 19).

These sentences show Tate reading *White Buildings* in the light of Crane's plans for a single long poem, the coherence of whose many parts would require the synthesizing action of "a central imagination." The issues of genre and unity thus raised by *The Bridge* return to the question posed in Tate's letters to Davidson: In the absence of a continuous tradition, how can the modern poet write major poetry? But that question takes a somewhat different form in Tate's introduction: How can the modern poet get beyond the serial discontinuity of Imagist lyrics? For Crane, at least, the answer comes in going *back* to the romantic imagination. Or so Tate suggests when he locates in Crane's work the presence of "a single evaluating power, which is at once the motive of the poetry and the form of its realization"—that is, a faculty Tate thinks of as being on the model of Coleridge's definition of organic form: "it shapes as it developes itself from within, and the fullness of its developement is one & the same with the perfection of its outward Form."[8] But what is understood historically as turning backward must be understood epistemologically as turning *inward*, and this inward turn represents a significant shift in the locus of poetic authority. For it is Tate's categorical distinction between perception and imagination that the one obeys the shaping force of the object while the other proceeds—again, in Coleridge's phrase—"under laws of its own origination" (Coleridge, *Collected Works of Coleridge*, 5:1, 495).

This definition of "a central imagination" as a counterempirical, self-regulating agency is very close really to Tate's notion of literary autonomy in "Whose Ox"; but it is an index of how far Tate has come from that text to this one that he can no longer classify the work of both Crane and Eliot in the same category. Indeed, as Tate's next paragraph discloses, abruptly qualifying the enthusiasm of his last, these two poets propose precisely antithetical alternatives:

> The poet who tries to release the imagination as an integer of perception attempts the solution of the leading contemporary problem of his art. It would be impertinent to enumerate here the underlying causes of the dissociation of the modern consciousness: the poet no longer apprehends his world as a Whole. The dissociation appears decisively for the first time in Baudelaire. It is the separation of vision and subject; since Baudelaire's time poets have in some sense been deficient in the one or the other. For the

revolt of Rimbaud, in this distinction, was a repudiation of the commonly available themes of poetry, followed by a steady attenuation of vision in the absence of thematic control. Exactly to the extent to which the ready-made theme controls the vision, the vision is restricted by tradition and may, to that extent, be defined by tradition. In The Waste Land, which revives the essence of the problem, Mr. Eliot displays vision and subject once more in traditional schemes; the vision for some reason is dissipated, and the subject dead. For while Mr. Eliot might have written a more ambitiously unified poem, the unity would have been false; tradition as unity is not contemporary. The important contemporary poet has the rapidly diminishing privilege of reorganizing the subjects of the past. He must construct and assimilate his own subjects. Dante had only to assimilate his. (Tate, "Introduction to *White Buildings*," 19)

Working backward from this paragraph we can piece together a historical analysis more systematic than Tate's quick shifts of focus and vocabulary might at first seem to permit. First, the antirhetorical strategies of Imagism overcame the excessive subjectivity of nineteenth-century poetry by grounding modern poetry in the objective authority of perception. But sense data could not stand in for the données of tradition, so Imagism left modern poetry stranded in the present, consigned to discontinuous and diminutive forms. Expecting to unite the new objectivity of Imagism with the subjectivity Imagism displaced, Crane "tries to release the imagination as an integer of perception." What Crane is up against, however, is "the dissociation of the modern consciousness," a fissure in the mental faculties Tate defines by substituting "vision" and "subject"—then "vision" and "theme"—for the prior set of terms, "imagination" and "perception." At first Tate declares that the causes of dissociation are too obscure—or too obvious?—to mention. But as he elaborates on the history of the dilemma, he arrives at an etiological statement. With Rimbaud illustrating the general point, Tate propounds an agonistic model of the relation between vision and theme in which the former, asserting its independence, rebels against the preexistent, distinctly institutional authority of the latter, which Tate identifies with tradition. This last gesture aligns Tate's opposition vision/theme with Eliot's much better known dyadic structures: creation/criticism, emotion/intellect, individual talent/tradition, each of which indicates a ratio of "revolt" and "control." These terms recall Tate's advocacy of the modernist break with "the tyranny of representation." But as the example of Eliot's dyads suggests, Tate is praising control, not revolt, and the contest between "the Moderns" and "the Tradition" is no longer at issue. Instead, the struggle between self-originating vision and "ready-made" theme discloses the Oedipal melodrama of two monolithic parties: romanticism and classicism.

Near the end of the introduction, Tate writes: "A living art is new; it is old" (Tate, "Introduction to *White Buildings*," 21). The proposition condenses a more complex statement of Eliot's in "Reflections on Vers Libre": "In an ideal state of society one might imagine the good New growing naturally out of the good Old, without the need for polemic and theory; this would be a society with a living tradition" (*Selected Prose of T. S. Eliot*, 32). That Eliot's organicism ultimately derives from Coleridge's (as Frank Kermode, among others, has shown)[9] should not keep us from seeing that in Tate's mind the two points of view are mutually exclusive. For Eliot, "a living tradition" is a collective body of beliefs undisturbed by the supervention of any *new* "theory," which is identified here with the divisive and contestatory force of "polemic"; it describes a condition of conformity and simultaneity in which the good New grows naturally "out of" the good Old and *not*, as Tate reads Crane's Coleridgean project, out of itself. The distinction concerns two notions of poetic authority, one locating it in the collectivity called *tradition*, the other locating it in the individual *work*, and thereby threatening the priority of the first. Tate's point is threefold: (1) Imagism produced a new poetry by cutting ties to the old (polemically, theoretically); (2) Crane correctly responded to "the 'new poetry' of a decade ago" by seeking out a model in the past; (3) but when he went back to romanticism, Crane went back to the *wrong* model—in fact, to the kind of poetry that, by seeking out its authorization, its control, merely *in itself*, had interrupted the organic continuity of Old and New in the first place. In Tate's view, the romantic error, comprehensible, even admirable as it may be, consists in the belief that imagination can of its own resources take the place of "a living tradition," the function of which is precisely the maintenance and regulation of imaginative resources, the natural propagation of the New. Like psychoanalysis, romanticism is itself a symptom of the disorder it purports to cure.

It is the deliberate decision to resist this error that is indicated by Tate's modifiers: "While Mr. Eliot *might have* written a *more ambitiously* unified poem, the unity would have been false; tradition as unity is not contemporary." To be contemporary in "the fullest sense," which is to display "vision and subject once more in traditional schemes," is to resist the "false" unity romantic theory ascribes to the individual work. To uphold tradition, when it is in ruins, is to resist the temptation to put tradition back together, which can only be done by substituting the intrinsic coherence of the work for the kind of coherence—extrinsic, "objective," officially sanctioned—that "a living tradition" supplies. As Tate understood it, this is Crane's ambition in both *White Buildings* and *The Bridge*. What Eliot achieves in *The Waste Land*, in his somehow less ambitious way, is the subordination of the work to tradition, the New to the Old, and vision to subject—a series of reconciliations that do not amount, however, to the restitution of that unity typical of texts produced in "an ideal state of society." Instead, "the vision for some reason is dissipated, and the subject dead."

Stepping back, we can see a sharp opposition taking shape. Romanticism, in Tate's account, is premised on individual vision, classicism on the corporate enterprise I will be calling "craft." Implicitly here, explicitly elsewhere, Tate links romanticism to the atomized world of mass culture—a democratic order in which the ideological priority of personal freedom produces a kind of standardized individuality. This is a society without a public center, which is organized around the private, peculiar, and plebian. By contrast, Tate sees classicism as the expression of aristocratic community, of a social order governed by shared intellectual discipline and received beliefs. It is impossible to reconstruct such an order, Tate believed. Yet it *is* possible to honor it—and to resist the imperatives of mass culture—by submitting the individual talent to tradition. Practically, this course of action requires the modern poet to submit to the formal "controls" of tradition, symbolized by traditional verse forms. For Tate, the literary community bound together by this formalist project is an elite fraternity or guild, and as such a remnant of "the closely-knit and homogeneous society" that engendered the "intricate formal patterns" of tradition in the first place.[10]

It should be clear at once that the terms "romanticism" and "classicism," insofar as they represent a vaguely art-historical classification of styles, are merely convenient; they are part of the general vocabulary of nineteenth-century aesthetics available to Tate and Crane when they needed names for themselves. T. E. Hulme once remarked, "If you asked a man of a certain set whether he preferred the classics or the romantics, you could decide from that what his politics were."[11] The two terms are code. They point in Tate's usage to two ways to locate literature socially: in the subway and the crowd; or in the museum or (as Tate proposes in "Ode to the Confederate Dead") the cemetery. But it would be misleading to treat these two points of view as distinct *choices*, equally plausible. In Tate's thinking, as in Hulme's, classicism is a stance arrived at specifically by going *beyond* romanticism; the romantic is a "stage" or phase that the clas-

sic presupposes. To understand Tate's classicism, therefore, we will need
to know more about what preceded it.

In his account of the dissociation of sensibility, Tate substi-
tutes "vision and subject" for Eliot's more familiar pair, emotion and intellect. In Chapter Two we considered Tate's use of "subject" and "theme":
more or less interchangeable, the two terms indicate Arnoldian data,
defined as the concrete legacy of tradition, and therefore closely related to
that most ambiguous and auratic word, "form." "Vision," an important
word in Tate's vocabulary in the 1920s, derived from Crane. "The modern artist needs gigantic assimilative capacities," Crane felt, "emotion,—
and the greatest of *all—vision*" (Crane, *Letters*, 129). In the following sonnet, written in the winter of 1923, Tate calls on Crane to instruct him in
this greatest of poetic capacities. The poem, as a gift to Crane, completed
an intimate exchange between the two poets; for Crane had just sent Tate
a photograph of the portrait of him made by William Lescaze, a Swiss-
French friend of Crane's who would later become a distinguished architect. Tate's poem begins by describing the portrayed face of his fellow
poet:

> Unweathered stone beneath a rigid mane
> Flashes insurgent dusk to ancient eyes
> Dreaming above a lonely mouth, that lies
> Unbeaten into laughter out of pain:
> What is the margin of that lovely stain
> Where joy shrinks into stilléd miseries?
> From what remembrance of satyrs' tippled cries
> Have you informed that dark ecstatic brain?
> I have not grasped the living hand of you,
> Nor waited for a music of your speech:
> From a dead time I wander—and pursue
> The quickened year when you will come to teach
> My eyes to hold the blinding vision where
> A bitter rose falls on a marble stair.

Tate placed "Sonnet: To a Portrait of Hart Crane" in the spring 1923
number of the *Double Dealer*.[12] The poem commemorates the exchange
that took place a year before when the *Double Dealer* first brought Crane
and Tate together; it is a public declaration of their private alliance.
"Please forgive me!" Tate wrote to Crane, announcing the poem's publication.[13] But Crane was not at all embarrassed. Rather, the sonnet trans-

Pencil portrait of Hart Crane by William Lescaze.

mits an image of Crane which, like Lescaze's portrait itself, Crane eagerly circulated among friends. In Gorham Munson's memory, "What Hart especially liked about the Lescaze drawing"—a copy of which Crane sent to Munson, followed by a copy of Tate's sonnet—"was the prominence of the right eye, for he had read in [P. D. Ouspensky's] *Tertium Organum* an assertion by Boehme that the right eye of a mystic was more seeing than the left; Boehme called it 'the eye of eternity.' "[14] Whether or not Crane saw himself as an Ouspenskyan seer, it is clear that Lescaze's sketch, emphasizing the intensity and abstraction of its subject's gaze in an intense and fashionably abstract pictorial language, precisely suited Crane's equation of the modern and the visionary. For both Crane and Tate, Lescaze's portrait would remain essential to Crane's image as a poet. When he lived with Tate and Gordon in Patterson in 1926, Crane glued it to the wall of the room where he worked on "Atlantis."[15]

Addressing himself to that portrait in 1923, Tate mythologized his own awakening, under Crane's influence, to the "revolutionary" cause of modernism. But what is most striking about Tate's poem, particularly by contrast to Lescaze's quasi-Futurist sketch, is surely its deliberate *archaism*— its recourse not only to rhyme and meter (which Tate almost never abandoned), but to that fin de siècle stage set of marble stairs and tipsy satyrs. What we find here is nothing like "abstraction"—the militant attack on representation that "Whose Ox," written a few months before, might lead us to expect. Rather, it is a poem Crane correctly called "a charming old-fashioned sonnet" (Crane, *Letters*, 122). So what has become of the young modernist? In fact, he has not really disappeared: Tate is offering another view of himself, a different framework in which to understand his modernism. The axis of self-definition here is not the vertical one of intergenerational confrontation (Tate's Oedipal standoff with Ransom and "the Tradition"), but the horizontal one of male comradeship— the kind of relation that Crane's letters and poems worked to bring into being. It is as if Tate's combat with the Father had disclosed, on the other side of the coin, an exhilarating, erotically charged bond with a brother.

For in its awkward flourishes ("a lonely mouth," "stillèd miseries," or that woeful "bitter rose") Tate's blazon situates itself, willy-nilly, within British Aestheticism's field of homoerotic codes, in effect evoking the "exquisite passion" that Walter Pater found in "any stirring of the senses, strange dyes, strange colours, and curious odours, or work of the artist's hands, or the face of one's friend."[16] Tate would quickly disavow in his own writing the encoding of male homosexual desire for which Pater's *The Renaissance* was variously deplored and admired.[17] But the fact that

Pater's prose *could* be read as a call to unlicensed pleasures, and the conclusion to *The Renaissance* therefore suppressed, indicates the proximity of Platonic appreciation to an elite male homosexual vernacular. The semiotics of Tate's poem are further complicated by the fact that Crane's "mysticism" functioned as a way for him to talk about homosexuality without openly doing so. As we will see in later chapters, "The Mystic" who envisions a beautiful world elsewhere was for Crane a role in which it was possible to imagine alternative spaces for the satisfaction (or sometimes the transcendence) of "impossible" desires: as "For the Marriage of Faustus and Helen" promises, *"There is the world dimensional for / those untwisted by the love of things / irreconcilable . . ."* (Crane, *Poems*, 26). Moreover, the subject of Tate's sonnet—Lescaze's portrait—was itself a particular and important link between the sexual and poetic dimensions of Crane's world.

For example, in an excited, drunken letter to Munson, written during the composition of "Faustus and Helen," Crane discusses (in succession) Greek vases that depict "satyrs with great erections [prancing] to the ceremonies of Dionysios," the "athletic style" of Lescaze's portrait of him, and the effects of an ether trance, during which "something like an objective voice kept saying to me—'You have the higher consciousness—you have the higher consciousness. This is something very few have. This is what is called genius' " (Crane, *Letters*, 91–92). In this chain of imaginings, Lescaze's "athletic" image of the poet links the big cocks of Dionysian initiates to the mystical "genius" of Crane's poetry, its claim to "the higher consciousness." Tate's poem about Lescaze's sketch retraces those associations—without, however, acknowledging the homoeroticism that suffuses the same series for Crane. Tate's letters to Crane in this period also permit, but do not avow, sexual interpretations. "I am coming to New York," Tate wrote to Crane a short time after composing his sonnet, "and I have no qualms about saying that the prospect fills me with an enthusiasm best described, perhaps, as somewhat pubic." This could be read as a provocative confidence. So could Tate's promise to send his own portrait to Crane (Crane, *Letters*, 120). But Tate had not yet "grasped the living hand" of Crane, he was not yet aware of Crane's sexual secret, and his "somewhat pubic" enthusiasm might seem merely "athletic" after all. The letter I just quoted from continues: "Swimming and tennis—these things we shall certainly do together, and some other things perhaps!"[18] Tate was not yet obliged to specify what "other things" might or might not be entailed.

For the same reason, I think, the homoeroticism of Tate's sonnet is not readily distinguishable from what one would have to call its romanticism. Behind or within the Aestheticist manners of this poem are a wealth of high Romantic texts; the sonnet is in fact so steeped in English Romantic poetry as to constitute a collage or pastiche of golden texts. To begin with, the poem's genre is that of Keats's epistolary sonnets to Haydon, Reynolds, Hunt, and others—the fraternity of Keats's artist-friends. But there are more concrete connections as well. For example, Tate's phrase "dark ecstatic brain" seems calculated to please Crane by its reference to Blake's "dark Satanic Mills."[19] Tate's adjectives "unbeaten" and "unweathered" and the questions that follow ("What is the margin of that lovely stain /Where joy shrinks into stilléd miseries? / From what remembrance of satyrs' tippled cries / Have you informed that dark ecstatic brain?") reverberate with Keats's questioning of his "unravish'd bride":

> What leaf-fring'd legend haunts about thy shape
>> Of deities or mortals, or of both,
>>> In Tempe or the dales of Arcady?
>> What men or gods are these? What maidens loth?
> What mad pursuit? What struggle to escape?
> What pipes and timbrels? What wild ecstasy?[20]

Tate's closing prospect of renewal ("From a dead time I wander—and pursue / The quickened year when you will come to teach / My eyes to hold the blinding vision") is powered by another Romantic address, this one Shelley's desperate imperative: "Drive my dead thoughts over the universe / Like withered leaves to quicken a new birth!"[21]

Romantic poetry is the medium through which Tate relates himself to Crane, the language in which he calls to him. This is the case with the particular words Tate chooses as well as his rhetorical formula, the apostrophe, which Tate uses in the same way Keats does: to make the mute speak, to bring an image to life. But Tate is, at the same time, asking Crane to give *him* speech, to lead *him* from death into life, and as a result, Tate and Crane exchange positions in the course of the sonnet. In the octave, that is, Tate speaks from the land of the living to Crane in the silent world of art; whereas, in the sestet, Tate appeals to the living Crane to help him escape the statuesque entrapment of "a dead time." Which one of these poets is "dead"? That is the question raised by Tate's most prominent echo of a romantic text:

> This living hand, now warm and capable
> Of earnest grasping, would, if it were cold
> And in the icy silence of the tomb,
> So haunt thy days and chill thy dreaming nights
> That thou would wish thine own heart dry of blood,

So in my veins red life might stream again,
And thou be conscience-calmed . . .

(Poems of John Keats, 503)

This darkest version of deathless art brings out the subversive suggestion in Keats's apostrophe to the urn: that the mute *will* speak, and do so by means of a ventriloquism that, in its turn, will deprive its auditor of speech.[22] In Tate's poem, a similarly uncanny transposition occurs. When he quotes Keats in addressing Crane ("I have not grasped the living hand of you"), it is as if Tate were replying to Keats himself, having brought Keats back to life through Crane. By the force of this symmetry, though, Tate depends on Crane's touch to infuse him with new life, and this in turn places *Tate* in the numinous position of the dead youth.

That exchange of positions leads us back to the erotics of Tate's relation to Crane. Tate told Crane he longed to escape "the malignant, personal sentimentalism of Nashville. Existence here amounts to intellectual castration."[23] Tate felt unmanned by the "sentimentalism" of the genteel South—a world he found soft, entrapping, feminine. Crane, who returned to New York City from Cleveland in the spring of 1923, promised Tate intellectual stimulation: under his sway, Tate would revive, be empowered, and escape. Tate's "Sonnet: To a Portrait of Hart Crane" longingly elaborates this fantasy of phallic renewal, which culminates in a sharing of "vision." But Tate's sonnet also calls that vision "blinding," and the power it assigns to Crane makes Tate passive, dependent on the other's guidance and touch. In these ways, the closing lines of Tate's poem hint at the fears of castration and feminization voiced in his letters to Crane. The prospect of meeting Crane—and grasping his hand—seems to renew, rather than resolve, them.

This reading is reinforced by a final echo, one which comes from Edwin Arlington Robinson's poem "The Gift of God." The poem treats a theme Tate knew intimately: a mother's overwhelming idealization of her son, "the firm fruition of her need." Like Hawthorne's "Feathertop," Robinson's poem would have suggested to Tate a comment on his relation to his own mother. It ends with this bitter prediction:

His fame, though vague, will not be small,
As upward through her dream he fares,
Half clouded with a crimson fall
Of roses thrown on marble stairs.[24]

Conveyed by Tate's memory of these lines, the repressed force of his mother's dreams returns in the otherwise cryptic conclusion to the sonnet:

"A bitter rose falls on a marble stair." This striking echo, which I assume is unintended, makes Tate appear less than confident about his future career (his pursuit of fame in poetry); it also associates Crane's visionary imagination with the demands and desires of Tate's mother. Tate's appeal to Crane seeks an alternative to the Oedipal struggle Tate staged in the Fugitive group. But behind this new relation to Crane, Tate's poem seems to fear, is a troubling old one—a son's sentimental attachment to his mother. Both relations raise doubts about the young poet's masculinity.

In Chapter One I suggested that the Fugitive group looked back to the amateur literary "society" of the nineteenth century at the same time that it looked forward to the English-department classroom of the twentieth. Tate's thinking was similarly Janus-faced. The notion of literary autonomy in "Whose Ox" is at once an early statement of New Critical doctrine and a return to the genteel view of poetry as a redemptive realm set apart from self-interest. As Frank Lentricchia has explained, Keats was the special exemplar of this ideal for the aesthetes who "dominated our poetry and criticism from the death of Whitman and the passing of the Fireside group to the emergence of the little magazines of modernism" (Lentricchia, *Ariel and the Police*, 160). For E. C. Steadman, G. E. Woodberry, and the other men of their circle, Keats stood for the power of poetry to transcend material determinations: sexuality, labor, the body. And when Tate's early poetry invokes Keats, it is this poet who appears. (Tate's preoccupation with Keats might have been intensified by Tate's tuberculosis, which forced him to enter a sanatorium briefly in 1922—at just the time he began corresponding with Crane.) But the same features of his life and work that made Keats an image of aesthetic freedom made Keats's masculinity seem compromised. "If 'Keats' was a word signifying freedom from bourgeois economic contamination," Lentricchia explains, "then, at the same time, and by the force of a deadly cultural logic, 'Keats' was also a word signifying sexual otherness to the econo-machismo of [modern American] culture"—an otherness that threatened the male poet with the loss of "a culturally readable and culturally acceptable masculinity" (Lentricchia, *Ariel and the Police*, 161).

The echo of "The Gift of God" in Tate's sonnet encodes his fear of that loss—a loss connected in Tate's work to the threats of passivity, paralysis, and premature death. Over the course of his career, Tate responded to those threats by committing himself to an antiromantic poetic, a position that roots the defense of a normative, "mature" heterosexual masculinity in the refusal to take romantic enchantments seriously. For example, in his only extended critical treatment of Keats, the essay called "A Reading of Keats," which appeared in 1945, Tate made this point about the speech assigned to the urn: "With the 'dead' mountain citadel in mind, could we not phrase the message of the urn equally well as follows: Truth is *not* beauty, since even art itself cannot do more with death than preserve it, and the beauty frozen on the urn is also dead, since it cannot move. This 'pessimism' may be found as easily in the poem as Keats's comforting paradox" (Tate, *Essays of Four Decades*, 276–77). This thorough demystification of prosopopeia reads the mute speech of art as mere delusion, as a kind of wishful thinking. (And yet Tate praises the "superior *dramatic* credibility" of Keats's "Ode to a Nightingale": it does not test one's credulity to suppose that a *text* can say something—only that an urn can do so.) The further implication, renouncing the infatuation of Tate's own early sonnet, is that Keats's work is itself "dead," because it moves only in the idealized world represented on the urn, not in the actual world of ordinary life. For "A Reading of Keats" concludes that the overwhelming defect of Keats's poetry—its morbid eroticism "or the compulsive image of erotic intensity realizing itself in dying"—is the sign of a mind unable to reconcile the idealizing force of desire with "the realization of physical love." The limits of Keats's poetry, it turns out, are those of the poet's own sexual immaturity.[25]

Crane's work, in Tate's judgment, was flawed in the same ways as Keats's. In an essay that compares *The Bridge*, in its "magnificence" and "failure," to Keats's *Hyperion*, Tate narrates Crane's career in the following terms, starting with a poem that praises, but does not purport to give speech to, a funerary urn:

> Crane had, in his later work, no individual consciousness: the hard firm style of "Praise for an Urn," which is based upon a clear-cut perception of moral relations, and upon their ultimate inviolability, begins to disappear when the poet goes out into the world and finds that the simplicity of a child's world has no universal sanction. From then on, instead of the effort to define himself in the midst of almost overwhelming complications—a situation that might have produced a tragic poet—he falls back upon the intensity of consciousness, rather than the clarity, for his center of vision. And that is romanticism. (Tate, *Essays of Four Decades*, 321)

Tate's map of Crane's itinerary locates the ideal and the actual—what is inside and what is outside—in childhood and adulthood, respectively, and the failure of Crane's passage from the one to the other signals the erosion of "the hard firm style," a kind of classicism "which is based upon a clear-

cut perception of moral relations, and upon their ultimate inviolability."
Because this story is ultimately that of the good son going to the bad
(going soft, transgressing "clear-cut" boundaries), it should not be surprising that Crane's "romanticism" is explained as a sign of his "narcissism."
In the still later essay, "Crane: The Poet as Hero," it is neither romanticism nor narcissism that Tate sees as Crane's problem, but homosexuality.
"What had happened to [Crane] morally between 1917 and 1926?" Tate
asks in that essay. The answer is clear: "He had been confirmed in his
homosexuality and cut off from any relationship, short of a religious conversion, in which the security necessary to mutual love was possible"
(Tate, *Essays of Four Decades*, 325).

   "Crane: The Poet as Hero" appeared in 1952. The essay is Tate's first
public mention of Crane's "homosexuality." When he does use the word,
it is as a medical term for a "neurosis" based in childhood trauma. In 1952,
Tate argues that Crane was unable to get away from his childhood; in
1932, in the passage I quoted above, Tate argues that Crane was unwilling
to give his childhood up. Tate's later essay assimilates Crane's sexuality
to—that is, draws it out of—the developmental narrative in which it was
always implicit. For Tate, the homoerotic indicates a failure to succeed to
maturity; like the romantic, it resists the reality principle; it tries to have
things its own way, but it is doomed to fail. That is the story of idealized
passion in "A Reading of Keats," where there is a blurring of the poet's
passion and his premature death—as if the one, fully indulged, caused the
other. In "Crane: The Poet as Hero," it is male homosexuality that is
linked to death. Crane, Tate assures his reader, was "an extreme example
of the *unwilling* homosexual"; indeed, Crane's struggle to overcome the
"alienated society of the committed [i.e., willing] homosexual"—which
Tate understood as a struggle to be straight—is produced as a paradigm of
the struggle against "alienation" in general (Tate, *Essays of Four Decades*,
327). Whatever motives Tate may have had for claiming that Crane was
"an *unwilling* homosexual" (whatever that is), Tate effectively represents
homosexuality as *a fate*, the consequences of which, it is hard not to feel,
are fatal. To this extent, Tate's thinking about Crane follows a familiar
system of association: from Tennyson's *In Memoriam* to media representations of the current epidemic, male homosexuality is defined—as Jeff
Nunokawa has argued—precisely as "that which dies young."[26]

   Crane's only hope for survival, Tate's late essay allows, was in "a religious conversion." That when he made this remark Tate had himself very
recently entered the Roman Catholic Church is of only a little less interest
than the fact that "a religious conversion" proposes a solution to two different disorders at once—homosexuality and romanticism—by a reinsti-

tuting of a source of authority outside the self. It would seem that the volatile bond between brothers can only be stabilized—and the integrity of "the individual consciousness" affirmed—by a denial of desire that returns each man to the regulation of the Father. What is evaded in this preemptory return is the inevitable frustration of desire (understood as both sexual exploit and literary ambition) that, in Tate's reading of Keats as well as of Crane, turns back on the poet with self-destructive force, committing the visionary imagination to the romance of death. This moral underlies Tate's submission to Eliot in the role of the master— Tate's recognition of the "realism" of *The Waste Land*. I would like to turn back at this point to that period in Tate's career when, unlike Crane, he elected to define himself as "a tragic poet." By 1926, it was clear to Tate that such a poet would also have to be a critic.

The meeting anticipated in Tate's sonnet did not take place until the summer of 1924 when Tate at last visited Crane in New York City. That fall, Tate returned to New York expecting to stay "rather permanently" (*Davidson and Tate*, 127). Yet only one year later Tate gave up his rooms in Greenwich Village (he had moved from Grove Street to Morton to Jones back to Morton) and rented half of the farmhouse in Patterson. During that year, the circumstances of Tate's life, personal and professional, had dramatically changed. Tate, we recall, came north with "an enthusiasm best described, perhaps, as somewhat pubic." One of Tate's romances in New York was with Caroline Gordon, a journalist whom Robert Penn Warren had introduced to Tate in Kentucky. In December 1924, Tate and Gordon conceived a child, and despite the father's reluctance, the couple were married in May. (Tate and Gordon usually dated their marriage to the autumn of 1924. When she was born, Nancy Tate was taken to live with her grandmother and namesake, Nancy Gordon. See Makowsky, *Caroline Gordon*, 57–65.) Meanwhile, Tate's literary enthusiasms ceased to seem "revolutionary." In Nashville, Tate had distinguished himself by challenging the authority of the older members of the group, and he had easy and prominent access to a magazine, the *Fugitive*, in which to carry out that challenge. When he came to New York, Tate was removed from direct confrontations with Ransom (who had come around to many of Tate's views), and the *Fugitive* was preparing to publish its last number. The combative energies that marked Tate's work as a Fugitive—now taken for granted or otherwise devalued in the metropolitan literary market—had lost their psychic focus and their public forum. When Tate moved to Patterson, these changes took shape in his description of the literary situation as a whole: the modern poet had been

cut off from his tradition and his audience at once. Tate's everyday life in
Patterson reinforced that sense of isolation. Because Patterson was a farming region depopulated by the relocation of labor to expanding urban cen-
ters like New York City (about sixty miles away), the free-lance intellectual who came there from Greenwich Village seeking cheap housing and
space for a vegetable garden might plausibly believe that "mind" and "culture" were moving in opposite directions. But even while the move to Patterson dramatized Tate's marginal or contrary position in American
culture, it promoted the ideal of intellectual solidarity and autonomy expressed in Tate's conviction that "our minds are as good as they ever
were." Gordon and Tate were not alone, after all—Crane was their guest,
William Slater Brown and Susan Jenkins lived nearby, and there were frequent visitors from New York, including Malcolm and Peggy Baird
Cowley, who purchased property in the area. Despite the differences of
temperament and background among them, these men and women shared
at least intimations of the romantic anticapitalism that would later lead
Cowley, for example, to the Left, Tate to the Right. But this was plainly
a period of retreat, not engagement.[27] The Patterson crowd drank bootleg
liquor and talked about *The Decline of the West*.

The move to Patterson marked a redefining of Tate's literary self-
image. In Manhattan, Tate had gradually shifted attention from the writing of poems to the writing of criticism and reviews, while he made money
working with Susan Jenkins for the Climax Publishing Company on a
steamy magazine called *Telling Tales*. When he left the city, Tate had accumulated enough commissions and connections to abandon the "pulp"
magazine and set up shop as "an independent free-lance" (*Davidson and
Tate*, 147). The move was an assertion of autonomy, freeing Tate from
the ignoble industry of mass culture (and an occupation he shared with a
woman). Consolidating his livelihood and literary work, then, Tate presented himself in the role of poet-critic. (Tate's preference was always for
the noble nineteenth-century phrase, "the man of letters.") More than an
acknowledgment of his work in contiguous disciplines, I use the hyphena-
tion to suggest the extent to which each of Tate's practices informed and
depended on the other. Eliot, as a poet-critic, had to both make and "sell"
his work, Tate told Davidson in 1925. The "selling" in question can be
taken literally: criticism was a way for poets to make a living *as poets*. For
Tate, like Ransom, could use his identity as a poet to distinguish himself
from the university scholar by emphasizing a practical ("hands-on")
knowledge of texts, as well as a commitment to contemporary literature.[28]
On the other hand, like Eliot, Tate could use his identity as critic to dis-

tinguish himself from other poets by emphasizing a scholarly knowledge of tradition and a philosophically sophisticated skepticism. The strategic uses of this role were only realized, of course, over a period of years. But its ideological significance, its claim to *coordinate* in one author, one mind, the faculties of intellect and emotion, criticism and creativity, and thereby to ensure the psychological autonomy of "the man of letters," was already securely in place by 1926.

The poet-critic was "the whole man" Ransom dreamed of: he who makes of poetry a legitimately professional labor, even as he defends imagination against the reductive rationality of science and bureaucracy. Yet it must be stressed that "criticism" had, psychologically speaking, a police function. That is, for Tate, the ideal of the "whole" or balanced mind, which is a mind free of delusion, did not promise to release creative potential, but to control it. In his correspondence with Davidson, as we saw in Chapter Two, Tate declared that the modern poet's *critical* faculty could only be reclaimed—and a balance between criticism and creation effected—at the cost of the radical curtailment of *creative* possibility, viewed as the expression of a historical imperative: you cannot write epic. I described this deliberate curtailment as Tate's submission to tradition; it could also be called the subordination of "vision" to "theme." Pragmatically, personally, these operations came down to Tate's identification with Eliot and his repudiation of Crane.

We can watch these transactions taking shape, along with a new definition of romanticism, in Tate's letters. For example, in late November 1925, just before he moved to Patterson, Tate told Davidson about his inability to get beyond the "defeatism" that had marked the poetry of the Fugitives as a group. "I am not writing any poetry now," Tate confided, "and the reason is obvious: I have no idiom for a Vita Nuova, for it will take a long time for me even to understand it. For poetry is the triumph of life, not a commentary on its impossibility" (*Davidson and Tate*, 148). This letter shows Tate still looking for the renovative "idiom" Crane had called for more than three years before: "Let us invent an idiom for the proper transposition of jazz into words!" (Crane, *Letters*, 89). It shows Tate still committed to a Shelleyan "triumph of life" and not, as he would soon declare himself, to an Arnoldian criticism of life (defined here as "a commentary on its impossibility"). But even as the letter demonstrates Tate's intensified experience of obstruction, its reduction of possible options to two opposed alternatives—triumph and commentary—points to the exit Tate found. That is, "defeatism" implies an ongoing struggle, "commentary" a qualified objectivity—a detached perspective on the combat and submission of other minds. If, in November, "the blinding vision" seemed somehow beyond him, by April Tate had conclusively put it behind him: as Tate wrote in a letter to Mark Van Doren, "there is no *noumenon* and Imagination doesn't exist."[29]

This commentary on impossibility announces a position that, because it anticipates (and thereby "includes") the failure of any poetry grounded in imagination, both surpasses and depends on Crane's position as a stage, or phase, in its own articulation. For Tate's definition of himself as a poet-critic entailed the assignment to Crane of a complementary role—that of the "genius"—which, moralized in Tate's hands, indicated both what Tate had sacrificed and why he had chosen to make that sacrifice. No longer a model of the poet Tate wished to become, Crane became a model of the poet that, in another era, Tate might have been. The poet-critic's career begins where the genius encounters his permanent obstruction.

We have already gained some sense of these complementary roles from Tate's introduction to *White Buildings*—a document whose mere physical relation to the poems it precedes raises questions about the relation of critic to poet: Who takes priority? Who gets the last word? Can either one do without the other? In the paragraph below, which comes near the end of the introduction, these questions are further complicated by Tate's effort to talk about both poetry and criticism at once.

> There is the opinion abroad that Crane's poetry is, in some indefinite
> sense, "new." It is likely to be appropriated by one of the several esoteric
> cults of the American soul. . . . It is to be hoped, therefore, that this state of
> mind . . . will not at its outset be shunted into a false context of obscure
> religious values, that a barrier will not be erected between it and the rational
> order of criticism. For, unless the present critic is deceived as to the struc-
> ture of his tradition, the well-meaning criticism since Poe has supported a
> vicious confusion: it has transferred the states of mind of poetry from their
> proper contexts to the alien contexts of moral and social aspiration. The
> moral emphasis is valid; but its focus on the consequences of the state of
> mind, instead of on its properties as art, has throttled a tradition in poetry.
> The moral values of literature should derive from literature, not from the
> personal values of the critic; their public circulation in criticism, if they are
> not ultimately to be rendered inimical to literature, should be controlled by
> the literary intention. There have been poetries of "genius" in America, but
> each of these as poetry has been scattered, and converted into an *impasse* to
> further extensions of the same order of imagination. (Tate, "Introduction to
> *White Buildings*," 21)

Tate's concern at this moment is the reception of *White Buildings*, a process the introduction itself inaugurates by attempting to forestall Crane's "likely" appropriation "by one of the several esoteric cults of the American soul." Tate is writing here against Gorham Munson and Waldo Frank in particular. Frank's review of *White Buildings* would in fact confirm Tate's fears by locating Crane's work in the Whitmanian mode of cultural prophecy that Frank himself practiced in *Our America* and *Virgin Spain*. (Tate ridiculed Frank's review—not so unfairly—as a "belligerent and, in places, nonsensical apocalypse" [*Davidson and Tate*, 197].) In a sense, the "appropriation" Tate is fighting had already occurred, when Frank, taking Tate's place as Crane's advocate, had accompanied Crane to the Isle of Pines after Crane left Patterson in April 1926. Tate's hope that a barrier not be erected between Crane's work and "the rational order of criticism" reads on this level like a request for Crane to turn around and come home. But the threat that is represented here as, at least implicitly, Crane's induction into "an esoteric cult" rewrites the recent past, a period marked not by Crane's apostasy but by Tate's conversion to a new kind of *orthodoxy*—by which I mean a view of the "literary" that rigorously and categorically excludes "the personal values" (moral, social, religious) of poet and critic alike.

The tenets of that orthodoxy are, of course, those which Tate advanced in his version of the New Criticism, and Tate's effort to distinguish his own practice from "the well-meaning criticism" since Poe entails formulations to which he would return throughout his career. For Tate, the distinction is one of purification: against those types of criticism that transfer "the states of mind of poetry from their proper contexts to the alien contexts of moral and social aspiration" Tate upholds the integrity of the literary as a domain that includes its ends (or "consequences") in itself. "The moral emphasis," Tate allows, "is valid," but only insofar as the moral values in question "derive from literature itself," and then only valid insofar as "literature" designates an autonomous—and an oddly *corporate*—entity. Tate's position is obviously indebted to "Tradition and the Individual Talent." Chris Baldick puts the point correctly, for Tate as well as for Eliot, when he summarizes Eliot's position on the place of "ideas" in poetry: "The poet in Eliot's view has to deal with ideas, if at all, when these ideas take their place in a more or less *finished* system, when they are absorbed, filtered unconsciously into a society's habits of perception. . . . He is not asking that all philosophy be banished from poetry—which could be the more or less consistently held position of an advocate of 'art for art's sake.' His argument is rather that only those philosophies which are traditional and accepted can be put to use by the poet."[30] As Baldick also makes

clear, Blake provided Eliot with a countermodel, with an example of the
poet committed to decidely untraditional philosophies, as well as to the
disruption of "society's habits of perception." Because it is wholly relevant
to Tate's criticism of Crane's poetry—which Tate, following Crane himself, consistently compares to Blake's—we ought to pause over Eliot's
reading of Blake. Of particular importance is Eliot's claim, put forward in
The Sacred Wood, that Blake's poetry, marred as it is by "formlessness,"
eccentricity, and "a certain meanness of culture," demonstrates the aesthetic consequences of operating under a "home-made" philosophy.[31] The
problem is not that Blake employed ideas in poetry, but that he had
had to fabricate them himself (whether out of perversity of will or force
of circumstances is never really clear in Eliot's argument). Thus Eliot
concludes: "The concentration resulting from a framework of mythology
and theology is one of the reasons why Dante is a classic, and Blake only
a poet of genius" (Eliot, *The Sacred Wood*, 158). The next and final essay
in the book is "Dante." The distinction between these two poets is presented as one of form—"concentration" against "formlessness"—but
Eliot's apparently technical discrimination reflects Dante's access to an
"impersonal point of view" and Blake's lack of such. And it is this lack,
common to all poets writing in the absence of "a more continuous religious history," that drove Blake inward to the resources of his own "genius" for compensation.

By 1927, when he entered the Church of England, Eliot had found for
himself an extreme, perhaps even eccentric, solution to the cultural dilemma behind Blake's eccentricity. Tate came to his own solution, following Eliot's early example, by replacing the ideal of a continuous religious
history with the ideal of a continuous *literary* history—the institution, mi-
raculously intact until the intervention of romanticism, that Tate usually
refers to simply as "tradition." In Tate's introduction, it is "the rational
order of criticism" that submits itself to the "control" of "the literary intention" (rather than the merely personal intentions of poet and critic)
that is properly aligned with tradition. This new sort of criticism, which
finds its creative analogue in the poetry of Eliot, opposes not only "the
well-meaning criticism since Poe" (including Frank's), but also the American "poetries of 'genius'" (of which Poe's is probably Tate's most frequently, even obsessively adduced example). For in Tate's introduction, as
in Eliot's "Blake," "genius" stands for the sum of individual talent; it is
linked to the power Coleridge called "imagination," and it offers itself as
a substitute for tradition. The poetries of genius that Tate mentions—
they include those of Crane's "avowed masters": Whitman, Melville, and

Poe—therefore constitute a sort of antitradition. The line they form is a discontinuous one of repeated beginnings, each of which provides—in its ultimate break with the poetry of the past—only "an *impasse* to further extensions of the same order of imagination."

With this particular phrase Tate turned one of Crane's own sentences against him, since it had been Crane's conviction, when he began corresponding with Tate in 1922, that "Eliot presents us with an absolute *impasse*, yet oddly enough, he can be utilized to lead us to, intelligently point to, other positions and 'pastures new' " (Crane, *Letters*, 90). By "other positions" Crane had in mind "spiritual events and possibilities as real and powerful now as, say, in the time of Blake" (Crane, *Letters*, 115). To affirm such possibilities, Tate decided, is to task poetry with goals that lie outside it, and so to confuse *literary* possibility with "moral and social aspiration." It is this project that, quite legitimately, Tate sees in Whitman's "range," a capaciousness that was "possible in an America of prophecy," Tate argues, but impossible in the "complex present" that Crane's America represents. "The great proportions of the myth have collapsed in its reality," Tate writes. "Crane's poetry is a concentration of certain phrases of the Whitman substance, the fragments of the myth" (Tate, "Introduction to *White Buildings*, 20).

Tate's image of architectural collapse implies a severe reading of Crane's Whitmanian vision of a sublime structure vaulting the sea, and it looks ahead to Tate's later exposition (in an essay deeply indebted to Eliot's "Blake") of formal discontinuity in *The Bridge*: "The fifteen parts of *The Bridge* taken as one poem suffer from the lack of a coherent structure, whether symbolic or narrative: the coherence of the work consists in the personal quality of the writing—in mood, feeling, and tone. . . . In 'Cape Hatteras,' the airplane and Walt Whitman are analogous 'bridges' to some transcendental truth. Because the idea is variously metaphor, symbol, and analogy, it tends to make the poem static. The poet takes it up, only to be forced to put it down again *when the poetic image of the moment is exhausted*" (Tate, *Essays of Four Decades*, 315). Without "an objective pattern of ideas" to depend on—the sort of framework that, Tate goes on to point out, Dante provides—Crane's poetry, like Blake's, breaks up into the subjective units of personal utterance; the epic whole gives way to a disjunctive series of lyric parts. The serial discontinuity of *The Bridge* (which returns Crane to the discontinuities of Imagism and "*the poetic image of the moment*") thus recapitulates in its own form the serial discontinuity that is the history of romantic poetry. For in its substitution of subject for object, imagination for perception, and desire for control, romanticism exceeds

the limits of the literary to take on the burden of "moral and social aspiration" under which it can only collapse. "Genius," like the hero of Crane's
"Legend," can only spend itself repeatedly.

For Tate, to recognize the limits of the literary is to acknowledge what
T. E. Hulme called "the closing of all roads"—an impasse, at once moral,
social, and religious, that discloses "the *tragic* significance of life" (Hulme,
Speculations, 34). This impasse, which announces the restitution of rational
order *and* of "the religious attitude" (a state of mind in which "things are
separated that ought to be separated"), is the basis for what Hulme called
"classicism." This classicism is not the one romanticism rebelled against,
but a classicism that is seen as romanticism's *successor*. Ransom offers an
especially instructive statement of this position, although his word is not
classicism (nor even neoclassicism) but "irony":

> Irony may be regarded as the ultimate mode of the great minds—it
> presupposes the others. It implies first of all an honorable and strenuous
> period of romantic creation; it implies then a rejection of the romantic
> forms and formulas; but this rejection is so unwilling, and in its statements
> there lingers so much of the music and color and romantic mystery which
> is perhaps the absolute poetry, and this statement is attended by such a dis-
> arming rueful comic sense of the poet's own betrayal, that the fruit of it is
> wisdom and not bitterness, poetry and not prose, health and not suicide.
> Irony is the rarest of the states of mind, because it is the most inclusive; the
> whole mind has been active in arriving at it, both creation and criticism,
> both poetry and science.[32]

Ransom's propositions arise from a reading of Robert Frost, and they fully
apply only to poems of his own (for instance, to the lyric that we looked
at in Chapter Two, "Blackberry Winter"), but their relevance to Tate's
break with Crane should be clear. Note that Ransom is talking about a
mode of figuration, but that he is primarily concerned with the moral, not
the tropological, action of irony. Indeed, we are told that irony represents
a psychological operation in which the *whole* mind—"both creation and
criticism, both poetry and science"—has cooperated. But note, too, that
irony is constituted by a temporal series in which the activity of antithetical faculties is not simultaneous but *consecutive*, with creation giving way to
criticism (however much of the former's music, color, and mystery may
stay behind). Charted along the lines of psychological development, Ransom's concept of irony is a formula for literary maturity—a maturity that
Crane, thwarted in his passage from childhood to responsible adult life,
from homosexuality to heterosexuality, was never able to achieve. Charted

along the lines of literary history, the same concept is a formula for "the right kind of modernism": it is the supercession—the reluctant but wise rejection—of romanticism.

That, at any rate, is what I would like to call the plot of "The Subway," one of the best-known lyrics collected in Tate's *Mr. Pope and Other Poems*. In the summer of 1924, on his first visit to New York City, Tate described the subway ride to Crane's Brooklyn Heights room in a letter to Davidson: "I'm greatly thrilled at the mere *physique* of this great city! The subway is simply marvellous. Fancy going under a huge river at 40 miles an hour!" To these exclamations, though, Tate immediately added another, qualifying response: "The sheer wonder of it is almost atonement for its significance as a phase in the triumph of the Machine" (*Davidson and Tate*, 120). Three years later, Tate clarified the relation between these competing responses by assigning them to two distinct positions in the poem. Those positions correspond to the roles of the genius and the poet-critic; they can be observed in the visionary speaker whose monologue comprises "The Subway" and the ironic craftsman whose perspective, silently but powerfully signified in the poem's strict adherance to the sonnet form, implicitly frames the speech of the other:

> Dark accurate plunger down the successive knell
> Of arch on arch, where ogives burst a red
> Reverberance of hail upon the dead
> Thunder, like an exploding crucible!
> Harshly articulate, musical steel shell
> Of angry worship, hurled religiously
> Upon your business of humility
> Into the iron forestries of hell:
>
> Till broken in the shift of quieter
> Dense altitudes tangential of your steel,
> I am become geometries—and glut
> Expansions like a blind astronomer
> Dazed, while the worldless heavens bulge and reel
> In the cold revery of an idiot.[33]

Like Tate's "Sonnet: To a Portrait of Hart Crane," "The Subway," begins in the high romantic register of the apostrophe, but Tate invokes this figure in the second poem in a different spirit. In the first sonnet, Tate enthusiastically passes from the invocation of Crane's face as artifact ("Unweathered stone beneath a rigid mane") to Keatsian interrogation of the silent object: "From what remembrance of satyrs' tippled cries / Have you informed that dark ecstatic brain?" It is a mythologizing rhetoric that uses apostrophe to break down the antinomies of imagination and perception, subject and object, self and other. And in "The Subway," apostrophe is enlisted in the same tasks. But the representation of the speech it elicits as mechanical thunder doubles back on the speaker to render his own speech as bombast. For what is "Harshly articulate" about this "musical steel shell" is the accuracy with which it echoes the visionary's delirious claims, giving his words back as pure sound, pure force. The subway is an echo chamber for a programmatically *de*-mythologizing rhetoric designed to expose apostrophe as sheer *projection*—as an instance of the anthropomorphizing imagination that mistakes "the triumph of the Machine" for the sublime proportions of a heroic "*physique.*"

Of course, the particular mode of apostrophe being parodied here is Crane's. In fact, Tate's sonnet includes a variety of Crane's characteristic effects: those somewhat recherché "ogives"; a typically intransitive verb, such as "burst," made transitive (which is also a Keatsian usage); the multiplication of appositives; the crowding of like consonants—and syntactic compression—of a line like "Dense altitudes tangential of your steel"; the iambic pentameter scheme modulated by trochaic substitutions; and, finally, the Latinate epiphany—"I am become geometries"—which recalls, among many instances, Crane's climactic exclamation in "The Wine Menagerie": "New thresholds, new anatomies!" But the exact object of Tate's appropriation is obvious: it is Crane's address to the bridge *over* the East River in "To Brooklyn Bridge" and "Atlantis." Crane's vision of heroic ascent "through the cordage shaking its white call / From arch to arch"[34] is rewritten in Tate's poem as mock-heroic descent "down the successive knell / Of arch on arch" into "the iron forestries of hell," on the far side of which "the cold revery of an idiot" awaits. Crane's ecstatic transport is transformed into a sort of urban roller-coaster ride, and the eroticized ascent is demystified—desublimated—as mechanical violence.

In its appropriation and rejection of Crane's rhetoric, then, Tate's sonnet precisely reverses the action of identification in the sonnet on Crane's portrait. It is as if the second poem were expressly designed to undo the first. The crux of Tate's sonnet, that moment when the craftsman and the visionary, Tate and Crane, are emphatically distinguished, comes in the last four lines:

> I am become geometries—and glut
> Expansions like a blind astronomer
> Dazed, while the worldless heavens bulge and reel
> In the cold revery of an idiot.

The assertion in the first part of line 11 derives from Crane ("I am become geometries"), whereas the second part of that line ("—and glut") expresses Tate's view of such a claim. In effect, the dash distinguishes the first-person form of the preceding lines and the oddly detached, third-person perspective that follows, an "impersonal" point of view from which the visionary intelligence is unambiguously defined as a solipsist—as "a blind astronomer," "an idiot." The movement here is the one that Ransom describes as creation giving way to criticism, or poetry to science, but there is nothing wistful about Tate's exposition. Instead, those closing monosyllables—"glut," "Dazed," "bulge and reel"—disavow the authenticity of visionary experience with a degree of violence or polemical overstatement that makes it impossible to mistake Tate's position. The Cubist "geometries" of Crane's face, brought to the foreground in Lescaze's sketch, now signify the decomposition—the mechanical abstraction—of human form and reason. "The blinding vision," it turns out, is just that—blinding—and the modern mystic is a madman.

This mode of negation is not very different from Tate's contention that "Imagination doesn't exist," and it gives us an idea of how such a statement might get into a poem. Above all, it is important to note that the faculty I have been calling "criticism" indicates the presence *in the poem* of an interpreter—or better, an ironist—and that this position is established by rejecting—by ironizing—another position, that of the genius or visionary, who represents the impossible promises of an anterior poetry (romanticism) and of an anterior self (in Ransom's words, "a period of honorable and strenuous romantic creation"). "The Subway" manifests this process of ironization in a strikingly schematic manner, and it reminds us of the active struggle—the violent action of subjection—at the center of a narrative that Ransom preferred to understand as an uninterrupted, "natural" passage into maturity. For "the rational order of criticism," understood in this sense as the superior lucidity, or sanity, of the ironist, is affirmed by the *subordination* of "genius"—just as the integrity of "The Subway," its tacit claim to coordinate criticism and creation, poetry and science, is affirmed by the appropriation and rejection of Crane's rhetoric. The language of modernism gained authority by separating itself from the lan-

guages of everyday life. This linguistic opposition, which recapitulates the
basic opposition between modernism and mass culture, is recast here as
the difference between classical "order" (or reason) and romantic "dissolution" (or madness)—a difference maintained, in Tate's poetry, as a ratio of
"revolt" and "control."

The violence such a ratio requires is apparent throughout *Mr. Pope and
Other Poems* in Tate's closing lines. The last line of "The Subway," with
its blunt designation of the speaker as "an idiot," should be placed beside
the following examples, each of which comes from the conclusion of a
poem in *Mr. Pope and Other Poems*:

> There is a calm for you where men and women
> Unroll the chill precision of moving feet.
>
> ("Death of Little Boys")

> . . . and then the towering weak and pale
> Covers his eyes with memory like a sheet.
>
> ("Idiot")

> Crushed in the terrible stoop you loved so much . . .
>
> ("Obituary")

> Alert, with the careful energy
> Of a dream, the forward curse
> Of cold especial eyes—
> In the headlong hearse.
>
> ("Light")

> Where she stopped once with stricken eyes
> Bitterly, then closed an iron door.
>
> ("Resurgam")

> One rumor straight comes huddling on another
> Of death, and death, and death!
>
> ("Procession")

All of these poems end by "dying." Thematically, closure entails a deideal-
izing gesture, an acknowledgment of mortality (seen as cold, shock, or
calm, not only "death!"), which coincides in each case with the rejection of
one kind of poetic statement in favor of another. The final stanza of "Procession" gives the clearest and most compact illustration:

> The laughter and the shouting of delight
> Of children, flexed into a summer noon,

Chatter of women striating the crisp dark,
The crinkled light of an imprisoned moon,
Stop and foregather, hesitate, until
One rumor straight comes huddling on another
Of death, and death, and death!

On one level, "Procession" is simply another rendering of (as the poem puts it) "the good life's burial in the West"—the story, obsessively told and retold in Tate's work, of the dissolution of Western culture. On another level, though, this is specifically a story of the male poet's struggle to distinguish his own mature voice from the "laughter" and "shouting" of children and the "chatter" of women—the story, that is, of Tate's ongoing effort to produce an elite and distinctively masculine modern poetry, a poetry purified of the feminine, the "immature," and the popular. In this case Tate associates such verse with the consolations of perfunctory rhyme ("summer noon / imprisoned moon")—a form that he conspicuously, polemically departs from in the last lines by refusing to rhyme. In this case, the suspension of rhyme enacts an abrupt rupture, a sign of formal control, which is more often achieved (as in the other examples from *Mr.Pope*) by fulfillment of the rhyme scheme.

In "The Subway," the recognition of limits—expressed as a withdrawal from visionary experience as it devolves into "the cold revery of an idiot"—is thus confirmed by the completion of the form. The result is the promotion of verse form as an end in itself, an action identifying the poem's final perspective with that of its craftsman, and reminding us of Tate's defense of "the literary intention" apart from moral, social, or religious claims (each of which, of course, is typically associated with the sort of popular verse "Procession" eschews). Still, as Winters made plain in his commentary on the poem, the claims being made for this final perspective considerably exceed that of any merely technical control.

> The sonnet indicates that the author has faced and defined the possibility of . . . madness . . . (a possibility from the consideration of which others as well as himself may have found it impossible to escape) and has arrived at a moral attitude toward it, an attitude which is at once defined and communicated by the poem. This attitude is defined only by the entire poem, not by the logical content alone; it is a matter not only of logical content, but of feeling as well. The feeling is particular and unparaphrasable, but one may indicate the nature of it briefly by saying that it is a feeling of dignity and self-control in the face of a situation of major difficulty, a difficulty which the poet fully apprehends. This feeling is inseparable from what we

call poetic form, or unity, for the creation of a form is nothing more nor less than the act of evaluating and shaping (that is, controlling) a given experience. It should be obvious that any attempt to reduce the rational content of such a poem would tend to confuse or even to eliminate the feeling: the poem consists in the relationship between the two. (Winters, *In Defense of Reason*, 20–21)

This paragraph comes from "The Morality of Poetry," the introduction to *Primitivism and Decadence*, Winters's 1937 study of "the Experimental School in American Poetry," and it offers Tate's poem as an example of— from an ethical standpoint—what poetry can and should accomplish. In particular, it holds up "The Subway"—above all, it holds up the "unity" of its form—as an alternative to the "limp versification of Mr. Eliot and Mr. MacLeish" (which is "inseparable from the spiritual limpness that one feels behind the poems") *as well as* an alternative to the "fragmentary, ejaculatory, and over-excited quality of a great many of the poems of Hart Crane" that "is inseparable from the intellectual confusion upon which these particular poems seem to rest (for examples, *The Dance, Cape Hatteras,* and *Atlantis*)" (Winters, *In Defense of Reason*, 22). But what does that unity consist in? What distinguishes Tate's poem from the chatter of women or the "ejaculatory" laughter and shouting of a boy? Winters's answer, which Tate would approve, is the sustained "relation"—Tate's own word would be "tension"—between "feeling" and "rational content," a relation achieved by "evaluating and shaping (that is, controlling) a given experience." Once more we are referred to the poem as a psychological process, a process that claims to coordinate the mental faculties, but which in fact constitutes an embattled defense of a particular definition of reason.

There is no doubt that, despite his efforts to resist paraphrase (in the case of the "looser" forms of either Crane or Eliot, we learn, "the process of paraphrasing would constitute a much slighter act of betrayal"), Winters's ethical emphasis distinguishes these remarks from the strictest exercises of the New Criticism. But this emphasis only makes explicit the distaste for "decadence" contained in Tate's account of Crane's departure from "the hard firm style" of his early poems. In the poetry of Winters and Tate, which is marked by the adjectives "cold," "hard," and "strict," form signifies a stoic discipline—a discourse of closure—that affirms "the rational order of criticism" *at the expense of* "genius." This discipline invokes the scarifying energies of male homophobia, and it issues in the election of a scapegoat—the victim identified as "Orpheus" in the title of Winters's elegy for Crane and, less plangently, as "a blind astronomer" and an "idiot" in "The Subway." It also issues in a conception of poetry as a kind of silent language, an "unparaphrasable" form, whose deprivation of speech is a function of its absolute closure: a condition that, as we have already seen, Tate's lyrics persistently represent as one of rigor and chill. To explore this condition we must pass on now to the poem placed immediately following "The Subway" in Tate's *Collected Poems*, "Ode to the Confederate Dead."

FOUR

The Burial of the Confederate Dead

The long poem, or sequence of poems, that Davidson described to Tate in May 1926 was completed by the end of that year, and
Davidson promptly forwarded a copy of the manuscript to Tate, asking
him, a little fearfully, "to come down hard in the old Fugitive way" but "to
be charitable in the general view" (*Davidson and Tate*, 179). Davidson had
reason to be worried; for although Tate himself subscribed to the "ideas"
or "doctrines" in Davidson's work—in Tate's more or less accurate summary, "that Southerners are better men than Yankees, that the fall of the
South meant a State for the pig, and that some sort of love is the keynote
of ethics"—Tate found Davidson's verse "disordered, . . . mixed, repeti-
tive, and abounding in over-emphases." "In fact," Tate continued, "I do
not believe it was your intention to write a poem; you wished to do something else. Had you done it outside of poetry it may well have succeeded"
(*Davidson and Tate*, 181). A week later, appealing to the judgment of another friend, Tate expanded on these comments:

> I agree with a comment of Mark Van Doren's on the two poems you
> sent him. He says that while you think the subject-matter is important
> for you, the failure of the poems *as poetry* proves that it is not. . . . This
> is identical with something I wrote you long before I saw the poems, to
> the effect that our past is buried so deep that it is all but irrecoverable. The
> result of this remote stratification of the material is that you offer a product
> which is neither bird, nor beast, nor fowl: it is not poetry, it is not
> philosophy, it is not sociology: it is a little of all three, and none. (*Davidson
> and Tate*, 182–83)

What did Davidson wish to do that could only be done outside of poetry? On the basis of Tate's letter, we might think: write philosophy—or sociology; but a reading of Davidson's poem, called "The Long Street" at this point, and published as *The Tall Men*, suggests something different. Here is Davidson's account of the settlement of Tennessee:

> In twos and threes the tall men
> Strode in the valleys. Their palisades were pitched
> In the Cumberland hills. They brought their teeming wives
> To rock the hickory cradles and to mould
> Bullets for words that said: "Give way, Red Man.
> You have lived long enough. The seed is sown and covered
> Which like the dragon's-teeth in a new soil
> Will sprout full-armed in tall men who fight
> With a lazy smile, speaking from long rifles."[2]

Although he embellishes his argument here with an allusion to "the dragon's-teeth" of Ovid's *Metamorphoses*, Davidson evokes a language that would bypass language, substituting "Bullets for words," "long rifles" for pens, force for discourse. This rude fantasy of racial power is obviously aligned with the nativist violence and immigration quotas of the mid-1920s, however remote Tate might find Davidson from "the minds of Tennesseans."[3] And in its quest for a premodern, local, and heroic idiom, a phallic language of "long rifles," Davidson's poem is a polemical attack on the ironized, deracinated, elite dialect of modernism. Yet Davidson's position is continuous, of course, with that of other white modernists writing in praise of the primitive. Indeed, as Daniel Joseph Singal points out, "[Davidson's] glorification of primitivism and attack on cultural elitism sprang directly from the Modernist strain in his thought. Certainly no nineteenth-century southern writer would have willingly claimed the violent frontier as his heritage" (Singal, *The War Within*, 223).

When Tate says Davidson is writing philosophy and sociology, then, Tate is talking about the protopolitical ambition of *The Tall Men*, its conscious effort to create a racial and regional myth with real political and social force. Tate is talking about Davidson's desire for direct access to facts, to a language referenced to the world and not—emphatically—to itself. The "blunt" talk of rifles (which is not so different, really, from William Carlos Williams's reply to Greek and Latin "with the bare hands")[4] leads Davidson away, Tate suspects, from the discipline of craft and the purely "literary intention"—an abnegation of *literary* responsibility that leaves Davidson's poem unrecognizable "*as poetry*" (it is "neither bird, nor beast, nor fowl"). Keep in mind: this exchange between the two men occurs before any notion of *I'll Take My Stand* has been discussed. Tate is accusing Davidson of trying to do in poetry the kind of work Tate himself will take up in prose.

Tate's criticism of *The Tall Men* adheres, in other words, to his demand for a poetry purified of moral, social, and religious aspirations. But Tate's notion of a past "buried so deep that it is all but irrecoverable" refers less to the strictures of Tate's criticism than to the figures of his poetry, above all "Ode to the Confederate Dead." Whether or not Tate began the ode during the spring of 1926, he had substantially completed the poem by the time he sent a copy to Davidson on January 5, 1927 (with the letter that explained Tate's and Van Doren's views on the "failure" of Davidson's work). Davidson, worrying Tate, took two weeks to acknowledge the letter, three more to respond. When he did, Davidson had had time to compare his own poem about Southern history with Tate's. Davidson applauded "just as I might for a difficult series of Liszt cadenzas, performed with great skill, but my enthusiasm has no passion in it."

> I think the reason is this. Your poetry, like your criticism, is so astringent that it bites and dissolves what it touches. You have decided that the opposite sort of poetry (say, an *expansive* poetry) can no longer be written in an age where everything is in a terrible condition. But this attitude does not merely lie behind the poetry; it gets *into* it, not in the form of poetry but of aesthetics, so that poem after poem of yours becomes aesthetic dissertation as much as poetry. . . . [W]hen you deal with *things themselves*, the things become a ruin and crackle like broken shards under your feet. The Confederate dead become a peg on which you hang an argument whose lines, however sonorous and beautiful in a strict proud way, leave me wondering why you wrote a poem on the subject at all, since in effect you say (and I suspect you are speaking partly to me) that no poem can be written on such a subject. . . .
>
> The poem is beautifully written. . . . But its beauty is a cold beauty. And where, O Allen Tate, are the dead? You have buried them completely out of sight—with them yourself and me. God help us, I must say. You keep on whittling your art to a finer point, but are you also not whittling yourself. What is going to happen if the only poetry you can allow your conscience to approve is a poetry of argument and despair. Fine as such a poetry may be, is it not a Pyrrhic victory? . . .
>
> You see I refuse to wield your favorite word—*failure*. With the utmost assurance you say on every possible occasion: [Archibald MacLeish's] *The*

Pot of Earth is a *failure*; my poems are a *failure*; so-and-so is a *failure*,—
thereby assuming a remarkable critical responsibility.

Your poem, I say, is a success, and if you want that particular kind of
success, nobody should say no. (*Davidson and Tate*, 186–87)

Even sixty years later, Tate's poem has not received a reading as severe
and probing as Davidson's wounded, almost lyrical remarks. We will return to a number of questions raised by this letter in the following pages.
At this point I want to reflect on just one of Davidson's assertions: namely,
that Tate's "success" amounts to "a Pyrrhic victory."

Briefly, what Davidson finds victorious about the ode—in its own
terms, but also in competition with *The Tall Men*—is its level of *formal*
achievement, which is viewed as a function of the poem's perfect closure,
completion, or coherence. "I do not quibble over a single word," Davidson declared; "it is coherent, structurally unimpugnable" (*Davidson and
Tate*, 186). But what is Pyrrhic about that victory is the poem's claim that
its "content" (or "subject-matter") cannot be recovered. This is the condition treated specifically as a failure of vision in lines Tate called the "germ"
of the poem (*Davidson and Tate*, 212). There are, in effect, two versions of
the ode: the one printed in *Mr. Pope and Other Poems* in 1928; and the one
that appeared in *Selected Poems* in 1938, and which is dated "1937" in *Collected Poems*. Unless otherwise specified, I will be quoting, as in this case,
from the later text:

Turn your eyes to the immoderate past,
Turn to the inscrutable infantry rising
Demons out of the earth—they will not last.

As this vision withers, Tate is left alone, as Davidson suggests, with the
mere rectitude of resignation—with the "cold beauty" of an "unimpugnable" structure. (The integrity of the structure is emphasized in this instance, as elsewhere, by Tate's insertion of an end-stopped rhyme.) This
is, ostensibly, an admission of defeat and a reason for grief. But Davidson's
point, it seems to me, is that Tate *never set out to raise the dead*, but rather
to bury them "completely out of sight," and that this failure of vision is
therefore, in an important sense, designed. It is as if Tate's poem had
achieved its claim to formal coherence not despite—but because of—the
inaccessibility of (in Davidson's terms) its "content." I would like to test
these propositions now with a reading of the ode. Following Davidson,
my aim will be to demonstrate that the value of the container is predicated
on the evacuation of the thing contained—what Davidson's calls "*things*

themselves." I should add that "Ode to the Confederate Dead," besides its doomed soldiers, is vitally concerned with the fate of another figure. He is exhumed in Tate's criticism as Narcissus, but we might also recognize him as Hart Crane.

We might begin by observing that the effects of completion and coherence Davidson praises in Tate's poem cannot be isolated from the dissolving, corrosive, or whittling action to which he objects. Consider the tendency of Tate's poem to bring itself, repeatedly, to a stop. That tendency is immediately apparent in Tate's preference for end-stopped lines, the majority of which represent complete syntactic units, often reinforced by rhyme; but it is probably most prominent in Tate's various techniques for closing off or demarcating the individual verse-paragraphs. The 1928 text of the ode consists in nine verse-paragraphs, each of which ends in a full stop. Each of these stops gives a sense of completion, either through a clear affirmation of the metrical scheme:

> They sough the rumor of mortality.

—or through a comprehensive, summary statement:

> Here at this stile, once more, you see them all.

—which, more often than not, includes some figuration of death or deprivation:

> You shift your sea-space blindly, like a crab.

—or again:

> You have cursed the setting sun.

The poem's commitment to closure coincides with its preoccupation with death, as is the case with so many of the poems in *Mr. Pope*. Here death is seen as a state of completion—or even plenitude (in the 1937 version: "the inexhaustible bodies that are not / Dead, but feed the grass row after rich row"); but because death also signifies mutilation, disfigurement, and interruption (e.g., "the uncomfortable angels that rot / On the slabs, a wing chipped here, an arm there"), it is not surprising to find that certain verse-paragraphs conclude with conspicuous *incompletion*, achieved either through the abrupt termination of a line (this time in the 1928 version):

> . . . the silence which
> Engulfs you like a mummy in time, whose niche
> Lacks aperture.

—or through the tense suspension of a question:

> Shall we, more hopeful, set up the grave
> In the house? The ravenous grave?

It makes little difference, though, whether Tate chooses to tie the thread, break it off, or leave it hanging: these techniques of closure (really a catalogue of the devices we considered at the end of Chapter Three) simultaneously underscore the coherence and integrity of individual verse-paragraphs (remember Davidson's remark: "I do not quibble over a single word") *and* threaten to dissolve or interrupt the continuity of the poem as a whole (its capacity, in Davidson's terms, to *expand*).

The first verse-paragraph, which opens the poem as a sort of preface or introit, but which might just as easily stand on its own, as persuasively finished as it is, is a model of the formal procedure I am trying to describe.

> Row after row with strict impunity
> The headstones yield their names to the element,
> The wind whirrs without recollection;
> In the riven troughs the splayed leaves
> Pile up, of nature the casual sacrament
> To the seasonal eternity of death;
> Then driven by the fierce scrutiny
> Of heaven to their election in the vast breath,
> They sough the rumor of mortality.

As I mentioned, the clearly articulated iambic pentameter of line 9 brings this sentence to a decisive conclusion. Now, with the stanza before us, we can also read the heroic measure *back* into lines that otherwise exhibit a variety of impulses (the four-beat variations of lines 3 and 4, the anapestic substitutions in lines 5, 6, and 8)—in effect, retrospectively recognizing the strict coherence of the meter. The same point could be made about the usually understated but insistent rhyming (especially *within* the line where "driven" picks up "riven"; "mortality," "eternity"; and, in one of Tate's idiosyncratic and somewhat fussy choices, "sough" picks up "troughs"). We see the same sort of reflexivity operating, on still another level, in the chiasmatic syntax at the center of the stanza: "of nature the casual sacrament / To the seasonal eternity of death," a winding back and forth that leaves the genitive phrases ("of nature" and "of death") in symmetrical positions at the beginning and end of their respective lines, as if freezing these lines in an isolated tableau. (As we will see below, Tate sees "death" and "nature" in this poem as essentially the same thing.) Of course, these are not *unusual* features of poetic language, but that is just the point: Tate's array of formal effects introduces a poem that, in the rigor of its self-reference, in its predilection for turning back on itself as it moves forward, is unusually concerned to present itself *as* poetic language and not something else. These opening lines exemplify the poet's will to produce a self-sufficing structure.

The military graveyard, a clearly demarcated, semisacred site, suggests a metaphor for such a structure. Consider for a moment only the first two lines of the poem: "Row after row with strict impunity, / The headstones yield their names to the element." Here the dignity of martial discipline points to the metrical strictures of the lines themselves, to the poem's ordering of its own rows. In this context, "Row after row" describes a design comprehending both literary craftsmanship and military discipline: it is the form parts assume when they enter into a whole. What is lost in this form, evidently, is the name—or individuality—of each part, and this loss or defacement is seen here as nothing less than death, however willingly headstones or soldiers *yield* to "the element." (It is worth noting that between 1928 and 1937 Tate substituted "yield" for "barter" in line 2, in effect accenting the sense of a deliberate sacrifice. These headstones, to the extent that they stand for the soldiers they commemorate, are also heads-turned-to-stone; they are emblems of the human transformation wrought by martial discipline, the stoic refusal of sentiment.) What, on the other hand, is *gained* in this extreme ascesis is the confirmation of a corporate order—an articulation of the whole that depends upon the subordination of the parts. This economy obviously informs Tate's definition of the unitary, organic society, instantiated in the heroic codes of the Confederate South, but it is just as obviously the economy of that other unitary structure, the organic text. For the process by which the dead give up their names also figures that process by which the personal enters into and is effaced by the "element" of poetic form.

That process is one of defeat—passively, or perhaps impassively, the headstones *surrender* their names—and yet it is also one of victory, since the markers surrender "with strict impunity." That phrase neatly condenses the oxymoronic victory-in-defeat we are concerned with here, and it points to the kind of "unimpugnable" structure Davidson speaks of in his letter to Tate. Throughout his poetry, Tate's fascination with what is "strict," tight, or narrow, evokes a style of contained power, a kind of crabbed violence, that is very different from the "lazy smile" Davidson ascribes to his erect heroes. In the following lines, from the title poem of *Mr. Pope*, Tate evokes a poet bent over in his "wit and rage":

When Alexander Pope strolled in the city
Strict was the glint of pearl and gold sedans.
Ladies leaned out more out of fear than pity
For Pope's tight back was rather a goat's than man's.

Tate wrote "Mr. Pope" in 1925, his first year in New York. Pope is a man of strict bearing whose "tight back" is, paradoxically, a sign of rectitude in crooked times; and as such, he is a model for Tate's own eccentric neoclassical postures. But even though the dazzle of the city—Pope's London, Tate's Manhattan—is seen as fool's gold, there is nostalgia in Tate's poem for a period of wealth and polished forms. Tate's Pope disdains the ladies, but his ability to frighten them poorly conceals a would-be gallant's fantasy of attracting them. (There is a similar erotic scenario in Ransom's frequently anthologized "Piazza Piece.") As the poem proceeds, it takes up an apparently unrelated matter, the complete impersonality of Pope's work.

Often one thinks the urn should have more bones
Than skeletons provide for speedy dust,
The urn gets hollow, cobwebs brittle as stones
Weave to the funeral shell a frivolous rust.

And he who dribbled couplets like a snake
Coiled to a lithe precision in the sun
Is missing. The jar is empty; you may break
It only to find that Mr. Pope is gone.

What requisitions of a verity
Prompted the wit and rage between his teeth
One cannot say. Around a crooked tree
A moral climbs whose name should be a wreath.

(Tate, *Collected Poems*, 6)

If in Tate's ode the replacement of the dead by their headstones, which are in turn defaced—made anonymous—by "the element," is an image of aesthetic impersonality, we encounter the same story here in the replacement of the poet by his poem—a poem, what Tate calls a "jar" or "funeral shell," that is a type of the well-wrought urn exalted in the criticism of Cleanth Brooks. In the ode, the disappearance of the dead implies willed *submission*, whereas, in "Mr. Pope," the disappearance of the poet is a feat of *escape* (incongruously in the manner of Houdini). On the level of the text, then, the evacuation of Pope's urn is a corollary of Pope's eccentricity, which is the social sign of his power to stand outside history. This eccentricity is both imposed and elected in the poet's defense of a "verity" beyond "the glint of pearl and gold sedans." That this ultimate verity is inaccessible (something of which we "cannot" speak) does not impugn—but rather sustains—its value, because this is a male fantasy of negative power, of potency preserved and enhanced because withdrawn, a fantasy in which the memorialization of the poet-hero's name should make us doubt its assertion that he has vanished. (The poem looks ahead to some of the central motifs and problems of the New Criticism: for example, to the tendency among Tate and his colleagues to devalue the merely personal and biographical as tools of literary analysis even as they insist on the individual author as the origin of the texts they analyze. "The Intentional Fallacy" does not imply that criticism must have nothing to do with authors; it makes a case for valuing a certain kind of author and not others: one who, in the words of Wimsatt and Beardsley, has gotten the "lumps" out of the pudding and the "bugs" out of the machine.)[5] In short, the very emptiness of the urn—its hollowness, its silence—is adduced as evidence of the master's transcendence.

The emptiness of Pope's urn also returns us to the problem of the place of "ideas" in poetry. In a sense, the poetic form to which Tate aspires at least purports to have no content. In Chapter Three I mentioned Tate's quasi-scientific objections to the speech Keats ascribed to the urn in his ode. "It is here that the poem gets out of form," Tate complains of the famous equation between truth and beauty, "that the break in 'point of view' occurs; and if it is a return to Samuel Johnson's dislike of 'Lycidas' (I don't think it is) to ask how an urn can say anything, I shall have to suffer the consequences of that view" (Tate, *Essays of Four Decades*, 276). The consequences of such a view, I have argued, include a commitment to antiromantic, countervisionary poetry—a commitment most consistently and complexly exemplified, in Tate's own poetry, in "Ode to the Confederate Dead." What Tate's commentary on Keats adds to our reading of the ode is a sense of "form" as that which is broken—as silence is broken—by speech; broken by speech or, in Keats's ode, by "what the mathematicians call an extrapolation, an intrusion of matter from another field of discourse," which is "not a visible function of what the poem says."

From what field of discourse? From philosophy or sociology—those discourses whose intrusion on *The Tall Men* Tate censured? Tate suggests an answer in his response to Davidson's accusation that he had prematurely, dogmatically sacrificed the possibility of writing "an *expansive* poetry":

I have by no means decided that an expansive poetry can't be written. I say that none is being written—successfully. Crane's is the most expansive poetry of the age; but for some reason it fails to expand, except line by line. Why didn't Keats finish Hyperion? It is idle to say because he got sick and lovesick. . . . Keats had, I daresay, a finer talent than either you or I; but both Hyperions are failures, from the point of view of their intentions. And— here's the dogma—there has not been a successful expansive poetry in English since Keats. The Victorians fell on the rock of scientific doctrine—as if Keats, in giving up the second Hyperion, hadn't shown them the whole fallacy of injecting 18th century philosophy into poetry, to take the place of the myth. As for your poems, I don't mean that the material is irrecoverable in the spatio-temporal sense; but that it is epistemologically . . . (*Davidson and Tate*, 188)

The failure of both of Keats's epic ventures, no less than of the last stanza of "Ode to a Grecian Urn," comes down to a faulty hypothesis: that "18th century philosophy" could be put *into* poetry "to take the place of myth." And eighteenth-century philosophy—the empiricism whose logic Tate frequently reduces to "pearl and gold sedans," to the utilitarian confidence behind the modern capitalist's car—is little different, it turns out, from the ideas Crane and Davidson invoke in their efforts to produce a mythopoeic poetry. Instead of such an injection of ideas—the extrapolation that gets Keats's poem "out of form"—Tate consigns himself to an absence that designates "the place of myth." The result is a defiantly minor poetry, whose deliberately strict refusal to "expand" (remember, from Chapter Three, "The Subway" 's "blind astronomer" who *gluts* "expansions") preserves the absolute silence of the poetic text—its lasting reluctance to tell us either what we want or what we need to know.

This intense aestheticism might look like an abdication of the traditional injunction to instruct—like an elevation of beauty *over* truth—but it is in fact an assertion of the primacy of that truth which is inaccessible. When Tate concludes about Keats's ode, "Truth is *not* beauty, since even art cannot do more with death than preserve it" (Tate, *Essays of Four Decades*, 276), Tate is advocating an art which not only submits to death, fate, or, in Hulme's phrase, "the closing of all roads," but that, as it comes to this impasse, confirms—indeed enters into—a structure of meaning outside itself. Such "a structure of meaning" can only refer, again, to "the religious attitude," but Tate refuses to make this reference explicit. Indeed, as Ransom acknowledged in a letter to Tate written in 1926, "For you and I and the elite whom I know, art is the true religion and no other is needed."[6] But this truth could not be spoken in public, in either poetry or in literary criticism, without it constituting a shift in "the field of discourse," and thus a breaking of form. Poetry's efficacy as religious truth required that its sacred work be kept secret, implicit, available only to "the elite," not the vulgar. It was imperative that modern poetry appear not only "difficult," but untranslatable—impossible to paraphrase. For the truth of "tradition" was available to the poet not as a body of doctrine or belief, but as a system of forms, as a practice or *techne*, not a theory.

The limits of the literary are the central question in the exchange between Tate and Davidson. "I said all I had to say," Tate told his friend with satisfaction. "You can take me to task in a moral sense for not having more to say; but not for refusing to exceed my material. That was my whole quarrel with your new poems: you exceeded your material" (*Davidson and Tate*, 189). Tate's qualification, "in a moral sense," must be taken to mean "in an extra-literary sense," for Tate is in fact defending the ethical position of a poetry that strictly complies with the limits imposed by its "material"—as, in Chapter Three, we found Tate advocating the subordination of vision to theme. In "Ode to the Confederate Dead," this ethic is implied in the techniques of closure we began by examining, in the poem's recurrent figures of silence, entombment, and constriction, and in the poet's station *outside* the cemetery itself. That liminal position effectively dramatizes the poet's relation to the heroic dead *as well as* his relation to tradition, represented here as a monumental ground walled off from modernity and therefore beyond change. As the emblem of a poetic text from which the poet has *himself* been excluded, the cemetery also figures an empty container like the funerary urn in "Mr. Pope," the emptiness of which signifies the successful effacement of individual talent—the "extinction of personality"—by which the maker of this ode has been absorbed into the consecutive and simultaneous, timeless and time-bound order of tradition ("Row after row," "Rank upon rank"). "The gate is closed," Paul H. Fry has observed, "but precisely because it is closed we discover the formal consolation of a whole in which to dwell."[7]

Headstones that yield their names to the element, "splayed" leaves driven "to their election in the vast breath"—ironized and anonymous, these are representations of the work of art that is cut off from its human origins and preserves at most the traces of intention. Admittedly, I am describing an exaggerated version of the autotelic text typical of the New Criticism, but this sketch does bear comparison with the poem Tate is discussing when, in the essay called "Narcissus as Narcissus," he tells us that he is unable to give a *genetic* account of "Ode to the Confederate Dead," or at least that he is uninterested in doing so. "Poets," Tate informs us, "in their way, are practical men; they are interested in results" (Tate, *Essays of Four Decades*, 594). And "results" means the verse on a page, and nothing else. (In the case of the poet, at least, a certain positivism is not only to be condoned but demanded.)

"I say all this," Tate says, dismissing "the geneticists of poetry,"

> because it seems to me that my verse or anybody else's is merely a way of knowing something: if the poem is a real creation, it is a kind of knowledge that we did not possess before. It is not knowledge "about" something else; the poem is the fullness of that knowledge. We know the particular poem, not what it says that we can restate. In a manner of speaking, the poem is its own knower, neither poet nor reader knowing anything that the poem says apart from the words of the poem. I have expressed this view elsewhere in other terms, and it has been accused of aestheticism, or art for art's sake. But let the reader recall the historic position of Catholicism: *nulla salus extra ecclesiam*. That must be religion*ism*. There is probably nothing wrong with art for art's sake if we take the phrase seriously, and not take it to mean the kind of poetry written in England forty years ago. Religion always ought to transcend any of its particular uses; and likewise the true art for art's sake view can only be held by persons who are always looking for things that they can respect apart from use (though they may be useful), like poems, fly rods, and formal gardens. (Tate, *Essays of Four Decades*, 595)

The poem does not offer knowledge "about" something else, since that difficult preposition would open up a space or gap—another area of enclosure—*within* the poem, which consists precisely and tautologically only in "the words of the poem." To be sure, Tate is describing "fullness," not emptiness, here, but because that plenitude cannot be articulated apart from its own articulation, it is fundamentally occult: it is present to us as an absence—as what it says that we cannot restate. And, in this sense, the inaccesibility of the poem's *origins* corresponds to its lack of *consequences* or uses. It does not tell us what we know or need to know; it is an ostensive object directing our attention first and last to itself.

This definition of the poem relies upon, in John Guillory's phrase, "the perceived muteness of the literary work"—a state of affairs that is replicated, in turn, by "the gestural aphasia of the teacher" or critic (Guillory, "Ideology of Canon Formation," 188). The poem's "perceived muteness" would seem to be entirely at odds with "the historic position of Catholicism: *nulla salus extra ecclesiam*," which is nothing if not an explicit directive. And yet Tate's analogy (reinforced by the New Testament resonance of the phrase, "the fullness of that knowledge") reminds us that the very silence of the poem issues an injunction, a call to discipline that is analogous to the Church's directives: from priest and believer, the Church requires the conservation of ritual; from poet and reader, the poem requires the conservation of form. Of course, neither ecclesiastical ritual nor poetic form, each understood as a *commemorative* vessel, presents itself in the place of ideas, doctrine, truth, or content, but this is precisely the negative knowledge they impart as expressions of practice.

Perhaps such a practice does not constitute aestheticism, nor even "religion*ism*," but it is essential, surely, to Tate's modernism—at least as Tate understood that literature which, in its dedication to the enhancement of its own formal mediations (what I have been calling its "difficulty"), proposed to reclaim for literature the hieratic distance once associated with the sacred text. The collapse of that distance (which romanticism exemplifies for Tate) means a confusion of subject and object, a trespass of limits, which, in his ode, Tate treats as solipsism or "Narcissism, or any other *ism* that denotes the failure of the human personality to function objectively in nature and society" (Tate, *Essays of Four Decades*, 595–96). The point for Tate is that "isms"—viewed as theories of experience (whether Communist *or* Agrarian)—impose a version of the self on what should be other—"nature and society"—and so recapitulate the condition that, in principle, these theories are intended to redress. "Isms," Tate believes, merely reinforce the hypertrophy of the intellect, and therefore "the cut-off-ness of the modern 'intellectual man' from the world" (Tate, *Essays of Four Decades*, 598).

That condition, Tate explains, is represented allegorically by the blind crab and the jaguar in the ode. But the quotation marks around "intellectual man," like the manifest impatience in "any other *ism*," indicate Tate's overriding reluctance to make his poem be about "something else," particularly about something like "the cut-off-ness of the modern 'intellectual man'" in which Tate might have a personal, perhaps even narcissistic investment. "As a citizen I have my own prescription," Tate explains, "but as a poet I am concerned with the experience of 'solipsism.' And an experience *of* it is not quite the same thing as a philosophical statement *about* it" (Tate, *Essays of Four Decades*, 596). Tate has a politics, in other words, but it is essential to Tate to keep his politics out of his poetry (i.e., to keep out the sort of "doctrines" that Davidson wanted to put *in*). The purpose of this strategy, which is continuous with Tate's dismissal of "genetic theories" of poetry, is to sustain the objectivity of the poem, to resist, as Davidson did not, the distorting force of "ideas"; but its effect is precisely to enforce the "cut-off-ness" of the poem itself. Folded into the perfect unity of content and form, the ideal poem is "its own knower." Which is to say that the poem Tate describes sounds a good deal like Narcissus.

This conclusion is the opposite of what Tate is claiming, but it really only restates the principle we have seen at work in "Ode to the Confederate Dead"—above all, in its preoccupation with technical effects of closure. For "cut-off-ness" is precisely the goal of a literary method that, in its refusal to exceed its material, defines the poem *as* poetic language and not something else. Behind this method—or discipline—is simply the proposition we started out with: that the integrity of the poem *as form* depends upon its inaccessibility *as content*. I want to show now that the valorization of form over content Tate defends in "Narcissus as Narcissus" points, in the ode, to the story we examined closely in Chapter Three: that is, to the replacement of the visionary poet by the craftsman.

This plot can be glimpsed, I think, in Tate's progress from second-person singular to first-person plural constructions in the course of the meditation. The second-person emerges for the first time in the poem when, in the second verse-paragraph, the man at the gate looks into the eyes of one of the angels inside:

> The brute curiosity of an angel's stare
> Turns you, like them, to stone,
> Transforms the heaving air
> Till plunged to a heavier world below
> You shift your sea-space blindly
> Heaving, turning like the blind crab.

Like the Ozymandian statue Tate once saw in Lescaze's portrait of Crane, this angel—demonized as a kind of animal or brute—turns its admirer into stone. In this case, the transformation more or less explicitly expresses Tate's censure of his own visionary ambitions. For the disfigured stone angels, in contrast to the headstones in the first lines of the poem, provide an image of *personalized* art, of the preservation of the human form beyond death, which, in this naturalizing setting, merely recapitulates the knowledge derived from Keats's urn: that "art cannot do more with death than preserve it." To believe otherwise, as the "you" of the poem is, at least at times, rather desperately trying to do, is to confront the "natural" limits of desire, to see desire turned back, with vengeance, on the self. On the level of the image, this experience of limits is pictured in the mutilation of the cemetery's statues, later as the suppressed "rage" of "muted Zeno and Parmenides." On the grammatical level of the pronoun, it can be seen in the emergence of an alien- or dummy-self, the ironized "you" of internal colloquy.

This dummy-self is the victim and agent of the violence in the three verse-paragraphs that follow, each of which generates a hallucinatory vision of battle before arriving at an admission of defeat. In these central sections of the poem, Tate coordinates the charge of the Confederate soldiers and the effort of the man at the gate to renew, as a visionary act in poetry, the heroism of that charge. Here the command to *praise* "the vision" and "the arrogant circumstance" of the dead, seen as martyrs, defines the man's heroism as the heroism of utterance, or in this case as the making of a classical ode—an activity, we are led to feel, whose chance of success is surely no greater than that of the Confederate cause. In fact, in the version he showed Davidson in January 1927, Tate classified the poem as an elegy; he only later settled on the familiar title. "I suppose," Tate reflected on the change in "Narcissus as Narcissus," "in so calling it [i.e., in calling it an ode] I intended an irony: the scene of the poem is not a public celebration, it is a lone man by a gate" (Tate, *Essays of Four Decades*, 602).[8] This "irony," if that is the right word for the poem's attitude toward its own generic claims, is already unmistakably expressed in the failure of the speaker to be heard. This is the silence, I take it, that surrounds him at last—before Tate presents us, in lieu of his corpse, with an old dog trapped in the cellar:

> You hear the shout, the crazy hemlocks point
> With troubled fingers to the silence which
> Smothers you, a mummy, in time.
>   The hound bitch
> Toothless and dying, in a musty cellar
> Hears the wind only.

This entombment "in time," mourned by a miserable mother, ends the action of the second-person singular. The last, closing movement of the ode is introduced next by an elaborately framed question, stated in the first-person plural:

>   Now that the salt of their blood
> Stiffens the saltier oblivion of the sea,
> Seals the malignant purity of the flood,
> What shall we who count our days and bow
> Our heads with a commemorial woe

> In the ribboned coats of grim felicity,
> What shall we say of the bones, unclean,
> Whose verdurous anonymity will grow?

The substitution of "we" for "you" marks a move beyond visionary failure toward the definition of limits, presented as a question of possible speech: What shall we say—implicitly, What *can* we say—of the dead? Or, as the poet himself usefully paraphrases the passage in "Narcissus as Narcissus," "In the midst of this naturalism, what shall the man say? What shall all humanity say in the presence of decay?" (Tate, *Essays of Four Decades*, 606). The defeat of the poem's heroic commitment to praise introduces, in short, an ethical question of bearing, of comportment, that is necessarily a matter of practice and discipline (and therefore a matter to be determined and regulated by an authority over and outside the self). Of course, as Tate's return to a normative meter indicates, completing the unfinished line ("Hears the wind . . .") with what he calls "a formal rhythm" ("Now that the salt . . ."),[9] this is also a matter of received form: the rigor of the heroic dead, who strangely alter the element they enter, in effect stiffening, sealing, and *formalizing* nature, provides the correct example for those who confusedly mourn in "the ribboned coats" of the New South's—or, indeed, of the New World's—"grim felicity." If not in life, the Confederate Passion can still be imitated in death.

That this question can be framed in the first-person plural, announcing a principle of conduct governing self and other, and therefore the recovery of audience, recalls us to the victory-in-defeat adumbrated in the first lines of the poem: the entrance into form is an entrance into an impersonal—perhaps we should now say *trans*personal—medium. What can be said in this medium, it turns out, is merely the affirmation of "naturalism" that Tate offers when the ode's "refrain," those two-line fragments about the flying and the plunging of the leaves, previously interjected between verse-paragraphs, joins the body of the argument:

> We shall say only the leaves whispering
> In the improbable mist of nightfall
> That flies on multiple wing . . .

This is presented as a minimal statement, an accommodation to the limiting case, and it effectively restates the directive Tate issued to Davidson in May 1926: "We must be subjective." On the face of it, this is an unlikely place for Tate's meditation to wind up. But the subjectivity that is affirmed in these lines has been distinguished from "the experience of solipsism" by its recognition of "the failure of the human personality to function objectively" either in life or in literature—a failure that does not liberate the individual talent, of course, but enforces a collective imperative.

Accordingly, the threat of narcissism—and behind it, that of the homoerotic—can now be relegated to the remote violence of an apotropaic gesture:

> Night is the beginning and the end
> And in between the ends of distraction
> Waits mute speculation, the patient curse
> That stones the eyes, or like the jaguar leaps
> For his own image in a jungle pool, his victim.

An apotropaic gesture, because the self-consuming jaguar enacts the possibility of self-destruction that the poem has itself, up to this point, only partially resisted. In one sense, this possibility can now be represented—and thus disposed of—because the poem has definitively passed beyond it: a commitment to form has been restored just when the frustration of its visionary impulses had threatened to destroy it (to render the poem *merely* a failure—and not a Pyrrhic victory). But the poem really only gets beyond that threat *by* representing it: stylized as moral exemplum, the fate of the jaguar-Narcissus confirms the wisdom of Tate's fated withdrawal into the controlling discipline of form.

The brief appearance of the jaguar immediately raises the possibility of deliberately *choosing* suicide:

> What shall we say who have knowledge
> Carried to the heart? Shall we take the act
> To the grave?

And yet Tate's new access to a rule of conduct determined outside the self has prepared him to pass on at this point to the more urgent question posed by the ethos of ancestor worship itself:

> Shall we, more hopeful, set up the grave
> In the house? The ravenous grave?

But even these questions can be left behind, finally, by leaving the grave where Tate found it:

> Leave now
> The shut gate and the decomposing wall:
> The gentle serpent, green in the mulberry bush,
> Riots with his tongue through the hush—
> Sentinel of the grave who counts us all!

That is, behind a gate that, even by the end of the poem, has yet to be opened. I suppose Tate's desire to enter the cemetery returns here in a fear that the "decomposing" wall will *not* hold and the phallic serpent-sentinel will advance to claim him. But this fantasy is not a last-minute reprieve, saving the poem from the inaction it suffers under and deplores. Its final action is delegated to a serpent who "riots with his tongue" only; and even this violence must be enacted in silence, transmitted "through the hush."

          In response to Davidson's complaints about his "accusation of failure on all sides," Tate explained that the standards he brought to modern poetry were simply those of "all the poetry of the past which I have read": "My attempt is to see the present from the past, yet remain immersed in the present and committed to it. I think it is suicide to do anything else. From the attitude of my own criticism (perhaps from that of others' too!) my own poems are 'failures' " (*Davidson and Tate*, 189). This is, in fine, the argument of "Ode to the Confederate Dead"—a summary that is alert, even, to the danger of disregarding the claims of the present (or of setting up the grave in the house). But what Tate describes as measuring the poetry of the present by that of the past might be more accurately described, in the case of his own poem, as measuring the poetry of Hart Crane by that of T. S. Eliot. For in its ironization of the visionary mode, "Ode to the Confederate Dead" recapitulates Tate's identification with Eliot and his repudiation of Crane.

The ode brings these choices to the fore by its conspicuous appeals to Eliot's poetry. David Bromwich has described "Ode to the Confederate Dead" as a pastiche of Eliot's "Gerontion."[10] The ode is indeed indebted to "Gerontion" in several ways: there is Tate's rephrasing of Eliot's question ("After such knowledge, what forgiveness?"), the theme of "reconsidered passion," the wind that blows through both poems, and the dramatic monologue form. But this list, considerable as it is, only begins to suggest the ode's debts to Eliot's poetry in general. For instance, there are borrowings as unmistakable as the blind crab from "Prufrock" (and Tate's symbolic bestiary—crab, bitch, jaguar, spiders, owl, and serpent—is always used in Eliot's *manner*), and then there are borrowings whose force, if palpable, is only cumulative. Words like "nightfall," "murmur," "lean," and "whispering" do not constitute specific allusions to *The Waste Land*, but they can all be found in "What the Thunder Said." Taken together, these and other words present themselves as signs of a shared vocabulary, a collective idiom. Tate's cut-and-paste method, his oddly obvious and multiple debts to Eliot and other poets,[11] is ultimately an expression of the poem's commitment to *conformity*—or what I have called Tate's ethical commitment to received forms. On the level of style, Tate's submission to an impersonal order comes down to the imitation of Eliot.

To Crane, who in 1923 advised Tate to improve his poetry by "willfully extracting the more obvious echoes of Eliot" (Crane, *Letters*, 123), Tate's crowding of the poem with echoes of Eliot must have signified the elimination of his own presence in Tate's work. But despite all of its explicit appeals to Eliot, I would maintain that "Ode to the Confederate Dead" is unlike Eliot's poetry in ways that it is much more like Crane's. Except in the most attenuated modernist sense of these genres, for example, I doubt that Eliot ever thought of "Gerontion" as *either* an ode or an elegy. Nor can one imagine Mr. Silvero, Hakagawa, or Fraulein von Kulp, the cartoon characters in "Gerontion," turning up in Tate's poem. Being cut off from the past really *is*, for Tate's man at the gate, an experience of grief; and, in the end, this disappointment links him, in defeat, with the heroic dead, not Eliot's little old man.

It also links Tate with Crane. To say that Crane is the elegiac subject of the ode, we would have to uncover the evidence that Davidson could not when he asked, "And where, O Allen Tate, are the dead?" But Crane's presence in the ode is perceptible as "form," if not "content." Despite the ways in which Tate's poem links itself with Eliot, it never fully sounds like Eliot, because it sounds so much like Crane. For Eliot is not primarily or distinctively a pentameter poet, while Crane is, and above all in the major lyrics from the mid-1920s (poems such as "Recitative," "Possessions," "For the Marriage of Faustus and Helen," "Voyages," and "At Melville's Tomb"). Tate responded to several of those poems in draft, and he absorbed their meters in his own work—typically an iambic scheme modified by free-verse variations.[12] That metrical combination of tradition and modernity suggested to both Tate and Crane the possibility of writing a heroic modern poetry, a poetry "at once contemporary and in the grand manner" (as Tate put it in the preface to *White Buildings*). Against Eliot, the meters Tate heard in Crane's work argued that traditional forms were not in fact "dead." To align himself with Eliot, Tate had to give up that argument—which Tate did, even though he retained its formal vehicle. Crane, it has been said, tried to write a poetry like Eliot's on Whitmanian themes. Tate set himself a similarly contradictory task: to put Eliot's ideas into a poetry like Crane's. When the man at the gate mourns the dead, he is also mourning Crane.

The association in Tate's mind between Crane and the dead heroes of the ode is brought out in "Narcissus as Narcissus," an essay written six years after the suicide of the only critic of the ode whom Tate mentions. Here is Tate's—and then Crane's—explication of the theme brought forward in the lines beginning, "You know who have waited by the wall":

> It is the theme of heroism, not merely moral heroism, but heroism in the grand style, elevating even death from mere physical dissolution into a formal ritual: this heroism is a formal ebullience of the human spirit in an entire society, not private, romantic illusion—something better than moral heroism, great as that may be, for moral heroism, being personal and individual, may be achieved by certain men in all ages, even ages of decadence. But the late Hart Crane's commentary, in a letter, is better than any I can make; he described the theme as the "theme of chivalry, a tradition of excess (not literally excess, rather active faith) which cannot be perpetuated in the fragmentary cosmos of today—'those desires which should be yours tomorrow,' but which, you know, will not persist nor find any way into action." (Tate, *Essays of Four Decades*, 599)[13]

Crane is introduced at this stage of the essay not simply because Tate is reluctant to tell us himself what his poem is "about" (although that is one reason); for Tate's quotation from Crane's letter also acts to renew—and remind the reader of—a friendship wholly relevant to the composition of the poem. The pathos of this renewal, of course, is that the friendship itself cannot be renewed: Tate has been cut off from his friend as emphatically and permanently as the man at the gate has been cut off from the Confederate dead. The effect is to link the dead poet and the dead soldiers, and to list, at least implicitly, Crane's own poetry of "excess" and "active faith" among "those desires which should be yours tomorrow," but which, Tate would have the reader know, "will not persist nor find any way to action."

At the same time, Tate is once again identifying himself—or, perhaps, an earlier version of himself—with Crane, who is made to speak here for a type of heroism that is inaccessible to both himself and Tate. Close to the surface of this argument, I would suggest, is an assertion that Crane himself is a model of "moral heroism," and the only sort of hero to be found in an age of decadence. (This view is explicit in the still later essay, "Crane: The Poet as Hero," as well as in Winters's late view of Crane as "a saint of the wrong religion.") Moral heroism is "personal and individual," whereas "heroism in the grand style" is impersonal and—one presumes—traditional. To choose between these kinds of heroism is to choose between romanticism and classicism, as Tate understood those terms, but there is in fact no choice to be made: Tate and his readers can

at best aspire, as Crane aspired, to a moral heroism that consists in imitation—in a "private, romantic" commemoration—of epic action. If Tate
diverges from Crane as much as "Ode to the Confederate Dead" diverges
from "Atlantis," the difference between them is effaced in "Narcissus as
Narcissus" in order to confirm what the two poets share: the belief that
the modern poet should be able to write—unironically and without quotation marks—"in the grand style."

For Tate, the denial of that right produces a parable of defeat. Although, in Tate's thinking, form takes precedence over content, and the
craftsman takes precedence over the visionary, form-making, as a refusal
to exceed imaginative limits, finally sustains the priority of that content
which is "irrecoverable." (The "buried" past Tate describes to Davidson
can be construed as the "active faith" of an earlier time or an earlier self.)
Form-making, as Tate sees it, is a commemorative and mimetic activity, a
mode of ritual that approximates, in an age of decadence, the heroism of
another era.

Although all the poems in Tate's *Collected Poems* are dated, the dates
"1927/1937" at the end of the ode have a special force. (The only substantial, rather than strictly local, change Tate made after the poem's first publication was the addition of the so-called refrain—an addition that Crane
thought necessary to the poem's "subjective continuity," and that Tate
hoped would make the poem "seem longer than it is." The refrain is in
each case a two-line, concentrated, imagistic statement, a series of variations on a theme beginning "Dazed by the wind, only the wind / The
leaves flying, plunge." That such a refrain was believed to enhance the
poem's continuity and make it *longer* emphasizes again the poem's competing impulses toward expansion and closure—or toward epic and lyric
utterances. The refrain, by drawing, as Hollander has pointed out, on the
leaves in Shelley's "West Wind" and on Hardy's revision of Shelley in
"During Wind and Rain," also emphasizes the poem's ambivalent relation
to romantic models: Shelley makes his way into the poem only under the
aegis of Hardy—a poet Winters recommended to Tate as a suitably un-
sentimental antidote to romanticism.) In fine, that dating of the poem is a
reminder of the *labor* of form—a labor that Tate's poem and his essay on
the poem constantly emphasize. Tate's form-making insists on the poet's
professional dedication to the task and on the technical expertise he brings
to it. But it is also imagined as heroic work: indeed, in Tate's hands, *the
duration of composition itself*, prolonged in revision, takes the place of the
irrecoverable duration of the epic work. "Ode to the Confederate Dead"
is Tate's terse reply to the long poems of Crane, Davidson, and others, but

it is not simply a rebuttal, a refusal to engage in the same competition; rather, Tate's poem preserves, through its protracted pursuit of an "unimpugnable" form, the heroic ambition it disavows on the level of "content."

The length of time Tate worked on the ode suggests a mind turning back on itself, unable to go forward. In Tate's life, the impasse he wrote about took concrete shape in a recurrent and increasingly severe writer's block, a block which, in the 1950s, kept him from finishing the projected long poem in terza rima of which "The Swimmers," "The Buried Lake," and "The Maimed Man" are the only completed parts. The limits of poetry, as Tate came to live them, were strict indeed. Tate adjusted to those limits, in part, by turning to criticism. The end of Tate's work on the ode in 1937 coincided with the beginning of the period in which he wrote his most important literary essays. Those essays are above all writerly performances, stamped not only by Tate's expertise but by his "wit and rage." The poet-critic's work as a critic begins, it seems, only once his primary work as a poet ends.

But I would argue that Tate's criticism simply continues the intensively self-reflective project of his poetry. For form-making is a fundamentally *critical* activity, as Tate viewed this process of, in Winters's words, "evaluating" and "controlling" a given experience, and it rightly culminates in criticism. The writing of "Narcissus as Narcissus" is the final step in the process of revision, the editorial discipline of self-scrutiny, that constituted the composition of the ode to begin with. But what is most striking about this conclusion to the poem is that it is no conclusion at all. Unable, that is, to evaluate either the consequences or the origins of his poem, just as he is unable to say what his poem is "about," Tate can only say what the poem says; he can only point, with the tools of prosodic analysis, to the metrical gestures with which the form of the poem mimes its content. (The alternation between "a formal regularity" and "a broken rhythm," Tate tells us, is meant to show the maintenance and collapse of "heroic emotion" in the poem. As Tate admits, "This is 'imitative form,' which Yvor Winters deems a vice worth castigation" [Tate, *Essays of Four Decades*, 603].) In the end, even the poet-critic can do no more than renew his poem's refusal to speak.

The attitude of Tate's poetry that I characterized at the end of Chapter Three as a discourse of closure should therefore be recognized, at the same time, as a discourse of incompletion—or perhaps *de*pletion, since it is exactly the hollowness of the urn that signifies the poet-hero's transcendence, his escape from the contingencies of merely personal expression. Emptiness, the blank space of Tate's poetry, is the trophy of this Pyrrhic victory, the mark of a successful failure. When, therefore, Tate reflects, in the closing sentences of "Narcissus as Narcissus," that "there is much to be said for the original *barter* instead of *yield* in the second line, and for *Novembers* instead of *November* in line fifteen" (609), it is more than a quibble. It is a sign of how great small things have become. It is a sign of just how much the poem has left out.

Let me step back to recapitulate the progress of this argument. I have been suggesting that "Ode to the Confederate Dead" articulates a movement of thought already familiar from our examination of Tate's shifting perspectives on Crane: that is, the poem records a passage beyond visionary failure toward the circumscription of what can be said in a modern poem. It is the task of Tate's ode, as it is of Tate's criticism, to represent these limits as *given*—when, in fact, such limits can only be constructed and prescribed. The recognition of limits Tate advocates, following Eliot and Hulme, evacuates modern poetry of other, potentially competing discourses, including the political and religious. What emerges in their place is Tate's concept of the poem as "its own knower"—an autotelic object that refers in an aphasic manner to the absence of transmissible doctrine (or "ideas") that its own access to authority has displaced.

Despite its claim to speak from a position of disinheritance (or "cut-off-ness"), Tate's poem itself enforces this condition on the levels of poetic form and argument. Indeed, in its own terms, the aesthetic value of "Ode to the Confederate Dead," which is also the value of a fly rod or a formal garden, *depends upon* the poem's independence from the historical determinations that otherwise inform Tate's definition of a cultural inheritance. The poem is a thing set apart, and quite deliberately so. As such, Tate's poem elevates defeat as the guarantor of the autonomy I am describing, whether it is the defeat of the rebel soldiers or of the poet who wishes to praise them. To identify the modern poet with the man at the gate is to represent the poet as declassed: Tate's poet-protagonist has been denied the prerogatives of his people, caste, and region not simply by the failure of the Confederate cause (which would be closer to Davidson's point), but also by the failure of traditional society to hold back modernity. ("The setback of the war," Tate explained, "was of itself a very trivial one.")[14] Yet this historical defeat, however catastrophic it is in Tate's account, successfully extricates the poet from ongoing entanglements of class interest: having lost everything, he has nothing to gain; and the poet who is cut off from the heroism of the past is also cut off from present social conflict. The autonomy of the text that demands our respect "apart from use" is finally a displaced representation of the disinterestedness that its author claims for his own social position.

The autonomy of the text is above all a function of its silence—its refusal to be "reduced" to (to be seen to serve) another discourse or system of "ideas." Poetry, as Tate came to define it, is an idealized mode of *experience*, an intimate, nonalienated way of knowing the world; it is the rational instrument of a practice that claims to transcend the merely instrumental rationality of science and commerce. (Remember Ransom's notion of poetry as a technical means of apprehending "the untechnical homely fullness of the world.") This definition, already clear in Tate's remark that "an experience *of*" solipsism is different from "a philosophical statement *about* it," opposes the experience of literature in general and poetry in particular to "ideology." For Tate and his colleagues in the New Criticism, "ideology" is precisely and only a system of "ideas," an abstract system that falsifies experience by simplifying it.[15] It was the role of poetry, Tate reasoned, to preserve the truth of experience, which is always concrete and particular, and therefore multiple and contradictory, like the range of meanings that cohere in a well-made poem.

That is the special claim Tate makes for poetry in the key essay from 1938 called "Tension in Poetry." Tate begins that essay by distinguishing poetic "tension" from "mass language," a category that comprises "lady-like lyrics" as well as "political poetry," modes of thought and feeling Tate found characteristic of mass culture. For an instance of both kinds of poem, Tate turns to "Justice Denied in Massachusetts" by Edna St. Vincent Millay, a poet whom (to judge from Ransom's "The Poet as Woman") the New Critics loved to hate. Millay's poem about Sacco and Vanzetti exemplified for Tate a public poetry of ideas. Tate's economical trick in using it was to make femininity, bleeding-heart politics, and a popular brand of free verse all seem like the same thing (Tate, *Essays of Four Decades*, 56–58). At the same time, Tate implicitly made formal rigor the sign of professional authority and a tough-minded, skeptical masculinity. As we will see in Chapter Eight, these symbolic values would win for Tate's formalism a privileged position in the intensively anticommunist literary culture of the postwar era. Tate's formalist principles and practice could be absorbed into English department pedagogy, under the rubric of technical expertise, as apolitical criteria. But Tate's formalism had been forged in "ideological" struggles with antagonists as different as Davidson and Millay, and it continued to do political work.[16]

The anticapitalist stance of Tate's Agrarian period, which was rooted in the critique of money rather than of property, had always had a vigorous anticommunist component: the title Tate suggested for *I'll Take My Stand* was, after all, "A Tract Against Communism." Tate's "proprietary ideal," which insisted upon the morally uplifting effects of owning property, including slaves as well as land, was always for Tate the special legacy of Western culture. "We must be the last Europeans," Tate had told Davidson at the beginning of his Agrarian phase (*Davidson and Tate*, 230); later, that cosmopolitan perspective became more prominent. It was when he turned away from Crane that Tate began the ode, and the ode led him into "the Southern movement"; but politics led Tate back to the ode, and to the hesitations of the lone man at the gate, quoting Eliot.

Henceforth, it seems to me, Tate's Southernism persisted primarily as a style, as a means of identifying himself among and in relation to other modern, cosmopolitan intellectuals. The Stars 'n' Bars over the mantel, grandfather's cane, a portrait of Stonewall Jackson, the pillared house above the Cumberland River that looked so much like "Tara"—however deeply Tate felt about them, those properties of his were also props, the machinery of a particular modernist drama. The general appeal of that drama is suggested by the lasting success of "the Southern renaissance" as a concept under which to organize and market modernist Southern writing, a concept that Tate was one of the first critics to promote.[17] Or consider the relish with which Eliot would perform for his friends "a ballad like 'The Reconstructed Rebel.' "[18] Trivially for Eliot, urgently for Tate, the Southern rebel dramatized the contradictions of modernist reaction. In his biography of Stonewall Jackson, begun at the same time as the ode, Tate analyzed the Confederate secession as a defense of the South's legitimate right to slavery, according to a historical and "literal" interpretation of the United States Constitution. "Secession was not revolution," Tate insisted; "it was Constitutionalism."[19] By maintaining the avant-gardist rhetoric of "secession" while they proclaimed the truth of the old ways, Tate's stories about the Confederate dead reconciled opposition and obedience, resolving in fantasy the contest between modernism and tradition. Like T. S. Eliot, the Confederate dead stood for "the right kind of modernism, which by opposing everything modern is reactionary."

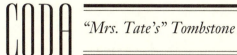

CODA

"Mrs. Tate's" Tombstone

IT IS FOR ADAM TO INTERPRET THE VOICES WHICH EVE HEARS.

—Jacques Maritain, "The Frontiers of Poetry"[1]

Before turning to a discussion of Crane's career, I want to make use of the hiatus between the two halves of this book to go back and reflect on the imaginative situation of the other member of the household in Patterson in the winter of 1926. It is not obvious where Caroline Gordon "fits" in the literary relationship between her husband and his friend, for each man's ambivalent and richly freighted interest in the other's writing was accompanied, for all appearances, by a lack of interest in hers. As we saw in Chapter Two, when Tate and Gordon quarreled with Crane in Patterson, Gordon was fighting with Crane *for* Tate; that is, both on behalf of her husband and for exclusive possession of him. But it is also important to see that Gordon was fighting *with both men*, and that she was fighting not for her marriage but for her right to be a writer. Gordon's everyday circumstances in the farmhouse in Patterson make the point clearly and forcefully enough: once Crane was gone, Gordon moved her writing out of the kitchen and into his study. The division of domestic and literary labor realized in that act made it possible, although still arduous, for Gordon to write. As she confided to a female friend in May 1926, "I find that having a room of my own enables me to write—I couldn't write a word all winter" (Gordon and Wood, *Southern Mandarins*, 22). In Gordon's case, the female fiction writer became an author—symbolically and pragmatically—by taking the male romantic poet's place.

Yet Gordon only gained access to a literary vocation by submitting, as Crane would not, to the traditional male authority embodied in her husband, the poet-critic. In a sense, Gordon's submission to Tate's authority was as essential to the forging of that authority as Tate's own submission to Eliot's. For Gordon, as it had for Tate, this act entailed a propitiatory

105

"extinction of personality," only it was her husband, not Eliot, to whom her sacrifice was presented. Gordon was at work on her second novel in 1926; the fate of her first novel is instructive. When Gordon showed it to Tate, she read disapproval in his face, and she destroyed it (Makowsky, *Caroline Gordon*, 70–71). There is no record of the novel's contents, other than Gordon's statement that it was autobiographical, like most of her fiction. Still, Gordon's Keatsian title, *Darkling I Listen*, tells us that she began her writing career by invoking a romantic poet (a romantic poet complexly linked to passivity and "the feminine") in order to name and validate her fiction (Makowsky, *Caroline Gordon*, 43). But Gordon permitted Tate to eliminate the romantic poet in her (apparently without a word) just as Tate had eliminated that poet in himself. Gordon thus ceded to Tate a more "advanced" position (intellectually and technically) and the power to pass judgment on her work. This is the position of the poet-critic in Tate's relation to Crane; in his relation to Gordon, it is the position of the husband. The latter allows us to recognize the gender assignments that are submerged in Tate's relation to Crane. For in Tate's relation to Gordon, the refined technique and superior rationality of the poet-critic explicitly and exclusively belong to the heterosexual male, the husband and father; whereas the irrational powers of mind associated with "genius," which require a skilled interpreter to shape and control them, are marked as female.

This hierarchical structure of authority informed Gordon's ties to a series of male mentors: her father, Tate, Ford Madox Ford, and Maxwell Perkins, her editor at Scribner's. With the guidance of these men Gordon developed her fiction according to the teachings and example of "the Master," Henry James. By emulating one of the few fiction writers Pound and Eliot had approved for emulation, Gordon sought to overcome the high modernist devaluation of women's writing and realist fiction. In Chapter One I described how Eliot adopted James's "fantasy of vocational upgrading" (Brodhead, *School of Hawthorne*, 113) to define his own form of professionalism, adding to James's emphasis on technique a strong ethical charge. Gordon adopted this fantasy as well in the course of her disciplined training in James; and it showed Gordon how to accommodate her fiction to the formalist aesthetics of her husband and his fellow New Critics. In the preface to *The House of Fiction* (a textbook and anthology designed as a complement to *Understanding Poetry*), Gordon and Tate praised the formal unity and dramatic effect of fiction in the Jamesian mode, "by means of which it has achieved something of the self-contained objectivity of certain kinds of poetry."[2] But the kind of poetry Jamesian fiction resembles is not, in the Tates' account, that of Keats or Crane. Rather, Jamesian fiction, in its claim to a position of authority "above and to one side" of its central character (Gordon and Tate, *The House of Fiction*, 626), is an example of the mature, ironic stance that Ransom recommended, and that Tate achieved by repudiating poets such as Keats and Crane.

Gordon's aspiring to the Jamesian ideal she defined in *The House of Fiction* made her access to literature conditional upon her identification with the masculinist values of "the right kind of modernism." Yet Gordon's submission to the literary judgment of her masters did not prevent her from finding grounds on which to contest it. Perhaps surprisingly, when she joined the Roman Catholic Church in 1947, Gordon's submission to traditional male authority itself provided the ground on which to challenge and resist her masculine literary models. In one sense, conversion merely extended the structure of discipleship across the whole of Gordon's life, affirming her view of patriarchy as the natural and eternal order of the universe. Yet because it duplicated the structure of her literary discipleship, conversion not only subordinated Gordon to the absolute authority of the Father, it also *identified* her with that authority, making Gordon independent of her mentors in a way she had not been before. In effect, by entering the Church in advance of her husband, Gordon climbed "above and a little to one side of" him: she placed herself in an intellectual and spiritual position to pass judgment on Tate and to hold out help for him in *his* career.

In *The Strange Children* (1951), a novel in which the Tate household is itself the subject of her fiction, Gordon worked to articulate this new position. The novel studies the lives of the poet Stephen Lewis and his wife, Sarah, from the "innocent" point of view of the Lewis's young daughter, Lucy. Lucy, who is set apart from the professional writers around her by her youth and by her deep feeling for nature, presents those writers to us in a manner sometimes comic, sometimes scathing. In the following passage, for example, we observe some of the Lewis's stranger houseguests through Lucy's eyes. The scene is based on Gordon's memory of the visit Ford Madox Ford and Robert Lowell made to the Tates in 1937 (to which we will return in Chapter Eight):

> The big Englishman and his wife and secretary and the young poet from
> Boston were all there then. . . . He [the Englishman] used to get tired of
> writing on his history of the world and would come out and go in the hen
> house a dozen times a day, to see if the hens had laid any eggs. The poet

lived in a tent in the yard and read poetry over and over to himself; it
sounded like a bumblebee buzzing. And then in the evenings they used to go
up on the gallery and have their drinks. Sometimes they would read poetry
to each other or sometimes they would just talk about their friends, but if
you lay down in the hollyhocks and looked up at them you could see each
one's face plain through the railings. It looked like they were animals that
had been put in a pen.[3]

Outside the cage of cocktail conversation, Lucy renders moral judgment
on her elders without ever being aware of having done so. Lucy merely
"wondered how they could sit there, hour after hour, talking. Talk was all
they seemed to care about. They would talk while Rome burned" (Gordon, *The Strange Children*, 114). Lucy's perspective is associated in this
way with the sacred point of view of the Psalmist, who provides the epigraph for the novel as well as its title: "Rid me, and deliver me from the
hand of strange children, whose mouth speaketh vanity" (Psalm 144). The
little girl and the Psalmist together suggest a point of view that is "naive"
and transcendental. These qualities are emphasized by the two sources for
Lucy's name—the Catholic saint and the subject of Wordsworth's "Lucy
poems." For when she links romanticism and religion in this way, Gordon
rejects all merely secular "talk" and chooses instinctual and mystical alternatives to discursive mastery. Through this choice Gordon deliberately
separates herself from the modernist intellectuals talking on the gallery
over drinks, among whom the most self-assured, skeptical, and vain are
the literary men.

On one level, *The Strange Children* is the story of Gordon's triumph
over those men. At least, before Stephen Lewis is ready to recognize the
spiritual path he needs to take, his vanity must be humbled, and his bonds
with other men broken. In the closing pages of the novel, these conditions
are met when "the friend of his youth" and "the most gifted of all his
intimates" suddenly leaves Lewis "without farewell." With Lucy pressed
against him and his wife beside them, Lewis has a kind of vision:

> Always when he thought of that friend a light seemed to play about his head.
> He saw him now standing at the edge of a desert he must cross: if he turned
> and looked back his face would be featureless, his eye sockets blank. Stephen
> Lewis thought of days, of years that they had spent together. He saw that
> those days, those years had been moving toward this moment and he won-
> dered what moment was being prepared for him and for his wife and his
> child, and he groaned, so loud that the woman and the child stared at him,
> wondering, too. (Gordon, *The Strange Children*, 303)

The future that Lewis wonders about here is revealed not to him but to Tom Claiborne, the poet-hero of Gordon's subsequent novel, *The Male-factors*. For Claiborne, the writing of poetry has always entailed an act of the rational will. "In the course of writing his first verses he had experienced a kind of inner illumination. The illumination had vanished, to reappear only sporadically. In its place had come a cold determination to write more verses."[4] Indeed, "cold determination" has made Tom Claiborne famous as a poet, critic, and editor (as it did Tate and Winters). But when we meet him in middle age, Claiborne has little determination left and no illuminations: the hypertrophy of his intellect has blocked all inspiration. Each day Claiborne locks the door to his study and reflects on the long poem that he is supposedly writing. Actually, he has given up on it with only eight pages written. He tries to console himself (as Tate would seem to have done in the case of his ode) by asserting the heroic value of the duration and difficulty of the labor itself.

> Well, they could not say (who was it he was always expecting to say something?) that he had not tried. He had sat there, day after day, hour after hour, or walked about the room, or stood looking out of the window, or had lain there on his sofa, with his eyes closed as now, sweating, sweating, until it seemed that all the sweat and all the blood had gone out of him and there was left only this dry manikin of skin and bone. (Gordon, *The Malefactors*, 134)

Claiborne's writing block has turned him into a "dry manikin," a figure like Hawthorne's Henry Feathertop, one of Eliot's hollow men, or the mummy in Tate's ode. Modeled on Tate in the depths of his poetic droughts, Claiborne is living a spiritual crisis at the limits of his will. He is proof that a man cannot make himself make poetry.

Gordon told Tate that Claiborne is "but a pale reflection of you but I think he's admirable."[5] In many ways he is. But when she made her husband's writing block the inspiration for her own writing, Gordon exacted a complex revenge, including revenge for Tate's sexual relationships with other women. As Tate repeatedly did (in Gordon's opinion),[6] Claiborne fights his imaginative failure with infidelity. Cynthia, the attractive younger cousin of Claiborne's wife, comes to Claiborne seeking his evaluation of her poetry. His potency aroused by her estimation, Claiborne has sex with her and then leaves his wife. The episode reflects on the master-disciple relationship between Gordon and her mentors: again a woman affirms the poet-critic's power by placing him in a position to judge her writing. In this instance, Gordon treats that structure as one of male narcissistic gratification. To be sure, Gordon blames Cynthia, but her more important concern is Claiborne's susceptibility to her wiles. For Claiborne is duped by Cynthia, the inconstant one, who has played on his vanity only to get ahead in the literary life (as everyone else could see). When she leaves him (because Cynthia quickly moves on to other projects), Claiborne is delusional, drunk, and alone.

As we might guess from her name, Vera, Claiborne's wife, is associated with Christian truth. At the start of the book, Vera is unconverted; but like Lucy in *The Strange Children*, Vera has a deep feeling for nature (she runs the Claibornes' farm), and this practical, intuitive aspect of her character, which distinguishes Vera from her "abstract," skeptical husband, leads her into the Church when Claiborne abandons her. In her faith Vera emulates Catherine Pollard, a friend of the Claibornes from their Bohemian days in Paris, who directs, as the Tates' friend Dorothy Day did, a shelter for the destitute in New York City and a communal farm upstate.[7] On the farm, which closely resembles Day's Maryfarm, patriarchal authority and female power are intimately connected. Near the end of the novel, when Claiborne arrives there seeking Vera, he is advised by a priest to stay and reclaim his rightful role as Vera's husband, to whom his wife owes obedience. This is the principle affirmed by Jacques Maritain in the sentence Gordon used as the epigraph to the novel: "It is for Adam to interpret the voices which Eve hears." The husband's responsibilities and privileges are continuous, it seems, with the poet-critic's. Yet Claiborne refuses to accept his kinship with the clay-born Adam. Instead, he leaves his wife and the farm: staying there would mean giving up his pretensions to cultural privilege and "sitting on the bench with the other bums" who have come to the farm for food and shelter (Gordon, *The Malefactors*, 312). All of the men there are or have been drunkards. The exception is a saintly old peasant: so decrepit he cannot speak, he is wholly dependent on the ministrations of Vera. This relationship (which seems to scare Claiborne when he encounters the two of them) is an example of the primacy of Catholic women throughout *The Malefactors*. The Father grants them power, and they act on His behalf, caring for men who cannot take care of themselves.[8]

Before he can return and take his place among those "bums," Claiborne needs the assistance of a most interesting and unlikely intermediary: Hart Crane. That is, Claiborne needs the help, in the form of a dream vision, of his long-dead friend Horne Watts, a poet systematically and conspicuously connected to Crane. As the change from "Hart" to "Horne" suggests, Gordon is interested in Crane's sexuality, specifically. In the context of the book's Catholicism, Horne is a great sinner. But Gordon believes that the secular raptures of the Lost Generation reveal, when properly understood, a deep yearning for Christian faith. Thus the author of *The Bridge* is Latinized: influenced (as no one guessed in the 1920s) by the work of a female Catholic seer, Horne's epic vision is called *Pontifex*. And Horne's homosexuality, translated in a similar way, can be seen as a vital Christian message.

Gordon makes this clear when Claiborne's thoughts turn to Horne early in his story. For Tate, Crane's homosexuality was a sign of his incomplete dedication as an artist—the lack of moral and intellectual discipline that ruined him; by contrast, Horne's homosexuality is a sign of his total sacrifice to art:

> Some men are born eunuchs, some men are made eunuchs by men, some men become eunuchs for the sake of the kingdom of God. The words were Jesus Christ's, but they came to him in Horne's voice. When he was drunk enough Horne spoke of himself as a "holocaust." The artist must sacrifice everything—including love of women—for the sake of his art, must burn himself on the Muse's altar. But it was the sea that got Horne in the end, and sharks, not flames, that picked his bones. (Gordon, *The Malefactors*, 121)

Horne's death haunts Claiborne throughout the book. In one dream Horne appears to Claiborne at the bottom of a cliff, his head cut off. The image recalls the eyeless stare Stephen Lewis receives from "the friend of his youth" in *The Strange Children*; it also recalls the dream figure encountered in "The Maimed Man," one of the sections of the long poem Tate never finished. Horne's fate is monitory, in the dream as in life. In the last of Claiborne's dreams, Horne appears again, this time gesturing toward a female figure, Catherine Pollard. Claiborne, prepared now to interpret Horne's example correctly, decides to seek Catherine and through her (we feel), salvation at the farm. Horne directs Claiborne to Catherine, who directs him to his wife.

Vera's closest associate is not really Claiborne, but Max, who was once Horne's lover and who lives with the Claibornes at the start of the book. Horne was Catherine's friend in Paris. Both of these relationships between a woman and a "eunuch" point to Gordon's alliance in *The Malefactors* with Crane.[9] She returns to him in this book to recover the romantic poet eliminated in her in the course of her professional training. Horne, Claiborne recalls, "had no mind. Just genius" (Gordon, *The Malefactors*, 81). Here Gordon allies herself with Crane's genius against Tate's intellect. Precisely because it is feminized in high modernist discourse, the romantic imagination has become available for this vision of female power. At the same time that Gordon returns to Crane, Gordon passes beyond Tate—as Vera moves beyond Claiborne—to a position from which his particular poetic and spiritual dilemma can be accurately surveyed. If the career of the poet-critic begins where the genius's stops, as I argued in Chapter Three, the Catholic visionary's career begins *where the poet-critic's is blocked*. Taking Crane's side, Gordon triumphs over the developmental narrative that fixes herself and Crane in the inferior, "feminine" position by placing Tate in a similar position in another such narrative, this one a story in which the man of letters must follow his faithful wife to be saved. In *The Malefactors* it is really Adam who hears voices and Eve who knows how to interpret them.

But if *The Malefactors* marks the beginning of the Catholic visionary's career, it is also, in Gordon's case, the end of it. It is significant that it is Cynthia, not Vera, who is the writer in *The Malefactors*. (In *The Strange Children*, Sarah Lewis is at best a sometime artist; the female author in that book is the mad Isabel Reardon.) This delegation of roles, implying that female authorship is incompatible with adherence to Catholic doctrine, points to the costs of Gordon's challenge to secular male power. Indeed, as if by contract, the terms on which Gordon gained her superior authority as a writer required her to give her writing up. Her late fiction twice tells the story of a pious woman who upholds the reputation and spiritual dignity of a man she loves (in one case a husband, in the other a father) by destroying his narcissistic art. In "Emmanuele! Emmanuele!" Madame Fay, the wife of the celebrated author Guillaume Fay, who writes looking into a mirror, secretly destroys the letters he writes to her every day; in *The Malefactors*, Vera is supposed to have destroyed the last paintings of her father—self-portraits of the naked artist. Yet in life it was Gordon who destroyed her own work. "Emmanuele! Emmanuele!"—a story Gordon liked and Tate did not—is the last short fiction she published; *The Malefactors*, which appeared in 1956, is the last novel she published. Gordon worked on two long manuscripts during the remaining twenty-four years of her life, but she could not reduce her mythological and autobiographical materials to a satisfactory form. In the role of Eve, who can hear voices but lacks the power and skill to interpret them, Gordon committed her late work, in effect, to the same end as *Darkling I Listen*.

Perhaps, after their second and final divorce in 1959, Gordon simply lacked Tate's shaping judgment, a resource she had relied upon in each of her published books. Gordon's silence entails ambiguities, however, like every other phase of her writing life. When Gordon stopped publishing, was she punishing herself, enforcing her own subordination, and refusing to accept her independence from Tate? (Gordon, who still liked late in life to be called "Mrs. Tate," resisted the second divorce.) Or was she, in the destruction of her work, destroying Narcissus—the male artist whose technique she was taught to prize and emulate? To the degree that Gordon's writing was never her own, it was not her own writing that Gordon destroyed. The sentence from Maritain that Gordon used as an epigraph to *The Malefactors* is inscribed on her tombstone. As a last word, it endorses the subordination of woman's imagining to the interpretive skill of the male. But it also can be heard as a dare.[10]

III.

CRANE: MODERNISM IN REVERSE

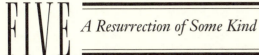

FIVE
A Resurrection of Some Kind

Having followed the progress of Tate's friendship with Crane as far as its oblique recuperation in "Narcissus as Narcissus," we are now in a position to tell the other half of this story—or perhaps, to tell the same story in reverse. For it was Crane's particular ambition to alter the course of modernism by reversing the direction it had taken in Eliot's work; and this decision propelled Crane on an imaginative path precisely and deliberately opposed to Tate's. In order to pose the questions Crane's "path" raises, which are questions about its logic and its costs, I want to turn to the series of letters in which Crane first defined his aesthetic goal and the course that he would have to take to reach it, starting in the spring of 1922 when he first wrote to Tate.

In his letters to Tate, Crane's imaginative independence is always conceived in opposition to certain authors, in solidarity with others (although Crane could change his mind about which authors belonged in which category). Replying, for example, to Tate's enthusiasm for Edwin Arlington Robinson, Crane agreed that Robinson was "very interesting—his work is real and permanent, yet it is also a tragedy—one of the tragedies of Puritanism, materialism, America and the last century. Wm. Vaughn Moody's beautiful tonality suffered in a kind of vacuum, too" (Crane, *Letters*, 89). In Crane's view, Robinson and Moody were victims of a culture dominated by genteel and commercial values ("Puritanism, materialism"), which forced them to develop in a "vacuum," and confined their work to social satire and private melancholy. Crane, who like Tate was born in 1899, and therefore had "a little toe-nail in the last century" (Crane, *Let-*

117

ters, 87), was determined to escape their fate. "The poetry of negation," he continues,

> is beautiful—alas, too dangerously so for one of my mind. But I am trying
> to break away from it. Perhaps this is useless, perhaps it is silly—but one *does*
> have joys. The vocabulary of damnations and prostrations has been devel-
> oped at the expense of these other moods, however, so that it is hard to
> dance in proper measure. Let us invent an idiom for the proper transposi-
> tion of jazz into words! (Crane, *Letters*, 89)

The idiom Crane imagines would insist that "one *does* have joys," and that they can be shared by those who move to the new rhythms of jazz (for instance, as rendered in the "crashing opéra bouffe" of "For the Marriage of Faustus and Helen," the second section of which Crane was working on).[2] This rhetoric is based on Crane's sense of himself as part of a gener-ation newly released from the "Puritan" sexual and economic disciplines of nineteenth-century America, bound to each other rather than to their parents and the past, in a mutually validating community of peers.[3] If Robinson and Moody lacked an audience, Crane was confident he could create one. When he first wrote to Tate, Crane was writing to Sherwood Anderson and Gorham Munson as well, and he would soon initiate ex-changes with Waldo Frank and Alfred Stieglitz. One letter to Stieglitz pledges, emphatically and typically, "*I am your brother always*" (Crane, *Let-ters*, 142).

The letter to Tate about "the poetry of negation," which Crane signed "Fraternally," affirms the same Whitmanian ideal of male comradeship. In the context of that letter, "the poetry of negation" is at least loosely associ-ated with late-nineteenth-century verse, a "beautiful" aestheticism stunted by the hostile climate of American capitalism. In subsequent letters to Tate, Crane associates the attraction and threat of "negation" almost ex-clusively with the work of their near-contemporary, Eliot. Crane's double perspective on Eliot led him to encourage Tate to read Eliot, then to dis-courage Tate from following Eliot's example. For himself, Crane under-stood Eliot's work as an obstacle that would require him to push his own work in a peculiarly double direction. As Crane put the matter to Tate, "I flatter myself a little lately that I have discovered a safe tangent to strike which, if I can possibly explain the position,—goes *through* [Eliot] toward a *different goal*" (Crane, *Letters*, 90). This is a more complex and perhaps even contradictory strategy than the one Crane outlined earlier since it requires Crane not only to "break away from" but also to pass "*through*" negation. Keep in mind, too, that a tangent does not in fact pass *through*,

as Crane suggests, but only converges upon the line or surface it inter-
sects. Crane somehow wants to write like Eliot and not to write like Eliot
at once.

The logic of this contradiction is extended, rather than clarified, when
Crane says that Eliot's work points out "the best" in the poetry of the past,
and so provides the grounds on which a future poetry might be constructed. In passing, the argument reminds Crane of Milton's meditation
on the premature end of a poetic career: "In his own realm Eliot presents
us with an absolute *impasse*, yet oddly enough, he can be utilized to lead us
to, intelligently point to, other positions and 'pastures new.' Having
absorbed him enough we can trust ourselves as never before, in the air or
on the sea" (Crane, *Letters*, 90). Crane's fleeting memory of Milton's
"Lycidas" and its final promise of a passage "Tomorrow to fresh Woods,
and Pastures new"[4] identifies Eliot not with "the uncouth Swain" who
sings Milton's poem but with the subject of that song, the young poet who
was lost at sea before his promise could be fulfilled. Because Eliot only
wrote verse, Crane claims, "between 22 and 25, and is now, I understand,
dying piecemeal as a clerk in a London bank" (Crane, *Letters*, 90), he suffers a fate not unlike the social tragedies attributed to Robinson and
Moody. Eliot has not been lost at sea but driven back to shore, and this
twist provides for a drastic revision of Milton's poem: death is to be feared
on land, not at sea. At the same time, however, Eliot is not merely another
example, like Robinson or Moody, to be avoided. For even though Eliot
himself may not have used them, Eliot provides Crane with the instruments he and others like him will need to navigate "in the air or on the
sea." What Crane admires in Eliot's work is his command of the technology of verse—imagined as his mastery of past models as well as the invention of new ones—all of which, in Crane's opinion, can be "utilized" and
"absorbed," appropriated as vehicles or tools for purposes quite different
from Eliot's.

Crane articulates this position more precisely when he returns, in January 1923, in a letter to Gorham Munson, to the problems of direction
explored in his first letters to Tate:

> There is no one writing in English who can command so much respect, to
> my mind, as Eliot. However, I take Eliot as a point of departure toward an
> almost complete reverse of direction. His pessimism is amply justified, in his
> own case. But I would apply as much of his erudition and technique as I can
> absorb and assemble toward a more positive, or (if [I] must put it so in a
> sceptical age) ecstatic goal. (Crane, *Letters*, 114–15)

The direction Crane charts in these sentences refines his earlier ambition to go "*through* [Eliot] toward a *different goal*"; he is now intent on "an almost complete reverse of direction" that will appropriate Eliot's "erudition and technique" as "a point of departure" toward a goal that is not merely "more positive" but "ecstatic." The confident assumption is that Eliot's form and content can be separated—Crane can "absorb" the one, reject the other—because they do not properly belong together in the first place. Eliot's technical achievement has pushed modern poetry forward at the same time that his "pessimism" has set it back.

In fact, Crane's "almost complete reverse of direction" is calculated to reverse what Crane sees as Eliot's own reverse of direction—specifically, the way in which the content of Eliot's poetry turns back from, in Crane's view, the promise of its form (which Crane defines both as technique and as the poetry's relations to techniques of the past). Ignoring the persistence of "certain spiritual events and possibilities as real and powerful now as, say, in the time of Blake" (Crane, *Letters*, 115), Eliot's poetry returns to the past only as an index to its distance from the present, a tactic that removes "the best" of the poetry of the past from the range of present possibilities. The burden of "For the Marriage of Faustus and Helen," by contrast, is precisely the simultaneous presence—the interpenetration—of past and present "possibilities" (exemplified stylistically, as I will be arguing, by Crane's unironic use of conspicuously outmoded verse forms and diction). The recovery of these possibilities, as this letter goes on to suggest, requires Crane to retrieve "hope" from the grave in which Eliot has buried it "as deep and direfully as it can ever be done" (Crane, *Letters*, 115). As he works to imagine this recovery, Crane shifts the axis of attention to the vertical one of height and depth, reformulating his figure of reversal in more urgent and extravagant language. "After this perfection of death—," Crane reasons, "nothing is possible in motion but a resurrection of some kind" (Crane, *Letters*, 115).

The figurative terms of Crane's criticism anticipate the language that Davidson uses in his criticism of Tate's ode, not only in the oppressive and oppressed imagination of burial they share, but in the quality of private injury they both express. Davidson thought Tate had buried the Confederate dead "completely out of sight—with them yourself and me" (*Davidson and Tate*, 187). In Crane's letter, it is as if Eliot had buried not only his own hope, but Crane's, "completely out of sight." Crane explains: "Everyone, of course, wants to die as soon and as painlessly as possible!" (Crane, *Letters*, 115). But as he summons the courage to continue his work—"All I know through very much suffering and dullness . . . is that it interests me to still affirm certain things"—the suggestion is in fact that everyone wants *Crane* to want to give up and die. For when he protests the general assumption that, "as everyone persists in announcing in the deep and dirgeful *Dial*, the fruits of civilization are entirely harvested" (Crane, *Letters*, 115), Crane is speaking from outside of a literary community that is very different from the "fraternal" one he imagines in his first letters to Tate. Crane's feeling, though, is not simply that he has been shut out by this community, but that his case has been *anticipated and rejected*—in such a way as to leave him only two alternatives, seen in this letter as resurrection and suicide.

Crane's isolation from the high modernist consensus is the position of promise and risk he fights to revalue in the major lyrics of *White Buildings*. It is also the position Crane came to adopt in his friendship with Tate. Perversely, perhaps, Crane introduced Tate to Eliot's work in order to lead his "disciple" away from it. But Crane instead precipitated, by the spring of 1926, a breach between himself and Tate that fulfilled the sense of personal exclusion expressed in the letter just mentioned. The following fragment of a draft of a letter to Tate, which Crane wrote during the quarrel in Patterson or shortly thereafter, demonstrates the convergence of Crane's literary argument with Eliot and his domestic argument with Gordon and Tate.

> You expect me to 'welcome' failings that haven't yet appeared in your work merely because I detect a certain narcissism in the voluptuous melancholies of Eliot—which you admire, and I don't. We should be able to agree to disagree about such matters without calling in dish pans, saws, and slop jars. . . .
>
> It's all wrong—all the way through—and unfortunate. Although I have no apologies to make—because I can't see my frequent vulgarities and assumptions as totalling the *real* causes you and Caroline have mounted against me—I don't see any use in being either defensive or ironic. . . . I'm sorry for my failings wherever they have incurred your inconvenience and displeasure, and ask you to forget them and me as soon as possible.[5]

Failure, narcissism, irony—as in a distorting mirror, the crucial terms from Tate's criticism of Crane's poetry appear here alongside the everyday objects of the house in Patterson: "dish pans, saws, and slop jars." As the movement from the one set of terms to the other—from Eliot's "voluptuous melancholies" to his friends' "inconvenience and displeasure"—indicates, Crane's departure from Patterson reenacts his break with Eliot, although the event is staged this time not as Crane's proud rejection of "the poetry of negation," but as his ignominious exclusion from the house of his peers; and that is a signal difference. In June 1922, Crane expected Tate to join him in the voyage out beyond Eliot "in the air or on the sea"; together they would go on where Eliot had turned back. In April 1926, Crane sets forth alone, propelled as much by Gordon's and Tate's rejection of him as by his own rejection of Eliot. The air and sea that signify the space of Crane's ambition now signify the space of exile and homelessness as well. And Crane's poetic objection to "the voluptuous melancholies" of Eliot, like his protest that "one *does* have joys," has become entangled with the "frequent vulgarities and assumptions," the extravagance, drunkenness, and personal demands, that made Crane at least temporarily unwelcome in the home of this heterosexual couple.

From one angle, Crane's departure from Patterson is a story about a homosexual man's exclusion from a heterosexual household, with the ramifications for Gordon and Tate we have considered now in some detail. But Crane's departure is also the story of his rejection of that home, his willing refusal of its shelter. This double perspective is plainly expressed in his fragmentary draft of a letter to Tate. On the one hand, the fragment is the message of a poet of impenitent song ("Lachrymae Christi"), who was never "ready for repentence" ("Legend"), who was willing to sacrifice the lesser satisfactions of civility, to tolerate "vulgarities and assumptions" in his life and in his work, in pursuit of "an improved infancy" ("Passage") or "a more positive, or . . . ecstatic goal." On the other hand, it is a message of self-pity and self-punishment, which not only offers an apology but also tells Tate "to forget" Crane and Crane's "failings"—he is not being ironic—"as soon as possible"; and in this sense, it has the disturbing quality of a suicide note. The path Crane embraced, which this document affirms, and which he imagined as a negation of negation, did not require Crane to choose *between* hope and despair, as he wished to believe; it required him to choose both.

Of course, the action that interrupts and completes Crane's career exemplifies this contradiction in its most extreme and provocative form. Crane drowned himself in April 1932 by jumping from the ship on his way to the United States from Mexico, where he had spent the preceding winter as a Guggenheim Fellow. When Crane leaped from the stern of the *Orizaba*, he refused to go in the direction of the homebound boat and again set forth alone (once more for Cuba, where he had come ashore the previous day); clearly and characteristically, Crane's final action was an effort to reverse an intolerable reverse of direction, although in this case the strategy led to his death. As John Irwin has remarked (commenting on the bedlamite's leap to death in "To Brooklyn Bridge"), Crane's suicide can be construed as "an act of despair" or "an act of affirmation"; it is a return to the sanctified space of Crane's ambition, renewing and affirming "the scope of the artist's desire," at the same time that it is a return to exile, indicating only that "it is better to be one of the dead than one of the living dead."[6] But there is really no question whether Crane's suicide expresses hope or despair—just as there is no question, in terms of Crane's own understanding and intentions, whether *The Bridge* is a success or a failure. The question is rather: Why did *The Bridge* have to be both? Or: Why does Crane's passage toward a "more positive" goal, which his letters envision as a state of "absolute music" or "tremendous rondure" (Crane, *Letters*, 267), entail figurations of the poet's death ("Voyages II") and the mutilation of the body ("The Dance")? Why did the hope of "a resurrection of some kind" direct Crane on a path whose progress concluded (as was foreseen) in suicide?

These are some of the questions readers have traditionally asked about Crane's death and poetry. By proposing them here I do not intend to attribute the private pathology of Crane's life to the logical demands of his work, as Winters did. I am asking, rather, why Crane's career is constructed in such a way as to fulfill the expectations that Winters, Tate, and other critics brought to it, to enact, finally, the scenario prescribed for Crane by a community of readers he rejected but did not (for he could not) cease to address. Of course, the further question to be answered concerns what is left over—what Crane achieves over and beyond, or perhaps within, the impasse he undoubtedly reaches (and reaches deliberately, insofar as his death was willed).

I plan to take up these questions in the next three chapters by attending primarily to the variety of texts (letters, poetics, poems) that Crane produced between the fall of 1925, before he moved to Patterson with Gordon and Tate, and the summer of 1926, which he spent in Cuba on the Isle of Pines. This is the pivotal period of Crane's career, not only because more than half of *The Bridge* was either drafted or completed during it,[7] but also because it is in this period that Crane's opposition to the high modernist project (as it was interpreted, particularly, by Tate) results in Crane's radical isolation from his peers.

To a degree, Crane has remained in that isolated position ever since. There has been general agreement since perhaps 1960 that Crane is a major modern poet, and that his work is worthy of sustained scholarly study. But the study Crane has received has provided few ways to read him in relation to other poets of the period. In the past three decades there

have been by my count sixteen books devoted exclusively to the explanation of Crane's poetry, published at a rate of roughly one every two years.
The regularity of their appearance is as striking as the uniformity of their
purpose: from varying perspectives and with varying levels of success, each
of these books might be called (as Warner Berthoff titles his 1989 book)
"Hart Crane: A Re-Introduction." Somehow, Crane's poetry is always
outside the paradigms that govern the field; it must be repeatedly "introduced" again, brought in, reclaimed. At the same time, though, these re-
introductions repeatedly leave Crane in need of the next critic's advocacy
and aid. Crane still does not have a place.

The most recent of these single-author studies, Thomas E. Yingling's
Hart Crane and the Homosexual Text, does the most to illuminate the poet's
anomalous standing and to contextualize his work. The success of Yingling's argument is to show that Crane's modernism was specifically a
homosexual writing, a gay semiotic that should be read in relation to
other minority codes in high culture and everyday life. Practically speaking, this means that Yingling has made Crane's sexuality complexly meaningful without circumscribing the meanings of his poetry (as have other
critics who, while correctly insisting on the centrality of homosexuality
in Crane's work, tend to approach homosexuality on the level of theme
and narrative, rather than "style").[8] In effect, Yingling has undone the
universality Crane's writing appears to claim for itself, and has analyzed
it as a minority discourse (as an example of "the homosexual text"). I
will assume and build on some of his arguments. I want to reverse the
general direction of Yingling's analysis, however, in order to examine
the ways in which Crane's homosexual writing was also a modernism. I
mean to emphasize the fact that (as Tate's case suggests) the naming and
minoritizing of gay male writing and experience was an important moment in the formation of literary modernism as a whole, an event that
brings into focus the dominant poetics of the emergent New Criticism as
clearly as it does the aberrant art of *The Bridge*. I will argue in particular
that Crane's roles as homosexual and poet were *not*, as Yingling holds,
"flatly contradictory sites" (Yingling, *Crane and the Homosexual Text*, 143),
but overlapping ones, whose complex relation was only unfolded over
time.

Crane came to modernism as a gay man. But this is not to say that
Crane was a gay man *before* he was a modernist; Crane had to learn homosexuality just as he had to learn modernism, and he frequently learned
both at the same time. This chapter will explore that double education by
way of two related topics: the imaginative expectations Crane brought to

modernism, and the narrative models he encountered in modernist texts. Both topics, it will become clear, concern bonds between men.

In an essay sensitive to the overlapping claims of Crane's art and life, Allen Grossman has observed that "modernism was in moral terms the treasonous friendship of which he obsessively complained."[9] For the time being, let me take Grossman's remark out of context in order to develop its suggestion that a story of bonding and betrayal between friends—a story played out between Crane and Tate—structures Crane's relations with high modernist writing generally. We will need to return to Crane's reading of Eliot, for Eliot's work was the treasonous friend of whom Crane most bitterly complained. But to understand how Crane's attitude toward Eliot developed, it may be useful to study the development of his attitude toward another modernist author, James Joyce.

From the start, Crane's comments on Joyce confront aesthetic questions "in moral terms." For example, in 1918, in a letter to the *Little Review* published under the title "Joyce and Ethics," Crane vigorously defended *A Portrait of the Artist as a Young Man* against charges of "decadence," "immorality," and "obscenity."[10] Crane begins by sorting out Joyce's relation to Swinburne, Wilde, and Baudelaire, linked together as "decadents" by another letter writer in the *Little Review*. Crane, reflecting high modernism's scorn for British Aestheticism, dismisses Swinburne and Wilde as insubstantial and unintellectual; but he accepts the comparison between Joyce and Baudelaire, on the grounds that both authors make "a thrust" into the reading public's "entrails." Significantly, Crane's defense of Joyce's contempt for genteel decorum values phallic vigor and the willingness to investigate forbidden territories, associated here with the anal. Implicit in this defense of the author is a defense of his hero, with whose resistance to bourgeois civility the young critic strongly sympathizes. "The character of Stephen Dedalus," Crane avers, rising to plead Stephen's case,

> is all too good for this world. It takes a little experience,—a few reactions on his part to understand it, and could this have been accomplished in a detached hermitage, high above the mud, he would no doubt have preferred that residence. *A Portrait of the Artist as a Young Man*, aside from Dante, is spiritually the most inspiring book I have ever read. (Crane, *Complete Poems and Selected Prose*, 200)

This is one of the earliest statements of the ethical code Crane obeyed—a code whose standards, Crane later wrote, in the course of rejecting the moral advice of Yvor Winters, "I reserve myself the pleasant right to define . . . in a somewhat individual way" (Crane, *Letters*, 299). It is specifically a code that effaces the boundary between art and life, hero and author, to praise the heroic action of the author who, in pursuit of an aesthetic absolute, disregards socially prescribed norms. For Crane and (Crane wished to believe) for Joyce, the goals of the artist's life validate, even require, "a little experience" in "the mud."

If Crane admired Joyce's first novel, he frankly coveted *Ulysses*. He sent to France to guarantee a copy in 1922; after United States Customs prevented distribution of the book, Crane asked Munson to smuggle back the copy he had ordered; and when Munson arrived in Cleveland with the contraband, Crane declined to take his unbound copy to the binder: "It sounds ridiculous, but the book is so strong in its marvelous oaths and blasphemies, that I wouldn't have an easy moment while it was out of the house" (Crane, *Letters*, 94). Along with this secrecy and cunning came the fantasy of membership in an elite world of letters. For *Ulysses* worked like a talisman or password connecting Crane and Crane's friends to the modernist experiments going on outside the United States—and outside United States law.[11] "It is quite likely," Crane boasted, "I have one of two or three copies west of New York" (Crane, *Letters*, 94). Through Lescaze, the friend who had drawn his portrait in Cleveland, Crane arranged for Tate to buy a copy of *Ulysses*, making Tate too one of the select.[12] The threat of attacks by a hostile public (at once actual and imaginary) energized and sustained Crane's image of an intimate league of like-minded authors. Crane feared "that some fanatic will kill Joyce sometime soon" and, in the next breath, dreamed of meeting Joyce himself: "He is the one above all others I should like to talk to" (Crane, *Letters*, 95).

The same letter continues directly: "I have been very quiet while Munson has been here. Tonight, however, I break out into fresh violences" (Crane, *Letters*, 95)—by which Crane meant the prohibited pleasures of alcohol and homosexuality. Crane's correspondent in this instance is Wilbur Underwood, a poet and an official in the State Department who had shared with Crane, when Crane visited there on business in 1920, the "violences" of his circle in Washington.[13] The rapid shuttle in Crane's letter between intellectual and sexual enthusiasms is characteristic of Crane's letters to Underwood, a correspondence in which Crane treats the nocturnal world of his sexuality (his exploits in the parks, at the theater) with the kind of pride and excitement that his semiclandestine adventures in modernism also evoked. Where *Ulysses* was concerned, Crane's reading was as prohibited as his drinking and sex; and he took special pleasure in those parts of the novel that had brought charges (legal ones this time) of decadence, immorality, and obscenity. For example, Crane typed and sent to Underwood sixteen "Pages Choisies" from the Nighttown chapter of *Ulysses*, starting with Bloom's meditation: "A man's touch. Sad music. Perhaps here."[14] Crane and Underwood had exchanged exciting, suppressed texts earlier, as when Underwood loaned Crane "the 'Satyricon' of Petronius (Arbiter), a rare and completely unexpurgated Paris edition, purported to have been translated by Oscar Wilde" (Crane, *Letters*, 44). In the case of Wilde's unexpurgated translation (authentic or not), the loan was an expression of gay male solidarity, connecting Underwood and Crane to the exiled author of *De Profundis*. In the case of Crane's "Pages Choisies" (Crane's phrase reminds us that *Ulysses*, like "Wilde's" Petronius, was sanctioned by the amiable French), the secret text accommodates gay codes in modernist ones (or seems to). Joyce's Nighttown not only resonated with the secret sexual experience of Underwood and Crane, it suggested a place for such experience in art. As Crane told Underwood, echoing his earlier claims for *A Portrait of the Artist*, "The 'Night-town' episodes are the most thrilling things intellectually that I have ever read."[15]

Indeed, Crane's tendency to read his own experience into *Ulysses*, which recalls his impulse to identify himself with the hero of *Portrait*, dissolves boundaries not only between art and life, but between intellectual and sexual stimulation. This tendency returns us to Crane's protest that, in fact, "one *does* have joys," and it allows us to specify the homosexual content of that protest. Crane's letters to Tate in 1922 on the necessity of breaking away from "the poetry of negation" should therefore be read alongside his letters from the same period to Underwood, for both correspondences record Crane's effort to validate his desires in the face of censorship. In different ways, Crane felt, Tate and Underwood were both susceptible to the threat of "negation." "Tate has a whole lot to offer when he finds his way out of the Eliot idiom," Crane told Munson, "which as you know, is natural to him, and was before he ever heard of Eliot" (Crane, *Letters*, 121). In Underwood, who had published two volumes of poetry early in life, but who had stopped writing since, Crane saw a poet whose creativity "the routine of uninteresting work has probably killed forever" (Crane, *Letters*, 44)—much as Crane would later suppose that the daily routine at the bank was doing to Eliot. In effect, Crane urged both poets, as he specifically urged Tate, "Launch into praise!" (Crane, *Letters*, 94).

"Praise" was Crane's plan for resisting the internalization of social discipline, for refusing the acceptance of expressive limits that led to a "vocabulary of damnations and prostrations." When Crane speaks of "breaking away" from the Aestheticist mode of his early work, therefore, he is also speaking of his will to overcome the homosexual despair he associated with Aestheticism, and with his youthful attraction to it. Despite the cool way he treats them in "Joyce and Ethics," Swinburne and Wilde are both present in Crane's early work, Wilde especially. The first poem Crane published was called "C 33"—a reference to the number of Wilde's cell in prison. Crane's poem about Wilde's "penitence" reminds one of a simple but central fact: that Crane began his writing life after Wilde's humiliation and imprisonment.[16] "C 33" is a double debut that links Crane's identities as poet and homosexual; and links them by encoding the latter in the former, for those who could read that code (and hiding it from whose who could not). The code name by which Crane names Wilde here—"C 33"— is in this sense a metonymy for the coded character of gay identity generally: it converts the imposed insignia of state punishment into a badge of male homosexual suffering, connecting Wilde and Crane and certain of Crane's readers.

One may say, optimistically, that suffering produces special literary skills, special powers of figuration and encipherment; and it gives rise to a community of readers and writers who share those skills and honor them in each other. But "C 33" emphasizes that Wilde's condition as a prisoner was finally one of "blight," from which issued only and inevitably a "song of broken, minor strain" (Crane, *Poems*, 135). By contrast, Joyce promised Crane a major music. The modernist movement Crane encountered in the early 1920s saw itself historically as a move beyond Aestheticism—a move exemplified by Yeats's stylistic transformation, or by Joyce's own progress from *Portrait* to *Ulysses*. Crane viewed the modernist break with Aestheticism not as a homophobic maneuver, but as a claim to cultural power and centrality on the part of a new "generation," a claim in which Crane felt he had a stake *both* as a poet and as a homosexual.

Before Crane met Tate, he arranged for Tate to meet Underwood, who treated Tate to the Nighttown pleasures of cross-dressing. As Tate reported to Crane, Underwood introduced him to one " 'Madame' Cooke" who "continually reminded me of the catamite at the Temple of Priapus in Petronius—his bullet head, thick knife-edged lips, and boxed chin. Oh!"[17] Crane arranged such a meeting between Underwood and Munson, but Munson was not amused, and Crane had to defend his devotion to Underwood: "My affection for him is based on a certain community of taste and pursuit we have which you will understand" (Crane, *Letters*, 105). Perhaps Munson did not understand, however; at least Crane did not enjoy his accustomed "violences" while Munson was his guest, as we have seen. Such discretion was often called for. Crane frequently censored himself, in one way or another, one effect of which was to generate significantly different styles of self-presentation in Crane's different correspondences. As Yingling has observed, Crane's sexual and literary "interests remained compartmentalized throughout his life, and one sees in Crane's letters unmistakable differences in style and vocabulary, in tone and persona, that speak to the differences between these two discursive communities," the gay community to which Underwood belonged and the modernist one to which Munson did (Yingling, *Crane and the Homosexual Text*, 81).

Yet one also sees in Crane's early poems and letters a desire to connect those "two discursive communities," or to override the boundary between them, as Crane's misguided efforts to establish bonds between Underwood, Munson, and Tate suggest. There are in fact some important *similarities* of style and vocabulary to be seen in Crane's letters to gay and straight friends. Crane wrote to Munson in 1923 describing the "mystic possibilities" of his new poem, *The Bridge* (Crane, *Letters*, 124); it is a significant letter, often mentioned by critics of *The Bridge*. Two days later, in a letter that is seldom mentioned, Crane describes to Underwood the start of a new love affair. Crane expects it to end soon, but he consoles himself "that *once*, at least, something beautiful approached me and as though it were the most natural thing in the world, enclosed me in his arm and pulled me to him without my slightest bid. And we who create must endure—must hold to spirit not by the mind, the intellect alone. These have no mystic possibilities" (Crane, *Letters*, 127). The return of "mystic possibilities" is striking. The phrase suddenly links sex and writing, body and mind, a way of talking to gay friends and a way of talking to straight ones, with the suggestion that the bridging work of Crane's projected poem will effect such linkages too.

I said in Chapter Three that Crane used the role of "The Mystic" as a cover, as a way of talking about homosexual desire without appearing to. "The Mystic" was also a role, identified with Whitman and, as we will see, Melville, in which Crane could see himself as a national poet and a homosexual one *at once*, a role in which he could imagine removing his cover, and doing away with the "compartments" in his life. This mystic possibility is not, I think, a fantasy about being "out"; it is a fantasy about the elimination of the closet and its inside/outside, either/or ontology. That fantasy energizes and connects Crane's appeals to to markedly distinct "discursive communities." In Crane's poems, the merging of those communities occurs in a utopian and specifically aesthetic space of relation, a place in which it is neither necessary nor possible to distinguish between sexual and nonsexual bonds. This is a continuum of personal relations that challenges the structure of male homosocial bonds—the wide range of social relations between men that proscribe and exclude the homoerotic.[18] It is also the continuum of personal relations visibly interrupted in *The Letters of Hart Crane* by the omission of Underwood's name.

We can get a fuller sense of this inclusive ideal by turning to "Episode of Hands"—a poem, written in 1920, that recounts Crane's attention to a worker injured in the factory owned by his father. We know from letters that the poem is unusually close to a record of Crane's lived experience, which is in keeping with Crane's efforts here to surmount obstacles between literature and life, and between men of different classes. Initially, the one man's attention to—or "interest" in—the other, and particularly a man of another class, causes the worker some additional pain:

> The unexpected interest made him flush.
> Suddenly he seemed to forget the pain,—
> Consented,—and held out
> One finger from the others.

Hands and eyes are the parts of the body that fashion bonds in Crane's poetry, and the marks that they frequently bear testify to the extreme difficulty of this task: "blamed bleeding hands" in "For the Marriage of Faustus and Helen," the swimmers' "lost morning eyes" in "Voyages V" (Crane, *Poems*, 32, 39). Here, in an instant of forgetting and consent, one pair of hands dresses the wound of the other, a pastoral vision supplants the workplace (as sunlight glitters "in and out among the wheels"), and the two men pause, bound together in one gaze:

> And factory sounds and factory thoughts
> Were banished from him by that larger, quieter hand
> That lay in his with the sun upon it.
> And as the bandage knot was tightened
> The two men smiled into each other's eyes.
>
> (Crane, *Poems*, 173)

The repetition of the simple conjunction "and," in contrast to the usually disjunctive and compressed syntax of Crane's verse, announces a new experience of continuity, and permits (as the same use of language does in "My Grandmother's Love Letters") a lucid expression of private feeling.

As it is exemplified by the shared pronoun "he" (in these lines, "his" hand is the hand of "the factory owner's son"), the bond ("the bandage knot") that is established is erotic and fraternal at once; and the smile connecting each pair of eyes to the other (a smile that is the expressive sign of covenant in all of Crane's poetry) recognizes a unity of feeling or assent overcoming the class distinctions of the workplace, figured as the wound that is incurred there. Note too that the class barrier that must be overcome derives in this case from the son's bond to the father, the capitalist.[19] It is not that the one man has been elevated to the other's place, or that the owner's son has joined ranks with the workers; rather, the two men have met as brothers (members of one generation) in a place apart.

Contrast this scene of solidarity and connection with that of another unpublished poem, this one written between 1924 and 1926, and left untitled:

> Thou canst read nothing except through appetite
> And here we join eyes in that sanctity
> Where brother passes brother without sight,
> But finally knows conviviality . . .
>
> Go then, unto thy turning and thy blame.
> Seek bliss then, brother, in my moment's shame.
> All this that baulks delivery through words
> Shall come to you through wounds prescribed by swords:
>
> That hate is but the vengeance of a long caress,
> And fame is pivotal to shame with every sun
> That rises on eternity's long willingness . . .
> So sleep, dear brother, in my fame, my shame undone.
>
> (Crane, *Poems*, 193)

The perfect lucidity of the early poem is met point by point by the obscurity of the later one. The scene, however, is entirely clear: this is Crane's Nighttown, the city of the body where men meet to inflict, not heal, the wounds "prescribed" for them by taking upon themselves the punishment that their crimes require. The gaze that linked the two men in "Episode of Hands" links these brothers too, but it is now "without sight"; the hand has been replaced by the sword; sentiment "baulks delivery through words"; and "conviviality" is a word for "turning" and "blame." In the stories they tell, the two poems could not be more different.

But the formal differences are equally striking, if not more so. For example, the loose accentual-syllabic scheme of "Episode of Hands," marked off in paragraphs of variable length, has given way to the most characteristic, highly charged, and ceremonial of Crane's verse forms— rhymed quatrains of iambic pentameter and, in the last stanza, hexameter lines. This decision about prosody is coordinated, moreover, with the heightened anachronism of the later poem's diction ("Thou canst read nothing," or "unto thy turning and thy blame"), its highly charged, ceremonial language. Indeed, in direct contrast to the narrative, prosody, and diction of "Episode of Hands," all of which, as Sherman Paul has noted, manifest Crane's desire for connection with authors like Whitman or Sherwood Anderson (to whom Crane in fact sent a copy of the poem),[20] the anachronistic formality of "Thou canst read nothing" declares no obvious allegiance to modernity. The poem's air of pastiche, its knowing deployment of Elizabethan and nineteenth-century French manners, may be indebted to modernist examples as various as those of Eliot and Stevens. But Crane's poem boldly distinguishs itself from other modernist texts by its refusal to ironize, qualify, or bracket (place into quotation marks) the high style it appropriates.

The logic of Crane's decision to cast such a poem in such a form is not immediately apparent, but it might be explained in this way. Crane's intention, here as elsewhere, is to deny the obsolescence of the high style as if the prohibition against it (conventional in high modernist verse, and particularly Eliot's) were not yet in effect; as if, in fact, it were *not yet an old style*. From the point of view of style, at least, Crane's declared allegiance to youth, liberation, and modernity entails a refusal to accept that "old" forms are outdated. These "fruits of civilization," Crane is saying, are *not* "entirely harvested"; his effort is to seize a position *prior to* the modernist claim of cultural belatedness. The high style, seen as the sign of an uncanceled promise, is appropriated in this way for Crane's expression of proscribed desires: it becomes the right language for a refusal to repent. The poem's elevated ceremony, in its devotion to officially disqualified forms, recapitulates, on the level of style, Crane's devotion to a prohibited sexuality. This is the convergence of sexual and literary exploit we see in the life envisioned in "Legend," as well as in the name Crane chose to adopt for his visits to waterfront bars: "Mike Drayton."[21]

The pseudonym is amusing but by no means trivial. It testifies again to Crane's drive to deny or dissolve the distance between his own experience and that of other authors, both actual and imaginary (authors like Drayton or Marlowe or Rimbaud, as well as Joyce's Stephen). The willed innocence of that impulse is consistent with the naïveté (at once willful, imprudent, and polemical on his part) of Crane's appropriation of the high style for "Thou canst read nothing." That is, Crane's appeal to the high style is intended to elevate and validate the imperatives of personal desire as it revives and approves the possibility of a poetry of uncompromised sublimity. Crane's effort to redeem his "low" subject matter—the decadence, immorality, and obscenity of "Thou canst read nothing"—both by and for the high style (what Tate called "the grand manner") at once sustains and restates his defense of the spiritual value of Stephen Dedalus's experience in "the mud."

The unlikelihood of success, however, is expressed as the likelihood of the project's reversal and debasement; or what Crane describes as a pivot between "fame" and "shame" destined to occur "with every sun / That rises on eternity's long willingness . . ." This complex figure is set off from the two prior stanzas by Crane's shift from pentameter to hexameter lines—as if it were intended to provide a moral or inscription for the foregoing stanzas. The prosodic variation signals the rising of Crane's rhetoric to an even more highly formalized mode, promising to confer honor and immortality as it attempts to recover and claim the high style. This is, again, an unironic strategy, but not an unambiguous one. For the moral these lines put forward connects the outcome of literary and sexual exploits in their depiction of desire as the rising of the sun on the horizon of eternity, where the promise of absolute satisfaction, permanence, and "bliss" is also evidence of the horizon's final inaccessibility. Like the "still imploring flame" of Crane's "Legend," "eternity's long willingness" solicits the rising sun (punningly magnifying and depersonalizing the desires of "the factory owner's son") even as that willingness survives "every" sun's decline (an enumeration stressing the inevitability and permanence of the sun's passing, not its renewal). At last, in the compression of the syntax Crane uses to describe the brothers' final coupling ("So sleep, dear brother, in my fame, my shame undone"), it is impossible to tell whether the poet's "fame" has "undone" his "shame" or the reverse. (The line could be paraphrased either: "So sleep, dear brother, now that my fame has undone my shame," or: "So sleep, dear brother, now that my shame has undone my fame." The further possibility, that "brother" is the subject of "undone," is also an implication of the interlocking of bodies and fates Crane wishes to commemorate.) But we are invited, in either case, to recognize "fame" and "shame" as inextricable terms—as words bound together in the nature of a proscribed bond. Two men, once more, have been brought together in a place apart. But this is not the transfiguration of relation imagined in "Episode of Hands"; it is much more like oblivion. The second poem desublimates the desires of the first. At the

same time, it moves into the sublime—in particular, into the archaic sublime of the high style. "Thou canst read nothing" is egregious in both its
language and its subject. It is at once too low and too high to find an
audience.

How do we explain the difference between the two poems? We have
already heard Tate's response to a similar question: "What had happened
to Crane between 1917 and 1926? He had been confirmed in his homosexuality and cut off from any relationship, short of religious conversion,
in which the security necessary to mutual love was possible" (Tate, *Essays
of Four Decades*, 325). Tate's answer is informative, if it is read not as a
statement about the natural order of the things, but as an example of the
discourse about sexual relations Crane lived through and under. This is a
discourse that isolates "the homosexual" both as an act and as a type of
person at the same time that it identifies such persons exclusively with that
act: "They may have affection *or* sex, but not both," Tate explains (Tate,
Essays of Four Decades, 326). Between Crane's arrival in New York in 1917
and his departure for Cuba in 1926—where he wrote to Underwood the
sentence Tate found especially degraded: "Let my lusts be my ruin, since
all else is a fake and mockery" (Crane, *Letters*, 264)—Crane learned that
he could not have sex with men *and* maintain the affection of friends such
as Tate. By 1926, when Crane left Patterson, his early hope of male "comradeship," the Whitmanian ideal that gave Crane a means to imagine his
place in a literary community of peers, was replaced by a new conviction
of personal betrayal, a conviction in which Crane's isolation as a homosexual coincided with his isolation as a romantic poet addressing modernist readers in the strange tongue of the high style. Crane's anachronistic
pursuit of an "ecstatic" goal ultimately engages both of these publicly discredited roles.

This is a story of Crane's sexuality, but it is also a story of his
modernism. Joyce's *Ulysses*, like *A Portrait of the Artist as a Young Man*,
helped Crane to locate his own writing in a movement, and to place himself in the company of other modern authors. Crane's possession of this
secret book—his ability to read himself into Joyce's story—signified
Crane's inclusion in the yet unrealized community he wished to affirm.
Yet, as early as February 1923, Crane would speak of Joyce as an author,
like Eliot, from whom he would have to break away to reclaim his hope
for the future: "After the complete renunciation symbolized in *The Waste-
land* and, though less, in *Ulysses* we have sensed some new vitality" (Crane,

Letters, 127). This sentence comes from a letter to Frank, with whose aid Crane expected to construct "some kind of community of interest." The view of Joyce here reflects Crane's reading of Munson's study of Frank, which presents Frank as a mystic who celebrates modernity, and Joyce as a "destroyer" and skeptic "tied to an old consciousness."[22] Crane is trying to please his correspondent, then, when he sets himself and Frank against Eliot and Joyce. But this is not to say that Crane does not believe what he is saying; rather, Crane is learning what he has to believe in order to make his way in the literary culture taking shape around him. If he wants Frank's help, Joyce cannot be part of the "community of interest" that Crane is asking Frank to help him form; and if Joyce must be excluded from their projected community, the implication is that Crane and Frank have already been excluded from Joyce's. In 1922, less than a year before he wrote this letter to Frank, Crane honored *Ulysses* as "easily the epic of the age," and he excitedly compared it to *Faust* (Crane, *Letters,* 94). After 1923, Crane's letters and essays make almost no mention of *Ulysses;* in 1927 he calls it merely "that bitter book" (Crane, *Letters,* 288). It is not clear that Crane came to read *Ulysses* as a homophobic text. But it is clear that he could no longer read about his own experience in Joyce's book.

Crane's changing view of Joyce follows a pattern that James Longenbach has described in Crane's view of Eliot. "Early on," according to Longenbach, "Crane cathected to the more passionate aspects of the older poet's work, and that passion fueled his poetry; later, as influential readers defined Eliot's achievement in different terms, Crane could no longer see his debt to the Eliot they denied."[23] The "influential readers" who defined the Eliot whom Crane could not recognize included Eliot himself—for example, in the notes to *The Waste Land* or in the essay "*Ulysses,* Order, and Myth," both of which were first published in the United States by "the deep and dirgeful *Dial.*" Longenbach argues that Crane discovered and admired not the "official" Eliot of *The Sacred Wood,* but "the Eliot of the awful daring of a moment's surrender," "the Eliot it has taken the rest of us another fifty years to know" (Longenbach, "Crane and Eliot," 84). This is the passionate poet who wrote these sentences distinguishing trivial imitation from another, deeper relation between poets:

> This relation is a feeling of profound kinship, or rather a peculiar personal intimacy, with another, probably a dead author. It may overcome us suddenly, on first or after long acquaintance; it is certainly a crisis; and when a

young writer is seized with a passion of this sort he may be changed, metamorphosed almost, within a few weeks even, from a bundle of second-hand
sentiments into a person. . . .

. . . We may not be great lovers; but if we had a genuine affair with a real
poet of any degree we have acquired a monitor to avert us when we are not
in love. . . . We do not imitate, we are changed; and our work is the work of
the changed man; we have not borrowed, we have been quickened, and we
become bearers of a tradition.[24]

These sentences come from an unreprinted essay of Eliot's published in
the *Egoist* in 1919. They have become, as Longenbach puts it, "a kind of
talisman for contemporary readers of Eliot," testifying (as does "The
Death of St. Narcissus," a poem Eliot suppressed, or the canceled drafts of
The Waste Land) to the complexity of an erotic imagination Eliot deliberately and only with difficulty concealed. Longenbach quotes them because
Crane quotes them—in the crucial letter to Tate in which Crane speaks of
his plan to go "*through* [Eliot] toward a *different goal*" (Crane, *Letters*, 90–
91).[25] Unhappily, Crane's quotation from Eliot breaks off before the passage above, because the remainder of the letter is lost; it is impossible to
say how much of the essay Crane quoted, or what he had to say about it.
One wonders if Tate lost the rest of Crane's letter deliberately; it is one of
few gaps in a correspondence Tate clearly cherished. Whether or not Tate
censored this text, however, we know, as Crane knew, that Eliot had censored his. It is not that Eliot excluded the *Egoist* essay from *The Sacred
Wood* (better known and quite "official"-sounding pieces were also left
out), but that Eliot replaced its model of literary affiliation with a fundamentally different account of how one enters into poetic community. For
"Tradition and the Individual Talent" rejects the homoerotic metaphor
and Paterian language of the *Egoist* essay in favor of institutional discipline, filial piety, and a poetics of renunciation.

Eliot's spooky qualification—"probably a dead author"—is meant to
emphasize the merely figurative status of his erotic conceit. Yet Eliot's
sense of the benefits to be gained from "a peculiar personal intimacy"
must have meant a great deal to Crane, who experienced his own love
affairs as transformative and imaginatively quickening events; indeed,
Crane found in them the impetus for particular poems and, as we will find
in Chapter Six, a model for the peculiar intimacy he wished to establish
with the readers of his poems. That Crane saw Eliot as a homosexual poet,
not simply as a young critic with a penchant for provocative figures of

speech, is the claim Tate made decades later in an interview with John Unterecker, Crane's biographer. Tate is speaking here of the beginning of his friendship with Crane:

> [Crane] said evidently I'd been reading T. S. Eliot, and he gave me some "signals," which I didn't understand at that time. He said, "I admire Eliot very much too. I've had to work through him, but he's the prime ram of our flock," which meant that in those days a lot of people like Hart had the delusion that Eliot was homosexual. "Ram of our flock" I didn't get onto until later, and when I knew Hart, much later, we joked about it. (Tate, quoted by Unterecker, *Voyager*, 240)

Now, this is intriguing—although Tate raises more questions than he settles. What exactly were Crane's "signals"? (That phrase, "the prime ram of our flock," does not appear in the letters Tate saved; in the letter quoted above, where Crane does say something like "I've had to work through him," he calls Eliot "our divine object of 'envy.' ") Did Crane—for that matter, did Tate—count Tate one of "our flock"? Who else shared Crane's "delusion that Eliot was homosexual"? *Was* it a delusion? Or was the delusion Tate's? Did Tate only think Crane thought Eliot was gay? After all, Tate thought he had misunderstood Crane in 1922; perhaps, "much later," he misunderstood Crane in a different way. What is certain is that Tate came to see Crane's letters about Eliot as freighted with sexual suggestion, as if they were saying, "Leave him and come with me." When he chose Eliot, Tate was not only rejecting Crane, he was rejecting a sexual invitation; and the Eliot with whom Tate chose to identify was not the author of the *Egoist* essay, but the scholar-poet who wrote "Tradition and the Individual Talent."

These intricate relations bring out the sexual subtexts entailed in the shifting alliances of American modernism in the mid-1920s. It is the same period during which, as we saw in Chapter Two, Tate changed his mind about the meaning of *The Waste Land*. In 1922, Tate saw *The Waste Land* as part of "the contemporary revolt against the tyranny of representation"; by 1926, Tate saw the same poem as evidence of "the death of our traditional forms." Rather than the beginning of a literature beyond representation, Eliot's work calls for a renunciation of epic and visionary modes, and thus aligns itself with the reality principle Tate had at first said it challenged. For Tate, this reading of the poem provides the foundation for a community of authors dedicated to an aesthetic of impersonality, authors bound together by the classical wisdom that promotes an accommodation to limits over romantic excess. For Crane, this is the foundation for a heterosexual community that excludes him and his desires, not incidentally but necessarily and expressly, even programmatically. This community is "treasonous," moreover, because it cancels the promises Crane once believed it had made to him. Modernism, when it calls for a "renunciation" that *even Joyce demands*, crosses over to the side of the social order that required the suppression of *Ulysses* itself. Fittingly, Crane's prized copy of *Ulysses* was stolen (or so he claimed) by his own friend, William Lescaze (*Letters of Crane and His Family*, 194–95, 197–200; Lescaze's name is censored by the editor). There is no evidence that Crane either recovered it or acquired another; and henceforth he cut Lescaze.

If Crane's shifting attitude toward *Ulysses* points to the homophobic structure of the literary culture that claimed it, it also points to the narrative structure of high modernist texts. This is the interpretation Allen Grossman urges when he reminds us "that, considered in the context of the poetic practice of his contemporary modernism, Hart Crane was not an experimental poet." Grossman goes on to explain this distinction in an essay from which I quoted earlier. His comments center on Yeats's career.

> Yeats' ironic distancing (as in "Adam's Curse" [1901]) of his own death-bound early ambition . . . made Yeats as a poetic speaker both the audience and the interpreter, in effect, of his own early motive, and announced that ironization of questioning that Eliot identified for his generation in the allusive poetics of "The Love Song of J. Alfred Prufrock" as the mark of high modern structural innovation in poetry. The voices at risk internal to Eliot's *The Waste Land* could no more have spoken the poem that quotes them than could Joyce's Stephen Dedalus have written *A Portrait of the Artist as a Young Man*. Crane, by contrast, spoke from the point of view not of the Daedelian survivor but of the Icarian over-reacher, spoke not as the survivor in retrospect but as the mariner in course of the unsurvivable voyage. Yeats feared . . . that he would come to speak "a tongue men do not know," and so he changed the rules of the game; Crane really spoke that obscure tongue, refusing to change the rules. (Grossman, "Crane's Intense Poetics," 224–25)

Grossman's exposition usefully links Crane's sense of betrayal by modernist literary culture to the narrative structure of that culture's paradigmatic texts. In the case of Yeats, this structure coincides with the narrative of a career; it consists in a contract according to which the poet is permitted to go on with his work on the condition that he renounce his youthful ambition—the "Celtic Twilight" period for Yeats—and assume instead the position of a commentator upon its impossibility. This is the contract Tate ponders when he decides between the alternatives of a Shelleyan "triumph of life" and an Arnoldian "commentary on its impossibility." For Joyce and Eliot, this structure is the narrative form not of the career but of the individual text, a text that presents itself as posterior to visionary and epic modes ("our traditional forms are dead") and thereby encodes, as irony and specifically as ironic allusion, the historicist ideology Crane deplored: "The fruits of civilization are entirely harvested." When this contract goes into effect in the individual text, Crane's poetic motive is not so much excluded as included and betrayed (that is, anticipated and rejected) because the consolidation of the position of the interpreter and critic is dependent on—can only take place after—the collapse of genius, or the failure of the quest. The authority of "the Daedelian survivor," understood as craftsman and father, narrator and critic, is explicitly derived at the expense of genius and son, "the Icarian over-reacher."

Grossman's primary example of this structure was Yeats, but Crane's, of course, was Eliot. Crane would not have needed to inspect the drafts of *The Waste Land*, as we can, to recognize section four, "Death by Water," as a deliberate renunciation—and ironization—of the visionary voyage, a voyage undertaken not only by Victorian questers like Tennyson's Ulysses, but by Eliot himself. The drafts of *The Waste Land* manifest the structure Grossman describes in an unusually visible way. For here the positions of genius and poet-critic are divided between two men, a situation that permits us to study an intratextual structure in the form of an intersubjective relation. Ezra Pound, not Eliot, takes up the position of the critic who is charged with the functions of audience, interpreter, craftsman, and censor; and Pound strikes from the poem—among other passages—an account of a disastrous voyage in the North Atlantic waters where Eliot had sailed as a youth.[26] The excised narrative calls back to early motives in at least two ways: as a record of the poet's first intentions and as a remembrance of the ocean of his youth. But it also calls back to earlier poets and poems: to Homer (*Odyssey*), to Dante (*Inferno*), to Tennyson ("Ulysses"), and to Eliot himself ("Prufrock"). Pound's action enforces a rupture between earlier and later texts of the poem, earlier and later moments in the poet's life, earlier and later poetries of voyage; it is an action, in other words, that can be understood in terms of textual, personal, or literary history. (In the poem on which "Death by Water" is based, "Dans le Restaurant," it is "sa vie antérieure" that Phlebas reencounters in death.)[27] The final assertion of craft that makes the poem a poem, controlling the chaos, hysteria, or excess of Eliot's first thoughts, consists in a suppression of text imposed by one man's pencil on another's typescript.

Wayne Koestenbaum, in a book about the erotics of literary collaboration between men, views Pound's work on *The Waste Land* as an imposition of phallic discipline, simultaneously arousing and restraining his partner's mobile desires and cathexes. For Koestenbaum, Pound's revisions initiate a tradition of reading Eliot's work that has masked "the affinities between the style of high male modernism and the discourse of the female hysteric"—in particular, the heightened discontinuities and rhapsodic excesses of her speech.[28] Pound, in Koestenbaum's analysis, effects for Eliot what Tate tries to effect for himself when, in a poem such as "Procession," he distinguishes his own voice from the "chatter" of women and the "laughter and shouting" of boys. This process of stylistic fortification, in Tate as in Pound and Eliot, entails not only a defense of normative gender roles, but also the creation of a new high-culture hero, a professional, protoacademic poet who disdains, under the category of the "feminine," the characteristic inflections of both genteel and mass cultural forms. *The Waste Land* is the paradigmatic expression of that new literary figure, the poet-critic.

As an indication (Valerie Eliot has suggested) of the loss of confidence caused by Pound's cuts, Eliot wondered if he should not go even further: "Perhaps better omit Phlebas also???" To which Pound replied: "Phlebas is an integral part of the poem . . . And he is needed ABsolootly where he is. Must stay in" (Eliot, *The Waste Land: Facsimile and Transcript*, 61, n. 2). Indeed, Phlebas had to "stay in" in order to indicate exactly what had been left out: his death by water is the necessary expression and trace of Pound's excisions; his corpse survives as the poem's proof of the unsurvivability of the voyage. When he is absorbed by "the deep sea swell," Phlebas is also absorbed, as Perry Meisel has noted, by the "dangerous afflatus of the oracular poet who wagers himself for the sake of revelation"—that is, the romantic poet who attempts to keep faith with and thus enact, in Grossman's terms, his own early motive. Meisel raises this question about "Death by Water" generally: "Is this short segment a movement of eternal return or of belated failure? Is Phlebas dead and gone or is he metamorphosed through the ages by the harmony of archetypal spheres?"[29] Although Meisel leaves the question open, I think it can be easily resolved: Phlebas is both "dead and gone" *and* "metamorphosed through the ages" because the drowning of Phlebas signals the replacement of the visionary motive of genius by the structural irony of the poet-critic.

We have studied this exchange in detail in "The Subway," a lyric in which Tate quotes Crane in order to pass judgment on his visionary motive. In "Death by Water," as elsewhere in *The Waste Land*, this narrative form gives Eliot access to an innovative principle of textual coherence and narrative authority entirely influential on Tate. Pound wrote: "Phlebas is an integral part of the poem; the card pack introduces him, the drowned phoen. sailor." This is Pound's version of a point Grossman makes differently: "The voices at risk internal to Eliot's *The Waste Land* could no more have spoken the poem that quotes them than Joyce's Stephen Dedalus could have written *A Portrait of the Artist as a Young Man*." This is, of course, an interpretation of *Portrait* precisely at odds with Crane's assumed equation between author and hero. In Phlebas, who is constructed in part from the voices of such earlier Eliot poems as "Dans le Restaurant" and *The Waste Land* drafts, we encounter again a narrative form that presents a hero-quester whose point of view is obviously distinct from that of the author; it is a structure engineered to abstract and schematize the voices it appropriates and, in so doing, to disqualify them from present utterance apart from quotation. This is a process of distancing, or ironization, that removes characters from the stories in which they are engaged and places them inside a larger narrative. For *The Waste Land*, if not for *Ulysses*, this larger narrative is the archetypal framework that is both provided and parodied, as Pound intimates in his letter to Eliot, by Madame Sosostris's "wicked pack of cards."

Eliot had in mind his own poems and Yeats's when he described Joyce's use of such a framework, in the essay "*Ulysses*, Order, and Myth," as "the mythical method." This method, which, Eliot contended, "has the importance of a scientific discovery," consists in "the manipulation of a continuous parallel between contemporaneity and antiquity"—with the intent not of revealing the continuity between past and present, but "of controlling, of ordering, of giving a shape and a significance to the immense panorama of futility and anarchy which is contemporary history" (*Selected Prose of T. S. Eliot*, 177). It is not, clearly, the "grafting process" that Crane had in mind when he described the composition of "For the Marriage of Faustus and Helen": "So I found 'Helen' sitting in a street car; the Dionysian revels of her court and her seduction were transferred to a Metropolitan roof garden with a jazz orchestra; and the *katharsis* of the fall of Troy I saw approximated in the recent World War" (Crane, *Complete Poems and Selected Prose*, 217). What Crane describes is indeed "a continuous parallel" between past and present. What Eliot describes is a relation of control in which the past presents a model, pattern, or standard (Eliot's own word is "foundation") *against which* the present is evaluated (and found to be inferior, unstructured). Eliot's emphasis is on the *incongruence* between past and present; and the opposition he constructs, which is one of "form" versus "formlessness," recalling his contrast between Dante and Blake, the classic poet and the genius, implicitly links Crane's work with "the immense panorama of futility and anarchy which is contemporary history." Eliot's relation to the modern "panorama of futility and anarchy," by contrast, is like Pound's relation to the drafts of *The Waste Land*. For the poet-critic achieves a perspective over and beyond the chaos of mass culture through an act of suppression, seen as an imposition of literary "form," which gives him a point of view over and beyond his own work. Thematized as the sacrifice of "the Icarian over-reacher," Eliot's valorization of the past validates the father at the expense of the son.

What Crane wanted from Eliot's "erudition and technique," finally, was the power of self-authorization, the accreditation, that Eliot claimed on the basis of his scholarship. Crane's opposition to Eliot was essential to establish his difference, but also his similarity—his right to speak on the same platform, to address the same audience. Crane wanted to "absorb" Eliot's authority, and in so doing overcome it. The awkward intellectual posturing in Crane's work—what Grossman calls "the phantom modernism" of *The Bridge*—derives from this strategy. Crane wanted to take over the powers Eliot had acquired for modern poetry, and use them differently. In the notes known as "General Aims and Theories," where Crane describes the pseudo-Eliotic structure of "Faustus and Helen" (a retrospective critical fiction that legitimates the poem by misrepresenting it), Crane admits that he is "utilizing the gifts of the past as instruments principally; and that the voice of the present, if it is to be known, must be caught at the risk of speaking in idioms and circumlocutions sometimes shocking to the scholar and historians of logic" (Crane, *Complete Poems and Selected Prose*, 222–23). The voice at risk in Crane's poems, as Grossman would say, is shocking because it violates the logic of scholar or historian or poet-critic by appropriating "the gifts of the past" as "instruments" for the articulation of "the voice of the present." This is not quotation, but the willfully naive appropriation, the claiming of other voices as Crane's own, that accounts for the anachronism of "Thou canst read nothing."

The method is continuous with Crane's ideal of unmediated relations between persons, and it is antithetical to Eliot's insistence on the distance between past and present, a distance Eliot indicates by (actual or implied) quotation marks and the addition to his poetry of scholarly (albeit mock-scholarly) notes. Eliot's goal is, as Hulme demanded, to keep things separated that ought to be separated.

Eliot's allusive techniques therefore deliberately renounce (that is, announce the demise of) those poetic "idioms and circumlocutions" in which Crane believed he was still entitled to speak (or should be so entitled). This stylistic strategy is linked in Crane's imagination to an experience of death and burial because Eliot's belief in "the death of our traditional forms" is reiterated, as it is later in Tate's work, in narratives of the death of the hero of romance quest. This hero is parodically diminished but recognizable in Eliot's St. Narcissus, Gerontion, Prufrock, and Phlebas. In Phlebas's case, Eliot is no longer working with the mock-heroic or parody (as he is in the earlier poems), but with a distinctively modernist kind of narrative. Here, the dissolution of personal identity in drowning transfers the hero's body from romance to an "anthropological" meditation on romance, from the personal order of romantic quest to the impersonal order of myth, archetype, and moral exemplum:

> Phlebas the Phoenician, a fortnight dead,
> Forgot the cry of gulls, and the deep sea swell
> And the profit and loss.
>
>   A current under sea
> Picked his bones in whispers. As he rose and fell
> He passed the stages of his age and youth
> Entering the whirlpool.
>
>   Gentile or Jew
> O you who turn the wheel and look to windward,
> Consider Phlebas, who was once handsome and tall as you.

(Eliot, Collected Poems, 65)

Phlebas's drowning emblematizes the failure of several kinds of progress at once: as a warning to those "who turn the wheel and look to windward," it is a reminder of the suprahistorical order overriding the eroticism of "the cry of the gulls," the poetic aspiration of "the deep sea swell," and the economy of "the profit and loss" (a phrase that is meant to resonate with the dissolution of Western culture as a whole). To forget these conditions of the voyage is to cancel the future and return, via the centripetal action of the whirlpool, to "the archetypal harmony of the spheres"—a vortex transporting the sailor out of Tennyson's "Ulysses," say, and into *The Waste Land*.

We can call this event the replacement of "narrative method" by "the mythical method," as Eliot does (in his best scientific manner), or the replacement of the genius by the critic, as Tate allows us to do. But we can also read it as the homophobic sacrifice of a brother or double or self "who was once handsome and tall as you." There are precedents for this reading. In 1952, John Peter proposed a homosexual subtext in "Death by Water" in a piece called "A New Interpretation of *The Waste Land*." Peter's essay appeared in *Essays in Criticism*—then disappeared, for Eliot's solicitors had been alerted, and copies of *Essays in Criticism* containing "A New Interpretation" were confiscated and destroyed. James E. Miller, Jr., who details this event in his book, *T. S. Eliot's Personal Waste Land*, sees in "Death By Water" an acknowledgment of Eliot's own homosexual experience.[30] Whether or not this biographical interpretation is founded, however, it seems rather beside the point. For Phlebas is already clearly implicated in the homoerotic desire of Narcissus, and Eliot's decision to drown him, seconded by Pound, is a judgment on the fate of such desire, as Crane understood.

Pound performed for Eliot the task Eliot's solicitors would later on; it is really the same task Eliot himself performed when he stopped *Poetry* from publishing "The Death of St. Narcissus" in 1915. "The surviving galley proof," Maud Ellmann has observed, "is 'scored through by hand with the manuscript directive "Kill" (i.e., suppress) in the margin of each section,' as if to emulate its suicidal hero."[31] Throughout Eliot's work, the subjection of Narcissus includes and implies the subjection of the homosexual, each of whom, like "the Icarian over-reacher," is destined to die. The denial of this fate is the denial of that "perfection of death" after which, Crane felt, "nothing is possible in motion but a resurrection of some kind." The resurrection Crane offered as a revision of "Death by Water," which expressly attempts to recover the "hope" buried by *The Waste Land*, is represented in lyrics such as "Voyages" and "At Melville's Tomb." In the next chapter, we will examine the mode of literary transmission imagined in "At Melville's Tomb"—a kind of compact between poet and reader that would rescue and revalue motives otherwise sacrificed, suppressed, or excised in high modernist practice.

SIX

Dice of Drowned Men's Bones

IF AFTER ALL THESE FEARFUL FAINTING TRANCES, THE VERDICT BE, THE GOLDEN HAVEN WAS NOT GAINED;—YET IN BOLD QUEST THEREOF, BETTER TO SINK IN BOUNDLESS DEEPS THAN FLOAT ON VULGAR SHOALS; AND GIVE ME, YE GODS, AN UTTER WRECK, IF WRECK I DO.

—Herman Melville, *Mardi*[1]

By the fall of 1925, the manuscript of *White Buildings* had circulated for more than a year without securing a publisher.[2] Nor, in this period, had Crane had much success placing his poems with magazines. Tate took "Legend" and "Lachrymae Christi" for the *Fugitive*, but Marianne Moore rejected "Passage" for the *Dial*, and Eliot rejected the same poem for the *Criterion*. When Eliot rejected "The Wine Menagerie" as well, Crane again tried Moore. This time Moore accepted Crane's poem, but with certain changes, which she took it upon herself to make; and these changes, it turned out, entailed the reduction of Crane's eleven pentameter quatrains to three much abridged, strangely Moore-like strophes, enigmatically retitled "Again."[3] Crane, it seems, would either have to see his work rejected by Eliot and Moore, or submit to their correction.

When he drafted "At Melville's Tomb" in late October 1925, Crane turned away from the modernist community represented by Eliot and Moore, as the speaker of this poem turns his back on the shore. At the same time, Crane turned toward the sea, toward the past, and toward Melville, the history of whose reception gave Crane a means to dramatize and interpret the vicissitudes of his own. Melville was an off-shore ally. His imaginative world gave literary sanction to Crane's erotic life, in particular to Crane's pursuit of sailors. In another sense, Crane's sexual voyages in Lower Manhattan or on the Brooklyn waterfront acted out literary motifs and ambitions, such as he found in Melville. "Under thy shadow by the

145

piers I waited," Crane says to Brooklyn Bridge; it is a scene of desiring that is neither merely sexual nor wholly literary (Crane, *Poems*, 44). Melville gave Crane ways to link the homosexual company he found by the piers and "the visionary company of love" he projected in his poems (Crane, *Poems*, 160). But Crane did not find in Melville healing and unity of the kind represented in "Episode of Hands." The Melville Crane addressed stood for boundless and despised desires.

"At Melville's Tomb" proposes a literary history in which Crane would have a place; in the act of reading Melville, the poem projects a reader for Crane. An intimate bond with the reader was essential to the kind of "obscure" poem Crane wrote. The difficulty of Crane's work calls forth—and is premised upon—an ideal reader; it is an appeal for aid and connection, as Crane explained during 1926 in a series of important and related documents, letters to Gorham Munson and to Harriet Monroe and the essay (or really the notes) called "General Aims and Theories." In this chapter, I plan to meditate on "At Melville's Tomb" and the prose texts that grew out of it in order to extract the basic terms of Crane's poetics and set them against those of Tate and Eliot. In conclusion, I will turn briefly to "Repose of Rivers." Written just after Crane left Patterson in April 1926, "Repose of Rivers" draws this stage of Crane's writing life to a close. It also looks ahead to *The Bridge*.

Who exactly was Melville in 1925? Whom did Crane invoke by that name? He was and was not the author who occupies a central position in the temple of the American Renaissance. That author was available to Crane in D. H. Lawrence's *Studies in Classic American Literature* (1923) or in writing influenced by Van Wyck Brooks's reevaluation of American romanticism, including Frank's *Our America* (1919) and Lewis Mumford's *The Golden Day* (1926). Crane, who sent his first draft of the poem to Frank, understood "At Melville's Tomb" as a contribution to this ongoing cultural labor, this search for "a usable past." But Melville was not an important figure in Brooks's canon, and less important still in "the genteel tradition" Brooks's canon was intended to displace. When Melville was revived in the early 1920s, it was later than Whitman, say, or Twain,[4] and under different circumstances: he had never been entirely alive. Melville was a minor author of sea tales whose appeal was closely associated with his own life as vagabond, *isolato*, and adventurer. Melville's later fiction, where it was known, was considered the imaginative failure of an embittered man; and *Moby-Dick*, if it was admired, was chiefly admired abroad.[5] In 1925, then, Melville carried with him the aura of an American *maudit*—

an obscure author with a criminal appeal not unlike that which attracted Crane to Joyce. Crane, known to dress himself as "an Indian" or "a cannibal" at parties, saw a brother in Melville, "who lived among the cannibals"; like Crane, Melville was a sailor and a symbolist—or, as the subtitle of Raymond Weaver's biography of Melville identifies him, a *Mariner and Mystic*.[6]

The epigraph with which this chapter begins comes from Melville's *Mardi* in a passage Weaver quotes to describe Melville's early ambition. Crane read Weaver's biography of Melville, which was published in 1921; he read *Moby-Dick* four times, read *White-Jacket*, *Typee*, *Omoo*, *Mardi*, and *Israel Potter*, read *Piazza Tales*, and read Melville's poems.[7] The life-narrative Crane found in these books is summarized by Weaver as an on-going conflict between the claims of desire and "reality":

> Throughout Melville's long life his warring and untamed desires were in violent conflict with his physical and spiritual environment. His whole history is the record of an attempt to escape from an inexorable and intolerable world of reality: a quenchless and essentially tragic Odyssey away from home, out in search of "the unpeopled world behind the sun." In the blood and bone of his youth he sailed away in brave quest of such a harbour, to face inevitable defeat. For this rebuff he sought both solace and revenge in literature. But by literature he also sought his livelihood. . . . Held closer to reality by financial worry and the hostages of wife and children, the conflict within him was heightened. By a vicious circle, with brooding disappointment came ill health. (Weaver, *Melville*, 19)

As Weaver's rhetoric rises to the level of Melville's in *Mardi*, he depicts Melville's literary project as "solace and revenge" for the failure of his youthful "Odyssey away from home," his longed-for deliverance from "the vulgar shoals" of "an inexorable and intolerable world of reality." Melville's youthful urge to escape the confines of bourgeois civility and "home" (later, the wife and children he holds hostage) is renewed in Melville's will to transcend "fireside literature," and produce a kind of writing that would mean more than his livelihood. Both of these quests, being dedicated to absolute satisfactions, necessarily encounter defeat, imagined as shipwreck, or as a writer's production of an unread (perhaps an unreadable) text. Weaver's Melville remains true to the "untamed desires" of his youth, but at the cost of becoming "the Devil's Advocate," a novelist created in the image of the Satanic Poet willing to commit himself to hell rather than repent. It is a version of the story Tate tells about Keats and Crane, but unlike Tate, Weaver does not endorse moral "realism"; Melville is for Weaver a tragic figure because he keeps faith with his desires, not because he gives them up.

This is the moral and history of Crane's Melville too. But to refuse to repent, to abandon the consolations of "home," is not, in Crane's poem, to cut oneself off from all bonds; it is to enter into a different kind of community, a league of "drowned men," from which it is possible to draw hope. In the first stanza of Crane's poem, the persistence of this community across time, even in "defeat," is figured in the repeated action of the waves as they rise and fall, breaking on the shore.

> Often beneath the wave, wide from this ledge
> The dice of drowned men's bones he saw bequeath
> An embassy. Their numbers as he watched,
> Beat on the dusty shore and were obscured.

(Crane, Poems, 33)

The trochaic substitutions in the first and fourth feet of line 1 introduce a tension between iambic and trochaic schemes, the metrical norm and its reversal, which, as we will see, is encoded on another level in Crane's images of rising and falling, lifting and sinking. In this first instance the metrical alternation, a movement of arrest and renewal, is coordinated with the action of the waves. The trochaic word "Often" locates this action in time while the phrase "wide from this ledge" locates it in space. That initial phrase invokes a recurring possibility of vision—at once enduring *and* discontinuous—of the kind invoked in the first line of *The Bridge*: "How many dawns, chill from his rippling rest" (Crane, *Poems*, 43). In fact, the beginning of *The Bridge* specifically reworks the beginning of Crane's draft, "How many times the jewelled dice spoke."[8] In both cases, Crane begins a poem in such a way as to place his own action within a *series* of beginnings. The effect, here, is to emphasize the continuity between Crane's and Melville's perspectives even as it emphasizes the discontinuity, or seriality, of this perspective as such. In the preface to *White Buildings*, Tate faults Crane's "masters"—Whitman, Melville, and Poe—for establishing only a discontinuous tradition of false starts, repeated beginnings; in "At Melville's Tomb," Crane claims that discontinuity as a sign of generative power and a principle of historical connection.

The vision Melville and Crane share—"wide from this ledge"—introduces an expanded field of possibility. "Wide" is a peculiarly Cranean modifier, a *positional* term, implying breadth, lateral movement, and scope. It points to both separation and extension, and it turns up repeatedly in Crane's poems about the sea, which are also poems about Crane's relation to nineteenth-century American male authors like Melville and Whitman. "Wide" (sometimes "widening" or "wider") occurs four times in "Voyages," once in "The Harbor Dawn" and in "Ave Maria," and twice more in both "The River" and "Cape Hatteras." In "Voyages I," the word describes the danger of engulfment by "caresses / Too lichen-faithful from too wide a breast" (Crane, *Poems*, 34); and in "Voyages II," this threat is matched and overcome by "The seal's wide spindrift gaze toward paradise" (Crane, *Poems*, 35).

Here, in the first line of "At Melville's Tomb," "wide" describes the poet's latitude of vision across the extrasocial space of the sea, a place without limits, of "rimless floods, unfettered leewardings" ("Voyages II" [Crane, *Poems*, 35]), an imaginative domain very different from the strictly circumscribed and highly structured space of Tate's cemetery.[9] The sea's boundaries, defined by the tides, are continually in flux; as Crane imagines it, the sea is destructive—or not so much destructive as destructuring, a medium of transformation, process, and change. For these reasons, as Lee Edelman has argued, the sea in Crane's poems can be discussed in Lacanian terms as a "maternal" space unmediated by—and unconstrained by—the symbolic coordinates of the Father (Edelman, *Transmemberment of Song*, 135–37). In the fragment "The Sea Raised Up," from the winter of 1927, the sea is the site of a regressive, incestual fantasy of union, collapsing male poet and mother in the compound identity "—me—her":

> The sea raised up a campanile . . . The wind I heard
> Of brine partaking, whirling into shower
> Of column that breakers sheared in shower
> Back into bosom, —me—her, into natal power . . .
>
> (Crane, *Poems*, 213)

The "natal power" spoken of here is a mother tongue; it suggests that the anachronistic language of Crane's high style is not (in contrast to the "grand manner" Tate coveted) a language of the fathers. Rather, it is a transgressive discourse cut loose from—"wide from"—the proprieties of conventional reference, and therefore "shocking to the scholar and the historians of logic."

Crane's decision to locate Melville's tomb at sea—as if the author had been lost at sea—has not sufficiently surprised his critics. To deny Melville his actual resting place on land is to rededicate his spirit to the youthful quest Weaver describes; to deny, in effect, that Melville ever had or could come home. For Crane's *cimetière marin* is imagined in such a way as to refuse, as Tate's cemetery does not, the possibility of representing and enclosing the heroic dead. Tate's headstones ("Row after row," "Rank upon rank") depict a static temporality Eliot conceived of as an ideal order of monuments. They are first of all *containers*—like Mr. Pope's well-wrought urn; they *stand for* bodies; and they describe a poetics, exemplified by "Ode to the Confederate Dead," wherein the poet cannot be present, cannot act, except as the disembodied intelligence that contemplates the scene from this side of the gate. The charge brought by Davidson against this poetics—that it assigns the poet to a point of view which, in its absolute removal from the site, is structurally analogous to that of the dead—was freely, although unhappily, admitted by Tate. The charge brought by Tate against Crane's poetics is exactly complementary: that the poet in Crane's poems cannot be assigned a point of view outside of them, and thus is not in a position to control and interpret his materials, only to be absorbed by them. Crane's "pantheism," Tate explained, "is necessarily a philosophy of sensation without a point of view" (Tate, *Essays of Four Decades*, 319). Despite the moral that clings to it, Tate's remark touches Crane's deepest ambition; for the poet in Crane's poems seeks to fully participate in the visionary events he describes.

This ambition places the reader of Crane's poems—unnervingly, disorientingly—in a position conventionally assigned to the poet. R.W.B. Lewis defines this effect when he quotes and comments on the aims Crane stated in defense of "At Melville's Tomb": " 'Fresh concepts, more inclusive evaluations . . . added consciousness and increased perceptions.' There is the vital essence of Crane's theory, and an abstract of his practice. . . . Aiming at those things, Crane's poems are persistently *about* them, and about aiming at them; when, with our active cooperation, they succeed, they increase our consciousness of what is involved in the effort to increase our consciousness" (Lewis, *Poetry of Crane*, 206). In Lewis's account of Crane's practice, Crane's reader is placed in the position of the speaker on shore in "At Melville's Tomb," a position in which the reader is charged with receiving and thus completing the message or "embassy" that the drowned men's bones "bequeath." If Lewis's logic looks circular, or his language convoluted, it is because Crane's contract with the reader is imagined as a circuit, as a circulation of energy and meaning, which is figured, in subsequent stanzas, in Crane's vortical images of "shells," "calyx," and "coil." These are images of the structure of the poem itself, because the poem's circular forms, its inward "corridors of shells," represent in spatial terms the vision Crane and Melville—and Crane's reader—share across time. That vision is discontinuous, despite its endurance across time, because it is continually passing—and continually renewed—with every reading of the poem. Meaning is repeatedly promised and deferred in Crane's poems; it is virtual, preludial, prospective—intended to increase "our consciousness of what is involved in the effort to increase our consciousness"; and it is carried to shore, like "the dice of drowned men's bones," only in the moment before it is "obscured."

Lewis describes Crane's aims ("Fresh concepts, more inclusive evaluations") by quoting from Crane's own statement of them in "A Letter to Harriet Monroe," a reply to the editor of *Poetry*, which appeared in the magazine with "At Melville's Tomb" in October 1926. The obscurity of Crane's meanings, apparently, had made the poem all but unpublishable; it circulated for almost a year before Monroe, somewhat grudgingly, accommodated it along with Crane's explanation. That explanation is, as he knew it would be, Crane's most widely known performance as a critic and theorist, and it bears the strain of Crane's obligation to prove his sophistication, intelligence, and good faith to several audiences at once. Privately, Crane ridiculed Monroe; "Aunt Harriet" was a recurrent figure of fun in communications with Tate. Crane's antipathy toward Monroe, as well as Moore, whom he called names like "the Rt. Rev. Miss Mountjoy" (Crane, *Letters*, 218), leagued him with other modernist men. In his letter to Monroe, Crane took the side of his male colleagues by defending modernist "difficulty" against genteel standards, which are seen here as, at least implicitly, female ones. But one function of Crane's obscurity, as of his misogyny, was to disguise his sexual desires, and this motive divided him from Tate and Monroe both. Defending obscurity, Crane was defending his right to a language in which the unspeakable could be spoken.

Crane's metaphor "the dice of drowned men's bones" vexed Monroe particularly. Crane's gloss remains cogent:

> Dice bequeath an embassy, in the first place, by being ground (in this connection only, of course) in little cubes from the bones of drowned men by the action of the sea, and are finally thrown up on the sand, having "numbers" but no identification. These being the bones of dead men who never completed their voyage, it seems legitimate to refer to them as the only surviving evidence of certain messages undelivered, mute evidence of certain things, experiences that the dead mariners might have had to deliver. Dice as a symbol of chance and circumstance is also implied. (Crane, *Complete Poems and Selected Prose*, 238)

"Dead letters! does it not sound like dead men?" (Melville, *Writings of Herman Melville*, Vol. 9, *Piazza Tales*, 45). It is hard not to hear Crane's gloss as an affirmative reply to the pained exclamation of the narrator of Melville's "Bartleby." We can see the "dice of drowned men's bones" as a figure for "the homosexual text," in Yingling's terms, insofar as the "obscurity" imposed on and by homosexual desire presents a fable for the textualization of the self. On the one hand, Crane's mariners cannot deliver their messages—they are converted to "numbers," perhaps as Wilde is when he becomes "C 33"; on the other hand, their experience is precisely and narrowly textual—in code, accessible only through reading. The writing they do here—their transmissions of self as text—is identified with dying, and specifically with death by water. The metaphor follows the consequences of wagering the self in literary exploit to the marking not of paper, but of bone—as if the attempt to put oneself into words could only issue in the fragmentation, formalization, and inscription of the body. Rather than expression, then, what is recovered is the impression of the transforming medium itself—"the action of the sea"—which is equated with the pure form manifest in poetic "numbers." The mariners of "At Melville's Tomb" are absorbed into and changed by a textual process Crane associates with the determinate structure of metrical order and the nonhuman violence of the waves.

The contrast between Crane's account of this process and the drowning of Eliot's Phlebas, or the erosion of Tate's headstones in the ode, is worth contemplating. In Eliot, the death of the handsome sailor removes him from quest-romance and places him in an archetypal framework from which his failure could be foreseen. In Tate, the headstones that "yield their names to the element" figure an effacement of personal identity consistent with the submission to an ethical order outside the self. In both cases, we encounter representations of the sacrifice of self that is necessary for the integration of parts into a whole; whether this whole is imagined as "the harmony of archetypal spheres," or the harmony of the so-called traditional society, it is located in a remote and idealized past. In *The Waste Land*, the passage from the present to the past is represented by the regressive vortex of the whirlpool, a circular movement that reverses the drowned mariner's direction, returning Phlebas "through the stages of his age and youth" to a point at which individuality dissolves into the scholar's archetype.

Eliot's vortex returns in "At Melville's Tomb," but Crane's interest is in the centrifugal force of the whirlpool, its power to cast up and disseminate traces of the voyage it consumes:

> And wrecks passed without sound of bells,
> The calyx of death's bounty giving back
> A scattered chapter, livid hieroglyph,
> The portent wound in corridors of shells.

(Crane, *Poems*, 33)

The vortex or whirlpool (in other poems, the waterspout and the hurricane) symbolizes the rhetorical operations of expanding and compacting, widening and winding, that structure Crane's condensed and overtaxed poetry. John Irwin explains: "In Crane's verse the metaphoric relationship 'A is B' takes by ellipsis the form of a complex word or phrase 'AB,' and this complex word or phrase becomes in turn part of the metaphoric relationship 'C is AB,' and so on, with mounting complexity."[10] The will to activate and include all "the so-called illogical impingements of the connotations of words on the consciousness" (Crane, *Complete Poems and Selected Prose*, 234) results in the excess and eliding of references for which Crane's work remains notorious. "This crowding of the frame," Grossman writes, "came to constitute a trope peculiar to him—not the modernist 'ambiguity,' which hierarchizes, or ironically totalizes a plurality of meanings—but a singularly naive rhetoric of shadowed wholeness (the impossible simultaneity of all the implications of desire) that struggles merely to include all meanings in the one space of appearance" (Grossman, "Crane's Intense Poetics," 230). What emerges from that struggle, the failure of which Crane images as a shipwreck and descent into the whirlpool, is not "shadowed wholeness" but the isolated fragments of this whole, "A scattered chapter, livid hieroglyph, / The portent wound in corridors of shells." This cycle of absorption and redistribution represents a narrative of poetic composition in which the whole, as it is engrossed in the part ("the one space of appearance"), which cannot possibly sustain it, is both torn apart *and* disseminated. The "wholeness" Crane envisions is "shadowed," or "obscured," precisely in the sense of "foreshadowed"—still waiting to be constituted and received; its destruction (simultaneous with its arrival on shore) is also the condition of its postponement, its transmission as a "portent." Unlike the "unity of sensibility" Eliot and Tate looked for in the past, Crane's deferred harmony refers to the future.

The distinction can be clarified by examining the difference between Tate's sense of poetic structure as container and Crane's sense of poetic structure as "portent"—as a sign both necessary and inadequate to the expression of its referent. For example, Harvey Gross has shown the extent to which the intelligibility of Crane's poems *depends upon* verse form—and particularly meter—to mitigate "uncertain, almost haphazard syntactical progression."[11] Gross's insight is borne out by the poem at hand to the extent that the multiple figures in the second stanza's substitutive chain (wrecks—calyx—chapter—hieroglyph—portent) are organized *as* a chain and not as a random series less by logic or grammatical relation than by the catena of pentameter. This is frequently the state of affairs in Crane's poems, where meter takes over the work of grammar in the construction of an elaborate apostrophe or an extended series of appositive phrases. Yet even metrical order, however necessary to intelligibility, remained for Crane a compromise of his intentions. "Poetic structure, whether the phantom modernism of *The Bridge* or the nineteenth-century French formality of 'The Broken Tower,' was unaccommodated to [Crane's] meaning because no structure, the function of which is to bear meaning into the world of appearance, is free from the finitizations that are the sufficient condition of appearing at all" (Grossman, "Crane's Intense Poetics," 239).

In "The Broken Tower," Crane represents the costs of this compromise, of the "finitizations" attendant on poetic structure, as an engraving of "Membrane through marrow," which recalls the inscription of "numbers" on "the dice of drowned men's bones." The "scattered chapter" that these bones constitute returns, in the same stanza of "The Broken Tower," as "my long-scattered score / Of broken intervals" (Crane, *Poems*, 160). This is, in Crane's "final" poem, a retrospective reflection on the shape of Crane's career, an embittered comment on the intermittency of writing. But it also describes the disseminative violence that Crane's poems, from the beginning, participate in and celebrate. For Crane, the entrance into poetry is imagined as a breaking or scattering of the whole of his desire, ambition, identity; it is a passage into structure that is, paradoxically, destructuring. Verse form, understood here both as abstract pattern and concrete instance, fragments Crane's utterance at the same time that it shapes and upholds it.[12] This is fundamentally the paradox of a discourse—a homosexual discourse for Crane—in which to speak is to be silenced. The point of the poet's appearance is also that of his disappearance, and the message of the drowned is communicated in the moment it is obscured.

"The dice of drowned men's bones" might be regarded, then, as emblems of Crane's own quatrains, which are forms fashioned in the tension between structure and flux, necessity and "chance," and which present the reader with "a livid hieroglyph." They are the decipherable but complexly encoded, complexly burdened parts of an inaccessible self, the fragments of a mutilated—because unrepresentable—whole. The question is: How did Crane find hope in this sea change? How does the fragmentation of word and self in "At Melville's Tomb" differ from the "song of minor, broken strain" in "C 33"? How could the mutilation of the body possibly anticipate its restoration?

In *American Hieroglyphics*, John Irwin suggests one answer to these questions when he calls attention to the way in which the drowning of

Bulkington, in "The Lee Shore" chapter of *Moby-Dick*, functions synecdo-
chically to describe the work of synecdoche in Melville's novel as a whole.
Bulkington, a handsome sailor in a line running beyond Billy Budd to
Phlebas and Crane's Melville, gives one "glimpses . . . of that mortally
intolerable truth" that the natural elements of the air and sea always drive
any "deep, earnest thinking" back upon "the treacherous, slavish shore."
Melville's Ishmael continues: "But as in landlessness alone resides the
highest truth, shoreless, indefinite as God—so, better is it to perish in that
howling infinite, than be ingloriously dashed upon the lee, even if that
were safety! . . . O Bulkington! Bear thee grimly, demigod! Up from the
spray of thy ocean-perishing—straight up, leaps thy apotheosis!" (Melville, *Writings of Melville*, Vol. 6, *Moby-Dick*, 107). The "six-inch chapter"
of "The Lee Shore," Ishmael tells us, is itself "the stoneless grave of Bulkington." Irwin, who interprets this epitaph as a prefiguration of the wreck
of the *Pequod*, writes: "What leaps up from the spray of his ocean perishing
is the phallic coffin/life preserver/book—the part-whole relation of the
phallic six-inch chapter to the body of the text prefiguring the symbolic
relationship of the book to the self."[13] The relation of the chapter to the
whole of the book, like that of Crane's own "scattered chapter" to "any
complete record of the recent ship and her crew" (Crane, *Complete Poems
and Selected Letters*, 239), is a relation of survival *through* dismemberment,
of the whole persisting in its parts. By the end of the novel, Bulkington is
returned whole, even as the *Pequod* itself is lost, when Ishmael rises from—
is cast up by—the vortex of its grave, buoyed by "the phallic coffin/life
preserver/book." Ishmael, at the same time, survives the unsurvivable voyage not by renouncing but by reaffirming the moral imperative of the
quest, allowing us to identify character and narrator in a way we could not
in the case of modernist narratives like *The Waste Land* or *A Portrait of the
Artist as a Young Man*.

The structure of Melville's novel presents a narrative unfolding of
Crane's desired union of author and hero, self and text. As Irwin indicates
in his comments on "The Lee Shore," the English word "chapter" derives,
like "capital," the architectural term for the crown of a column, from the
Latin *caput* for "head." It is possible, with this etymology in mind, to read
Crane's "scattered chapter" as a simple restatement of the initial figure
of "the dice of drowned men's bones," and to see both phrases as early
versions of the architectural collapse announced in the title of "The
Broken Tower." In each of these phrases, the dismembering of the body,
conceived of as structure, instrument, or vehicle, is identified with the dismembering of texts, because word and flesh are fractured under the pres-

sure of Crane's effort to lift and connect them, to turn each one into the other. It is not at all an admission of failure, therefore, when a petulant Crane tells Monroe that she should expect "about as much definite knowledge" to be had from a "scattered chapter" and "livid hieroglyph" "as anyone might gain from the roar of his own veins, which is easily heard (haven't you ever done it?) by holding a shell close to one's ear" (Crane, *Complete Poems and Selected Prose*, 239). For Crane is willing to sacrifice claims to a conventional mimesis (claims that he is at pains to defend elsewhere in this letter) in order to interpret the sound of the sea, remembered in the form of the shell ("The portent wound in corridors of shell"), as the present sound (and not the echo) of "the roar in his own veins."[14] The poem does not simply record the passions of the body; it *consists in* those passions, and magically transmits them.

This turn of mind anticipates Crane's identification of Shakespeare with a Prospero absorbed into the fury of his own creating: the author that Crane apostrophizes in "To Shakespeare" is "pilot,—tempest, too!" (Crane, *Poems*, 131). In a letter to Munson written in March 1926, and more or less contemporary with "General Aims and Theories" (which was based upon, if it did not in fact constitute, the notes that Crane sent Eugene O'Neill for his undelivered preface to *White Buildings*),[15] Crane described his poems as "incarnate *evidence*" of a kind of knowledge that can be experienced but not properly named, since one enters—as writer or reader—so fully into that experience: "Poetry, in so far as the metaphysics of any absolute knowledge extends, is simply the concrete *evidence* of the *experience* of a recognition (*knowledge* if you like). It can give you a *ratio* of fact and experience, and in this sense it is both perception and thing perceived" (Crane, *Letters*, 237). Despite Crane's confidence about poetry's unmediated access to experience, there is nothing very simple about this definition. Indeed, as Edelman has shown in a fine deconstruction of the passage, the "concrete *evidence*" Crane writes of, because it refers us to a prior "*experience* of recognition," "must be founded not on the presence, but on the absence of the experience to which it refers; it presents itself, that is, as a mediated version of an originally unmediated vision" (Edelmen, *Transmemberment of Song*, 33–34). This is not an indication of the inadequacy of Crane's exposition so much as an accurate description of the contradictory character of its claims. It is consistent, that is, with the impossible condition of a poetry that seeks to become both sign and signified, "both perception and thing perceived," a poetry projected by a poet who imagines himself as "pilot,—tempest, too!"

Grossman, who claims that Crane's poetry, in the absence of "new structures" of its own to deploy, "tends to hallucinate or thematize" such structures (Grossman, "Crane's Intense Poetics," 224), and Edelman, who shows how "the structural principles that generate Crane's figures also generate recurrent narrative and thematic concerns" (Edelman, *Transmemberment of Song*, 14),[16] both point to Crane's lack of a language—apart from the figural and formal operations of the poetry itself—that would be capable of explaining and legitimating those operations. Crane has this problem in mind when, in a letter to Otto Kahn, he says it is "next to impossible to describe [*The Bridge*] without resorting to the actual metaphors of the poem" (Crane, *Letters*, 241). This is the case both because Crane's poems leave vacant the position of the poet-critic established in modernist convention and because Crane's poems specifically seek a language *prior* to criticism, a language Crane connected (misleadingly or not) with "experience." Crane's stylistic anachronism is a sign of this primary language. I compared it earlier to a "mother" tongue; Crane usually called it "a logic of metaphor." This logic, Crane argued, "antedates our so-called pure logic, and . . . is the genetic basis of all speech" (Crane, *Complete Poems and Selected Prose*, 221); yet it does not refer, strictly speaking, to the past. Crane preferred to describe it, as he does in "General Aims and Theories," as a language of "*causes* (metaphysical)" and "spiritual consequences" (Crane, *Complete Poems and Selected Prose*, 220). It is a nonnarrative language condensing beginnings and ends, "causes" and "consequences," signs and signifieds, in a medium that exists outside history in the timeless present that Crane invokes at the beginning of "At Melville's Tomb" and of *The Bridge*.

In this sense, the archaic language Crane seeks is also radically "new." "It is as though," Crane speculates in "General Aims and Theories," "a poem gave the reader as he left it a single, new *word*, never before spoken and impossible to actually enunciate, but self-evident as an active principle in the reader's consciousness henceforward" (Crane, *Complete Poems and Selected Letters*, 221). Never before spoken, that is, *because* it is "impossible to actually enunciate"; it can only be transmitted as an *event*, as a transaction between the poem and a reader who retains this new word as fragment or token, as the kind of "self-evident" and untranslatable sign that Crane describes simply as "mute evidence of certain things, experiences that the dead mariners might have had to deliver." The mystical "new *word*" is a secular synecdoche of a sacred Word, colored by Crane's experience with the subliminal codes of both advertising and gay culture. But what that word means is hard to say. Crane's own critical language typically falls mute when called upon to specify the content of his poems' prophecy (merely "certain messages," "certain things," "certain spiritual events and possibilities"). Munson, Winters, Tate, and Blackmur, echoing

Arnold's evaluation of the Romantic Poets, judged that reticence harshly; they claimed Crane did not know enough. But what they called a lack of knowledge was Crane's commitment, in his life, to the role of the autodidact, and his decision, in his work, *not* to arrive at "definite knowledge," not to submit to the various forms of doctrine that were required by his critics.[17]

In "General Aims and Theories," Crane speaks of his search for "a morality essentialized from experience directly, and not from previous precepts or preconceptions" (Crane, *Complete Poems and Selected Prose*, 221). Crane's statement is the basis for an ethics, linked to his defense of Joyce's *Portrait*, and a poetics, linked to his defense of "At Melville's Tomb." "If the poet is to be held completely to the already evolved and exploited sequences of imagery and logic," Crane wrote to Monroe, "—what field of added consciousness and increased perceptions (the actual province of poetry, if not lullabies) can be expected when one has to relatively return to the alphabet every breath or so?" (Crane, *Complete Poems and Selected Prose*, 237). The point of novelty, of Crane's "new *word*," is to liberate the poet's language from "precepts or preconceptions," the received order of "the alphabet." The "new *word*" is new, therefore, because it is obscure, and it is obscure because it breaks with "already evolved and exploited" systems of reference, which Crane sees as sequential ("already evolved") systems. "Obscurity," Barbara Johnson has written, ". . . is not encountered on the way to intelligibility, like an obstacle, but rather lies beyond it. . . . Obscurity is an excess, not a deficiency, of meaning."[18] Johnson's comments refer to Mallarmé's *Mystère dans les lettres*, but they are also a statement of the issues at stake in Crane's letter to Monroe, an essay in which Crane defends himself from the charge of obscurity by asserting his right to language that exceeds and transgresses (goes "beyond") normative expectations, which are experienced by Crane as proscriptions. To write a "new word," which is also to write a forbidden word, is to violate the sequential order Crane ascribes to both "history" and "logic."

To deny the poet this transgressive authority, Crane told Monroe, is not simply to circumscribe present possibilities; it is "to limit the scope of the medium so considerably as to outlaw some of the richest genius of the past" (Crane, *Complete Poems and Selected Prose*, 235). In "At Melville's Tomb," Crane seeks to recover an outlaw and genius of the past, a venture in which he is motivated by his sense of himself as a poet whose faith in the authority of personal "genius" had been cast into disrepute, if not outlawed, by "the rational order of criticism." Behind this project is Crane's ongoing struggle to find sanction for a criminalized homoeroticism that he fetishistically identified with the sailor—a marginalized man, like the hoboes of "The River," who is not at home in the productive economies of home and workplace, but who remains dedicated, in exile, to the sexual community of other "drowned" men.

The codes and conditions of male homosexual fellowship inform Crane's projection of a relation between reader and poet that is not properly sexual, perhaps, but peculiarly, even transgressively intimate, secretive, and physical. Recall the way Crane's "new *word*" is transmitted: it remains unspeakable ("impossible to actually enunciate") even while it continues to operate, like a password, "as an active principle in the reader's consciousness henceforward." In "A Letter to Harriet Monroe," Crane expands on this notion with a question: "In the minds of people who have sensitively read, seen, and experienced a great deal, isn't there a terminology something like short-hand as compared to usual description and dialectics, which the artist ought to be right in trusting as a reasonable connective agent toward fresh concepts, more inclusive evaluations?" (Crane, *Complete Poems and Selected Prose*, 237–38). What Crane describes as a "short-hand" code, or "connective agent," is the rhetorical strategy he elsewhere calls "inferential mention." The special persons sensitized to such inferences form a kind of league, and they seek each other. The examples of this rhetorical strategy Crane gives come from Blake and Eliot. In effect, Crane makes Blake a modernist, and claims a place in modernism for Crane's Blakean stance; he is also trying to show how Blakean Eliot is, or could be. Implicitly, Crane is trying to validate his own early readings of both Blake and Eliot.

Crane explains Eliot's simile in "Rhapsody on a Windy Night," "Every street lamp that I pass / Beats like a fatalistic drum," in this way: "There are plenty of people who have never accumulated a sufficient series of reflections (and these of a rather special nature) to perceive the relation between a *drum* and a *street lamp—via* the *unmentioned* throbbing of the heart and nerves in a distraught man which *tacitly* creates the reason and 'logic' of the Eliot metaphor" (Crane, *Complete Poems and Selected Prose*, 237). Whatever value this has for reading Eliot, it has a great deal of value for reading Crane. Metaphor works in Crane's account as a relation between two terms the logic of whose connection is to be inferred or implied by those who are in a position to infer it on the basis of their own experience; and what is implied, in this case, is most significant: it is the throbbing of the heart and nerves of a distraught man—a highly private ("subjective") sensation, a tremor located in the male poet's body as he walks the Nighttown streets. To read Eliot's line rightly, one must have "read, seen, and experienced" enough to recognize in one's own body the unmentioned but urgent and inferred sensations in the poet's.

Unmentioned and unmentionable: the tawdry streets and urban night of Eliot's "Rhapsody" are both a homosexual and a modernist topos for Crane. Linking that scene with the scene of reading as such, Crane imagines the act of reading a modern poem—when it is successful, when the reader and poet really "spark" (a slang word Crane used)—as a tryst. Reading is like cruising; it calls for shared recognitions; it communicates pleasure and pain. Even the arbitrariness of the union between a modern poet and a reader, the necessary impersonality of their bond, becomes the ground of a profoundly personal relation, a communication that exceeds the demands and conventions of civil reference. When a poem is truly and fully read, poet and reader encounter each other as equal and kindred, "twin shadowed halves"; they recognize an essential relation beyond their random connection, assuaging the loneliness each of them feels in his body. For Crane, the intelligibility of Eliot's "obscure" poems, as of his own, ultimately presumes a transaction or pact like the unspoken, physical connection (the meeting of smiles and eyes) that concludes "Episode of Hands."

The bond between speaker and addressee in "At Melville's Tomb" dramatizes another version of this mutuality. Earlier I talked about the problem of perspective in Crane's poem as if only time separated Melville and this speaker, who are otherwise bound by a shared vision. The problem is more complicated. The opening lines of the poem do not make it clear whether Melville "watched" the waves from "this ledge" or from a position somehow "beneath the wave" itself. This ambiguity is coordinated with that of the poet's own perspective. Although he speaks "from this ledge," he is clearly identified with the drowned mariners, and speaks "for" them, from their point of view. For Crane's poet is charged with receiving and reading the messages of the drowned; yet his own message does not represent a decoding, so much as a repetition, of theirs; and this repetition in turn places the reader in the position of receiver, the poet onshore. If, in Tate's poems, the poet takes up the position of the reader or critic, the reader in "At Melville's Tomb" is invited to take up the position of the poet. But the completed communication or communion (implicitly, a kind of rescue) that the message's transmission would mean is repeatedly deferred through repetition of the event; and the reciprocity that author and reader demand and project results in the

oscillation between their two positions, which is figured as the bond between those on shore looking out to sea and those still at sea appealing to
the shore.

In the first quatrain, this oscillation is implicated in the recurrent rising
and falling of waves; in the third quatrain, in the lifted gaze of the mariners as they sink to their deaths:

> Then in the circuit calm of one vast coil,
> Its lashings charmed and malice reconciled,
> Frosted eyes there were that lifted altars;
> And silent answers crept across the stars.

> (Crane, *Poems*, 33)

The vortex imaged in the second quatrain as "The calyx of death's
bounty" is triumphant here in its expansion to the point of "one vast coil,"
the point of "calm" arrived at beyond the violent competition ("lashings")
of regressive and progressive currents. This "circuit calm" designates, if
not a moment of rescue, then one of suspension, of reconciliation, which
is induced under the sway of a specifically aesthetic "charm." The communication between these starlike "Frosted eyes" and the gazing stars above
them is perhaps an instance of the "new *word*" Crane speaks of; it is certainly a "silent" communication, "impossible to actually enunciate," which
extends the figuration of the author's appeal to the reader to the vertical
axis Crane invokes when he wrote to Munson about "a resurrection of
some kind." Here, it is not a matter of exchanging a message between sea
and shore, but between earth and heaven.

Syntactically, the inversion in the third line of the third quatrain—that
is, the placement of "Frosted eyes" *before* "there were"—suggests a similar
kind of exchange in the construction of the line itself. Compare the published with the draft version of lines 8 and 9:

> Frosted eyes there were that lifted altars;
> And silent answers crept across the stars.

> Some frosted altar there was kept by eyes
> Unanswering back across the tangent beams.

One effect of the revision is to eliminate the enjambment and stabilize
both lines as individual units. (The only enjambments in the published
text come in the first and fourth quatrains, deferring the objects of the
verbs "bequeath" and "contrive.") The other effects produced by the ex-

change of "altars" and "eyes" *across* line 8 are more subtle. Even the process by which Crane came to a final version of this line enacts the sort of substitution, the reciprocity and reversibility, that the line itself evokes: one feels that, in whatever order Crane deploys them, there will be "eyes" and "altars" here so long as subject and object continue to reciprocally sustain each other across the line—which, as Crane's placement, in both cases, of "eyes" and "altars" at each end suggests, is itself "a tangent beam."

The revision shifts Crane's sentence from the passive to the active voice, as it introduces the key verb "lift," and so gives definite expression to Crane's faith that (as he said to Monroe) "a man, not knowing perhaps a definite god yet being endowed with a reverence for deity—such a man naturally postulates a deity somehow, and the altar of that deity simply by the very *action* of the eyes *lifted* in searching" (Crane, *Complete Poems and Selected Prose*, 239). In Crane's gloss, it is "the eyes," not "altars," that are "lifted." The grammatical shift that comes with Crane's rendering of the line into prose again enacts the reciprocity we are concerned with, which, in Crane's account of his "faith," is understood as the power of the human subject to construct, of its own action, the object of its desire. This is a "mystic" claim, validating stylistic, spiritual, and sexual goals disallowed in the theory and practice of Crane's peers. The phrase "definite god" specifically recalls Crane's refusal of the demand—central to Tate's literary criticism—for "definite knowledge"; and "the eyes *lifted* in searching"—rejecting Eliot's skepticism as well as his later orthodoxy—approve the autodidact's decision to proceed without "precepts or preconceptions." Whether the stars give "silent answers" to these searchers or are "Unanswering," is a question that the poem does less to resolve than to retain in suspension.

This state of suspension is momentarily audible in the metrical structure of Crane's line. I mentioned, early on, the tension between iambic and trochaic impulses in the first line. In the revision of line 8, Crane not only moves from a passive to an active construction, but from an iambic to a trochaic pattern. The draft version, "Some frosted altar there was kept by eyes," is consistent with the iambic scheme of the whole, whereas the published text, "Frosted eyes there were that lifted altars," introduces a line of trochaic pentameter. In this strongly iambic context, the alternation represents a halt, a moment of resistance or reversal, before the meter of line 9, "And silent answers crept across the stars," returns the poem to its normative cadence (and emphasizes, by contrast, the dominance of that cadence). The metrical alternation is itself a structure of inversion, then, which interrupts, if it does not really suspend, the progress of the poem at that moment when the mariners, fixing their eyes on the stars, can still resist the fact of drowning.

Crane's poems create enclosed spaces *that offer no shelter* because the structural features of their enclosure (the specular identity of eyes and stars, the chiasmatic exchange of sea and shore, the simultaneity of past and present visions) are figures for an endless and impossible circulation. This circulation is sometimes represented in Crane's poems as the poet's power to speak to readers from beyond the grave. In the fragment beginning, "So dream thy sails, O phantom bark," whose pentameter quatrains make it an uncanny companion piece to "At Melville's Tomb," Crane imagines a power of posthumous speech such that "I thy drowned men may speak again" (Crane, *Poems*, 214)—a phrase that, again according to an Elizabethan formula, equivocates as to whether "drowned men" is an appositive subject or an object (i.e., the poet may be speaking *as* or on *behalf* of "thy drowned men"). The position of the posthumous speaker in this and other Crane poems is not like that of Whitman's poet in "Crossing Brooklyn Ferry," whose life in time is perpetuated by the poem's enduring power to address a future audience, but like that of Dickinson's poet in "I heard a Fly buzz—when I died—," whose speech comes to us from a station outside of time, a place that Crane and Dickinson both call "Eternity."[19] Unlike Whitman's democratic address to the crowd, the mode of address Crane shares with Dickinson is strangely private or elite, intimating, as Crane puts it in his sonnet "To Emily Dickinson," "Some reconcilement of remotest mind" (Crane, *Poems*, 128).

This remote "reconcilement" is the kind of agreement between poet and reader that Crane looks for in "At Melville's Tomb," in which Crane imagines reading as the recovery of a message the drowned "bequeath." In "Voyages II," we encounter another bequest, only this time the speaker of Crane's poem is not the inheritor but that which is inherited:

> Bind us in time, O Seasons clear, and awe.
> O minstrel galleons of Carib fire,
> Bequeath us to no earthly shore until
> Is answered in the vortex of our grave
> The seal's wide spindrift gaze toward paradise.

> (Crane, *Poems*, 35)

To be bound "in time" is to be bound by a vortex consuming and renewing the self as it casts up, out of time, as bequest, "The seal's wide spindrift gaze toward paradise." Both "spindrift" and the odd word—

"findrinny"—that it replaced in Crane's revision are "new" words from Melville's *Moby-Dick* (Unterecker, *Voyager*, 389); and the sentence they complete is a reimagining of the conclusion of that book, placing the speaker in the position at once of Tashtego, the last sailor to be drowned, and of Ishmael, who survives to tell the story. This is an impossible position in which the poet imagines speaking both from death and beyond it—as if, by passing through this form of "negation," he might affirm his original, "more positive" goal—and it calls to mind Crane's contradictory plan to undo the direction modernism had taken in Eliot's work. Perhaps the unusual, winding syntax in the subordinate clause, in which the verb ("Is answered") supplants and defers the subject ("The seal's wide spindrift gaze"), exemplifies the reversal Crane sought; certainly it is a reordering of grammatical sequence, a substitution of beginning for end ("cause" for "consequence"), which evokes, in this case, the substitution of life for death. The poem closes, then, with an image not of the shut "grave," but of the open "gaze," as a visionary action of lifting—or postulation—issues from the whirlpool of *The Waste Land*. The "answers" Crane submits here, as in "At Melville's Tomb," are "silent" ones; and the paradise his seal seeks remains a remote destination. But the structure of Crane's syntax is such that the answer (of the grave) precedes the question (of the gaze) with the effect of affirming, in and through death, the survival of the latter.

The end of "Voyages II" is a striking and deliberate contrast to the end of "Procession" and other Tate poems that define closure as "death, and death, and death!" In the final quatrain of "At Melville's Tomb," Crane offers another kind of resurrection. The initial conceit of Crane's poem—that Melville is buried at sea—is surprising, but it merely prepares for the more daring claim that Melville is to be found neither at sea nor on land but in the "azure steeps" shadowed by the rolling sea.

> Compass, quadrant and sextant contrive
> No farther tides . . . High in the azure steeps
> Monody shall not wake the mariner.
> This fabulous shadow only the sea keeps.

> (Crane, *Poems*, 33)

Remember Crane's intention to appropriate "the gifts of the past" (among them, Eliot's "erudition and technique") as "instruments" with which to catch and fix "the voice of the present." This Daedalian definition of language as *techne* should be contrasted with "the voice of the present" in the resonant sentence that ends "General Aims and Theories": "Language has built towers and bridges, but itself is inevitably as fluid as always" (Crane, *Complete Poems and Selected Prose*, 223). As structure or *techne*, language

operates in time; as "itself," language operates in the eternity of the continuous present ("is . . . always"), imagined as the fluid and destructured
space of the open sea. Here, in the final quatrain of "At Melville's Tomb,"
Crane arrives at the point at which instruments ("Compass, quadrant and
sextant") no longer function but cede control to the medium ("farther
tides") as it exists by and for itself—the vanishing point of infinity that
Crane designates simply and characteristically by an ellipsis.

In this final quatrain, for the first time in the poem, Crane shifts from
the past into the present tense—a change that is coordinated with Crane's
elevation of Melville from the place he seems to occupy "beneath the
wave" to somewhere "High in the azure steeps." As John Hollander observes, "steeps" takes the place of the rhyming antonym a reader expects:
"deep" (Hollander, *Figure of Echo*, 141), in a final instance of the kind of
specular reversal we have been studying in the poem. The use of the word
here resonates with Crane's image for the "high" interior of the sea at the
epiphanic center of "Voyages":

> where death, if shed,
> Presumes no carnage, but this single change,—
> Upon the steep floor flung from dawn to dawn
> The silken skilled transmemberment of song;
> Permit me voyage, love, into your hands . . .
>
> (Crane, *Poems*, 36)

The point where the "floor" of the sea is made "steep" by, or is "flung" by,
the embrace of the lovers "from dawn to dawn," establishes the enclosed
circuit of a single day in which two bodies, as they submit to "this single
change," can know "transmemberment" by and in "song." Crane's phrase
"azure steeps" reconstitutes this interior space in the air, and identifies the
voyager-lover of "Voyages III" with the voyager-author Melville (trans-
membered, once he is finally and fully "steeped" in the medium of his
quest). If, in the third quatrain of "At Melville's Tomb," the searching
eyes of the mariners found only the "silent" response of the stars, in the
final quatrain of the poem Crane's poet is given a vision of human connection through song, which, although it "will not wake the mariner," still
reconciles height and depth, present and past.

Crane's term "monody" places this poet and his poem in the line of
several songs and singers of the past, invoking as it does the subtitles of
Milton's "Lycidas" and Matthew Arnold's "Thyrsis" (Arnold's elegy for
Arthur Hugh Clough) as well as Melville's own title "Monody"—the
brief, late elegy for Hawthorne collected in *Timoleon* (Hollander, *Figure of
Echo*, 92). In the cases of Arnold and Melville, the allusion to Milton's

elegy draws some of its force from the special power of a friendship mourned, allowing the generic marker—monody—to indicate a state of private isolation and bereavement: only one is left to sing. The same marker in Crane resists the separation of the living and the dead—as Crane's draft version, employing the first-person plural, suggests:

> Our monody shall not wake the mariner
> Whose fabulous shadow only the sea keeps.

"Monody," in this sense, reverberates with those "beating leagues of mono-tone" that a shell is said to "secrete" in "Voyages VI" (Crane, *Poems*, 39); it is a song of unity and of union that is achieved by every singer steeped in the sea; and it presumes no disjunction but that "single change" that Crane calls "transmemberment."

As a figure for historical relation, the neologism "transmemberment" eschews the lesser reconcilements of memory to affirm the transfiguration of the past in the present. As a rhetorical strategy, the term indicates the mode of transumptive allusion that Hollander, Edelman, Irwin, and Bloom have studied in Crane's work.[20] For Crane, the goal of such a strat-egy is to admit no distance—or rather: no distance that cannot be spanned—between his own song and, in this instance, Melville's, which, under the auspices of the reciprocity we have been discussing, is itself shown, retrospectively, to be an elegy and interpretation of *Crane's* song. By the most curious kind of reversal, Melville emerges here, in Gross-man's suggestive phrase, as "a hermeneutic friend" (Grossman, "Crane's Intense Poetics," 227), a version of the ideal reader who is able to receive the message Crane bequeaths. He does so, again, in the space of "eter-nity," identified here with "the azure steeps," the earthly shadow or type of which only the sea "keeps." In choosing to break his syntax at the pen-ultimate line, excise the possessive "Whose" and admit the demonstrative "This," Crane again chooses to suspend reference. "*This* fabulous shadow" might designate either Melville's shade or Crane's—or, for that matter, the poem itself, which is given over to the sea in a form of ritual burial recalling the ceremonial scattering that concludes Shelley's "Ode to the West Wind" or Crane's own "Praise for an Urn." "At Melville's Tomb" is commended to the sea as the shadow of the fable that connects Crane and Melville, and that together they transmit.

"At Melville's Tomb" was probably completed before Crane came to live with Tate and Gordon in December 1925. Blaming Gordon for the dispute that made him leave four months later, Crane told Under-wood, in a postcard from Cuba, that she and Tate were jealous over the money Kahn had given him to work on *The Bridge*; they had gossiped about him with other friends, he said, and betrayed his "faith" in them, causing Crane in turn to lose "faith" in the "material" of *The Bridge*. "It's all been very tiresome—," Crane complained, "and I'd rather lose such elite for the old society of vagabonds and sailors—who don't enjoy chit-chat" (Crane, *Letters*, 264). With the sailor, in contrast to that "elite," "no faith or such is properly *expected* and how jolly and cordial and warm the tonsiling *is* sometimes, after all" (Crane, *Letters*, 264). Crane would return several times to Mrs. Turner's house in Patterson—Tate and Gordon left in the summer of 1926—and he returned to Brooklyn as well. But Crane remained in no place long—and for the most part he remained unemployed—during the final five years of his life (a period Crane spent in Cuba, New York, Connecticut, Ohio, California, England, France, and Mexico in rented rooms, in the homes of friends and family, on trains, and aboard ships).

The state of exposure and mobility that Crane chose when he left for Cuba in 1926 is the subject of "Repose of Rivers."[21] The poem's alliterative title introduces antithetical terms, linking stasis and motion, the singular and the plural, in anticipation of the oxymoronic figures that dominate the poem. There is in "Repose," I think, a connotation of putting things *back* into place—as if Crane's use of the word were modeled on "return." But what is returned to here—the great mouth of the river, where the river meets the sea and is absorbed by it—is not an origin but an end. The poem is an account of a career, identifying the course of the poet with that of a river, through the ancient association of eloquence with fluency, and the progress it traces is a story of immersion in the liquid Crane called "language itself," an itinerary—at once homosexual and visionary—that concludes at the point of the speaker's engulfment.

Because the power of poetic utterance depends, in the mythology of this poem, on its unimpeded flow, the seaward course of the river-poet requires him to resist or escape from a series of traps. These are the burden of the second and third strophes:

> Flags, weeds. And remembrance of steep alcoves
> Where cypresses shared the noon's
> Tyranny; they drew me into hades almost.
> And mammoth turtles climbing sulphur dreams
> Yielded, while sun-silt rippled them
> Asunder . . .
>
> How much I would have bartered! the black gorge
> And all the singular nestings in the hills

Where beavers learn stitch and tooth.
The pond I entered once and quickly fled—
I remember now its singing willow rim.

(Crane, *Poems*, 16)

These are all sites of seduction—versions, perhaps, of possible "homes"—
which threaten to draw the poet down and "into" their enigmatic enclosures. The human experience in this narrative is highly fraught, and hard
to decode, but Harold Bloom provides a good starting place: "Embowered
by steep alcoves of cypresses, intensifying the dominant noon sun, Crane
nearly yields to the sexual phantasmagoria of 'flags, weeds,' and the sound
play alcoves / almost intensifies the narrowness of the escape from a primary sexuality, presumably an incestuous heterosexuality." In Bloom's account, what Crane "would have bartered, indeed did barter, was nature for
poetry," in such a way as to relate "the inevitability of sexual orientation to
the assumption of his poethood" (Bloom, "Introduction," *Crane: Critical
Views*, 4–5). This is useful, because it defines the relation between Crane's
poetry and his sexuality by the opposition to "nature" that they share, linking Crane's rejection of his place as son in the Oedipal succession to his
"unnatural," visionary poetics, a way of writing that was always a refusal to
reproduce the world as he found it.

For this reason, homosexuality is difficult to find on the level of plot. As
Yingling explains, building on the readings of Bloom and Robert K. Martin, "Repose of Rivers" does not "depict an actual relationship between
two men; it focuses instead on the problem of homosexual self-authorization as an issue of internal resolution where one comes to maturity
through a rejection of Oedipal models of development and an adoption of
homosexual ones" (Yingling, *Crane and the Homosexual Text*, 139). With
this genetic model in mind, Yingling reads the "mammoth turtles" of the
second strophe as emblems of "Oedipal masculinity," enacting sexuality as
a drama of "division and competition" under the "tyranny" of the midday
sun, "a trope for the overpowering but false authority of patriarchal reality" (Yingling, *Crane and the Homosexual Text*, 141). This is compatible
with Bloom's reading, in which the scene calls up the lure and threat of "a
primary sexuality, presumably an incestuous heterosexuality." But one
could also view Crane's "steep alcoves" as a kind of closet in which homosexual desire has been confined under a Circean spell. As Bloom remarks,
these turtles seem to recall Melville's "The Encantadas," a tale concerning
the "emphatic uninhabitableness" of the Galapagos Islands and, among
their unlikely inhabitants, the gigantic tortoises. These, it is reported, sailors held to be "wicked sea-officers" transformed after death ("in some

cases, before death") and about whom there was "something strangely self-condemned" (Melville, *Writings of Melville*, Vol. 9, *Piazza Tales*, 128–29).[22] The giant creatures in Crane's poem, seen in this light, belong among his other representations of homosexual banishment, imprisonment, and metamorphosis, from "C 33" to a cryptic late lyric like "The Mermen" (Crane, *Poems*, 113).[23]

But Crane's anthropomorphic beasts resist the impulse to decode them in human terms, even psychoanalytic ones, because "Repose of Rivers" is not an autobiography, but a refusal of autobiography. The poem is about breaking bounds. Its action is indeed one of "homosexual self-authorization," but it identifies Crane's particular homosexual poetics with boundlessness—or with the pursuit of boundlessness, a pursuit that overrides the representational means by which identities are conventionally fixed and counted, including that of the homosexual. "Repose of Rivers" converts the "negation" under which homosexuality takes its place in culture—its unrepresentability—into the motive for a poetry that eschews representational aims. What Crane's poet reclaims from his river-voyage, therefore, is a remembrance of thresholds behind which the object of desire—and reference—is withdrawn, as "the pond" is supplanted by the poet's memory of "its singing willow rim."

Memory supplants event in this poem ("remembrance of steep alcoves," not the alcoves themselves), but the memory is not of the past, as in Tate's or Eliot's nostalgic modernism; it is a memory *of the future* in which, Crane says in the fourth strophe, "all things nurse":

> And finally, in that memory all things nurse;
> After the city that I finally passed
> With scalding unguents spread and smoking darts
> The monsoon cut across the delta
> At gulf gates . . . There, beyond the dykes
>
> I heard wind flaking sapphire, like this summer,
> And willows could not hold more steady sound.

The sexual arts and violence of the city ("scalding unguents," "smoking darts") are a prelude to the poet's entrance into the gulf, the poem's ultimate space of enclosure beyond all enclosures, out "beyond the dykes," where a "monsoon" cuts across the delta. The cutting action of the hurricane, like the wind that "flakes" the "sapphire" sky ("breaking up," Bloom writes, "and yet also distributing the Shelleyan azure of vision" [Bloom, "Introduction," *Crane: Critical Views*, 5]), recalls the mowing of the wind in the first strophe:

The willows carried a slow sound,
A sarabande the wind mowed on the mead.
I could never remember
That seething, steady leveling of the marshes
Till age had brought me to the sea.

(Crane, *Poems*, 16)

The actions of mowing, leveling, cutting, and flaking described at the beginning and end of the poem emphasize that the recovery of origin that "Repose of Rivers" projects is an apocalyptic event, connecting origin and end in a vision of unity that is acquired at the cost of a radical reduction of life, imaged in the grasses Crane has drawn as much from Proverbs as from Whitman. Still the actual articulation of that unity, like the ineffable present moment of composition Crane alludes to as "this summer," remains outside and beyond the limiting structures of the poem, past "gulf gates." Beginning with the images it ends with, therefore, and ending with those it begins with, "Repose of Rivers" turns on itself in a circulation of figure and energy, a "circumlocution" that refers us again to Crane's hurricane and vortex, as well as to the controlling figure of *The Bridge*. What emerges from this perpetual motion is, curiously enough, repose, or "steady" sound, a song that is figured as a "sarabande," or dance, both sexual and elemental, and that is also represented as the "singing" of the pond's willow rim. Beyond that threshold is the "absolute music" of "Atlantis."

TIME AND SPACE, SUCCESSION AND EXTENSION, ARE MERELY
ACCIDENTAL CONDITIONS OF A THOUGHT. THE IMAGINATION
CAN TRANSCEND THEM AND MORE, IN A FREE SPHERE OF
IDEAL EXISTENCES. THINGS, ALSO, ARE IN THEIR ESSENCE
WHAT WE CHOOSE TO MAKE THEM. A THING IS, ACCORD-
ING TO THE MODE IN WHICH ONE LOOKS AT IT. "WHERE
OTHERS," SAYS BLAKE, "SEE THE DAWN COMING OVER THE
HILL, I SEE THE SONS OF GOD SHOUTING FOR JOY."

—Oscar Wilde, *De Profundis*[1]

Few critics of *The Bridge* have remarked on the fact that
most of Crane's "mystical synthesis of 'America' " was not written in the
United States but on the Isle of Pines in Cuba. It may seem that the
circumstances of its composition are irrelevant to the reading of a poem
in which Crane intended to "transfigure" "History and fact, location,
etc., . . . into abstract form that would almost function independently of
its subject matter" (Crane, *Letters* 124). But the transcendental aims of
The Bridge need to be understood in relation to the isolation in which
Crane's poem was actually written. In 1923, when he first conceived of
The Bridge, Crane saw himself as part of a new aesthetic community in
the United States; through his relationships with men like Frank and
Stieglitz, Munson and Tate, Crane felt "directly connected to Whitman"
(Crane, *Letters*, 128). Crane saw himself as part of the nation described in
Frank's *Our America*, and he fully expected *The Bridge* to win for him a
place in the national literature. By 1926, however, when he arrived in
Cuba, Crane's identification with Whitman had permanently divided him
from friends like Tate, and he had fled the nation he wished to speak to
and on behalf of. Ending in expatriation, then, Crane's flight from Patterson extends the meaning of his break with Tate: he is symbolically

171

excluded not only from the heterosexual household, but also from the nation.

Writing his poem on the Isle of Pines, Crane lives out the principle of cultural organization Yingling calls "the structural necessity of the separation of the homosexual and the national" (Yingling, *Crane and the Homosexual Text*, 11). Yingling points to the traditional alliance of patriotism and homophobia in American politics, but he is particularly concerned with the ways in which American transcendentalism, as a nationalist literary discourse, and the intellectual origin of American studies, has excluded the homosexual. Indeed, "the ideology of literary and cultural authority under which Crane wrote would have made homosexuality an inadmissable center from which to write about American life" (Yingling, *Crane and the Homosexual Text*, 27); and in this sense, Crane could never, as a homosexual poet, become a national poet. But in another sense, and precisely because he could not declare himself a homosexual poet, Crane could *only* become a national poet. That is, because Crane could not speak of or as "himself," he was able to speak to and on behalf of "America"; because Crane could not specify his desire, he spoke of his desire in a language of universals. He was not the first author to do so. One has only to name Whitman, Melville, and Thoreau to identify a national tradition that could also be claimed as a male homoerotic one.[2] These majority and minority traditions are not compatible, perhaps, but they intersect—in such a way as to make male homosexuality seem at once possible and impossible as a "center from which to write about American life."

The many stages of *The Bridge*'s development, the expansion and contraction of Crane's plans for it, the stops and starts of composition, record Crane's ongoing experience of that dilemma, his vacillation between hope and despair. In Chapter One, I said that Crane's manic-depressive swings enact the contradictions of professional "merit"; they also enact the contradictions of male homosexuality—its possibility and impossibility—as a ground of poetic authority. The depth of despair into which homosexuality plunged Crane—his sense, sometimes, of having *disappeared* from public life—reflects the outrageous height to which his desire also carried him, the particular prominence it allowed Crane to claim. In the chapter that follows, we will examine these dizzy alternatives as they appear in the earliest drafts of "Atlantis," which are also some of the first writing Crane did on *The Bridge*. The "arching path" represented in the final text of this part of *The Bridge* symbolizes, I will argue, the sublimative process by which the homoerotic both enters into and is eliminated from the poem as a whole. The continuous willed elevation of "Atlantis" is the high style of a poet who proposes to rise above desire on the strength of it, a project that is always shadowed by Crane's fear of descending into mere disclosure and "piteous admissions" (Crane, *Poems*, 18); the extraordinary hyperbole of "Atlantis" is both an ecstatic leap upward and a desperate effort to keep from falling down. To emphasize the centrality of Crane's fears for his own dignity in the composition of *The Bridge*, I want to turn now to a letter Crane wrote to Frank during his first month in Cuba, a letter in which Crane imagined, in advance, the public reception of *The Bridge*.

Since 1923 Frank had remained for Crane, as Luis de San Angel and Juan Perez remain for Crane's Columbus in the "Ave Maria" section of *The Bridge*, one of the "faithful partisans of his quest" (Crane, *Poems*, 47). Frank's demands on the poem, however, were incompatible with Tate's, and the competing expectations of these critics produced in Crane an internal rift or division of the kind he described (and expected to overcome) in "Recitative." "Emotionally," Crane confided to Frank, "I should like to write *The Bridge*; intellectually judged the whole theme and project seems more and more absurd." The distinction Crane draws between the emotional dignity of his work and its intellectual absurdity shows the extent to which Crane had internalized Tate's criticism of *The Bridge*. That criticism is audible in this letter's voice of "intellectual" censure, which insists that "the bridge as a symbol today has no significance beyond an economical approach to shorter hours, quicker lunches, behaviorism, and toothpicks." However sustaining his friendship with Crane had been and remained, Frank could not effectively answer this argument. Crane knew that, by the mid-1920s, Frank was himself an isolated figure, whose opposition to Eliot, unlike Crane's, ignored his technical achievement. By offering Crane "emotional" rather than "intellectual" support, Frank reinforced the divided condition Crane describes in this letter. Crane recognized that his challenge to *The Waste Land* could not rely on the collective assent or "equal pride" of his peers, only on the strength of his own convictions. He had placed himself in an exposed and even dangerous position.

In another passage from the same letter, Crane turns from his own experience of isolation to the problematic isolation of *The Bridge* in literary history: "The form of my poem rises out of a past that so overwhelms the present with its worth and vision that I'm at a loss to explain my delusion that there exist any real links between that past and a future destiny worthy of it. The 'destiny' is long since completed, perhaps the little last section of my poem is a hangover echo of it—but it hangs suspended somewhere

in ether like an Absalom by his hair" (Crane, *Letters*, 261). Crane's fear
that the readers his poem needed did not in fact exist generates the ghostly
image of *The Bridge* as an inadequately supported structure that "rises out
of the past" but finds no ground in either the present or the future. Or, if
the bridge Crane envisions really is the epic span of America's spiritual
"destiny," this destiny must be "long since completed," leaving the "little
last section" of *The Bridge* as a mere residue or "hangover echo." Crane's
impulse here is to identify the fate of the last section of *The Bridge* ("Atlantis," but at this point simply called "The Bridge" [Crane, *Letters*, 241])
with the fate not only of the poem, but of the poet. That is the implication, at least, when Crane describes "Atlantis" as "an Absalom" hanging by
his hair (2 Samuel 18 specifies: "between the heaven and the earth"). Suspended in "ether," "Atlantis" is like a man trapped in a tree, stranded,
helpless, and laughable in the moment before he is killed.

What motivates Crane's comparison of "Atlantis" to Absalom? To
begin with, it glosses Crane's weary admiration, elsewhere in the same
letter, for the "increasingly lonely and ineffectual" confidence of Whitman, and implies that Crane saw his solidarity with Whitman as a martyrdom, at once terrifying and ridiculous. The ridiculousness derives from an
untenable position: Absalom, as he enters into battle with the forces of his
father, King David, is prematurely thwarted when "his head caught hold
of the oak, . . . and the mule that was under him went away" (2 Sam. 18:9
in the King James translation). The point is that Crane's "mule"—the
basis Crane posits for *The Bridge*, following Whitman, in "organic and
active factors in the experience of our common race, time and belief"—
has disappeared; Whitman's America has become (as Tate saw it) a grossly
utilitarian culture of "shorter hours, quicker lunches, behaviorism, and
toothpicks." In such a world, projects such as Crane's are hopelessly naive
and belated. Not to have recognized this state of affairs is an intellectual
and professional embarrassment, with implications for Crane's masculinity. Indeed, it leaves Crane feminized and dissolute, feeling like "a
drunken chorus-girl" unable to go on with the show "in a totally undig-
nified mind and undress" (Crane, *Letters*, 262). Opposing the high modernist consensus and the claims for its new type of masculine hero, the
poet-critic, Crane fears he will be seen as a show girl, a poet reduced to
vulgar sexual display, a drunk. Finding himself in a version of Absalom's
unlikely or even "absurd" position in the oak, Crane is unable to defend
his poem in the life-and-death contest he has initiated; and he imagines
the reception of *The Bridge* as a repetition of the ritual murder by the
jealous Joab, as well as the "ten young men that bare Joab's armour," of

Israel's princely exile, rebel, and son. Ironically, perhaps, Absalom's name means "Father of Peace."

The ritual murder Crane imagined was eventually enacted by Tate and Winters. It may seem lurid to describe the reception of *The Bridge* in these terms, but the comments on Crane's poetry by Tate and Winters are themselves lurid; they describe *The Bridge* not only as a failure, but as a site of death and destruction. The extravagance of Winters's judgment is more famous: "The flaws in Mr. Crane's genius are, I believe, so great as to partake, if they persist, almost of the nature of a public catastrophe";[3] but Tate warned of an imminent calamity as well: "Beyond the quest of pure sensation and its ordering symbolism"—that is, in Tate's opinion, beyond *The Bridge*—"lies the total destruction of art" (Tate, *Essays of Four Decades*, 323).[4] Moreover, the apocalyptic vigor of these critics expressed their sense that *The Bridge* had come at the end of a moribund tradition, and amounted to the kind of "hangover echo" Crane had feared it would. For Winters, *The Bridge* demonstrated "the impossibility of getting anywhere with the Whitmanian inspiration": "No writer of comparable ability has struggled with it before, and, with Mr. Crane's wreckage in view, it seems highly unlikely that any writer of comparable genius will struggle with it again" (Winters, "Progress," 31). For Tate, *The Bridge* marked "the end of the romantic movement" as a whole. "If this impulse is dying out," Tate added gallantly, "it is as fortunate for its reputation as it is remarkable, that it should be represented at the end by a poetry so rich, finely wrought, and powerful as Hart Crane's" (Tate, *Poetry Reviews*, 104).

Epitaphic and admonitory, these readings of Crane's poem retroactively illuminate the extreme pathos of "Cape Hatteras," virtually the final section of *The Bridge* to be completed, and that moment in the poem at which Crane explicitly turned to Whitman to address—to take hold of—an audience he knew he did not have. Predictably, the audience Crane *did* have, at least as it was constituted by Tate and Winters, questioned this fraternal show of feeling. Tate, who once wrote a poem in which he spoke of his desire to grasp Crane's hand, found Crane's grasping of Whitman's hand sentimental;[5] and Winters called Crane's attitude toward Whitman in *The Bridge* "desperately sentimental" (Winters, "Progress," 29). For both critics, Crane's address to Whitman was symptomatic of his effort throughout the poem to substitute personal feeling for the "objective pattern of ideas" (Tate) or "definite significance" (Winters) required by the epic form, without which *The Bridge* collapsed, as Whitman's own poems had. (In Winters's judgment, "The book as a whole has no more unity than the *Song of Myself*" [Winters, "Progress of Hart Crane," 25]). It

is as if Crane, when he extended his hand to Whitman, at the last moment,
for support,

> Not soon, nor suddenly,—no, never to let go
> > My hand
> > > in yours,
> > > > Walt Whitman—
>
> > > > > so—

(Crane, Poems, 84)

had instead been pulled down by his massive and embarrassing pre-
decessor.

In a letter to Tate, Crane replied to the charge of "sentimentality" in his
address to Whitman by reaffirming his allegiance to "the positive and universal tendencies implicit in nearly all of [Whitman's] best work." He then
reminded Tate: "You've heard me roar at too many of his lines to doubt
that I can spot his worst" (Crane, *Letters*, 354). This is a complex gesture
on Crane's part, since he uses his alliance with Whitman to define and
sanction his "emotional" differences with Tate, even as he calls to mind
time spent with Tate ("*You've* heard me roar") to assert his "intellectual"
differences with Whitman. It is a version of the argument Crane presented at the end of an essay he wrote in 1930 called "Modern Poetry":
"The most typical and valid expression of the American *psychosis* seems to
me still to be found in Whitman. His faults as a technician and his clumsy
and indiscriminate enthusiasm are somewhat beside the point" (Crane,
Complete Poems and Selected Prose, 263). At once brave and hedging, such
double assertions did not resolve, so much as restate, Crane's dilemma.
The fact that R. P. Blackmur would later seize on Crane's pseudotechnical
use of "psychosis" as an instance of the sloppy, untrained thinking that
Crane shared with Whitman, and that finally drove Crane mad,[6] is a sign
of the dilemma Crane faced: he could not affirm "the positive and
universal tendencies" of Whitman without *also*, in the eyes of Blackmur
and critics like him, giving himself over to "clumsy and indiscriminate
enthusiasm."

This contradiction refers to a stylistic problem in Crane's writing, but
it also points to the problematic status of Crane's homosexuality. For
Crane could not appeal to Whitman without also implicating himself, as
Eric Sundquist puts it, in "the 'joke' of homosexuality which Crane felt
enclosing himself as it had the loafing and laughing Whitman."[7] Even
among authors such as Van Wyck Brooks, who identified themselves with
Whitman against the "Puritanism" of genteel culture, Whitman's sexual-

ity remained a vexing matter, difficult to square with his otherwise whole-some democratic inclinations.[8] For Tate, Whitman's social vision, his po-etics, and his homosexuality were always linked and equally distasteful. "Why [Crane] wanted to identify himself with Whitman, I don't know," Tate reflected in an interview with John Unterecker. "Hart had a sort of megalomania: he wanted to be The Great American Poet. I imagine that he thought by getting into the Whitman tradition, he could carry even Whitman further. And yet there's another thing we must never forget—there was the homosexual thing, too. . . . The notion of 'comrades,' you see, and that sort of business" (quoted by Unterecker, *Voyager*, 431). In-deed. As these retrospective, confiding comments make clear, Tate's os-tensibly stylistic objections enforced under the rubric of taste his objec-tions to Crane's ways of putting sexuality into writing. In particular, Tate, like Winters, objected to Crane's attempt to connect "private" and "pub-lic" expression by projecting, on the model of Whitmanian comradeship, a relation between persons that would include sexuality—or that would not exclude Crane's homosexuality. Crane's inability to embrace Whit-man's "positive and universal tendencies" *without* embracing his "clumsy and indiscriminate enthusiasm" effectively restates, in the register of Crane's work, his inability to maintain *both* erotic and social bonds in his life. The visionary comradeship that is the principle of Crane's identifica-tion with Whitman—of his *inclusion* in the human community Whitman projected—can be seen at the same time as the principle of Crane's *exclu-sion* from "the only group of people whose verbal sophistication is likely to take on interest in a style such as mine" (Crane, *Letters*, 236). The terms under which Crane sought community were also the terms under which he chose exile; and the quest for personal relationship Crane undertook in *The Bridge* called for a passage beyond sanctioned forms of address in which erotic and linguistic aberration converged.

The problem could be put this way. On the one hand, *The Bridge* searches for the idealized whole of a redeemed body, that total integration of erotic and linguistic experience which Crane meant when he said of his lovemaking with Emil Opffer: "I have seen the Word made Flesh" (Crane, *Letters*, 181). On the other hand, *The Bridge* proceeds toward this goal by means of the most radical of linguistic disfigurations, a violence of logic and style that coincides, on the level of the narrative, with the recurrent sacrifice and disappearance of the quester's body—an event figured in the proem as the bedlamite's leap to death, in "The River" as the tide of "floating niggers," in "The Dance" as Maquokeeta's ritual mutilation, in "Cape Hatteras" as the wreck of the "Falcon-Ace," in "The Tunnel" as

Poe's "retching flesh." This apparent discrepancy between Crane's ends and means is in effect another version of Crane's sense of poetic form as both an obstacle and an instrument. "Atlantis" sets out to resolve these contradictions by proposing as its terminus a point of *suspension*—the point arrived at in "At Melville's Tomb" when the drowning mariners lift their eyes to the stars. The same point is reached in "Atlantis" with the completion of the suspension bridge to "Love," effecting the release of the poet's body into the object of desire, which shelters and upholds Crane's "floating singer" (Crane, *Poems*, 107). On the level of linguistic practice, the floating singer's song signals the achievement of an "abstract form," a condition in which Crane's language, like the singer's body, is "trans-figured"—elevated and sustained, that is, by a system of reference func-tioning without a ground in "History and fact, location, etc.," functioning almost "independently of its subject matter." This is Crane's fantasy of perfect reception—of a complete and permanent response. At the same time, though, "Atlantis" encodes the actual conditions of its composition and reception by insisting on the *expiration* of this singer, who is "sus-pended somewhere in ether like an Absalom by his hair," and who disap-pears from Crane's text as an ambiguous "inheritance," the final figure to be sacrificed in the making of *The Bridge*.

These remarks summarize the reading of "Atlantis" that I am going to present here. But by beginning at the end of my argument I have ne-glected Crane's curious and important decision to begin, with "Atlantis," at the very end of *The Bridge*, and we ought to examine that decision be-fore we look at the text.

Crane worked on "Atlantis" from 1923 until 1930—the span of time during which he produced almost all of his major work. The com-pletion of "Atlantis" was as protracted as its beginning was precipitous; the impatience with which Crane began *The Bridge* by writing the last section first turned into reluctance to bring the process of composition to an end. In fact, Crane continued to make changes in the text of "Atlantis"—some-times significant ones, as we will see—in the few months between the pub-lication of the Black Sun and the Liveright editions of *The Bridge*. Follow-ing scholarly convention, I will use the final text of "Atlantis" as the basis for discussion. But I do so with the knowledge that Crane's practice of radical and ongoing revision, exaggerated in "Atlantis," resists resolution in a single authoritative form. The manuscript history of "Atlantis" is sufficiently complex, finally, to show that Crane did not write, so much as *rewrite*, "Atlantis." Crane's worksheets are the visible and virtually illegible record of a poetics that validates metamorphosis and process over the conventional order of linear sequence, at the cost of the continual undoing of a poem's text.

The manuscript history of "Atlantis" reflects Crane's impulse throughout his work to shuttle back and forth between "causes and consequences," origin and goal. The circular narrative this shuttling action produces in "Repose of Rivers" is manifest on a grand scale in Platonic myth, according to some versions of which the sinking of Atlantis is the origin of history, and the future restoration of Atlantis is history's goal.[9] The Atlantean myth retains this cyclical structure in the narrative form of *The Bridge*, where Atlantis is the site of the generative Word that the poet-quester must obtain *before* he writes *The Bridge*, and the goal *toward* which, as the story of his quest, *The Bridge* proceeds (and proceeds, in this respect, in reverse). The many New World visions encountered in *The Bridge*, from "Ave Maria" to "The Tunnel," have the same status in the structure of the poem, therefore, as they do in history: these visions refer us—typologically, as it were—both backward and forward in time to "Atlantis"; they are the multiple signs of this single signified; and the historical figure they reveal is the "arching path" of the bridge itself.

"The bridge," Crane wrote to Frank in January 1926, "in becoming a ship, a world, a woman, a tremendous harp (as it does finally) seems to really have a career" (Crane, *Letters*, 232). The "career" of the bridge as it unfolds in "Atlantis," which is more extended and bizarre than Crane's letter avows, effectively concludes the metamorphic sequence of New World visions (in the course of which Crane's means of transport has become "by turns, a curveship, waking dream, train, covered wagon, sailing ship, airplane, subway, and tunnel") at the instant when, in Donald Pease's words, the historical avatars of the bridge "drop away and *longing itself assumes the appearance of a world*."[10] The poet-quester's desire at this moment in the poem takes priority over any possible object of desire; the ground of historical reference is systematically withdrawn; and the conclusion of *The Bridge* is converted into a wildly extended apostrophe, in the course of which one name cancels and supplants the next, and no word is adequate to the world "longing itself assumes."

The New World of "Atlantis" does not refer, then, to the empirical world of a conventional mimesis but rather, as John Irwin puts it, to a "counterworld" of its own making. Irwin has argued that the "language of internal coherence" in Crane's work, "because it always begins with and is built out of the language of external correspondence, is in a sense a language of reverse correspondences" that connects "things through a similarity in their names rather than in the things themselves" (Irwin, "Naming Names," 297, 294). Irwin's notion of a "countermimesis" composed of "reverse correspondences" is a suggestive account of Crane's poetry. It calls to mind the mirror motifs of homosexual writing (remember the "plate of vibrant mercury" in "Recitative"); it also calls to mind Crane's plan to challenge the "realism" of *The Waste Land* by means of "an almost complete reverse of direction" (Crane, *Letters*, 114). As we found in Chapter Five, Crane told Tate that this reverse of direction would require him to "strike" a "tangent" that "goes *through* [Eliot] toward a *different goal*" (Crane, *Letters*, 90). This spatial image and its complex burden of literary positioning are also behind the "arching path" Crane takes toward the "counterworld" of "Atlantis."

In "General Aims and Theories," Crane quotes from Blake's "Auguries of Innocence" to explain the difference between his visionary practice and the conventional mimesis he identifies with "impressionism," "realism," or even "classicism": "We are led to believe in a lie / When we see *with* not *through* the eye."[11] This is in effect another version of Crane's plan to go "*through*" Eliot, the logic of which is clarified, I think, by the particular program Crane extracts from Blake: "It is my hope to go *through* the combined materials of the poem, using our 'real' world somewhat as a springboard, and to give the poem *as a whole* an orbit or predetermined direction of its own" (Crane, *Complete Poems and Selected Prose*, 220). It is only by first passing "*through* [its] combined materials" that the poem is then propelled *upward* (as if from "a springboard") into a perpetual, parabolic "orbit." On the level of poetic plot, this double movement corresponds to the revisionary history Crane writes in *The Bridge* by returning to the historical past in order to recover its utopian promise for the future. Such a promise is inaccessible to those, like Eliot, who see history only "*with* the eye," and who therefore see only what is already there, not what will be. The meaning of the linguistic discontinuities in *The Waste Land*, as a representation of history in *decline* or decay, is precisely opposed to that of similar effects in *The Bridge*, which represents history in the process of ascent or *becoming*.

It is the culmination of this historical process—both the liquidation of history and its fulfillment—that the "orbit" of "Atlantis" represents. "Through," significantly, is the first word of "Atlantis"; and it specifically indicates a process of becoming, which Crane imagines, in the course of the first three stanzas, as a passage beyond "our 'real' world" into a visionary system of reference:

Through the bound cable strands, the arching path
Upward, veering with light, the flight of strings,—
Taut miles of shuttling moonlight syncopate
The whispered rush, telepathy of wires.
Up the index of night, granite and steel—
Transparent meshes—fleckless the gleaming staves—
Sibylline voices flicker, waveringly stream
As though a god were issue of the strings . . .

And through that cordage, threading with its call
One arc synoptic of all tides below—
Their labyrinthine mouths of history
Pouring reply as though all ships at sea
Complighted in one vibrant breath made cry,—
"Make thy love sure—to weave whose song we ply!"
—From black embankments, moveless soundings hailed,
So seven oceans answer from their dream.

And on, obliquely up bright carrier bars
New octaves trestle the twin monoliths
Beyond whose frosted capes the moon bequeaths
Two worlds of sleep (O arching strands of song!)—
Onward and up the crystal-flooded aisle
White tempest nets file upward, upward ring
With silver terraces the humming spars,
The loft of vision, palladium helm of stars.

(Crane, *Poems*, 105)

The "combined materials" passed "through" here are first of all the material structures of the suspension bridge itself, its wires and strings, "granite and steel," materials progressively animated in the course of these stanzas, as Crane's text assigns them agency and even voice, until "tempest nets file upward"—as if the cables of the bridge ascended of their own intention, in a fantastic procession toward "The loft of vision, palladium helm of stars." The upward thrust of the opening stanzas, it should be emphasized, does not dispense with conventional mimesis so much as, in Crane's terms, pass *through* it, in such a way as to convert the "combined materials of the poem" into the agents of the action they represent. The animation of the architectural "materials" of the bridge is at once analogous to and dependent upon the animation of the linguistic materials of the poem; and progress "Through the bound cable strands" turns into both an instance and an allegory of the "transfiguration" of reference propelling "Atlantis" into "an orbit or predetermined direction of its own."

The "orbit" "Atlantis" enters can specifically be understood as a series of self-reflexive verbal chains of reference in which separate words are connected to each other, like the mutually supporting cables of the suspension bridge, through appositive structures of interdependent elements. In the first stanza, for example, we find the following phrases—"bound cable strands," "the arching path," and "the flight of strings," and then "the index of night," "granite and steel," "Transparent meshes," and "the gleaming staves." Each of these noun phrases is linked to and isolated from the grammatical subject of the sentence ("Taut miles of shuttling moonlight," "Sibylline voices") by means of Crane's characteristic and ambiguous punctuation mark, the dash, which signifies connection and interruption at once. It is the case in "Atlantis," as Harvey Gross has said of the proem, that "the apostrophe requires no explicit grammar; the understood subject of every sentence is The Bridge, and every verb links the poet to his love" (Gross, "Crane and Stevens," 49). Yet Crane's refusal to definitively indicate the "understood subject" of his prepositional clauses ("Through the bound cable strands," "Up the index of night," "And through that cordage," "And on, obliquely") is calculated less to imply than to *elide* the mimetic subject of this visionary action, and thus to operate without reference to a "natural" or human ground. In place of such a ground, "Atlantis" presents merely a "direction" or "tangent," an orbit expressing the capacity of language to "almost function independently of its subject matter" (Crane, *Letters*, 124).

To understand the bridge in this way is not only to recognize it *as a poem*, as numerous critics have observed, but to recognize it as a poem in its purely "material" (or linguistic) presence—and specifically, I think, in its material presence *as verse form*. In this sense, the poem's passage through "the bound cable strands" of the bridge explicitly allegorizes, as musical "flight," the passage of "Atlantis" through its own material structures. The "bound cable strands" of line 1 become "arching strands of song" in the third stanza, and both phrases can be construed as figures for Crane's pentameters, which coordinate, draw "taut," and "bind" together the individual elements of each line, in effect serving as a kind of grammar. So, too, the "New octaves" evoked in the third stanza are both diatonic intervals of eight degrees and the eight-line units before us on the page, which organize, in material and immediately visible structures, the progressive ascent of Crane's ecstatic utterance. What Crane is seeking in these self-descriptive tropes is not the "imitative form" of "Ode to the Confederate Dead," where the action of the verse mimes or replicates, in a mode of commemorative ceremony, heroic events unavailable to the poet; in "Atlantis," the action of Crane's language is itself the heroic event it describes. For Tate, verse form became an end in itself—the horizon of literary speech; for Crane it was always a *means*, the premise or condition of utterance.

In the opening of "Atlantis," the event we witness is the conversion of the stable structure of poetic "numbers" into a *"swift / Unfractioned idiom"* (Crane, *Poems*, 44), which is also the "arching path" of the bridge. That upward arc of the bridge consists in a peculiar double movement, which could be drawn on a sheet of graph paper as a sequence of perpendicular lines passing across and upward on the page. By enjambing the first line of "Atlantis" ("the arching path / Upward"), Crane isolates this movement in the movement of his own syntax—as if to move across one line and down to the next were in fact to move *upward* on the page. The upward leap the lines enact—this fiction of moving up the page—depends upon the actual physical progress of the poem *down the page* in such a way as to first draw on and then deny the strictly material properties of a text. The empirical presence of the poem is made to signify in this way the transcendence of its "materials" that Crane speaks of in "General Aims and Theories." If, as his comments in "Narcissus as Narcissus" suggest, Tate's versification is a mimesis of possible actions in the world, the action Crane's verse performs is *only possible in a poem*.

Crane's meditation on the material properties of verse in "Atlantis" converts the "combined materials of the poem" into the "springboard," then, for a visionary event. The doubleness of the movement this event involves expresses Crane's sense of the doubleness of his poetic "materials." For Crane, verse form is the material sign of the poem's "materials" generally. It is a sign of all the restrictions to which the poem must submit (pass "through") before the poem can achieve release (what "Atlantis" calls "upward" movement)—a synecdoche for the conditions to be met, the regulations to be observed, before a poetic voice can be released. In the first stanza of "Atlantis," this movement is figured in the play of constriction and release whereby "miles" of "moonlight," as they are drawn "taut," are made to "shuttle" back and forth in a cyclical motion, vibrating to the "syncopated" voice transmitted in this "whispered rush, telepathy of wires." The syncopation of that voice implies the systematic interruption or contraction of the motion Crane is concerned with—a motion made visible in the dashes that connect the appositive phrases in this stanza, but that also act like ellipses to indicate a telegraphic series of gaps: "the index of night, granite and steel— / Transparent meshes—fleckless the gleaming staves—" (Crane, *Poems*, 105). The discontinuities of grammar here and elsewhere in "Atlantis" are a linguistic instance of "shuttling moonlight" or "gleaming staves," and they mark the emergence of an intermittent and discontinuous presence, a subject audible as the multiple "Sibylline voices" that "flicker" and "waveringly stream / As though a god were issue of the strings," in the last two lines of the first stanza.

The voice of the god that emerges in this manner is both multiple (fractured by the poem's many strictures) and unitary (the "issue" of the poem's "*combined* materials"). Such a voice suggests, I think, the phenomenology of a self that is wholly mediated—indeed, created—by the instruments and process of its own expression. Donald Pease has described a related effect in Whitman's "Song of Myself": "When Whitman wrote 'I sing myself' he literally meant that his singing brought a self into being"; and the self brought into being by this singing, Pease specifies, is not "Whitman's empirical ego," nor the "dramatic" subject in a conventional mimesis, but an "inter-subject," by which he means a *relation*, or a process of relation, between self and other, body and voice. In this sense, the "inter-subject" Whitman's singing creates, like "the sexualized self" represented in his homoerotic narratives, is a preeminently *erotic* relation that "incarnates the relation between persons rather than any individual identity" (Pease, "Blake, Whitman, and Crane," 212).

This formulation of Whitman's practice begins to explain the paradoxical status of a voice that is both multiple and unitary, a voice that is the "issue" of the discreet, material parts of the poem, and yet whose emergence as a motion, or as "a process of relation," dissolves the integrity of those parts—in the way Crane's "numbers" approach an "*Unfractioned idiom.*" With this making of many voices into one, and of one voice into many, the text of Crane's "Atlantis" itself approaches the condition of the "multitudinous Verb," which, the sixth stanza explains, "the suns / And synergy of waters ever fuse, recast / In myriad syllables" (Crane, *Poems*, 106). Like Whitman, Crane's "Verb" contains multitudes, and the continual breaking and binding, fusing and recasting, of its elements refers us to the unity of song Whitman discovered in the flow and ebb of his own voice. In the second stanza of "Atlantis," where the "arching path" of the bridge has become a "call" that fuses and uplifts, from the water below, the "labyrinthine mouths of history," Crane sees this unity of voice as "One arc synoptic of all tides below—." At this point, the bridge is recognized precisely as an overarching structure—as the recurrent (and in this sense stable) trajectory of the multiple voices that constitute the history written in *The Bridge*. Those voices assume their full, collective resonance only when they are heard as "all ships at sea" (implicitly as all of the lovers who ever voyaged in those ships) "Pouring reply" to the singer brought into being by "Atlantis": "Make thy love sure—to weave whose song we ply!"

This reply answers Crane's search throughout *The Bridge* for voices that will sustain and participate in the song of his own desire, and it expresses the fantasized fulfillment of the poem's search for a fully erotic basis of communication, binding all speakers in one call, making love a medium of sure connection. Tate held that *The Bridge* fails in its attempt to convert a lyric sequence into epic, but that was never Crane's intention; as the second stanza of "Atlantis" suggests, Crane wished to convert epic *into lyric*—in particular, into the kind of love lyric Crane practiced, a poem both homosexual and visionary in mode. Crane's wish was to bear witness to the visionary direction of American history as it is revealed in the erotic trajectory of an ideal lyric voice, a voice that would realize and secure ("make sure") the absolute relation between persons Crane sought, and thereby enact the peculiarly American promise of Whitmanian comradeship.

This one voice, like Whitman's "valved voice," gathers to it and contains all the desiring voices in *The Bridge*, including the heroic exclamations of Columbus, the muffled "tide of voices" in "The Harbor Dawn," and the ship names that "Cutty Sark" taps out in Morse code:

> *Rainbow, Leander*
> (last trip a tragedy)—where can you be
> *Nimbus*? and you rivals two—
>   a long tack keeping—
>   *Taeping*?
>   *Ariel*?
>
> (Crane, *Poems*, 73–74)

These ships, like "all ships at sea" in "Atlantis," constitute an unusually literary fleet, their names invoking various powers of poetry, all of which Crane calls on to enforce his triumphant claims in the second stanza of "Atlantis." Yet the fictive boats in "Cutty Sark" are also lost, or separated from each other, at sea, and the reunion that these questions portend is the arrival on shore of the drowned mariners in "At Melville's Tomb." The epigraph for "Cutty Sark" comes from Melville's naval elegy "The Temeraire": "O, the navies old and oaken, / O, the Temeraire no more!" Crane quotes these lines in a letter to Wilbur Underwood, written in January 1927, in which Crane describes his longing for his "faithful," and his feelings about the death of a homosexual friend of his and Underwood's, Harry Candee (Crane, "Wind-blown Flames," 365). The presence of Melville's ships in Crane's letter about the loss of gay friends and lovers— men whose loving solidarity across the separations enforced upon them has heroic power for Crane—implies the presence of those friends and lovers (under code names, as it were) in "Cutty Sark." In "Atlantis," the ships separated at sea are nonetheless bound together by the fate they share, a fate that Crane makes explicit in the draft version of the ships' "cry" in "Atlantis": "Make thy love sure, to lift whose song we die" (Weber, *Hart Crane*, 438).[12] The "arc synoptic," which is the perpetual form of the song of the lovers here, is lifted only by their death, according to the logic of a compact into which Crane's "floating singer" must also enter. In order to explore that logic further, I will interrupt my comments on "Atlantis" at this point and go back to the origins of this text in drafts and letters.

Crane's pursuit of a purified medium of communication, of a language that would bind together the many voices of American history and provide the basis for new community, casts the singer of *The Bridge* as—in the words of Alan Trachtenberg—"the true mediator of a true cultural history." Trachtenberg is describing the mediating role Crane found for himself in the criticism of Brooks, Mumford, and Frank, a prophetic cultural criticism that envisioned "an aesthetic self, a poetic sensibility," at the center of American history. Indeed, Trachtenberg asks, "How else are we to understand the epic scale of *The Bridge* except as the effort of the poet to discover *himself* in all of American history . . . ? To discover himself as the redemptive consciousness of the history as a whole, as a totality" (Trachtenberg, "Cultural Revisions in the Twenties," 59). The text Trachtenberg uses to exemplify this motive comes from Crane's earliest worksheets for "Atlantis"; it is probably the first passage Crane wrote for *The Bridge*, and it locates Crane's singer at the organizing center of his culture—"midway" on the bridge:

> And midway on that structure I would stand
> One moment, not as diver, but with arms
> That open to project a disk's resilience
> Winding the sun and planets in its face.
> Water should not stem that disk, nor weigh
> What holds its speed in vantage of all things
> That tarnish, creep, or wane; and in like laughter,
> Mobile yet posited beyond even that time

The Pyramids shall falter, slough into sand,—
And smooth and fierce above the claim of wings,
And figured in that radiant field that rings
The Universe:—I'd have us hold one consonance
Kinetic to its poised and deathless dance.

                              (Crane, in Weber, *Hart Crane*, 425)[13]

Crane's resilient "disk" is an image of the symbolic totalization Trachtenberg describes: it is an image of the poem as orb or sphere, as a type of
"the radiant field that rings / The Universe" itself, and it is also an image
of the *poet* as he opens his arms to demonstrate the circumference of a
circle, which is doubled in the river flowing beneath him. This fixed image
projected upon—and retrieved from—flux reveals the poet as the "aesthetic self" that is both the subject and the object of historical process.
More precisely, Crane's solar disk, "Winding the sun and planets in its
face," has been retrieved from literary history, and specifically from that
moment in "Crossing Brooklyn Ferry" when Whitman tells us that he too

Saw the reflection of the summer sky in the water,
Had my eyes dazzled by the shimmering track of beams,
Look'd at the fine centrifugal spokes of light round the shape
                              of my head in the sunlit water,

—and from this position saw "the flags of all nations" and the chimneys
casting light on both shores.[14] As Whitman's face replaces the sun's, the
poet recognizes himself at the center—the focal point—of "the fine centrifugal spokes of light" that radiate across the harbor and then rebound
from each shore. The position is that of "the true mediator," whose solar
body links and illuminates both shores of this visionary community, and it
is the position Crane takes up when *his* face replaces Whitman's in a sacrament of poetic succession that validates the homoerotic gaze of Narcissus.

The sacramental nature of the occasion is emphasized in Crane's fragment by the extension of the poet's arms—a gesture of connection, which
imitates the structure of the bridge, and signifies a priestly benediction. At
the same time, however, the gesture suggests crucifixion, and it points out
that the poet's position midway on the bridge is also that of the bedlamite
who, in the final text of *The Bridge*, leaps to death in the proem:

Out of some subway scuttle, cell or loft
A bedlamite speeds to thy parapets,
Tilting there momently, shrill shirt ballooning,
A jest falls from the speechless caravan.

                              (Crane, *Poems*, 43)

Crane works to erase, but in fact draws out, a potential confusion between his prophetic speaker and the suicides and daredevils for which the Brooklyn Bridge was famous when he specifies, without an obvious reason for doing so, that the poet's position is *not* that of a "diver."[15] The specification, raising this possibility rather than setting it to rest, does not distinguish so much as *superimpose* the positions of the visionary and the suicide—as if these two positions, for all appearances, were simply identical.

The ambiguity of the poet's position is underscored when we consider this fragment in light of where it first appeared—as the postscript to a letter Crane wrote to Underwood, in February 1923, announcing his plan to write *The Bridge*. The letter, which we looked at briefly in Chapter Five, begins by detailing Crane's attraction to a male companion at the theater; by the end, when Crane turns from prose to verse, the letter has passed through a dizzying meditation on love and art:

> O yes, I shall see him again soon. The climax will be all too easily reached,—
> But my gratitude is enduring—if only for that *once*, at least, something beautiful approached me and as though it were the most natural thing in the world enclosed me in his arm and pulled me to him without my slightest bid. And we who create must endure—must hold to spirit not by the mind, the intellect alone. These have no mystic possibilities. O flesh damned to hate and scorn! I have felt my cheek pressed on the desert these days and months too much. . . . I long to go to India and stay always. Meditation on the sun is all there is. Not that this isn't enough! I mean I find my imagination more sufficient all the time. The work of the workaday world is what I dislike. I spend my evenings in music and sometimes ecstasy. I've been writing a lot lately. . . . I'm on a synthesis of America and its structural identity now, called *The Bridge*. I quote the last lines—
>
> And midway on that structure I would stand . . .
>
> (Crane, *Letters*, 127)

Consider the sequence of association: self-consciously world-weary, Crane anticipates the climax and passing of his passion; he consoles himself, then, with the memory of his lover's binding touch (or a fantasy of it, to judge from the rest of the letter); and then Crane passes from this image of loving enclosure to the moral assertion: "And we who create must endure—must hold to the spirit," by which Crane means not "the mind, the intellect alone," but also that flesh which is "damned to hate and scorn." In sum, the vacillation here between hope and despair charts a series of oppositions organized around the trials of homosexual men. On one side is damnation of the flesh, the desert of the homosexual lover's isolation, and the redundant routine of "the work of the workaday world"; on the other side is the sufficiency of the imagination, "meditation on the sun," and the promise of passage to India. The one set of terms promises to redeem the other, as the spirit will redeem the flesh. Yet the redemption Crane imagines does not imply the transcendence, so much as the restoration, of the claims of the male homosexual's body. For Crane's letter specifically looks forward to the restoration of touch and the orgasmic reunion of bodies projected in Whitman's "Passage to India":

> Reckoning ahead O soul, when thou, the time achiev'd,
> The seas all cross'd, weather'd the capes, the voyage done,
> Surrounded, copest, frontest God, yieldest, the aim attain'd,
> As fill'd with friendship, love complete, the Elder Brother
> > found,
> The Younger melts in fondness in his arms.
> > (Whitman, *Leaves of Grass*, Vol. 3, 573)

Crane's selection of the second of these lines as the epigraph to "Cape Hatteras" is one measure of the endurance of this vision throughout the making of *The Bridge*; and it insists that the goal of poetic quest in *The Bridge* is a point at which distinctions between self and other, the elder and the younger, the spirit and the flesh, have dissolved (or "melted away") in the achievement of a bond that is sexual and fraternal at once. "Those who have wept in the darkness are sometimes rewarded with stray leaves blown inadvertently," Crane told Underwood, playing upon metaphors from both Whitman and Underwood (Crane, *Letters*, 126).[16] That promise of consolation is also biblical, deriving from Psalm 126: "Those who go forth weeping, bearing the seed for sowing, shall come home with shouts of joy, carrying their sheaves." Crane read this sacred text through Wilde's martyrdom; Wilde had read it, in turn, through Blake, as the quotation from *De Profundis* that I have used as an epigraph to this chapter suggests. It is a reminder that the transcendental impulse in Crane's work is always also a homoerotic one. As Yingling explains, Crane's "homosexual dream of perfect metaphysical union is not so much a reflected heterosexual ideal as it is the compensation for having wept in the darkness, for the loss of meaning in a world governed by spiritually bankrupt institutions" (Yingling, *Crane and the Homosexual Text*, 90); it is an image of the redemption, not the renunciation, of male homosexuality.

But if the spiritualization of male bonds redeems the flesh, it entails the mortification of the flesh as well. That is the suggestion, I think, when, writing to Frank in 1924, and shouting with joy for his new relationship with Emil Opffer, Crane presents another account of the erotic embrace of brothers:

> I have seen the Word made Flesh. I mean nothing less, and I know now there is such a thing as indestructability. In the deepest sense, where flesh has been transformed through intensity of response to counter-response, where sex was beaten out, where a purity of joy was reached which included tears. . . . And I have been able to give freedom and life which was acknowledged in the ecstasy of walking hand in hand across the most beautiful bridge in the world, the cables enclosing us and pulling us upward in such a dance as I have never walked and never can walk with another. (Crane, *Letters*, 181)

This letter both summarizes the human narrative of "Atlantis" and suggests why that narrative is inaccessible to us. That is, when Crane writes about "the ecstasy of walking hand in hand across the most beautiful bridge in the world, the cables enclosing us and pulling us upward," he is writing about the passage "Through the bound cable strands" we have just been considering. And yet, as we have seen, the linguistic procedures of "Atlantis" refuse access to the human subjects of Crane's grammar; we are presented not with two men "walking hand in hand" (as we are at the end of "Cape Hatteras") but with the "abstract form" of a text's own "orbit." What happens when flesh is made into words in this way can be understood according to the way in which the Word is made into Flesh. Incarnation is above all an *erotic* event for Crane, and yet it is an erotic event in which the flesh is "transformed by intensity of response to counter-response" until sex itself is "beaten out." The body is the necessary condition—the material vehicle—of this event, but the body is, for the same reason, an obstacle that the lovers must overcome. In this respect, Crane and his lover have to pass *through the body* in the same way Crane must pass "*through* the combined materials" of "Atlantis."

The relation I am suggesting between erotic and linguistic practices may be clarified by reviewing the drafts of "Atlantis." Over the long course of its composition, as the poem's text moved toward "indestructability," "sex was beaten out" in an obvious and practical sense. For example, in the fragment quoted above, "And midway on that structure I would stand," Crane introduces a first-person speaker; and in its final couplet, "—I'd have us hold one consonance / Kinetic to its poised and deathless dance," the first-person singular becomes plural. Six months later, the first-person plural discloses a companion who is urged to touch the "cloudy buried throat where light"

> Is branched like prayers unspoken that await
> Your deepest thrusting agony for answer: strike
> Its breast precipitate, its lust-forbidden flanks,
> Sleek with your sweat's erosion,—til we hear
> The sound of waters bending and astride the sky:
> Until, as though an organ pressing doom
> Should set this nave of time atremble, we feel
> Though brimming clay and signalling upright,
> Beneath us lift a porch, a living concourse
> Whose alignment rears from equal out to equal,
> Yielding mutual assumption on its arches
> Fused and veering to the measure of our arms.
>
> (Crane, in Weber, *Hart Crane*, 428)

Like other early fragments of "Atlantis," this passage contains phrases Crane later reworked in different contexts. "The sound of waters bending and astride the sky" reverberates as part of a pentameter couplet in the penultimate strophe of "The Tunnel" (Crane, *Poems*, 101); "an organ pressing doom" reappears in the eighth stanza of "Atlantis" (Crane, *Poems*, 107); these "arches / Fused and veering" return in "the arching path / Upward, veering with light." This redistribution of verbal elements, by which Crane's word is "recast" and "fused" in new forms, is typical of the compositional process of "Atlantis." But the reappearance of these and other lines from otherwise discarded drafts should be examined in relation to the *disappearance* of those lines that present the bridge as a figure for that "living concourse" raised "from equal out to equal" in the sexual union of two male bodies—its "arches" representing simply and recognizably "the measure of our arms." When the bridge is first lifted, it is a figure clearly arising from a ground in human action—indeed, it images two men making love, "fused and veering" in the rear alignment of anal intercourse. But before the bridge's full extension in the final text of "Atlantis" is realized, the human subjects of this action vanish, revealing, in their place, merely the "concourse" (earlier, the "consonance") they created together.

Sex is "beaten out" of "Atlantis," then, in the same way that linguistic reference to "History and fact, location, etc.," is "transfigured" in the repeated acts of erasure and revision by which "Atlantis" is itself raised. "For poetry," as Crane explained in "Modern Poetry," "is an architectural art" (Crane, *Complete Poems and Selected Prose*, 260); and yet it was Crane's procedure to build structures by taking them apart. This is, manifestly, the textual history of "Atlantis"; it is also the poetic history of Crane's search for the new structures that he called "white buildings." The color of those buildings is a sign not of their innocence but of the process of purification—the acts of reduction and erasure—by which the architect lifts them into place before us. For the whiteness Crane pursues throughout his poetry is not the color of an unmarked point of origin; it is the color of the "positive, or . . . ecstatic" goal Crane sought by means of that deironization of terms I have been calling "the negation of negation." That double negation is represented in the double movement of "the arching path" of "Atlantis" as well as in the double action of erasure and revision, the discarding and recasting of the poem's elements, by which Crane brought the text of "Atlantis" into being.

The muse of these double movements is the seagull glimpsed in the first quatrain of *The Bridge*:

> How many dawns, chill from his rippling rest
> The seagull's wings shall dip and pivot him,
> Shedding white rings of tumult, building high
> Over the chained bay waters Liberty—

(Crane, Poems, 43)

The gull rises through a series of dipping and pivoting motions that call to mind the cyclical nature both of this daily ascent ("How many dawns") and of the quest Crane himself engages in *The Bridge*. The gull's spiral ascent is an act of "building," but also "shedding," because the bird climbs up by throwing down the "white rings" of his "tumult." The unusual participle "shedding" invokes that signal moment in the third part of "Voyages" when Crane writes of the "transmemberment of song" achieved when the lovers have "shed" death. In this case, which is itself another "resurrection of some kind," the gull throws off the "chill" of the night's rest and once again converts its body into a vehicle of flight. The gull's ascent is a visible instance of the double movement across and upward in "Atlantis"; it is an *ascetic* action—a process Crane colors "white"—in which the extravagance of upward flight is achieved by stripping away, or throwing off, the gull's ties to earth.

"Shedding" mixes a suggestion of metamorphosis (the snake's shedding of its skin is a central figure in "The Dance") with a suggestion of bleeding, in a way that makes bleeding seem like a means to metamorphosis. In the proem, the gull's wings, "with inviolate curve, forsake our eyes / As apparitional as sails"; in "Atlantis," those saillike wings return when "White tempest nets file upward, upward ring," and the intensity of longing leads the eyes themselves (isolated, abstracted from a human agent) to set out on the bird's course:

> Sheerly the eyes, like seagulls stung with rime—
> Slit and propelled by glistening fins of light—
> Pick biting way up towering looms that press
> Sidelong with flight of blade on tendon blade
> —Tomorrows into yesteryear—and link
> What cipher-script of time no traveller reads
> But who, through smoking pyres of love and death,
> Searches the timeless laugh of mythic spears.
>
> (Crane, *Poems*, 105–6)

The successive trochaic substitutions at the start of each of the stanza's first four lines mark a sudden sharpening of the poem's angle of ascent, giving rhythmic force to the new violence of this fourth stanza. The eyes climb upward "Sheerly," one feels, because the climb entails the cutting or "slitting" of the eyes, which in turn "Pick" and "bite" their way through the resistant, material structures of the bridge. A human subject at last emerges in this action, but only in the concentrated, synecdochic form of the visionary's "eyes," which are also compressed and cut, violated, "propelled" by the "glistening fins of light" that disfigure them. The disfiguration of the visionary's eyes "stung with rime" recalls the whitening process by which "Frosted eyes . . . lifted altars"; it is also a dramatization of Blake's command to see "*through* the eye," making evident the ecstatic, castrative violence to the natural body this injunction demands (and allows) for Crane.

Crane sometimes saw himself, and he has very often been seen, as the poet of "the machine"—as the propagandist and advocate of industrial technology. Indeed, Crane felt that if poetry cannot "absorb the machine," it will have "failed of its full contemporary function" (Crane, *Complete Poems and Selected Prose*, 261–62). But "absorb" means, in this case, what it means when Crane says he plans to "apply as much of [Eliot's] erudition and technique as I can absorb and assemble toward a more positive, or . . . ecstatic goal." Crane is always interested in technology, whether Eliot's or Roebling's, as an instrument to be used and, in the process, used up: it is the middle term whose destruction propels a visionary leap from origin to goal. This is true in the case of the linguistic technology of verse form and in the erotic technology of the body. The purpose of these tools is realized only when they are transformed, as Crane suggests in "Cutty Sark," into "some white machine that sings" (Crane, *Poems*, 72). What needs to be recognized is the special violence—to the body, to "the combined materials of the poem"—that Crane's "white machines" require.

Above, in the fourth stanza of "Atlantis," the bridge is itself converted into a kind of "white machine," but a machine designed less for singing than for writing. The "towering looms" that weave the fabric of voices in the opening stanzas are presented here as a printing press, composing a text that Crane calls the "cipher-script of time." And the looms work in this way specifically by pressing, "Sidelong with flight of blade on tendon blade," "Tomorrows into yesteryear." This complex figure for the collapse of the future into the past, which composes an encoded history "no traveller reads" but one who passes "through smoking pyres of love and death," includes a peculiar rendering of the bridge as body, in which the looms produce a threshing action of "blade on tendon blade." In this phrase Crane converts the "strings" of the bridge into "tendons," which, like the "fins of light" above or the "mythic spears" below, figure a particular kind of erotic violence. The action of these interlocking blades images the full "intensity of response to counter-response"; and the phrase is itself an example of the symmetrical construction Crane uses in the third section of "Voyages" to evoke the union of two bodies: "Light wrestling there incessantly with light, / Star kissing star through wave on wave unto / Your body rocking!" (Crane, *Poems*, 36). But the union of bodies in "Atlantis" is not resolved in a "rocking" exchange of this kind; rather, it thrusts one "tendon blade" against another with the wounding force of erotic inscription that we saw in "Thou Canst Read Nothing": "All this that baulks delivery through words / Shall come to you through wounds prescribed by swords" (Crane, *Poems*, 193).

The figures in the fourth stanza that present writing as a kind of violence rendered by and to the body culminate in the fifth stanza when Aeolus, a name for the god who had emerged from the bridge's "strings" in the first stanza, is "splintered in the straits!" (Crane, *Poems*, 106). The note of triumph in Crane's exclamation expresses satisfaction in the text's passage beyond natural reference (in this case, the romantic mythology of the poem as Aeolian harp). To be the "issue of the strings," which is finally to pass through the "tendon blades" of the harplike bridge, is to see the body broken up and "splintered," no longer a totality. The instant of this fracture marks the end of the ascent recorded in the opening of "Atlantis." From this point onward the text is entirely given over to apostrophe—as if the "splintering" of the god were required before the bridge could emerge as a totality named in direct address.

The names that Crane gives this structure—for example, in the sixth stanza, "Tall-Vision-of-the-Voyage," "Bridge," "Choir," and "Psalm of Cathay!"—pass "through" sight and sound toward an entity that can neither be seen nor heard: "O Love, thy white, pervasive Paradigm . . . !" Each name in this sequence erases as it revises the last, and the address as a whole is built up by "shedding" one name after another, until the "white rings" of Crane's periphrasis arrive at an undefiled structure. (The sense in which the act of naming imitates the ascent of the gull in the proem is emphasized in the tenth stanza when "Deity's young name / Kinetic of white choiring wings . . . ascends." The name is not given to us here because it is "young," hence "inviolate.") "Atlantis" approaches the "white, pervasive Paradigm" of Love by means of a linguistic practice that, like the seagull's flight, is simultaneously ascetic and extravagant, and that gains access to the unnameable through an excess of names. The goal remains Whitman's "Psalm of Cathay!" But the human subjects recognizable in "Passage to India" as the Elder and the Younger Brother have been replaced in Crane's poem, through the erotic and linguistic violence we have been studying, by the purified technology of "an abstract form."

As if to rectify the absence of any actual lovers at the site of Love's "white, pervasive Paradigm," Crane introduces the first-person plural, for the first time in the poem's published version, in the opening lines of the next stanza: "We left the haven hanging in the night— / Sheened harbor lanterns backward fled the keel" (Crane, *Poems*, 106). Even here, though, the human subject emerges only in the past tense, and the lines refer to a departure from the shore (imaged by Crane, characteristically, in reverse) that has already taken place before "Atlantis" begins. In fact, Crane speaks at this point in "Atlantis" from midocean—a destination that is not a "haven," nor even a "place" in any usual sense of the word, but what I have been calling a "form" or a "structure." In the text of the Black Sun edition, Crane calls it the "fathomless," and in the Liveright edition, he calls it

> the circular indubitable frieze
> Of heaven's meditation, yoking wave
> To kneeling wave, one song devoutly binds—
> The vernal strophe chimes from deathless strings!

> (Crane, *Poems*, 106)

In the manner of Wallace Stevens's genitive phrases, which typically link abstract and concrete terms, Crane's lines suggest both that the frieze represents "heaven's meditation" and that it is itself the form that meditation takes. The structure Crane arrives at is something like the material form of a thought, therefore; and it reconciles, as both a material and a transcendental structure, the temporal and spatial antinomies of night and day and high and low, ultimately "lifting night to cycloramic crest / Of deepest day" (Crane, *Poems*, 106).

In the eighth stanza, in lines Tate particularly admired, Crane finds still other names for the impossible structure before us:

> O Thou steeled Cognizance whose leap commits
> The agile precincts of the lark's return;
> Within whose lariat sweep encinctured sing
> In single chrysalis the many twain,—
> Of stars Thou art the stitch and stallion glow
> And like an organ, Thou, with sound of doom—
> Sight, sound and flesh Thou leadest from time's realm
> As love strikes clear direction for the helm.

(Crane, Letters, 106–7)

Crane's "steeled Cognizance" is, like "the circular indubitable frieze / Of heaven's meditation," a concrete abstraction; and since the noun "Cognizance" is formed on the basis of a verb (in French and Latin), and in this sense specifies an act or state of knowing, the "Cognizance" Crane addresses compounds substance and motion as well. The line elaborates on the verbal element of the noun when this knowing is imagined as a "leap" that "commits" (etymologically, binds together; but also sends, wills, confirms, entrusts, or pledges) "The agile precincts of the lark's return." This "leap" answers—both rewards and materializes—Crane's leap of faith in *The Bridge*, because it establishes and sanctifies a space of "vernal" song, which is that point where time, seen now as "the circular indubitable frieze / Of heaven's meditation," turns upon itself, renewing the springtime singer's voice. The oxymoronic constitution of these "agile precincts" also points to a structure-in-motion, in such a way as to efface the distinction between Crane's tenor and vehicle. In one sense, that is, these "precincts" are the container both to and in which the lark returns; in another sense, the bird's return itself constructs its "agile" domain. The lark is in this way an image of the self-sustaining "floating singer" who will appear in stanza 11.

The binding action of the lark's flight also comments on the action of Crane's verse form. If, in the opening of "Atlantis," Crane figured the lines of his text as "arching strands of song" stretched "upward" by every turn down the page, those lines now do not "arch" so much as "encincture": an action of encircling, girding, or belting that is effected in the disposition of the eight-line stanza into four separate coupletlike structures whose integrity is emphasized at the end by rhyme. The "lariat" of the lark's song is a figure for the ways in which the material constrictions of verse enforce the unity of voice Crane seeks in "Atlantis," linked here to the image of the casing that binds "In single chrysalis the many twain." But because the song of the lark is like a lariat (notice how the same syllable in both words implies a connection between them—as if, say, "lariat" were simply the scientific name for a lark's song), it is also like a whip; and it has little to do with the reassuringly organic unity-in-metamorphosis of a butterfly.[17] ("Lariat" comes from the Spanish *la reata*—literally a "tyingback," which calls to mind, suggestively in this context, the etymologies of both "refrain" and "return.") The emphasis here is on the force that the poem's structures impose—the lariat it requires to create a butterfly.

The lark's song figures Crane's act of "wrapping harness" to the natural energies of his poem, to the sexual and specifically masculine energies imaged in the "stallion glow" of the stars. The "*st*itch" of those "*st*ars," threaded together by this "*st*eeled Cognizance" through the prominent alliteration, is one of Crane's most willful and outlandish assertions of a connection between words simply, it would seem, on the basis of a shared sound. "Of stars Thou art the stitch and stallion glow" is an unconstrained hyperbole, a wild boast of the power of naming, and a celebration of its own sound. The auditory splendor of this line, like the rhetorical and metrical excitement of this stanza as a whole, is the achievement of a poet who is reaching, boldly and directly, for the intensest sensual satisfaction poetic form is able to produce. This is fitting, since the eighth stanza of "Atlantis" concerns the permanent renewal, the perpetuation of the senses through song; but the aesthetic process of formalization by which the senses are perpetuated here entails a violent fragmenting of the phenomenal world. The space of the lark's return is, again, not a natural place, but a linguistic structure composed of the fragments (in Irwin's terms, the "reverse correspondences") of the totality normally present through the senses. The "stallion glow" of the stars is an important example. Elsewhere in Crane's work, wild horses are an emblem of male homoerotic vigor. In "Cape Hatteras," Crane's memories of his first reading of Whitman come to him mixed with images of "Cowslip and shad-blow, / flaked like tethered foam / Around bared teeth of stallions"; and in "Episode of Hands," the "beautiful" wounded hands of the worker reveal "the marks of wild ponies' play,— / Bunches of new green breaking a hard turf" (Crane, *Poems*, 82, 173). In both poems, Crane's wild horses place the male body and its pleasures in the natural world. In "Atlantis," however, the "stallion glow" of the stars does not refer to an object or an event in the world; the stars have an aura of earthly pleasures, the "glow" of them, but only that. The senses restored to Crane's singer have been detached from any possible natural context, and then reorganized—projected upward—according to linguistic principles such as rhyme, meter, and alliteration.

This practice produces the "disorganization of the senses" for which Crane's work is notorious, an effect his critics have attributed to influences as different as Rimbaud and alcoholism. Whatever causes one wants to ascribe, synesthesia in Crane's work points toward a mechanical, not an organic, totality, a totality arrived at by submitting experience to the fragmenting strictures of abstract form (passing "*through* the eye"). The satisfactions of the senses I spoke of above can only be poetic, which is to say linguistic, satisfactions; and they constitute the triumph of one kind of sense—one kind of *order*—at the expense of another. In the eighth stanza of "Atlantis," the "stitch and stallion glow" of the stars is a harnessing of the masculine eros in Crane's poem that functions on at least two levels. In its translation from earth to the stars, the "stallion glow" achieves permanent ("indubitable") form by a process analogous to the way in which the phrase itself has been made: Crane has removed it from natural reference ("stallion" as slang for a desiring and desirable man) and inserted it in the linguistic order of the text ("stallion" as an alliterative predicate of "stars"). The word signifies—it is not mere sound—but Crane's "counterworld" is as remote from the human world as the stars are from earth.

To constellate words in this way is a bravura, Marlovian act—the very definition of "the high style." The energy of that linguistic act is deployed in the service of tropes that fragment and reorganize the mimesis of sexual acts, in such a way as to interpret poetic composition as itself an ascetic act of self-binding or, to use Crane's trope, "beating." The "steeled" structure of the bridge is brought into being by a sacrifice of conventional mimesis identified in this case with a sacrifice of the body, producing a specifically masochistic mode of transport. Crane's intimate address of the bridge in the eighth stanza—"Thou," "Thou," "Thou," "Thou"—reverberates "with sound of doom" because the object of the quest (the bridge) becomes a subject when, as his senses are stripped away (that is, "shed"), the subject of the quest (the poet-quester) becomes an object. The bridge gains subjectivity by way of a process that objectifies the poet.

Crane narrates this ambiguous reciprocity in the closing, celebratory couplet of the stanza: "Sight, sound and flesh Thou leadest from time's realm / As love strikes clear direction for the helm." The Black Sun version of the last line—"And love, once suffered for, shall space o'erwhelm"—emphasizes that Crane is writing about the triumph of love, about the total collapse of distance between persons, a passage to India that would redeem those who have wept in the darkness. As in Whitman's poem, this passage promises to perpetuate the senses—to *lead* "Sight, sound and flesh" from "time's realm" to the permanent embrace of the Younger Brother in the Elder's arms. But this "transfiguration" of sense, like the transformation of flesh in which, Crane told Frank, "sex was beaten out," removes "Sight, sound and flesh" from the only medium or "realm" in which they exist. For this reason, as Bloom has remarked, "the pragmatic or merely natural burden" of this stanza is ultimately "quite suicidal" (Bloom, "Introduction," *Crane: Critical Views*, 13).

In the next stanza, Crane communicates the proximity of love's triumph and defeat in an unusually difficult address to the bridge: "Swift peal of secular light, intrinsic Myth / Whose fell unshadow is death's utter wound" (Crane, *Poems*, 107). As Edelman notes, "There is no certainty as to whether this 'Myth' wounds death or finds itself wounded by it," and the uncertainty is only complicated by Crane's definition of "secular light" as "fell unshadow." This "unshadow" is not, Edelman writes, "merely a trope for 'light'"; it is "a negative presence" that evokes, it seems to me, the negation of negation—the "not-not-light," if you will—that Crane usually presents as a "white" structure, or in the same stanza, "white escarpments" (Edelman, *Transmemberment of Song*, 244–45). To effect that double negation, Crane planned to "strike" a "tangent" that would go "through [Eliot] toward a *different goal*"; the plan is enacted in "Atlantis," finally and forcefully, when "love strikes clear direction for the helm." In each case, Crane's verb—"strike"—points to the special violence entailed by the "direction" he chose, a violence pledged to love that included destruction of the vehicles of language and the body. When, therefore, the bridge collapses into the river below it, in the course of the ninth stanza, the new, "River-throated" structure is "iridescently upborne / Through the bright drench and fabric of our veins"—as if the poem's two voyagers, having become the vessels of their own voyage (first bridge, then body), had themselves become the element from which those vehicles are ordinarily needed to protect them.

This fusion of "drench and fabric," dye and text, is an image of the poet's total immersion in the poem, and it portends what I called, at the beginning of this chapter, the elimination of the singer of *The Bridge*. This last event is postponed in the exquisitely suspended syntax of the penultimate stanza:

Migrations that must needs void memory,
Inventions that cobblestone the heart,—
Unspeakable Thou Bridge to Thee, O Love.
Thy pardon for this history, whitest Flower,
O Answerer of all,—Anemone,—
Now while thy petals spend the suns about us, hold—
(O Thou whose radiance doth inherit me)
Atlantis,—hold thy floating singer late!

(Crane, *Poems*, 107)

Crane has several "Migrations" in mind: the westward extension of epic tradition, and of the United States; the passage to India promised in Whitman's poetry; the passage of *The Bridge* itself—"this history"—toward its goal in "Love"; and the linguistic transport by which the poem approaches that goal. At the end of the prior stanza, that transport is represented as the ascension of "Deity's young name" on "white choiring wings"—a migration that "voids memory" because the building up of names, as we have seen, is also a shedding of names, erasing what has gone before. In stanza 11, the same double process is in effect, but it is associated not with the act of ascending but with the bridging—"Unspeakable Thou Bridge"—that carries this singer "to Thee, O Love." As a goal that is also an origin, Love "voids memory" by erasing personal history in the human subject's return into its source, which is another version of the incestual return in the fragment "The Sea Raised Up." This erasure of memory permits the singer himself to approach the condition of the "whitest Flower," and it grants "pardon" because it is the end of all error, past and future.

As the canceled line from stanza 8 suggests, the goal here is that point at which "love, once suffered for, shall space o'erwhelm." This is the transcendental rhetoric into which Wilde passes at the end of *De Profundis*, promising compensation for the suffering of love's martyrs. But "pardon" comes with punishment, in Crane as in Wilde. "Inventions that cobblestone the heart" destroy the body, not simply by passing beyond it, but by converting the body into the instrument by which such a passage is achieved. This bridge is "Unspeakable" because a "cobblestone heart" is monstrous, and because homosexuality cannot be named in civil discourse; Crane's periphrastic rhetoric (his method of "inferential mention") is both a visionary and a homosexual means of representing an unnameable love. Here, with Crane at the height of his rhetorical powers, Crane's language is afloat and ungrounded; it is at last nearing the undefiled, "*Unfractioned*," "Unspeakable" source existing outside of the discourse it makes possible—the original Word, that is, the pursuit of which (for Crane, a kind of incestual return) is intimated here by Crane's arrival at the original letter of the alphabet, "O Answerer of all,—Anemone,—. . . Atlantis."

As Edelman has shown, this series of names, in its renaming of the "whitest Flower" as "Answerer of all," signals a return to Whitman as well, by invoking Whitman's name for the poet in "Song of the Answerer." The identification is reinforced, I think, by "Cape Hatteras," where Whitman's power to "answer" the deepest "soundings" of the dead promises "a pact, new bound / Of living brotherhood" (Crane, *Poems*, 82). (Whitman's "Sea eyes" in "Cape Hatteras" link him with "The seal's wide spindrift gaze toward paradise" as that gaze is "answered" "in the vortex of our grave.") For Edelman, Crane's late return to the origin of *The Bridge* in Whitman functions to assert Crane's own originality, his difference from his precursor, in Edelman's Bloomian terms. This is the case, Edelman argues, because the appositive relation of "Answerer" to "whitest Flower" and "Anemone" ("daughter of the wind" in Greek) makes Whitman feminine, and thus removes Whitman from the Oedipal role of the "threatening paternal subject" and places him in the role of "the mother or maternal muse who has been the focus of Crane's desire since the dream of 'The Harbor Dawn.' " As a result, Crane is able to himself assume the self-authorizing status of the "paternal subject."

This is an elegant reading of intertextual complexity, but Edelman's emphasis on "Crane's struggle to discredit Whitman in 'Cape Hatteras' " and "Atlantis" (Edelman, *Transmemberment of Song*, 249–50) quite disregards the fact that, as we have seen, in the eyes of Crane's readers, Crane's Whitman was *already discredited*. For this reason, Crane's allusion to Whitman in "Atlantis," like his direct address to Whitman in "Cape Hatteras," asks Whitman to rescue Crane from the disgrace his identification with Whitman brings. Crane does not wish to stand alone; he fears he will be made to do so. The allusive link Crane makes between Whitman and the female muse does not aggressively disguise Whitman's gender, therefore; it projects a polymorphous addressee, someone who is both father and mother, brother and daughter, in whom differences of generation and gender have dissolved, fulfilling *The Bridge*'s goal of absolute relation and permanent response.

In the absence of the readers Crane required, Whitman presents himself to Crane as the fantastic, composite presence Grossman has called "a hermeneutic friend" (Grossman, "Crane's Intense Poetics," 227), a lover and reader who will read Crane rightly by loving him. In the special logic of this fantasy, Crane's "floating singer" does not acquire the authority of "the paternal subject"; rather, the first-person singular enters the published text at this point, in its first and only appearance, precisely as a grammatical *object*: "(O Thou whose radiance dost inherit me)." The preceding injunction, "Now while thy petals spend the suns about us, hold—," gives a first-person plural with several referents: the poet and the bridge, the poet and his lover, the poet and his reader, the poet and his reflected image. That Crane may also be speaking of himself and Whitman is suggested by the way Crane reworks Whitman's image of himself in the water in "Crossing Brooklyn Ferry" by converting "the fine centrifugal spokes of light" around Whitman's head into the solar halo of the sea flower embracing his "floating singer." The line also returns to the first of the two drafts we examined, in which Crane placed a speaker in Whitman's position "midway" between two shores. But Crane's final text is distinguished from Whitman's model and Crane's early draft by the removal of the first-person singular from its status as an active, indeed transcendental subject, and by the insertion of a self that is an object, held, suspended as if in "ether."

The suspension of Crane's "floating singer" briefly arrests the process by which the poet passes from the poem as an object (as a light like Whitman's solar glow) to be *inherited*, an event that culminates in the final conversion of substance to "radiance" begun in the first lines of "Atlantis." "Atlantis," both a poetic text and a mythic city, reappears from the waves just as Crane's poet anticipates his disappearance under them. He enjoins "Atlantis" to "hold"—both receive and sustain—its singer "late," in such a way as to cast him both back into the past (because the hour at which he speaks is already too late, and his voice the "hangover echo" of another era) and forward into the future (the hour still to come, later on, when he will be "inherited"). The "floating singer" is finally a voice existing in the dislocated, continuous present that Crane invokes at the beginning of *The Bridge* ("How many dawns"). This dislocated, continuous present is evoked in the last lines of *The Bridge*:

> So to thine Everpresence, beyond time,
> Like spears ensanguined of one tolling star
> That bleeds infinity—the orphic strings,
> Sidereal phalanxes, leap and converge:
> —One Song, one Bridge of Fire! Is it Cathay,
> Now pity steeps the grass and rainbows ring
> The serpent with the eagle in the leaves . . . ?
> Whispers antiphonal in azure swing.

(Crane, *Poems*, 108)

The "tolling" of this single, bleeding star is an accounting of the cost of the poem's arrival at a point "beyond time." For although the "orphic strings" of *The Bridge* as a whole "leap and converge" here, the unity of this ultimate song, the contraction of all vectors at one point, coincides with the dismemberment of Orpheus, the strings of whose lyre can be recognized now as "spears ensanguined"—as the parts of a structure that bear the mark of the poet's passage through them. That passage is completed in the interruption of the poem's concluding question, an ellipsis that leaves the question incomplete and, since the poet-quester has disappeared, unanswerable. The question can only be echoed, reiterated by the "antiphonal" whispers, which, crossing back and forth "in azure swing," terminate the text of "Atlantis" with a dialogue of disembodied voices in perpetual motion.

CODA

Unanswered Questions

People will love hart when he's dead.

—Kenneth Burke[1]

The ellipsis in the final question of *The Bridge* marks the expiration of Crane's singer, and it anticipates the interruption and completion of Crane's career in suicide two years after the publication of *The Bridge*. Crane chose to die in such a way as to remove his body from the world; he chose to disappear, that is, and to disappear into the sea, thereby living the dissolution of structures envisioned in the final stanzas of "Atlantis." It is possible to see Crane's suicide as the final effacement of his body, as a disowning of it, and therefore as the culmination of the sublimative, renunciatory process that is the textual history of "Atlantis." The transcendental aims of Crane's poetry always expressed an element of internalized homophobia, of homosexual self-hatred and shame, and a certain embarrassment about the body (reflected in the distaste his critics felt for his wish to take hold of Whitman's hand). When he killed himself, Crane had been a victim of homophobic violence; he had been beaten and robbed on shipboard; and his last sentence was, "I'm utterly disgraced."[2] But in another sense, Crane's suicide refused that disgrace, and *committed* him to his body: it was also a refusal to give his body up; by drowning, Crane kept his body to and for himself. The act made his exile permanent. Crane is "lost at sea" (as the marker in his birthplace, Garrettsville, Ohio, explains); he continues to forsake his native ground: Crane will not and cannot go home. Crane's suicide made him a *revenant*, one of the drowned men he wrote about, who cannot find peace.

"It's as if he asked a question which all of us tried to answer in our own terms," Malcolm Cowley wrote to Tate shortly after Crane's death.[3] What was Crane asking? Certainly he made demands on his friends. Crane asked them for friendship, money, shelter, patience, love; he asked them to have faith in his gifts and his intentions, especially when he failed to live up to

204

them. Crane's enormous pleasure in living, which he communicated to everyone who knew him, was itself a sort of question: Who could keep up with him? There was enormous pain in Crane's living too, and he imposed this on others as well, in small ways and large. Crane's "vulgarities and assumptions," his alcoholism, tantrums, accusations, and pleas, his loneliness—these were all desperate statements of a fundamental request: Crane wanted to be met, to be *joined*, to be "held." Crane's poems make the same request. Thematically, it is audible in their repeated call to solidarity: "And let us walk through time with equal pride" (Crane, *Poems*, 25). It is observable too in their "obscurity": Crane's poems dare their reader to follow, to keep up, to take part—which is also to say, they challenge their reader to be a poet, and to share in the act of poetry. Crane never forgot the promise of community he had heard in modernist writing. Like a conscience, he insisted on the early, "naive" motives of modernism—a visionary, romantic modernism Crane learned out of school; a transgressive modernism that high modernism grew out of and "beyond" in its progress toward public authority and institutional power. Modernism was, as Grossman puts it, "in moral terms the treasonous friendship of which he obsessively complained" (Grossman, "Crane's Intense Poetics," 225).

Among Crane's straight male friends (the "us" Cowley speaks of in his letter to Tate), Crane's "question" could be heard as a threatening sexual proposition. Gordon explored her own fantasy of such an invitation in *The Malefactors*; the following sentences describe the setting up of sexual boundaries between Horne Watts and Tom Claiborne, the two poets Gordon based on Crane and Tate.

> Horne had made his first—and last—pass at Tom Claiborne two days after [Claiborne] arrived in Paris. They were strolling down Monsieur le Prince late at night and Horne had stopped and, pointing to a light that burned dimly over the entrance to a cheap hotel, had suggested they go in and take a room. When Claiborne said no, that he wasn't that way, Horne had given an odd, defiant laugh and they had walked on, talking about *Le Bateau Ivre*. But the laugh had been followed by a sort of lowering of the bullet head, a hunching of the shoulders. [Claiborne] had the impression of a man trudging beside him buffeted by a storm invisible to mortal eyes.
>
> He had learned later that Horne was used to such rebuffs. Most of his friends, as he said once when he was drunk, he had "weighed in the balance and found wanting." Joe Tyrone, Bob Waite, Jim Wragge, and their wives [who fill out Gordon's "Lost Generation" cast], all testified that Horne "never let it make the least difference" . . . (Gordon, *The Malefactors*, 122–23)

There is no doubt that Crane's homosexuality made a difference; it separated him from friends like Cowley and Tate whether or not they "rebuffed" him in this manner. Cowley, remembering his last day with Crane, explains the successive "phases" Crane typically passed through while drunk: he pleased and flattered his friends; entertained them with "wild metaphors and brilliant monologues"; and then sank into paranoia and accusations. Passing out of that third phase, Crane took a train to New York City with Cowley and Muriel Maurer, a woman Crane and Cowley had just met, who would become Cowley's second wife. The three of them were returning from a weekend in Connecticut, as the guests of a married couple, in the spring of 1931:

> He slept in the train, then roused himself as it crawled into Grand Central. In the concourse he said good-bye to us, warmly but decisively, before hurrying off with his two heavy bags to find a taxi. I surmised that a fourth phase was about to begin, though I had never seen more than the beginning of it: the phase in which he cruised the Brooklyn waterfront in search of compliant sailors and was often beaten up or jailed. Something in my own life had ended. Hart and I had been close friends for seven years, but now he was not so much a friend as something more distant, an object of care and apprehension. He was living now by the iron laws of another country.[4]

The far reaches of Crane's alcoholism are also the remote region of his homosexuality, "another country" that Cowley implicitly equates with death. Standing with the woman who will become his wife, ready to go to work in the offices of the *New Republic* the next day, Cowley watches Crane leave, and feels something in his own life ending.

Cabbing downtown, Crane passes out of Cowley's life for good; his fourth "phase" led this time to Mexico, and to death. But even as he parts ways with Cowley, becoming something "more distant" than a friend, Crane moves into metaphor, legend, and memoirs, including such as Cowley's. The anecdote reminds us that Crane vanished from the lives of his literary friends only to reappear, almost at once, in their writing. Kenneth Burke was right: people *would* love Hart when he was dead. The grieving, sometimes guilty love of Crane's friends called him back to them repeatedly. Haunting the living, the question Crane posed was frequently reduced to his death. Why did Crane do it? What did he mean? Was it inevitable? These questions motivate the many published tellings of Crane's suicide. Cowley, Frank, Winters, Matthew Josephson, Munson, and Tate—each of them told the story of Crane's leap to death one or more times in essays on Crane. There is "The Last Days of Hart Crane," the personal memoir by Peggy Baird Cowley, Malcolm Cowley's first wife and Crane's friend and lover during the final months of his life, with whom Crane was traveling to New York at the time of his suicide. In addition, Crane's three biographers—Philip Horton, Brom Weber, and John Unterecker—offer their own accounts. Of these, Unterecker's is the most elaborate. It is a palimpsest made of several other accounts: the memoir by Peggy Baird Cowley; notes made by Henry Allen Moe, secretary of the Guggenheim Foundation, from his interview with "Mr. M. Seckendorf, Passenger Traffic Manager of the Ward Line," who had read to Moe "part of the report of the Master of the 'Orizaba' " (Unterecker, *Voyager*, 758); two postcards written by Crane and received after his death; and finally a letter from Morton Dauwen Zabel, editor of *Poetry*, telling Crane that *Poetry* had not received the poem he said he had submitted, "The Broken Tower"—a letter Crane himself never received. The proliferation of documents does not bring Crane closer, of course; instead, in Unterecker's effort to find final answers, one feels the mounting confusion of a frustrated search.

Fittingly, the document Unterecker produces on the next-to-last page of his book tells us nothing about Crane; it is simply about looking for him. It is a letter by Moe (not the first he wrote) requesting, in fact imploring a woman who knew Crane in Mexico, named Mary Doherty, to provide Moe with documentation of the days leading up to Crane's death. As he asks Doherty for a copy of Crane's will, Moe's voice strains: "Hart Crane on a certain night, I understand, dictated to you his 'will.' A copy of that document should be here (or elsewhere)—sealed, if you like—with a bald account of what happened that night. There were other epic happenings. What were they? What happened? What was said? Who was concerned? Facts, facts, facts" (quoted by Unterecker, *Voyager*, 772). Moe, Unterecker's surrogate, struggled to recover Crane's epic intentions, his will. But Doherty, whether or not she could help, did not reply.

The compulsion to represent Crane's death reappears in Unterecker's introduction to the edition of Crane's poems edited by Marc Simon. At the end of his biographical essay, Unterecker furnishes another, last document—a letter written to Unterecker thirty-five years after the event by a passenger on the *Orizaba* who witnessed Crane's suicide. Gertrude E. Vogt was among those passengers on deck just before noon "waiting to hear the results of the ship's pool" when Crane, looking "generally battered" in "pajamas and topcoat," walked to the railing, "took off his coat, folded it neatly over the railing . . . raised himself on his toes, and then dropped back," before vaulting over the rail and into the sea (Crane,

Poems, xxxvii–xxxviii). Vogt, enjoying the ship's scheduled entertainment within a sociable and presumably heterosexual group, watched in suspended disbelief as the battered homosexual, after a moment's urbane preparation, took his life. She was the representative of a society Crane left behind—of the friends Crane made onlookers, and the onlookers he made friends. But Vogt's account (aside from the question of its reliability) really tells one nothing that one did not know; it is a ritual retelling, placed there on the threshold of *The Poems of Hart Crane* for ceremonial purposes. As such, it comments on the general function of the many narratives of Crane's death: it consecrates and authenticates the poems; it explains why Crane cannot explain them himself; and, as an effort to find and fix the poet's body, and thereby specify his "point of view," it is an effort to solve the central interpretive problem of the poems. In a variety of ways, I think, all readings of Crane, including mine, repeat such a gesture. In the final section of this book I want to examine one further attempt—Robert Lowell's attempt—to recover Crane and make him speak. As we will see, the words that Lowell finds for him are Tate's.

IV.

BEYOND MODERNISM

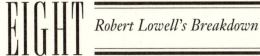# EIGHT *Robert Lowell's Breakdown*

THE NATIONAL LIFE SUFFERS FROM THE ILLS OF A SPLIT
PERSONALITY.

—Philip Rahv, "Paleface and Redskin"[1]

In 1959, the year in which he published *Life Studies*,
Robert Lowell recalled his first, unannounced arrival at Benfolly, the antebellum house Tate's brother Ben had bought for him and Gordon in
Clarksville, Tennessee. It seemed to Lowell that his career had really
begun there. "My head was full of Miltonic, vaguely piratical ambitions.
My only anchor was a suitcase, heavy with bad poetry. I was brought to
earth by my bumper mashing the Tates' frail agrarian mailbox post. Getting out to disguise the damage, I turned my back on their peeling, pillared house. I had crashed the civilization of the South."[2] When we add
that, before advancing any further on the Tates, Lowell stopped to mark
the territory with a piss,[3] we have recovered a ludicrous but instructive
episode in the transmission of modernism. The young man carried with
him "piratical ambitions," his ponderous, free-verse juvenalia, and a car
(no doubt manufactured in the North) that casually battered the mailbox
of this Southern Agrarian outpost. Lowell's feeling, in retrospect, is of
having conquered effortlessly and by accident. Yet the Southerners could
plausibly construe this "strangest visitation" as a victory of their own.
"Imagine," Gordon urged a friend, "a Lowell (yes, the poor boy's mother
is a Cabot)—imagine one coming all the way from Boston to sit at Southern feet" (Gordon and Wood, *Southern Mandarins*, 209).

This was April 1937. The twenty-year-old poet had left behind him
Harvard and the Cabots and the Lowells to pursue his study of literature
under Tate and Ransom.[4] He was following the advice of Ford Madox
Ford who, without informing the Tates, his hosts there, had invited
Lowell to visit him in Tennessee.[5] It is possible that Ford did not expect

211

Lowell to take the invitation literally. Certainly Gordon and Tate did not expect him to when they told Lowell that if he wanted to stay, he would have to pitch a tent on the lawn—which, since he was both an obedient and a contrary young man, Lowell proceeded to do. The simple literal-mindedness of these gestures is telling, it seems to me, since the same kind of literalism would make Lowell both an obedient and a contrary student of Tate. For Lowell began his career by systematically, literal-mindedly appropriating the rigorous verse forms and cultural pessimism in Tate's work, writing poems that satisfied his mentor's demand for symbolic art that could stand apart from and above personal experience. But Lowell later rejected Tate's teaching by turning to events in his own life, and above all to the ordeal of his psychological breakdown, in order to create a new kind of poetry, this one charged with the literal authority of fact. Lowell had destroyed Tate's symbols and discovered his own experience.

Or so Lowell came to understand his own career, and to narrate its progress. As I will suggest, the story that Lowell told—of generational struggle and succession, of obstruction, breakdown, and breakthrough—provided him and his readers with a compelling way to organize and interpret the relations between Anglo-American poetry of the 1920s and the 1950s. According to this story, the initial, experimental authenticity of modernism had by the middle of the century been supplanted by a narrowly technical practice, sapping poetry of its creative vigor and its adversarial force; and so it remained for a new generation of poets to undo the restrictions on them (as the modernists had once undone the restrictions of genteel culture) by putting the violence of their lives into their work. This is an effective story, and it has been applied to poets as different from each other and from Lowell as Sylvia Plath and Allen Ginsberg. I want to challenge its historical accuracy by showing how it naturalizes—or reproduces as fact—the poetic fictions it is meant to explain.[6] In particular, with Lowell's example before us, I want to question two closely related notions: one, that Lowell broke with Tate and the New Critical poetics he espoused in the process of writing *Life Studies*; two, that this poetic breakthrough was a result of Lowell's psychological breakdown.

I should emphasize at once that I am not concerned with anything like a clinical diagnosis of Lowell's mental states. My interest is in the ways in which Lowell's "breakdown" could be called a literary construction, a fiction created at a certain moment in Lowell's career with important consequences for both Lowell and his readers. Of course, I do not believe Lowell's madness had no extraliterary content; I believe that that extraliterary content has been mystified in ways it behooves one to understand. "No aberration can effect a real separation" between culture and the individual, Lionel Trilling insists; "even the forms that madness takes, let alone the way in which madness is evaluated, are controlled by the culture in which it occurs" (Trilling, *Beyond Culture*, xii). With Trilling's formulation in mind I will try to resist and reflect on the tendency of Lowell's critics to understand his "breakdown" as a transformative event—not only in Lowell's life, but in literary history. I will argue that Lowell's "breakdown," where it has been used to indicate and interpret historical change, reduces the passage between modern and postmodern poetry to a single moment of transformation in the same way that it reduces the history of Lowell's mental illness to a single moment of collapse.

At issue in these matters is the meaning of the impasse at which Crane and Tate, in their different ways, both arrived. If, as I have been proposing, modernism in American poetry is driven in contrary directions toward the two forms of stalemated silence we confront in Crane's leap and Tate's writer's block, what lies beyond it? As the focus for the final essay in this book, Lowell might be expected to provide a dialectical synthesis, that third term in which the opposition between modernism's "twin shadowed halves" is at last overcome. This promise is consistent with the self-definition of a poet who, by uniting the intense experience he associated with Crane and the intellectual discipline he saw in Tate, presented himself as the central, "complete" poet that neither Crane nor Tate was able to become. My claim, however, is that Lowell recapitulated, rather than resolved, the opposition we have been examining, and that his historical importance does not lie in his ability to move "beyond" modernism, but in his inability to do so.

Lowell's story should therefore be retold in this way. Lowell redefined his poetry during the 1950s in opposition to the "official" modernism of his mentor, a modernism that had by this time become strongly identified with the academic elites and private foundations that sanctioned it. In his rebellion Lowell reached back in time to unofficial or devalued modernisms, including the examples of Crane and William Carlos Williams, while also reaching out to his excitingly disreputable contemporaries, the Beats.[7] Yet Lowell could not recover the utopian energies sacrificed in the course of American poetry's integration into Cold War professional life; the divided features of modernism's "Janus face" were reassembled in Lowell's poetry, not made whole. Think of photographs of Lowell: he always has a tie on, and it is never tied on straight. The camera finds him smoking in his study, or standing in a circle of distinguished literary men (all of them in ties and jackets), but he looks off elsewhere—absently; he is really somewhere else. These images of Lowell manifest the tension between personal rebellion and institutional conformity at the center of his work. That tension made Lowell an icon of the "split personality"—of the division between "paleface" refinement and "redskin" vitality—that critics like Philip Rahv found in American culture as a whole.[8] Lowell's ambivalent relation to his own professional stature is part of the symbolic meaning, the peculiarly wide public resonance of Lowell's personal illness, schizophrenia.

And the resonance of Lowell's private suffering was once felt to be very wide indeed. As Irvin Ehrenpreis explained in 1963, "The course of [Lowell's] life became the analogue of the life of his era; the sufferings of the poet became a mirror of the sufferings of whole classes and nations."[9] Lowell's high social privilege, which was part of his representativeness for Ehrenpreis, would disqualify him from the same status for most readers today: at the very least, it is no longer plausible to call the postwar period "The Age of Lowell." That it ever *was* possible to do so remains, however, a fact of large interest, as this final chapter is intended to suggest. My view is that Lowell can be instructively discussed as a "representative," culturally central poet precisely because he set out to become such a figure, and because he made his way by permitting other persons to make him the poet *they* wanted him to become. Everyone knows that Lowell had a great influence on many poets; it is less often observed how many poets had a great influence on Lowell. Indeed, Lowell's writing is derivative in this incontestable and overwhelming sense: it continually uses other writers' words. Lowell formalized this principle of composition in *Imitations* (his controversial volume of translations); he later carried it to a limit in verse transcriptions of the letters of his second wife, Elizabeth Hardwick, after he had abandoned her. It is possible to view Lowell's rough disregard for the conventional boundaries between one's own words and someone else's as a form of the psychosis that sometimes made him speak and act as if he really *were* someone else. But I would prefer to see Lowell's drive to claim other speakers' voices for his own as a sign of the "piratical ambitions" that led him to pitch a tent on the lawn of Benfolly in 1937. Let me return to that episode now in order to explore the education Lowell gained from Tate. At the same time, of course, Tate had something to gain from Lowell.

Tate immediately impressed upon his student the absolute importance of technical competence in traditional versification. A good poem, Lowell learned, "had nothing to do with exalted feelings or being moved by the spirit. It was simply a piece of craftsmanship, an intelligible or *cognitive* object." Therefore Lowell dutifully "turned out grimly unromantic poems—organized, hard, and classical as a cabinet" (Lowell, *Collected Prose*, 59). These exercises were intended to imitate and confirm Tate's own rejection of romanticism in modern poetry. This included Crane's poetry of "exalted feelings," which Tate found deficient in the critical intelligence that "craftmanship" implied: by identifying his own technical rigor with a refusal of Crane's romantic vision, Tate was seeking a successor who would declare him the winner of this debate within modernism. Such is the circular logic by which Lowell was prepared to be recognized as the right heir for "the right kind of modernism." In the introduction to Lowell's first volume, *Land of Unlikeness*, Tate could point as if with surprise to an event so far removed from the merely coincidental that Tate had himself supervised it: "T. S. Eliot's recent prediction that we should see a return to formal and even intricate rituals and beliefs was coming true, before he made it, in the verse of Robert Lowell" (Tate, *Poetry Reviews*, 210).

The versification Lowell learned from Tate, passed on from one man to another, was in part a form of accreditation. Lowell had come to Tate for professional *training*, and he got it, as the "formal and even intricate metres and stanzas" in his first book amply testified. To this extent, the poems Tate taught Lowell to write exemplify the formalist, New Critical poetics that came to prominence in the decade after the war; they are the products of a method that would be distinctively suited to reproduction in the university. But Lowell's work has little of the elegance or ease usually associated with the university-based poetry of the 1950s. Rather, Lowell's versification was as "warped, fissured, strained, and terrific" as the hand-crafted black cabinet Tate exhibited, as an example of a well-wrought object, when Lowell first arrived at Benfolly. For when Lowell used traditional verse forms, he always did so for expressionistic ends: his willful performances, dramatizing self-imposed discipline, displayed a largeness of feeling by the level of force required to control it. As Randall Jarrell remarked about Lowell's poem "The Quaker Graveyard in Nantucket," "the coiling violence of its rhetoric, the harsh and stubborn intensity that accompanies all its verbs and verbals, the clustering stresses, learned from accentual verse, come from a man contracting every muscle, grinding his teeth together till his shut eyes ache."[10]

Lowell's clenched technique bears the burden of his fierce personal ambition. But Tate transmitted to Lowell, along with the mechanics of verse, an explicitly ideological struggle, and Lowell's verse bears this burden as well. When Tate and Lowell met, the Southern Agrarian project was all but defunct, and Tate, like Ransom, had turned his attention from politics and economics to literary criticism, as he worked to refine the New Critical doctrine of literary autonomy in "Tension in Poetry," "Narcissus as Narcissus," and other position papers. But the high formalism of this phase of Tate's thinking did not simply replace his anticapitalist and anticommunist polemics; rather, it absorbed and renewed those polemics on different grounds. Now Tate's primary enemies were Marxist literary critics, sociologists, and (in the words of the introduction to *Land of Unlikeness*) "the democratic poets who enthusiastically greet the advent of the slave-society" (Tate, *Poetry Reviews*, 211). Tate, as we have seen, argued that these parties relegated poetry to extrapoetic uses, according to the logic of utility permeating modern life. In response, Tate insisted that poetry be judged first by the received rules of its own making: preserved as a traditional craft, poetry could stand apart from popular taste and political interest, commerce and "causes." This is the premise of Ransom's fantasied "Institute of Literary Autonomy and Tradition." It is also the ascetic program of "Ode to the Confederate Dead"—a poem (not completed until 1937) in which Tate's defense of traditional society comes down to a defense of traditional verse forms.

In *Land of Unlikeness* and *Lord Weary's Castle*, Lowell used those verse forms in an attack on something as generalized as the state of civilization itself. In fact, once more literal-minded and fierce, Lowell pushed Tate's dedication to formal disciplines further than Tate was willing to commit himself by entering the Roman Catholic Church. Lowell took this step both on behalf of and in place of his teacher (whose protracted hesitation over conversion was so important to his marriage and to Gordon's later fiction). Catholicism was in this sense an obvious extension of Lowell's formalism; it is as if Eliot had *also* predicted that we should see a return to formal and even intricate rituals and beliefs. Significantly, Lowell's conversion entailed rebellion as well as conformity, since it was part of Lowell's rejection of his Episcopalian upbringing in Boston—the remaking of himself that Lowell undertook when he fought with his father, left Harvard, and drove south. But even as Lowell left his home behind, Tate made it newly valuable to him: Boston was Puritan, abolitionist, and haute bourgeois, the patrician center of nineteenth-century American culture, and Lowell himself was "part of a legend." As Gordon's pleasure in the "poor boy's" genealogy confirms, "the old deadweight of J. R. Lowell was now an asset. Here, like the battered Confederacy, he still lived and was history" (Lowell, *Collected Prose*, 59).

Tate's prolonged research into his own genealogy was nearing fruition in 1937 in *The Fathers*. To a man engrossed in the Civil War and its aftermath, Lowell's arrival would have been full of satisfying historical irony.

The North had come not only "to sit at Southern feet" but to recover its own culture there: Tate was teaching Lowell *who he was*, and Tate (not Harvard University) was in possession of the riches of English literary tradition, from Donne to Eliot. In this sense Lowell gave Tate a student (a privileged, Ivy League student) before Tate had any institution in which to profess; and the formalist training that Lowell received worked to accredit Tate as well as Lowell. That Tate was fully aware of this reciprocity is clear from his letter calling upon the Vanderbilt administration to prevent Ransom from moving to Kenyon: the decision of the "Lowell family of Boston and Harvard University" to send "one of its sons to Nashville to study poetry with Mr. Ransom" was the anecdotal evidence Tate gave of his friend's international stature.[11] But Lowell was more valuable to Ransom and Tate when they established themselves in the North (Ransom at Kenyon, Tate at Princeton and the University of Minnesota). The New Criticism offered institutional validation to Lowell, but it should be remembered that Lowell (the Puritan "legend") lent another kind of prestige to the New Criticism. *Lord Weary's Castle* won the Pulitzer Prize for 1946. Ransom, who virtually ceased to write poetry after the 1920s, did not win a comparable national prize for poetry until the 1950s; Tate did not receive such a prize until 1976.[12]

When, therefore, Lowell pitched his tent at Benfolly, a complex exchange took place. Lowell had claimed Crane's vacated position in the Tates' household: he could retain it if he put himself forward not as a rival or peer, but as a student and son. So Lowell opened himself fully to Tate's influence. As David Bromwich concisely describes it, "Tate may almost be said to have created Lowell. He gave him not only advice, friendship, and an idea of modernity, but a complete set of mannerisms to study, down to the very inflections of the Agrarian-Eliotic accent which Lowell picked up early and never wore out."[13] For his part Lowell gave Tate a student, a son, and an heir—a poet who was capable of reproducing the sound of his own voice. But as Tate should have expected from a foster son who knocked his real father down before he put himself up for adoption, Tate would become the object of Lowell's rebellion as well. In the course of that reversal, Lowell thrust upon Tate demonic versions of himself, turning against his teacher with a maniacal performance of the role Tate had created for him.

The convulsive events of Lowell's first manic breakdown dramatize the process I have in mind. In 1949, Lowell summoned Tate, by telegram, to join him in New York "to fight evil."[14] When Tate refused, Lowell took the train to see him and Gordon in Chicago, where Tate was teaching for the term; Lowell had "crashed" their lives once again. Tate described his protégé's state of mind in the following way. Tate refers to Lowell as "Cal," a nickname derived, according to different stories, from either Caliban or Caligula: "Cal is here, and in 24 hours has flattened us out. I do not know what we can do. . . . He constantly embraces us, and asks us to stand by him, since he is weak."[15] Accounts differ about what happened next. According to the most spectacular, Lowell decided that Tate should repent of his sins and reported his adulteries to Gordon; Lowell then picked up his diminutive mentor and suspended him from a second-floor window—while he recited "Ode to the Confederate Dead." Whether or not this last scene took place, the police came and handcuffed Lowell as he shouted obscenities from the windows of Tate's and Gordon's home. Afterward, Tate could authoritatively reflect: "[Lowell] has a purification mania, which frequently takes homocidal form."[16]

But Lowell's literary enactment of this attack on Tate is more famous, and famous precisely for effecting a "purification" of Lowell's style. There has long been a consensus among critics of this period that Lowell achieved "his own voice" in the middle of his career specifically by abandoning the traditional prosody, religious symbols, and heroic rhetoric that Tate had taught him how to wield: in the words of one critic, "The voice speaking in *Life Studies* is that of Lowell himself, off his stilts."[17] This consensus holds that Lowell made a significant departure from his mentor; that in the autobiographical project of *Life Studies*, in particular, Lowell discovered a vital and liberating alternative to the institutionalized formalism of the New Critics; and that Lowell thus established a definitively new, more "open" practice in American poetry.

The consensus I am describing draws on the psychoanalytic thematics of *Life Studies* itself in order to narrate American poetry's passage beyond modernism as a story of Oedipal violence in which fresh energies were released from confinement in old forms. This understanding of Lowell and his period revives the rhetoric of liberation that Tate, for example, once used to promote modernist poetry, and it does so deliberately, with the suggestion that postwar poetry restored the modernity of modernism. James E. B. Breslin provides a clear example: "At this moment of crisis, poetry once again became disruptive—critical of its culture, of its immediate past, of itself; by way of repudiating orthodox modernism, American poetry once again became modern, 'of the present.' "[18] This statement is a general report on American poetry in the late 1950s (Breslin discusses Ginsberg, Frank O'Hara, and others), but it explicitly draws on Lowell's own generalizations about the period. In particular, the model for Breslin's statement is an interview with Frederick Seidel in which Lowell complained about the excessive concern with technical compe- tence among poets of "my generation." Their work, Lowell charged, had "become too much something specialized that can't handle much experi- ence. It's become a craft, purely a craft, and there must be some break- through back into life" (Lowell, *Collected Prose*, 244). Here, of course, the meaning of "craft" is pejorative; it is a mark of professional specializa- tion—a symbol of the institutional walls that must be broken down or through before poetry can recover direct contact with "life." But by 1961, when he formulated the problem in this way, the author of *Life Studies* had already made the kind of "breakthrough" that he claimed his generation of poets needed to make as a whole. The result of Lowell's analysis is to make his own career representative—which Breslin affirms when he pre- sents *Life Studies* as the paradigm for the rediscovery by Lowell's "genera- tion" of literature's origin in "life."

"I thought civilization was going to break down," Lowell remembered in another interview, "and instead *I* did."[19] This marvelously compact re- mark not only suggests that Lowell had to "break down" before he could see his private life as a subject capable of replacing the public subject Tate had given him ("I thought civilization was going to break down"); it sug- gests that the "breakthrough" Lowell made at this pivotal moment—what he discovered for poetry—*was exactly his breakdown itself*. If *Lord Weary's Castle* pushed the apocalyptic theme of "the right kind of modernism" to its limit, *Life Studies* found a way to go on, then, by narrating the break- down not of tradition but of the individual talent; and Tate's conviction that "our culture is dissolving" was replaced by Lowell's startled recogni- tion of his own mental collapse. The analogy linking psychological and literary history here, which allows us to understand Lowell's "break- through" as a function of his breakdown, is essential to the story *Life Studies* tells, and it is essential to the story critics tell about "confessional poetry" generally. Experience authenticates poetry in this analogy, and suffering authenticates experience. Although the life Lowell recovered in *Life Studies* remained something to be studied, not simply lived, it was his own, and it presented itself to readers as fact.

Yet the facts of Lowell's breakdown were never available to readers apart from Lowell's fictions. The point becomes clear, I think, when we consider Breslin's sense of the structure—or plot—of *Life Studies* as a whole. For example, this is Breslin's explanation of the movement be- tween the first and second parts of the book: "The four poems of Part I describe cultural and historical disintegration in predetermined forms and all of these poems were written *before* Lowell's breakdown; in Part II Lowell begins again with the anecdotal prose of '91 Revere Street' dramatically breaking down the established boundaries of the literary—by moving toward the literal and contingent, the *data* of his own life" (Breslin, *From Modern to Contemporary*, 131). On one level, Breslin points to a thematic movement from cultural to personal "disintegration"; on another level, to a technical movement from "predetermined forms" to "anecdotal prose" (which in this scheme also represents a kind of disintegration). By implication, at least, Breslin sees these events as analogous both to each other and to the breakdown Lowell suffered between the composition of the texts arranged in these two parts of *Life Studies*. The suggestion is that Lowell's breakdown forced him to face his psychological condition in writing; this new subject required a new, "non-predetermined" form—prose; and in this way Lowell was able to break down "the established boundaries of the literary."

It might be objected that "91 Revere Street" did so little to test those boundaries that it was first published in the *Partisan Review*. Breslin and others have felt otherwise, I imagine, because family history in *Life Studies* presents itself as a ready metaphor for literary history. In Breslin's case, this means that the progress from one part of *Life Studies* to the next is seen to point to events actually going on in Lowell's life; and the book's progress from verse to prose (a sign of the formal direction in which American poetry generally moved from the 1950s to the 1960s) is coordinated with a particular psychotic break. This is a misleading idea, because it suggests by omission that the cycles of mania and depression Lowell suffered *before* the one Breslin mentions did not happen or did not matter. As a result, Breslin's interpretation converts a series of traumatic episodes into a single, narratively accessible event. Behind this appeal to a single moment of conclusive psychological change is the pressure of a specific literary historical framework. It shows Breslin's desire to see *Life Studies* as a conclusive break with Lowell's prior ways of writing, and to understand this break in terms of "the *data*" of Lowell's life—facts Breslin then imagines according to the fictive "data" *Life Studies* itself provides.

Breslin's use of Lowell's biography indicates one way *Life Studies* allows one to interpret the link between Lowell's mania and poetry. This is not the only way. It is true, for example, that a large portion of *Life Studies* was written after Lowell was hospitalized at the Payne Whitney Clinic in New York City in 1954, and that such famous poems as "My Last Afternoon with Uncle Devereux Winslow" were initially begun as part of the prose memoirs from which "91 Revere Street" derives. But it is also true that

Lowell was hospitalized before he finished his previous book, *The Mills of the Kavanaughs*, and that Lowell was again hospitalized after he wrote the poems about his family in *Life Studies*. Breslin views the family poems as evidence that Lowell had passed through a breakdown; Tate, as we will see, viewed the same poems as a sign that Lowell was *approaching* a breakdown. In a sense, Lowell's mania justified both points of view. But it is *Life Studies* that made Lowell's mania meaningful, and not the other way around.

Struggle over the meaning of Lowell's manic-depressive cycles has always been bound up with struggle over the meaning of his poetry. In an autobiographical fragment, Lowell called the cause of his hospitalization in 1954 "an attack of pathological enthusiasm" (Lowell, *Collected Prose*, 346). This category is potentially broad and suggestive enough to describe not only the delusions and physical violence that led to Lowell's confinement and alienated Tate, but also Lowell's conversion and his refusal to serve in the armed forces during the Second World War—actions that were strongly connected to the Catholicism and pacifism of *Lord Weary's Castle*. I am not saying that Lowell was always—or merely—sick; my argument is that the religious, political, and literary passions of Lowell's culture entered his "enthusiasm" and gave it shape, making his madness a nightmarish recapitulation and distortion of the roles in which he otherwise lived his life and wrote poetry. For this reason, Lowell's mania forced those who saw themselves as his literary allies, teachers, or peers to confront the features of the poet whom they knew and admired in fragmentary and caricatured forms. At stake was the authority with which they had invested him, and the implications of Lowell's poetic claims to represent them and *their* experience.

Consider the episode that culminated shortly after Lowell left Chicago in April 1949. Gordon and Tate put their guest on a train to Indiana, where he planned to visit the fiction writer Peter Taylor. Lowell's drafts for *Life Studies* record the depths of the madness he fell into next:

> The night before I was locked up I ran about the streets of Bloomington Indiana crying out against devils and homosexuals. I believed I could stop cars and paralyze their forces by merely standing in the middle of the highway with my arms outspread. Each car carried a long rod above its tail-light, and the rods were adorned with diabolic Indian or Voodoo signs. Bloomington stood for Joyce's hero and for Christian regeneration. Indiana stood for the evil, unexorcised, aboriginal Indians. I suspected I was a reincarnation of the Holy Ghost, and had become homicidally hallucinated.[20]

It is an extraordinary scene. The charismatic Catholic prophet, schooled in modernist texts and New Critical protocols, is able to discover Leopold Bloom *and* the Resurrection in "Bloomington." He stands in a place of public circulation, as the author of *The Bridge* wished to, with "arms outspread." But Lowell's gesture is not, like Crane's, intended to embrace modernity; it is intended to ward it off—or, in the form of the automobiles roaring around him, to bring it to a halt. Those cars are the dehumanized face of American mass culture; at the same time, they are "the evil, unexorcised, aboriginal Indians"—the red men whose interestingly phallic rear antennae link them in Lowell's mind to "devils and homosexuals." All of which is crazy, of course. But Lowell's madness formulated its grotesque utterances out of the literary vocabulary—the symbols, ideas, and anxieties—that he had acquired along with his professional training in modernism.

The episode that ended in these hallucinations began with another kind of red scare; and at this earlier stage, Lowell's friends could not firmly distinguish between his delusions and their own beliefs. Lowell had spent the previous winter at Yaddo, the artist's colony in Saratoga Springs, New York, working on the manuscript that became *The Mills of the Kavanaughs*. That February the *New York Times* printed a report that Agnes Smedley, a journalist, socialist, and longtime guest of Yaddo, was under suspicion as having been a spy for the Soviet Union. A week later the Army issued a retraction. At about the same time, though, FBI agents visited Yaddo and questioned the director, Elizabeth Ames, and two guests, Edward Maisel and Elizabeth Hardwick. The FBI's questions centered on the politics of Smedley and other former Yaddo guests. Hardwick and Maisel discussed the interviews with Flannery O'Connor and Lowell, the only other guests at the time, and the group together resolved that "Mrs. Ames is somehow deeply and mysteriously involved in Mrs. Smedley's political activities." This sentence is Lowell's, and it comes from the massive transcript of the courtroom proceedings that he and the others caused the Yaddo Corporation to hold. Lowell stipulated and directed the form of these bizarre proceedings, during which he presented charges on behalf of the other guests and then examined them himself. "I think two days will be necessary for a full hearing of this," Lowell said at the outset, "and perhaps a meeting again at New York, on a Saturday or Sunday." Yet Lowell could produce no more evidence of Ames's betrayal of Yaddo's ideals than Hardwick's intuition—"that at times there is a discrepancy between Mrs. Ames' surface behavior and her true feelings"—and Ames's own unmysterious admission: "I sometimes do not dare to say what I think."[21]

The political hysteria Lowell participated in at Yaddo was fully sanctioned by the United States government and the national press. Even Lowell's heterogeneous, seemingly arbitrary set of enemies—Communists, homosexuals, and "Indians"—were connected in the dream life of Cold War movies.[22] Yet it remains striking that the extraordinary zeal with which Lowell undertook the role of anticommunist crusader would only later be recognized by his friends as pathological behavior. The attack on Ames did not go uncontested: after the meeting of the Yaddo board, a letter with more than fifty signatures in support of Ames put an end to the affair (Hamilton, *Robert Lowell*, 151–52). But Lowell's admirers could still maintain that the charges against Ames were motivated by the disinterested principles that a few months before had led Lowell, Tate, and their fellow judges to give the Bollingen Prize to Ezra Pound, despite the poet's wartime broadcasts on fascist radio. The intensity of Lowell's "enthusiasm" at Yaddo, however misdirected, seemed continuous with the prophetic indignation of *Lord Weary's Castle*.

That is the argument Robert Fitzgerald made in a letter to George Santayana about the Yaddo affair. The case against Ames, Fitzgerald wrote, was "vaporous," but Lowell had determined "to strike hard, and there came into play an essential quality of his nature: the aggressive power that to the gentle must seem harsh and has indeed found, in his poems, violent images of strife: the harpoon that rips the sperm-whale's midriff into rags, the flintrock broken upon the father's skull."[23] That is, Fitzgerald turned to "The Quaker Graveyard in Nantucket" and "Rebellion" to interpret Lowell's actions: he needed the poet of *Lord Weary's Castle* to make sense of Lowell's mania; and he needed to defend that poet in the face of Lowell's discrediting actions.

Fitzgerald was struggling, above all, to preserve Lowell's authority as a Roman Catholic poet. Lowell's faith had lapsed in the late 1940s along with his poetic inspiration. After he left Yaddo, Lowell visited Fitzgerald in Connecticut and announced his return to the Church; by the end of the same week, Lowell had gone on a retreat with Trappist monks. Fitzgerald knew Lowell was psychologically disturbed, and he had no wish to pursue his prosecution of Ames. Yet Fitzgerald, as a poet and a deeply faithful Catholic, wanted to honor Lowell's claims "that God spoke through him and that his impulses were inspired." The case was sufficiently important to motivate Fitzgerald not only to write to Santayana, but also to send copies of his letter to Eliot, Tate, Ransom, and twelve other poets, fiction writers, and critics.[24] Not all of its recipients were sympathetic to Lowell or to each other, but the letter put the defense of Lowell's actions at the center of a distinguished circle of authors, a circle that was organized at that moment directly *around* Lowell. The letter's tacit assumption was that Lowell's reputation mattered to their own.[25]

After treatment, Lowell wrote to Fitzgerald acknowledging his efforts on Lowell's behalf, but Lowell's renewal of faith had passed with his mania; and the Catholic poet that Fitzgerald had sought to defend had all but ceased to exist. The poet that Lowell was in the process of becoming would not be fully evident until *Life Studies* was published in 1959. By that time Lowell had replaced his Roman Catholicism with existentialism, as his commentary on the spiritual drama of "Skunk Hour" makes explicit: "This is the dark night. I hoped my readers would remember John of the Cross's poem. My night is not gracious, but secular, puritan, and agnostic. Somewhere in my mind was a passage from Sartre or Camus about reaching some point of final darkness where the one free act is suicide" (Lowell, *Collected Prose*, 226). The extremity of Lowell's position, the "final darkness" he attains in "Skunk Hour," is arrived at specifically by replacing St. John of the Cross with Sartre, and "The Dark Night of the Soul" with a dark night in Maine. It is not that Catholicism ceased to be important to Lowell's poetry, but that the poet of *Life Studies* generated new authority by abandoning it. In *Lord Weary's Castle*, Catholicism gave meaning to Lowell's formal discipline. By the time Lowell wrote "Beyond the Alps," the first poem in *Life Studies*, the Roman Catholic Church was merely something to get "beyond," an institution. Having thrown off its doctrines, Lowell stood alone in the dark knowledge that "the one free act is suicide." This is the point of demystification "Skunk Hour" defines as breakdown:

> I myself am hell;
> nobody's here—
>
> only skunks, that search
> in the moonlight for a bite to eat.

(Lowell, Selected Poems, 96)

Understandably, Tate felt that Lowell had rejected his teaching. The ensuing conflict not only resembled a family quarrel; it specifically centered on Lowell's family poems. "*All* the poems about your family . . . are *bad*," Tate told Lowell, and they were bad (both aesthetically unsatisfactory and naughty) because they lacked the "formal ordering of highly intractable materials" that marked Lowell's "fine poems in the past." Tate's advice was severe and direct:

I do not think you should publish them. You didn't ask me whether you think they ought to be published, but I put the matter from this point of view to underline my anxiety about them. . . . The poems are composed of unassimilated details, terribly intimate, and coldly noted, which might well have been transferred from the notes for your autobiography without change. . . . Quite bluntly, these details, presented *in causerie* and at random, are of interest only to you. They are, of course, of great interest to me because I am one of your oldest friends. But they have no public or literary interest.[26]

To others, Tate claimed that the loosening of Lowell's prosodic structures and his immersion in family history were signs of the mounting excitement and loss of control typical of Lowell's psychotic behavior. Tate's alarm, though, was not confined to the free-verse poems about Lowell's family. On his own copy of "A Mad Negro Soldier Confined at Munich," a dramatic monologue in rhymed quatrains in which Lowell's GI exclaims, "Oh mama, mama, like a trolley pole / sparking at contact, her electric shock—the power-house!" (Lowell, *Selected Poems*, 58), Tate wrote in bewilderment or disgust, "author unknown."[27]

By thus disowning Lowell, Tate refused to acknowledge the author who was created through Lowell's identification with such figures as "A Mad Negro Soldier," the "thoroughbred mental cases" in McLean Hospital in Massachusetts, or "*Murder Incorporated's* Czar Lepke" in the West Street jail in New York City. What Tate did not foresee was that Lowell's new definition of himself as an author whose suffering had bound him to these social outcasts would be of *considerable* "public or literary interest." In fact, as the extraordinary success of *Life Studies* and then *For the Union Dead* indicates, Lowell had created a hero who would be celebrated by his society precisely for his suffering. This is the scapegoat figure Ian Hamilton memorializes at the end of his biography of Lowell by quoting Edgar's last lines from *King Lear* ("we that are young / Shall never see so much, nor live so long") beside William Empson's comment on the play: "The scapegoat who has collected all this wisdom for us is viewed at the end with a sort of hushed envy, not I think really because he has become wise but because the general human desire for experience has been so glutted in him; he has been through everything" (Hamilton, *Robert Lowell*, 474).[28] It was this poet who had "been through everything" who emerged from *Life Studies*. He stood for no general system of belief—he was not, in that sense, "wise"; he had simply "collected" in the story of his own life "the general human desire for experience."

It was of course Lowell "off his stilts," speaking from his experience as a particular, historical individual, who moved his readers in this way. Yet the type of hero one encounters in *Life Studies* was already securely established in Cold War culture *as a type*. Indeed, this hero is at the center of a plot so common in American fiction of the period that Richard Ohmann has given it a generic name: "the illness story" (Ohmann, *Politics of Letters*, 68–91).[29] As a rule, this plot is treated in a realist mode. It focuses on an individual (typically but not always white, educated, and male) whose questioning or rejection of approved professional and familial roles leads to a psychological crisis in which he passes through intensive self-examination toward a tentative recovery. In some versions, "the illness story" raises the possibility that the social order is unhealthy ("I thought civilization was going to break down"), but it moves toward a recognition that, in fact, the hero is ("and instead *I* did"). Recovery, when it occurs, takes the form of a personal adjustment—whether cynical, comic, or stoic—to "the way things are."

Persuasively, I think, Ohmann argues that this plot points to a common "structure of feeling" among the men and women who "wrote, published, read, and preserved" the writing in question—the literary culture, centered in New York City, that included Lowell's readership too. This "structure of feeling" reflected the discrepancy between the idealized, individual freedoms these intellectuals believed to be their right and the realities of competition, conformity, and personal powerlessness they faced in everyday life. For "the illness story" exposed the fault lines in the ideology of a social class that felt itself to be living in an era "beyond ideology." Essential to the self-image of this class was the high estimation of its own techniques and expertise. These were experientially based alternatives to the "abstract" theories of both the Left and the Right—tools that, in the hands of skeptical, realistic professionals, could resolve social conflict and enable Americans to pursue the satisfactions of private life. This was an impossible promise: intellectuals could not resolve conflicts crucially rooted in the occupational and educational hierarchies from which their own skills and status derived. "Yet myth, ideology, and experience assured the professional-managerial class that no real barriers would prevent personal satisfaction, so it was easy to nourish the suspicion that any perceived lack was one's own fault. If unhappy, one must be personally maladjusted, perhaps even neurotic" (Ohmann, *Politics of Letters*, 83).

This generic plot roughly informs the "plot" of *Life Studies* as critics such as Breslin interpret it. This is clear in the movement of the volume as a whole from the public concerns of "Beyond the Alps" to the private setting of, say, "Man and Wife." It is equally clear in the movement from social to psychological observation within poems such as "Skunk Hour"; that is, poems in which the poet's "outer" world is revealed as a mirror or frame or backdrop for his "inner" one. The conceptual priority of the latter is suggested by the fact that the first part of "Skunk Hour," which situates the poet's solitary anguish in the decay of a particular community, was actually the *last* part of the poem to be written (Lowell, *Collected Prose*, 228). And even that initial representation of the social world is constituted on the model of the psychological one, insofar as the Oedipal triangle remains visible behind the three characters assembled at the start of the poem—hermit heiress, summer millionaire, and fairy decorator.[30] Lowell's psychological experience is a structuring principle even when his poems open out onto "the suffering of whole classes and nations." It is a kind of bedrock, and it puts Lowell in touch with the essential meanings of experience, "beyond ideology."

But it is also because Lowell values "experience" in this way that *Life Studies* keeps faith with Tate's teaching. Lowell helps us to see why this is the case in the transcript of a talk he gave between the publication of *Life Studies* and *For the Union Dead*. Lowell is speaking here about the ideas he gained from his teachers in the late 1930s:

> We believed in form, . . . and for some reason we were very much against the Romantics. We would say that the ideal poet is Shakespeare, who is not a poet of ideology but a poet of experience, and tragedy, and the sort of villains to us were people like Shelley—that he used much too much ideology—and Whitman, the prophet, who was formless. And one felt that what poetry could do was have nothing to do with causes . . . and something like Aristotle's purging by pity and terror, that of going through a catharsis, that that is what was suitable, rather than to persuade people to do anything better or to make the world better.[31]

In its efforts to inspire "pity and terror," rather than to urge others "to make the world better," *Life Studies* sustains Lowell's teachers' belief in experience and their suspicion of ideology. Indeed, when he arrives at that point "where the one free act is suicide," Lowell may be felt to achieve (however ironically) the autonomy Tate demanded for the artist. And the new, heightened realism of *Life Studies* preserves poetry from the "distorting" effect of political interest far more successfully than the manic anticommunism of the Yaddo fiasco. What is changed in *Life Studies* is that Tate's ideas have themselves taken on the status of "ideology," and the poets Tate saw as "villains" now represent "experience." For all of these reasons, *Life Studies* is not a break with "the right kind of modernism"; it is Lowell's canny attempt to appropriate for his work the "exalted feelings" that he found in a poet like Crane, and that Tate had labeled the *wrong* kind of modernism.

"Words for Hart Crane" is an important poem in *Life Studies* in this respect, because it makes explicit Lowell's intention to get outside the modernism of his teachers by identifying himself with a poet they had themselves cast out. Lowell of course knew that Crane had lived with Tate and Gordon before he did, and he knew how that arrangement had ended. Lowell plays on that story here by imagining Crane as a sexual predator, as a man who has been shut out of American society because of his sexuality, and who returns in vengeance to take victims of his own. The last sentence can be heard as a taunt directed to Tate and Gordon.

> When the Pulitzers showered on some dope
> or screw who flushed our dry mouths out with soap,
> few people would consider why I took
> to stalking sailors, and scattered Uncle Sam's
> phony gold-plated laurels to the birds.
> Because I knew my Whitman like a book,
> stranger in America, tell my country: I,
> *Catullus redivivus*, once the rage
> of the Village and Paris, used to play my role
> of homosexual, wolfing the stray lambs
> who hungered by the Place de la Concorde.
> My profit was a pocket with a hole.
> Who asks for me, the Shelley of my age,
> Must lay his heart out for my bed and board.
>
> (Lowell, *Selected Poems*, 65)

These words are "for" Crane because they pay him the homage of identification: Lowell is speaking on behalf of Crane with the suggestion that, if he could, Crane would speak on behalf of Lowell. This places Crane in the gallery of literary portraits in *Life Studies* that includes Ford Madox Ford, George Santayana, and Delmore Schwartz—authors Lowell calls on as allies and models. Lowell did not know Crane in life, as he did the others, but Crane was a poet he had studied. Lowell's notebooks from his apprenticeship to Tate show that he copied down poems by Crane that Winters had singled out for approval in *Primitivism and Decadence*: "Repose of Rivers," "Voyages II," and "Faustus and Helen II."[32] And there are significant, sometimes intriguing traces of *White Buildings* in *Lord Weary's Castle*. For example, Warner Berthoff has noticed the precision with which the final, stunning line of "The Quaker Graveyard in Nantucket"—"The Lord survives the rainbow of His will" (Lowell, *Selected Poems*, 10)—echoes a line in "Recitative"—"A wind abides the ensign of your will" (Crane, *Poems*, 25).[33] The borrowing is instructive. Although Lowell has neatly preserved the *form* of Crane's line (its meter, its rhyme, the closure that comes with its placement at the end of a stanza in "Recitative"), Lowell has replaced Crane's Whitmanian promise of comradeship with an Eliotic, neoorthodox statement about the triumph of the Father. As a result, Lowell's line and Crane's mean very nearly opposite things. It is as if Lowell had been attracted simply by the *sound* of Crane. I would add that he was attracted to Crane without knowing it, because the heroic meter Lowell took from Tate's work was itself so full of the sound of Crane. As we have seen, Tate's meter was derived from the pentameter poems (such as "Recitative") that Crane showed him in the mid-1920s; and for this reason, Lowell's early work is indirectly but markedly indebted to Crane. When Lowell tried to break away from Tate's meter (as he was doing in "Words for Hart Crane," a transitional poem that is both colloquial and impossible to say aloud), Lowell was giving up that part of his writing most closely linked with Crane's.

What Lowell believed he was gaining when he appealed to Crane was a way out of the institutional walls symbolized for him at that time by meter. Lowell was not alone in this expectation. Written at about the same time as the first book-length critical reevaluations of Crane's work were begun, "Words for Hart Crane" sought out the poet for many of the same reasons that academic critics turned to him in the mid-1950s and early 1960s. Crane was an obvious alternative to the Eliotic, High Church formalism that had come to power in the American university. Identifying with him allowed one to dissent from the New Critical consensus without, however, giving up one's stake in tradition, patriotism, or "form." Above all, I think, the utopian current in Crane's poetry preserved visions of sexual desire and aesthetic community unqualified by the constraints and inequalities of professional life. Of course, that utopian element took different forms for different readers. We have already considered Crane's unlikely reappearance as a proto-Catholic mystic in Gordon's *The Malefactors*. In other cases, Crane's name came to signify not self-division and "dissociation of sensibility" (as it once had) but imaginative wholeness and a single-minded dedication to art. Those are in fact the terms in which Lowell praised Crane's poetry in 1961: "All the chaos of his life missed getting sidetracked the way other poets' did, and he was less limited than any other poet of his generation. There was a fullness of experience. . . . The push of the whole man was there" (Lowell, *Collected Prose*, 261–62).

The Crane Lowell evoked at this moment was not an exponent of pentameter, then, but a poet who had put the "push" of his own life into his work. In many ways, this was simply the scandalous poet of anecdote—a poet rather more like Gordon's "Horne Watts" than Hart Crane. Certainly this Crane "sounds" much more as Tate or Gordon might have gossiped about him than as Crane presented himself, either in his poems or his letters. The sense in which these words have simply been assigned to Crane is reinforced by a knowledge of the poem's compositional history. In an earlier form—a form that, nonetheless, is very near the last—the poem had nothing at all to do with Crane; instead, it was called "(An) Enlishman [*sic*] Abroad (1950)." I refer to a curious text Lowell sent to Pound in 1954 with no message except a Latin salutation and his nickname after the poem, "Vale, Cal."[34] That text is, with relatively few differences of rhyme or meter, the sonnet later called "Words for Hart Crane." But "(An) Enlishman Abroad (1950)" is about (that is, "for") another, unnamed poet, and the references are adjusted to his nationality: for example, "Stranger from England" (not "stranger in America"), "must pay pound sterling" (not "must lay his heart out"). The oddly mechanical character of these and other changes Lowell made suggests that Crane's name and example were later fitted, a little roughly, into a formula Lowell had on hand.

It is significant that Lowell made Pound the recipient of the poem. In the spring of 1954 Pound was still confined in St. Elizabeths Hospital in Washington, D.C.; Lowell, writing to him from Europe, had entered the initial phase of a manic cycle that culminated in his incarceration in the military ward of a Munich hospital—in the course of which Lowell met the prototype for another dramatic monologue in *Life Studies*, "A Mad Negro Soldier Confined at Munich." In one sense, Lowell must have sent the poem to Pound as a joke at the expense of a particular English poet (for our purposes his identity is unimportant). Pound, vulgar, vital, and intolerant, was the right audience for a poem that was at this stage little more than a homophobic doodle. "(An) Enlishman Abroad (1950)" is a case of the comic verse Lowell sometimes sent to other literary men; it has less in common with, say, Browning's monologues than with Eliot's privately circulated, deliberately obscene and racist "Bolo" poems. Yet Lowell was at this transitional moment in his career working to revalue certain objects of male modernist laughter and scorn: Jews, gays, blacks.

These figures, appearing in *Life Studies* as the repressed truth of modernism, provided Lowell with a way to define a new public role for himself—that of the scapegoat, "the man who had been through everything." On the verge of a violent breakdown, Lowell addressed this poem to Pound in the belief that the "Englishman," Pound, and "Cal" himself were all outcasts, "strangers," and pariahs.

Crane too appears in these roles in "Words for Hart Crane." We find him here at the center of a fantasy of homosexual rape (he boasts of "stalking sailors," "wolfing the stray lambs"), but the poem is not intended as an attack on Crane; rather, Lowell is interested in the criminal glamor of Crane's position, and he wishes to absorb it for his own. In so doing Lowell moves from an act of homophobic scapegoating ("crying out against devils and homosexuals," as he once did in the streets of Bloomington) to an identification with the scapegoat. Crane, like Lowell's soldier, has been punished and empowered by his punishment. The power he gains in this way is the freedom to express a primitive appetite, unconstrained by middle-class heterosexual norms. (In "Man and Wife," the husband "hits the streets to cruise for prostitutes," not sailors.) According to the same logic, Whitman and Shelley, the "villains" in Tate's essays on Crane, return in this poem as exemplars of authentic experience, identified here (as in "A Mad Negro Soldier") with the sexual violence of a tough-talking male. "Words for Hart Crane" makes explicit, then, the homophobic logic of Tate's repudiation of Crane, both personal and literary, in a manner calculated to affront Tate. The poem brings Crane forward in the role in which he was cast, making him talk back to Tate in a language Lowell learned from Tate.

This Crane, a poet who was capable, Lowell felt, of putting "the chaos of his life" into his work, comes to Lowell as the demonic double of his mentor, enabling the author of *Life Studies* to establish a point of view from which the chaos of his own life can be made into poems. Not incidentally, Lowell's alliance with Crane enables him to mock the Pulitzer Prize–winning "dope" who wrote *Lord Weary's Castle*—the poet Tate had so labored to create. The freedom Lowell claims on these grounds is privative, and it reflects a cultural moment decisively different from the one Crane knew. Consider only the circumstances of Lowell's own professional success. For the large part of the postwar period, Lowell dominated an intensively institutionalized literary scene, a world that was the immediate outcome of ideological struggles of the kind Crane and Tate enacted; it is after all Lowell, not Crane, who had an opportunity to "scatter Uncle Sam's / phony gold-plaited laurels to the birds." The voice of a poet who is beyond or outside the boundaries of the New Critical discourse of the 1950s does indeed speak in *Life Studies*, but that poet, like Lowell's version of Crane, has been derived from Tate, and he can only speak in quotation marks. Tate claimed that the author of "A Mad Negro Soldier" was unknown to him. It has been one of my aims in this book to show that Tate wrote that poem himself.

Notes

PREFACE

1. Crane, *The Poems of Hart Crane*, ed. Marc Simon (New York, 1986), 25.

2. Tate's "Euthanasia" and Crane's translation of Laforgue called "Locutions des Pierrots" appeared in the *Double Dealer* 3, no. 17 (May 1922): 261–62. "Rebels and Reactionaries rub shoulders amiably and in perfect harmony in the *Double Dealer*": this is the slogan the magazine used in its ads in the *Little Review* and elsewhere in the 1920s. For a brief history of this interesting and forgotten publication, which was based in New Orleans, see Frederick J. Hoffman, Charles Allen, and Carolyn F. Ulrich, *The Little Magazine: A History and a Bibliography* (Princeton, 1947), 10–14. The *Double Dealer* was a "Janus-faced" enterprise, mixing emergent and vestigial styles in instructive ways. For example, its covers featured the Beardsleyan drawings of Olive Leonhardt—until mid-1922, when British Aestheticism gave way to a modernist neoclassicism, and the drawings of Leonhardt were replaced by the image of an ancient coin face, which represented Janus.

3. *The Letters of Hart Crane, 1916–1932*, ed. Brom Weber (1952; Berkeley and Los Angeles, 1965), 87. All page references to this edition of the letters edited by Brom Weber will be identified as "Crane, *Letters*"; references to the volume of letters edited by Thomas S. W. Lewis will be identified as "*Letters of Crane and His Family*."

4. Raymond Williams, *The Politics of Modernism: Against the New Conformists*, ed. Tony Pinkney (London, 1989), 45.

5. For these and other uses of "modern" and "modernism," see *The Literary Correspondence of Donald Davidson and Allen Tate*, ed. John Tyree Fain and Thomas Daniel Young (Athens, Ga., 1974), 20–21, 29–30, 34–35, 189, 301. I will refer to this title as *Davidson and Tate*.

6. Tate to Davidson, February 5, 1933, and Tate to Davidson, April 16, 1931 (Heard Library, Vanderbilt University). In the letter from 1933, Tate is responding to an essay by Davidson: "I think your real argument is against the aimless experimentalism of the east that happens to fasten upon Joyce and Eliot as catchwords. Joyce himself is a provincial Irishman who has practically the same social and economic beliefs that we [the Southern Agrarians] have; and his work is the history of the moral horror in the individual when he is confronted with Modernism in all forms."

7. I am mindful of the anachronism involved in referring to Crane as a gay man—or even a homosexual; but I am also mindful of the importance of doing so. For an overview of sexual practices, ideology, and communities in the 1920s, see

233

John D'Emilio and Estelle B. Freedman, *Intimate Matters: A History of Sexuality in America* (New York, 1988). On the organization and naming of male homosexual relations in this period, including research into the particular forms of sexual community with which Crane was most familiar, see two essays by George Chauncey, Jr.: "The Way We Were: Gay Male Society in the Jazz Age," *Village Voice* 31, no. 26 (July 1986) and "Christian Brotherhood or Sexual Perversion? Homosexual Identities and the Construction of Sexual Boundaries in the World War I Era," in *Hidden from History: Reclaiming the Gay and Lesbian Past*, ed. Martin Bauml Duberman, Martha Vicinus, and George Chauncey, Jr. (New York, 1989). The latter essay shows that "straight" was a term for the penetrating partner in intercourse, whether homosexual or heterosexual; this is part of the evidence Chauncey draws on to show that, among the men under discussion in his study, whether a man took the "male" or the "female" position in sex was a more important indicator of his sexual identity than whether the gender of his partner was male or female.

8. A valuable exception is Albert Gelpi, *A Coherent Splendor: The American Poetic Renaissance, 1910–1950* (Cambridge, 1987). Gelpi's wide-ranging study pairs modern poets, including Crane and Tate, as examples of the "Janus-faced" tension between Romantic and Modernist poetics in twentieth-century American poetry.

9. Allen Tate, *Memoirs and Opinions 1926–1974* (Chicago, 1975), 32.

10. Walter Benjamin, *Charles Baudelaire: A Lyric Poet in the Era of High Capitalism*, trans. Harry Zohn (London, 1983), 75.

I. *JANUS-FACED MODERNISM*

ONE. *Toward the Institute of Literary Autonomy and Tradition*

1. *The Letters of T. S. Eliot*, ed. Valerie Eliot, Vol. 1, *1898–1922* (New York, 1988), 58.

2. Lionel Trilling, *Beyond Culture: Essays on Literature and Learning* (New York, 1965), xii–xiii.

3. Houston A. Baker, Jr., *Modernism and the Harlem Renaissance* (Chicago, 1987), 4. Baker chooses to define himself in relation to Trilling in particular: "I am certain that I shall never place *Ulysses* in a group of texts that I describe, to use Trilling's words, as 'spiritual' if not 'actually religious.' Perhaps the reason I shall not is because the questions Trilling finds—correctly or incorrectly—intimately relevant to his life are descriptive only of a bourgeois, characteristically twentieth-century, white Western mentality." Baker refers to Trilling's sense that modern literature "asks us if we are content with our marriages, with our family lives, with our professional lives, with our friends." He continues: "As an Afro-American, a person of African descent in the United States today, I spend a great deal of time reflecting that in the world's largest geographies the question Where will I find water, wood, or food for today? is (and has been for the entirety of this century) the most pressing and urgently posed inquiry" (Baker, *Modernism and the Harlem Renaissance*, 7).

4. Sandra M. Gilbert and Susan Gubar, *No Man's Land: The Place of the Woman Writer in the Twentieth Century*, Vol. 1, *The War of the Words* (New Haven, 1988), 135.

5. Andreas Huyssen, *After the Great Divide: Modernism, Mass Culture, Postmodernism* (Bloomington, Ind., 1986), vii.

6. As Huyssen points out, "In the age of nascent socialism *and* the first major women's movement in Europe, the masses knocking at the gate were also women, knocking at the gate of a male-dominated culture" (Huyssen, *After the Great Divide*, 47).

7. Wyndham Lewis, *Blasting and Bombardiering* (London, 1967), 250.

8. I adopt the phrase "Male homosexual panic" from Eve Kosofsky Sedgwick as she develops it in two books: *Between Men: English Literature and Homosocial Desire* (New York, 1985), 88–90, and *Epistemology of the Closet* (Berkeley and Los Angeles, 1990),182–212. For Sedgwick, the phrase names a mechanism of social discipline, supplemental to gay-bashing and the law, which enforces the prohibition against male homosexuality by means of paraniod male self-surveillance: "Not only must homosexual men be unable to ascertain whether they are to be objects of 'random' homophobic violence, but no man must be able to ascertain that he is not (that his bonds are not) homosexual" (*Between Men*, 88–89). This phrase (which, like "homophobia," is perhaps regrettably pathologizing) has also had a juridical career: it has been used as part of a responsibility-reducing defense for men charged with anti-gay violence (*Epistemology of the Closet*, 18–21).

9. For a historical overview, see *The Invention of Tradition*, ed. Eric Hobsbawm and Terence Kanger (Cambridge, 1983).

10. Richard Ohmann, *Politics of Letters* (Middletown, Conn., 1987), 34.

11. Alvin Gouldner, *The Future of Intellectuals and the Rise of the New Class* (New York, 1979), 21. Gouldner's global framework, to which I will refer again, can be usefully complemented by the extensive scholarship on the rise of the professional-managerial class in the United States. See, for example, *Between Labor and Capital*, ed. Pat Walker (Boston, 1979).

12. Marcus Klein, *Foreigners: The Making of American Literature 1900–1940* (Chicago, 1981), 12.

13. Magali Sarfatti Larson, *The Rise of Professionalism: A Sociological Analysis* (Berkeley, 1977), 51.

14. "You have the higher consciousness. . . . This is something very few have," an inner voice told Crane in the winter he first conceived of *The Bridge* (Crane, *Letters*, 92); the consciousness of the poet of *The Bridge* is a collective one, however, speaking for the future of "our people" as a whole (Crane, *Letters*, 124). Waldo Frank, who significantly influenced Crane's self-definition as a poet, speaks of America "as a democratic nation led by an aristocracy of spirit" in *The Re-discovery of America: An Introduction to a Philosophy of American Life* (New York, 1929), 4.

15. Ransom to Tate, September 17, 1936 (Princeton University Library).

16. T. S. Eliot, "The Metaphysical Poets," in *Selected Prose of T. S. Eliot*, ed. Frank Kermode (New York, 1975), 65.

17. Pound quoted this description of himself, from a review of his own *Exultations* in the *Spectator*, in order to praise Eliot (*Letters of T. S. Eliot*, 101).

18. Louis Menand, *Discovering Modernism: T. S. Eliot and His Context* (New York, 1987), 99.

19. For a discussion of the transition between the genteel and modernist marketplace, with particular reference to Frost and Pound, see Frank Lentricchia,

"Lyric in the Culture of Capitalism," *American Literary History* 1, no. 1 (1989): 63–88.

20. Menand continues: "But the irony is easily cheapened if too much store is set by it. For even an activity that undertakes to stand in an independent and critical relation to the life of the group as a whole, as modern high-culture art once proposed to stand, requires for its effectiveness a legitimacy that can only come from an appeal to the standards of the group itself." This seems to me to unnecessarily limit the implication of Menand's own insight.

21. Jonathan Freedman, *Professions of Taste: Henry James, British Aestheticism, and Commodity Culture* (Stanford, 1990), xix.

22. Richard H. Brodhead, *The School of Hawthorne* (New York, 1986), 113.

23. Ezra Pound, *The Literary Essays of Ezra Pound*, ed. T. S. Eliot (New York, 1954), 299–300.

24. Ezra Pound, "The Audience," *Poetry* 5 (1914–1915): 30. *Poetry* had chosen the quotation from Whitman as its motto.

25. In context, Eliot's remark is tinged with regret, since he is talking about the probability that he will not return to France, except to visit. In this sense, Eliot's remark means, "I would prefer to go on living and writing in France, that exciting and romantic place, but practical considerations make that unlikely, so I plan to make do here instead."

26. Gouldner makes use of this distinction, derived from Basil Bernstein, to describe the "intensive linguistic conversion of students [in the new school system] from casual to reflexive speech" (Gouldner, *The Future of Intellectuals*, 3). Invoking the linguistic concept of "diglossia," John Guillory presents a far-reaching theory of the opposition between "literary language" and "the demotic" in his essay, "Canonical and Non-Canonical: A Critique of the Current Debate," *ELH* 54, no. 3 (Autumn 1987): 483–527.

27. Raymond Williams connects this relation to language with the experience of three distinct immigrant groups in the modern city: colonial subjects (perhaps anyone from a region economically dominated by metropolitan capital); those who come from "linguistic borderlands"; and exiles from "rejecting or rejected political regimes. For in each of these cases, though in interestingly different ways, an old language had been marginalized or suppressed, or else simply left behind, and the now dominant language either interacted with its subordinate for new language effects or was seen as, in new ways, both plastic and arbitrary: an alien but accessible system which had both power and potential yet was still not . . . the language or the possible language of a people but now the material of groups, agencies, fractions, specific works, its actual society and complex of writers and game-players, translators and signwriters, interpreters and makers of paradoxes, cross-cultural innovators and jokers" (Williams, *Politics of Modernism*, 78). This is a suggestive description of the London—the multicultural Bloomsbury—to which Eliot expatriated. Williams's model becomes more useful for understanding the situation in the United States if we extend the notion of a "dominant" language to include not only national tongues but those of the privileged sociolects that higher education creates.

28. As Michael H. Levenson has shown, Imagism was, from a business point of view, an amusingly vexing success. When Amy Lowell, a sort of corporate raider,

used the group name Pound had created for her own anthology, *Some Imagist Poets*, Pound protested the appropriation and, in his view, the vulgarization it represented. According to Levenson, "Lowell quickly became impatient with Pound's proprietary attitude, observing wryly at one point that he could not copyright the name." But *Some Imagist Poets* was so successful in the United States as to immediately produce many new Imagists; as a result, "Lowell was confronted with the circumstance that had tormented Pound, the loss of literary identity in the wash of imitators. Fearing that she might lose control of the movement, she herself considered copyrighting the name 'Imagist,' forming a 'business association' which would be able to exclude the casual imitator." Michael H. Levenson, *A Genealogy of Modernism: A Study of English Literary Doctrine 1908–1922* (Cambridge, 1984), 148.

29. For the same reason, though, Pound had more investment in the ideal of patronage than did Eliot. See Frank Lentricchia, "Lyric in the Culture of Capitalism," 80.

30. This is the premise of Frank Lentricchia's reading of the poet in *Ariel and the Police: Michel Foucault, William James, Wallace Stevens* (Madison, Wis., 1988).

31. Wallace Stevens, *Opus Posthumous: Poems, Plays, Prose*, ed. Samuel French Morse (New York, 1957), 165.

32. John Irwin, "Hart Crane's *The Bridge* (II)," *Raritan* 9, no. 1 (1989): 113. The first part of Irwin's essay appeared in *Raritan* 8, no. 4 (1989): 70–88.

33. Grace Hart Crane to her son Harold, March 29, 1917: "In signing your name to your contributions & later to your books do you intend to ignore your mother's side of the house entirely? . . . It seems to me that Hart or at least H. should come in some where— I understand that the Cranes say you get all your literary talent from them—uncle Fred for instance being the example they point to. If you feel that way leave 'Hart' out—but if not, now is the time to fix it right. How would 'Hart Crane' be. No partiality there— You see I am already jealous, which is a sure sign I believe in your success." *Letters of Hart Crane and His Family*, ed. Thomas S. W. Lewis (New York, 1974), 55. Crane always remained "Harold" to his father's "side of the house."

34. Guy Hocquenghem, *Homosexual Desire*, trans. Daniella Dangoor (London, 1978), 95.

35. "Greenwich Village," as I use it here, refers to the Bohemian community of Lower Manhattan generally. When Crane first came to New York City, he lived on the Lower East Side, later at a number of addresses in or near the Village, including 24 West 16th Street, where Crane rented rooms above the offices of the *Little Review*.

36. Caroline F. Ware, *Greenwich Village, 1920–1930: A Comment on American Civilization in the Post-War Years* (Boston, 1935), 71.

37. Edward Abrahams, *The Lyrical Left: Randolph Bourne, Alfred Stieglitz, and the Origins of Cultural Radicalism in America* (Charlottesville, Va., 1986), 8. See also Arthur Frank Wertheim, *The New York Little Renaissance: Iconoclasm, Modernism, and Nationalism in American Culture, 1908–1917* (New York, 1976), 65; Wertheim reproduces Sloan's sketch, "The Arch Conspirators."

38. Stuart Ewen, *Captains of Consciousness: Advertising and the Social Roots of the Consumer Culture* (New York, 1976), 184. There are many other versions of this argument. Malcolm Cowley, *Exile's Return: A Literary Odyssey of the 1920's* (New

York, 1936), and Lewis A. Erenberg, *Steppin' Out: New York Nightlife and the Trans-formation of American Culture* (Westport, 1981), both examine the role of Manhattan pleasure seeking in the shaping of a consumption ethic for the United States as a whole. Essays that explain these cultural developments with reference to the "disaccumulation" phase of capitalism include Martin J. Sklar, "On the Proletarian Revolution and the End of Political-Economic Society," *Radical America* 3, no. 3 (1969): 1–42, and Fred Block and Larry Hirshorn, "New Productive Forces and the Contradictions of Contemporary Capitalism," *Theory and Society* 7, no. 3 (1979): 363–90.

39. Roland Marchand, *Advertising the American Dream: Making Way for Modernity, 1920–1940* (Berkeley, 1985), 42, 44.

40. Allen Tate to Hart Crane, April 4, 1923 (Columbia University Library). Tate's early letters to Crane are remarkably different from his letters during the same period to Donald Davidson. Tate is as self-abasing in relation to Crane as he is self-assured in relation to Davidson. In the letters to Crane, Tate is contemptuous of the Fugitives and of the South.

41. Veronica A. Makowsky, *Caroline Gordon: A Biography* (Oxford, 1989), 48–49. As Makowsky makes clear, Tate's link to the idealized patriarchal South in his poems and in his novel *The Fathers* was always through the maternal line.

42. *The Fugitive* 1, no. 1 (1922): 1.

43. Twelve Southerners, *I'll Take My Stand*, intro. and ed. Louis D. Rubin, Jr. (New York, 1930; Baton Rouge, 1977), xxxviii.

44. See Michael O'Brien, *The Idea of the American South, 1920–1941* (Baltimore, 1979) 208–9, and Daniel Joseph Singal, *The War Within: From Victorian to Modernist Thought in the South, 1919–1945* (Chapel Hill, 1982), 220–31.

45. Paul Bové, "Agriculture and Academe: America's Southern Question," *boundary* 2, 14, no. 3 (1986): 180. Despite the disagreement I register here, I find Bové's study of the Agrarians' political situation and their later careers as literary critics one of the most suggestive of the many scholarly treatments of the subject. The essay is, in part, a revision of Bové's argument about the New Criticism in his earlier study, *Intellectuals in Power: A Genealogy of Critical Humanism* (New York, 1986). *Intellectuals in Power* emphasizes the New Criticism's extension of "the very social modernity whose bureaucratic scientism and anomie it claims to reject" (55)—to a degree that makes the New Criticism (at least as practiced by I. A. Richards) seem *merely* "a servant to forces it doesn't understand" (75). I find more accurate the point Bové makes in his treatment of the Agrarians. When they abandoned Agrarian agitation to pursue their academic careers, Bové suggests, the Agrarians were not "bought off": "On the contrary, the State we may say met some of the real needs of these intellectuals by allowing them to carry on their struggles in the international, cultural arena of literary studies and production" (182). For a treatment of the Agrarians closer to Bové's earlier point of view, see John Fekete, *The Critical Twilight: Explorations in the Ideology of Anglo-American Literary Theory from Eliot to McLuhan* (London, 1977).

46. Gerald Graff, *Professing Literature: An Institutional History* (Chicago, 1987), 155.

47. John Crowe Ransom, *The World's Body* (New York, 1938), vii.

48. John Crowe Ransom, "What Does the South Want?" in *Who Owns America?*, ed. Herbert Agar and Allen Tate (Boston, 1936), 186.

49. For example, see "A Note on Criticial 'Autotelism,' " in Allen Tate, *Essays of Four Decades* (Chicago, 1968), 169–72. In a paper forthcoming in *Sagetrieb*, "Poet-Critics and Professionalism in the 1930s," Alan Golding stresses that those New Critics, like Tate, who "were poets first," preserved "an amateur or non-academic" concept of criticism, and that "they therefore felt a certain conflict over the project of professionalizing criticism, even as they saw the necessity of that project." For another, widely suggestive treatment of the poet-critic, see Robert von Hallberg, "American Poet-Critics Since 1945," in *Reconstructing American Literary History*, ed. Sacvan Bercovitch (Cambridge, 1986), 280–99.

50. Roy Harvey Pearce, *The Continuity of American Poetry* (Princeton, 1961), 322.

II. *TATE: THE RIGHT KIND OF MODERNISM*

Two. *The Realism of* The Waste Land

1. Henry James, *The American Scene*, ed. Leon Edel (Bloomington, Ind., 1968), 232.

2. John Unterecker provides a useful and detailed account of this period in *Voyager: A Life of Hart Crane* (New York, 1969), 417–35. Brief versions of the story, told from Gordon's point of view, can be found in Makowsky, *Caroline Gordon*, 64–68, and Ann Waldron, *Close Connections: Caroline Gordon and the Southern Renaissance* (New York, 1987), 45–49. In addition to the published and unpublished letters cited in the following notes, there are two relevant memoirs: Susan Jenkins Brown, *Robber Rocks: Letters and Memoirs of Hart Crane, 1923–1932* (Middletown, Conn., 1968), 47–58 and passim; and Malcom Cowley, "Two Winters with Allen Tate and Hart Crane," in *Allen Tate and His Work: Critical Evaluations*, ed. Radcliffe Squires (Minneapolis, 1972), 26–33. Susan Jenkins and Slater Brown lived a short walk from the Tates and Crane; other writers and artists, including Malcolm Cowley, eventually moved to the area. As Unterecker notes, the houses occupied by "the Tates" and "the Browns" were both on South Quaker Hill in Pawling, close to the Connecticut line, although Crane "always spoke of them as in Patterson" (Unterecker, *Voyager*, 402). I will follow Crane's practice, and Unterecker's, in calling the place "Patterson."

3. Crane sent ten stanzas of "Atlantis" to Waldo Frank on January 18, 1926. These as well as Crane's worksheets from the spring and summer have been collected by Brom Weber, *Hart Crane: A Biographical and Literary Study* (New York, 1948), 425–40.

4. Eliot's response is dated March 16, 1926. Tate excitedly wrote to Davidson about it on March 24. "Incidentally," Tate said, "you can't afford to miss the 'Criterion' (I should have said this all along, even before Eliot's cordiality), for it's the finest journal of ideas in the language" (*Davidson and Tate*, 160). In a second letter that spring, Eliot compared Tate's verse to Baudelaire's; he also cautioned Tate against making too high or too emphatic an utterance. Eliot's correspondence with Tate is collected in the Allen Tate Papers, Princeton University Library. Curiously enough, Crane appeared in the *Criterion* before Tate. "The Tunnel" was accepted in 1927; Eliot accepted Tate's first contribution, "Emily Dickinson," an essay, in late 1928.

5. Crane to Cowley, March 28, 1926 (Beinecke Library, Yale University).

6. Tate dated the ode "1927/1937" in Tate, *Collected Poems, 1919–1976*, (New York, 1976), 23. Radcliffe Squires places the start of composition of the poem in the winter of 1926. See Squires, *Allen Tate: A Literary Biography* (New York, 1971), 61. Louis D. Rubin, Jr., contends that "Tate began the Confederate ode in 1925–26." See Rubin, *The Wary Fugitives: Four Poets and the South* (Baton Rouge, 1978), 99. For further, very detailed speculation, see Edward J. Brunner, *Splendid Failure: Hart Crane and the Making of "The Bridge"* (Urbana, Ill., 1985), 124 and 268, n. 12.

7. For Tate's review, see Tate, *The Poetry Reviews of Allen Tate, 1924–1944*, ed. Ashley Brown and Frances Neel Cheney (Baton Rouge, 1983), 47–51.

8. Reported by Garry Mitchell, "Allen Tate Says Southern Writing Still Distinct," *Minneapolis Star*, April 17, 1974, 8C. The details of Tate's memory seem closer to his feelings about Crane than to the facts. I am grateful to Thomas Underwood for a copy of this newspaper story.

9. Gordon and Wood, *The Southern Mandarins: Letters of Caroline Gordon to Sally Wood*, ed. Sally Wood (Baton Rouge, 1984), 22.

10. For Crane's letter to his mother, written at the peak of the crisis, see *Letters of Crane and His Family*, 478–83. Crane here seems to be blaming one woman—Gordon—in order to gain aid and sympathy from another—Grace Hart Crane.

11. It may seem curious, Makowsky remarks, "that a couple beginning married life would want a third party, but actually the invitation to Crane established a pattern in the Tates' married life. They often had others living with them, those who needed help, whether financially, emotionally, or artistically. The third party acted as a buffer between them and ultimately as the lightning rod that would receive the blast of their mutual tensions, the blame for the failure of the extended household" (Makowsky, *Caroline Gordon*, 65).

12. While, as we will see, Tate's essays of the period center on Eliot, his letters to Davidson reveal his efforts to publish Crane in the *Fugitive*. Ransom, who was always suspicious of Eliot, nonetheless conceded ground to Crane by praising Tate's friend as the "free-est mind" among contemporary poets. Ransom, "A Doctrine of Relativity," the *Fugitive* 4, no.3 (1925): 93–95.

13. Lee Edelman, *Transmemberment of Song: Hart Crane's Anatomies of Rhetoric and Desire* (Stanford, 1987), 2.

14. Harold Bloom, "Hart Crane's Gnosis," in *Agon: Towards a Theory of Revisionism* (New York, 1982), 264–65. The essay serves as the introduction to *Hart Crane: Modern Critical Views*, ed. Harold Bloom (New York, 1984); subsequent references to the essay will employ this edition.

15. On this subject see Jonathan Culler, "Changes in the Study of the Lyric," and Jonathan Arac, "Lyric Poetry and the Bounds of the New Criticism," collected in *Lyric Poetry: Beyond the New Criticism*, ed. Chaviva Hošek and Patricia Parker (Ithaca, 1985), 38–54 and 345–55. Two of the changes that Culler mentions, "the shift from symbol to allegory and the change in the status of self-reference," demonstrate, Arac argues, "that New Criticism and its successor remark exactly the same 'places' and 'moves' in the poems they are reading, but they give different *values* to the features they agree in discerning. If allegory emphasizes distance and difference rather than the intimate reconciliation effected by the symbol, and if self-reference no longer performs a comforting embrace but instead opens up ver-

tiginous abysses, this is all to register an inversion in what we may call the plot of criticism" (*Lyric Poetry*, 346–47).

16. Davidson replied: "I admit your point about themes. But I must refute other implications by declaring that I am not writing an epic (good Lord, surely not an *epic*) for Tennesseans. I will merely use your phrase and say that I'm writing the history of a mind—my mind, to an extent" (*Davidson and Tate*, 170).

17. Matthew Arnold, "The Function of Criticism at the Present Time," in *Lectures and Essays in Criticism*, ed. R. H. Super (Ann Arbor, 1962), 262–63. My sense of Arnold's cultural project has been shaped by Chris Baldick, *The Social Mission of English Criticism 1848–1932* (Oxford, 1983), and Raymond Williams, *Culture and Society 1780–1950* (New York, 1950). Tate, like Eliot, both relies upon and disparages Arnold's position. For a somewhat later treatment of the issue, see Tate's essay "Literature as Knowledge," written in 1941, in Tate, *Essays of Four Decades*, 72–77.

18. From a review of Spengler's *The Decline of the West* in the *Nation* 122, no. 3175 (May 12, 1926): 534.

19. Tate to Davidson on March 16, 1928: "It all happened in one day—not only the Guggenheim, but Balch's acceptance of my poems for publication this fall. Old Jack did it all. Before even a copy is in circulation, he has paid for himself" (*Davidson and Tate*, 208). "Old Jack" refers to Tate, *Stonewall Jackson; the Good Soldier: A Narrative* (New York, 1928) Minton, Balch & Co. published Tate, *Mr. Pope and Other Poems* (New York, 1928) as well as the biography.

20. *Fugitive* 1, no. 4 (1922): 99–100.

21. *Secession* 1 (1922): 19. Despite Crane's advocacy, Munson did not publish any of Tate's work.

22. *Fugitive* 2, no. 5 (1923): 2.

23. John Crowe Ransom, "Waste Lands," *Literary Review* of the *New York Evening Post*, July 14, 1923. Part of the edge of this exchange had to do with the relative insecurity of Ransom's position at Vanderbilt, where he had to constantly prove the value of his particular intellectual values and procedures. See Thomas Daniel Young, *Gentleman in a Dustcoat: A Biography of John Crowe Ransom* (Baton Rouge, 1976), 152–55. See also Rubin, *Wary Fugitives*, 22–29 and 82–87.

24. Allen Tate, "Waste Lands" [letter], *Literary Review* of the *New York Evening Post*, August 4, 1923.

25. John Crowe Ransom, "Mr. Ransom Replies" [letter], *Literary Review* of the *New York Evening Post*, August 11, 1923.

26. Discussing the vexed question of Robert Frost's status as a modern poet, Richard Poirier lucidly describes the relation between *The Waste Land*'s "realism" and its canonicity: "Condescensions directed at Frost by many admirers of the classical texts in English of twentieth-century modernism derive in part from the assumption that modernist literature was made inevitable by historical realities of the twentieth century. It has been assumed that Joyce and Eliot are therefore closer to the central 'significances' of their age than is Frost. Works like *The Waste Land* that originally seemed 'incoherent' to the general reader finally, therefore, imposed themselves on consciousness as 'realistic.' " Poirier, *Robert Frost: The Work of Knowing* (New York, 1977), 39. Erich Auerbach provides an exemplary statement of the position Poirier is discussing: "At the time of the first World War and after—in a Europe unsure of itself, overflowing with unsettled ideologies and ways of life, and

pregnant with disaster—certain writers distinguished by instinct and insight find a method which dissolves reality into multiple and multivalent reflections of consciousness. That this method should have been developed at this time is not hard to understand." Auerbach, *Mimesis: The Representation of Reality in Western Literature*, trans. Willard R. Trask (1946; repr. Princeton, 1968), 551.

27. I. A. Richards, *Practical Literary Criticism* (Cambridge, 1926), 235.

28. Pierre Bourdieu, *Distinction: A Social Critique of the Judgment of Taste*, trans. Richard Nice (Paris, 1979; Cambridge, Mass., 1984), 3.

29. John Guillory, "The Ideology of Canon Formation: T. S. Eliot and Cleanth Brooks," *Critical Inquiry* 10, no. 1 (1983): 176.

30. Tate's identification with Eliot was complicated and intense. "Eliot—*I have known it all along!*—is the most intelligent man alive," Tate wrote to Davidson in July 1925. "Of course I say that because he agrees with me; more so, because he writes up my own ideas better than my poor skill permits me to do for myself" (*Davidson and Tate*, 141). When Tate later recalled with pride Crane's initial remark, in 1922, that he wrote poetry like Eliot's, Tate emphasized that he had not yet read Eliot. (Commentators on Tate's poetry invariably revive this anecdote.) It was important to Tate both that he wrote like Eliot and that he wrote like Eliot before he had read Eliot.

31. John Crowe Ransom, *Selected Poems* (New York, 3rd ed., 1978), 54. For another treatment of heroic combat and submission, see Ransom's "Man Without a Sense of Direction." Both this poem and "Blackberry Winter" were first collected, appropriately, in *The Manliness of Men* (1927; contained in *Selected Poems*).

THREE. *Genius and the Rational Order of Criticism*

1. T. S. Eliot, *The Sacred Wood* (1920; repr. London, 1960), 58.

2. See Unterecker, *Voyager*, 415–17, 427–28, 448–49. O'Neill was one of the references Crane gave Otto Kahn, and he did compose a blurb for the jacket of *White Buildings*.

3. Crane to Tate, July 25, 1926 (Princeton University Library).

4. There is a copy of Tate's preface bearing O'Neill's name in the Eugene O'Neill Papers in the Berg Collection of the New York Public Library; this document may have been submitted to O'Neill for his perusal before it was decided that the essay would bear Tate's name (which of course was virtually unknown at the time). Tate's generosity in this matter should not be forgotten. But it is worth noting that Tate had an essay on Crane already written, or at least planned. At least that is the implication of the letter Tate wrote on March 18, 1926, to Gorham Munson: "Your note on Hart, *as far as it goes*, is better than mine" (Princeton University Library). Tate's introduction to *White Buildings* was his first appearance in book form.

5. Yvor Winters, "The Significance of *The Bridge*, by Hart Crane; or What Are We to Think of Professor X?," in *In Defense of Reason* (Chicago, 1947), 602.

6. Allen Tate, "Introduction to *White Buildings*," in *Hart Crane: A Collection of Critical Essays*, ed. Alan Trachtenberg (Englewood Cliffs, N.J., 1982), 18–19.

7. Carol Christ, *Victorian and Modernist Poetics* (Chicago, 1984), emphasizes the continuity of nineteenth- and early-twentieth-century practices. An example of the older and still widely influential model, which holds that Imagism is a decisive break with Victorian poetry, is David Perkins, *A History of Modern Poetry*, Vol. 1

(Cambridge, Mass., 1976). In Tate's case, the deprecation of Imagism is pointed specifically at Winters, who was dedicated to it at this stage of his career.

8. *Collected Works of Samuel Taylor Coleridge*, ed. Kathleen Coburn. Vol. 5:1 *Lectures 1808–1819* (Princeton, 1980), 495.

9. See Frank Kermode's concluding chapter in Kermode, *Romantic Image* (London, 1957). Raymond Williams, from the perspective of social and political thought, also underlines the continuity between Eliot's and Coleridge's position in Williams, *Culture and Society 1780–1950*.

10. This is Eliot's account of the origin of "intricate formal patterns" in poetry: "Only in the closely-knit and homogeneous society, where many men are at work on the same problems, such a society as those which produced the Greek chorus, the Elizabethan lyric, and the Troubadour canzone, will the development of such forms ever be carried to perfection" ("Reflections on Vers Libre," in *Selected Prose of T. S. Eliot*, 36).

11. T. E. Hulme, *Speculations: Essays on Humanism and the Philosophy of Art*, ed. Herbert Read (1924; 2nd ed. London, 1929), 114. The particular "set" whose use of these terms Hulme drew on here included Charles Maurras, Pierre Lasserre, and other figures in the protofascist Action Française. See Levenson, *A Genealogy of Modernism*, 82–84.

12. *Double Dealer* 5, nos. 27–28 (March–April 1923): 123.

13. Tate to Crane, March 18, 1923 (Columbia University Library).

14. Gorham Munson, *The Awakening Twenties: A Memoir-History of a Literary Period* (Baton Rouge, 1985), 199. Munson, a follower of Ouspensky and G. I. Gurdjieff, is a less than reliable guide to Crane's mysticism. (He is given to phrases like "What collided with us was a C Influence.") But Munson is correct that Crane was strongly stirred by his reading of Ouspensky. Crane praised *Tertium Organum* in a letter to Tate after receiving the sonnet. Crane added dryly and a little flirtatiously, "Its corroboration of several experiences in consciousness that I have had gave it particular interest" (Crane, *Letters*, 124).

15. The author's interview with William Slater Brown, July 1990.

16. Walter Pater, *The Renaissance: Studies in Art and Poetry*, ed. Donald L. Hill (1893; Berkeley and Los Angeles, 1980), 237.

17. Tate's sonnet on Crane's portrait belongs among the intensely idealizing representations of literary fraternity elsewhere in his poetry and prose, none of which is intended as a profession of sexual desire. For example, Tate's letter to Davidson congratulating him on the publication of his first book of poems in March 1924 uses the same sort of "old-fashioned," ceremonial, and richly suggestive rhetoric that we find in his sonnet: "It is the occasion for a renewed consciousness of the meaning of our compact. . . . It is a compact of the understanding, the seal of a love unsuspected by those who are so inured to the mere materials of life that they cannot speak of it impartially in art. . . . This attitude grown out of loneliness in an alien world is so secret that it must exult a little when it recognizes a brother. . . . And so to your bow of burning gold I bring, in my meager way, what arrows of desire I can make for us in the momentary cessations of clamor in the physical world" (*Davidson and Tate*, 96–97). See also note 19 below.

18. Tate to Crane, April 16, 1923 (Columbia University Library).

19. *The Poetry and Prose of William Blake*, ed. David V. Erdman (Garden City, N.Y., 1965), 95. This famous phrase comes from the prefatory lyric of Blake's

"Milton." Tate's familiarity with it is made clear by his claim to bring "arrows of desire" to Donald Davidson's "bow of burning gold" (*Davidson and Tate*, 97). The third quatrain of Blake's prefatory lyric begins: "Bring me my Bow of burning gold: / Bring me my Arrows of desire."

20. "Ode on a Grecian Urn," in Keats, *The Poems of John Keats*, ed. Jack Stillinger (Cambridge, Mass., 1978), 372.

21. "Ode to the West Wind," in Shelley, *Shelley's Poetry and Prose*, ed. Donald H. Reiman and Sharon B. Powers (New York, 1977), 223.

22. According to Paul de Man, this disturbing symmetry is "the latent threat that inhabits prosopopeia" generally. Paul de Man, *The Rhetoric of Romanticism* (New York, 1984), 67–81.

23. Tate to Crane, April 4, 1923 (Columbia University Library). In this letter Tate sent a photograph taken of him in 1921.

24. Edwin Arlington Robinson, *Collected Poems* (New York, 1954), 7–8. "The Gift of God" was printed in Robinson's *The Man from the Sky* in 1916. I am indebted to John Hollander for hearing this echo and pointing it out to me. Hollander comments on it in a discussion of Tate's sonnet and Lescaze's portrait in his forthcoming study, *The Gazer's Spirit* (tentative title).

25. Tate's point restates as an accusation the defense of Keats made by the aesthetes Lentricchia discusses. "Not surprisingly," Lentricchia relates, "the publication of the Fanny Brawne letters made passion, apparently not of the ethereal sort, the riveting issue of genteel commentary (public and private) on Keats. Keats's sexual innocence had to be protected at all cost—it was the symbolic mark of what poetry had to be: the safe haven of ideality in a world that the genteel cultural critics found epitomized by the marketplace" (Lentricchia, *Ariel and the Police*, 162). The solution was to treat Keats as neither sexual nor nonsexual but presexual. Tate takes over this developmental model directly.

26. Jeff Nunokawa, "*In Memoriam* and the Extinction of the Homosexual," *ELH* 58, no. 2 (1991): 436. Nunokawa extends this argument to readings of contemporary texts in another essay, " 'All the Sad Young Men': AIDS and the Work of Mourning," *Yale Journal of Criticism* 4, no. 2, (1991): 1–12.

27. I take the category of "romantic anti-capitalism" from Georg Lukács as expounded by Robert Sayre and Michel Löwy, "Figures of Romantic Anti-Capitalism," *New German Critique* 32 (Spring/Summer 1984): 42–92. For a useful overview of patterns of retreat and engagement among American intellectuals of the 1920s and 1930s, see Warren I. Susman, *Culture as History: The Transformation of American Society in the Twentieth Century* (New York, 1984), 184–210.

28. For a measure of Tate's exceedingly ambivalent attitude toward the university scholar, consider his response to Warren's pursuit of an advanced degree at Yale: "Red is determined to stick it out and get his union-card emblazoned *Ph.D.* I feel like writing an essay on this subject, showing how a worthless idea dressed up with pious research can produce a monstrosity like [John Livingston] Lowes' [*The Road to*] *Xanadu*. . . . Why such nonsense should be respected because it is garbed in learning is beyond me. Hinc illae lacrimae" (*Davidson and Tate*, 204). For a discussion of the intellectual tradition in which Tate defined his work, see Lewis P. Simpson, *The Man of Letters in New England and the South: Essays on the History of the Literary Vocation in America* (Baton Rouge, 1973).

29. Cited by Squires, *Allen Tate*, 65. The letter was written on April 11, 1926—a week before Tate and Crane quarreled. Tate was specifically referring to Ouspensky's concept of the "*noumenon.*"

30. Chris Baldick, *Social Mission of English Criticism*, 128–29.

31. I am quoting from the essay entitled "Blake." "We have the same respect for Blake's philosophy," Eliot writes, ". . . that we have for an ingenious piece of home-made furniture: we admire the man who has put it together out of the odds and ends about the house. England has produced a fair number of these resourceful Robinson Crusoes; but we are not really so remote from the Continent, or from our own past, as to be deprived of the advantages of culture if we wish them" (Eliot, *The Sacred Wood*, 156–57).

32. John Crowe Ransom, "Thoughts on the Poetic Discontent," *Fugitive* 4, no. 1 (March 1925): 64. For Ransom, Frost's "Birches" and "The Need of Being Versed in Country Things" exemplify this movement.

33. *Mr. Pope and Other Poems* (New York, 1928), 10. Tate's *Collected Poems*, which gives the date of the poem's composition as 1927, has no comma in line 4 and a comma, not a dash, in line 11.

34. These are the first lines of stanza 2 from the draft of "Atlantis" that Crane sent to Waldo Frank on January 18, 1926, from Patterson—a version of the poem that Tate could, therefore, be expected to have had in mind or on hand. Weber, *Hart Crane*, 429.

Four. *The Burial of the Confederate Dead*

1. Cleanth Brooks and Robert Penn Warren, *Understanding Poetry* (1938; 3rd ed., New York, 1960), xiv.

2. Donald Davidson, "The Tall Men," in *Lee in the Mountains and Other Poems* (Boston, 1938), 66. Houghton Mifflin published *The Tall Men* in 1926.

3. For example, consider the argument on behalf of instinct against "intellectualism" by Hiram Wesley Evans, the Imperial Wizard, in "The Klan's Fight for Americanism," *North American Review* 223 (March-May 1926): 33–63.

4. From the epigraph to *Paterson*: "*a local pride; spring, summer, fall and the sea; a confession; a basket; a column; a reply to Greek and Latin with the bare hands; a gathering up; a celebration.*" William Carlos Williams, *Paterson* (New York, 1958), 2.

5. W. K. Wimsatt, Jr., *The Verbal Icon: Studies in the Meaning of Poetry* (Lexington, Ky., 1954), 3–20. Wimsatt's essay, "The Intentional Fallacy," was co-authored with Monroe C. Beardsley.

6. Quoted by Singal, *The War Within*, 219. Singal's treatment is an excellent guide to Ransom's understanding of his own clerical aspirations. "I am the son of a theologian, and the grandson of another one, but the gift did not come down to me" (Singal, *The War Within*, 203), Ransom wrote in 1930, emphasizing the entanglement of religion and patriarchal identity that characterizes most of Ransom's—and Tate's—meditations on inheritance. Singal draws this conclusion from Ransom's 1927 venture into theology, *God Without Thunder: An Unorthodox Defense of Orthodoxy* (Hamden, Conn., 1965): "Rejecting Catholicism and Anglicanism as foreign faiths unavailable to anyone of his ethnic stock, he settled on a simple set of injunctions that may be fairly paraphrased as 'Restore orthodoxy to the church of your choice' " (Singal, *The War Within*, 216).

7. Paul H. Fry, *The Poet's Calling in the English Ode* (New Haven, 1980), 2. The sentences just preceding this comment on the ode should be cited as well: "There is a uniquely modern comfort in taking it for granted that the gate is closed. We would like to go through, it troubles our metaphysics that we cannot 'cross the bar,' but still, happily, we do have our proper bounds marked off by the neat map, or replica, that is our poem." I would add that there is a uniquely high modernist comfort in this impasse.

8. Fry concisely summarizes the generic distinction at stake: "The ode differs from elegy ... chiefly in coming upon death while meaning to talk about birth; whereas in the typical movement of an elegy it is the other way around" (Fry, *Poet's Calling*, 13). For further commentary on the generic complexities of the modern ode, see the last chapter of *Poet's Calling*, and Alistair Fowler, *Kinds of Literature: A Theory of Literary Modes* (Cambridge, Mass., 1982).

9. Tate spends the next-to-last pages of "Narcissus as Narcissus" in detailed metrical analysis of the transition between "Hears the wind only" and "Now that the salt of their blood" (605–6), providing ways in which we can read these two lines together *and* individually. The difficulty, it seems to me, arises from Tate's desire to preserve the integrity—or isolation—of the individual verse-paragraphs *at the same time* that he is seeking to show the continuity of the poem as a whole. These pages of "Narcissus as Narcissus" summarize the poem's formal dilemma: when the drive to create a self-sufficing structure is carried to the smallest units of a poem, how can the coherence of the whole be preserved?

10. David Bromwich, "Parody, Pastiche, and Allusion," in *Beyond the New Criticism*, ed. Hošek and Parker, 333. Bromwich, who argues on behalf of the legitimacy and value of literary imitation, is not censuring so much as categorizing Tate's poem.

11. John Hollander indicates the range and depth of allusion in Tate's poem when he points out borrowings and recastings from Stevens, Donne, Hardy, Shelley, Crane, and others—all of which, I think, can be heard as modulations in (as Hollander puts it) "the constant sound of Eliot." See Hollander, *The Figure of Echo: A Mode of Allusion in Milton and After* (Berkeley and Los Angeles, 1981), 96–98, 121. For Tate's relations to another poet, see Jefferson Humphries, "The Cemeteries of Paul Valéry and Allen Tate: The Ghosts of Aeneas and Narcissus," *Southern Review* 20, no. 1 (1984): 54–67. Tate denied Valéry's direct influence on the ode.

12. For brief but suggestive comments on Tate's technical debts to Crane, see R. K. Meiners, *The Last Alternatives: A Study of the Works of Allen Tate* (Denver, 1963), 100–101.

13. Tate is citing a letter from Crane written sometime in early January 1927 (Crane, *Letters*, 281–83), which provides a rather detailed critique—concentrating on Tate's "obscurities"—of the draft that, presumably, Tate had also just sent to Davidson. Yet Davidson refers to "your *Elegy*" while Crane refers to "your *Ode*."

14. Tate, "Remarks on the Southern Religion," in Twelve Southerners, *I'll Take My Stand*, 175. The sentence I quote here completes the following, rather curious meditation: "The South would not have been defeated if it had possessed a sufficient faith in its own kind of God. It would not have been defeated, in other words, had it been able to bring out a body of doctrine setting forth its true conviction that the ends of man require more for their realization than politics."

15. For a useful treatment of the opposition between "ideology" and "experience" among the so-called New York Intellectuals, see Alan M. Wald, *The New York Intellectuals: The Rise and Decline of the Anti-Stalinist Left from the 1930s to the 1980s* (Chapel Hill, 1987), 226–63.

16. An adequate assessment of Tate's "politics" would have to take into account the pragmatic, institutional authority he exerted in the middle and later phases of his career. Although this obituary comment may overstate the performative capacity of his "word," it rightly reminds us of the network of professional relations through which Tate exercised power: "during the height of his career as Man of Letters (not as a poet; that came a little earlier), in the 1940s and 1950s, Allen Tate was a major and formidable presence in the American literary scene. His word could get books of poetry published, procure fellowships, set up literary awards and secure financial grants, arrange reviews, and assure academic appointments. There was no more influential presence in the province of poetry." Louis D. Rubin, Jr., *A Gallery of Southerners* (Baton Rouge, 1982), 108.

17. See, for example, Allen Tate, ed., *A Southern Vanguard: The John Peale Bishop Memorial Volume* (New York, 1947).

18. This anecdote, related by Herbert Read, is mentioned by Cleanth Brooks in his essay "T. S. Eliot and the American South," in *'The Southern Review' and Modern Literature, 1935–1985*, ed. Lewis P. Simpson, James Olney, and Jo Gulledge (Baton Rouge, 1988), 198. According to Brooks, the ballad goes like this: "O, I'm a good old rebel / Now that's just what I am / For the 'fair land of freedom' / I do not care a damn."

19. Allen Tate, *Stonewall Jackson*, 60. Richard J. Gray stresses the continuity between Tate's arguments and those of nineteenth-century apologists for slavery in Gray, *Writing the American South: Ideas of an American Region* (Cambridge, 1986), 122–64.

CODA. *"Mrs. Tate's" Tombstone*

1. Jacques Maritain, *"Art and Scholasticism" and "The Frontiers of Poetry,"* trans. Joseph W. Evans (New York, 1962), 141. This translation by Evans differs somewhat from the epigraph, which, as I will explain, was presumably translated by Gordon.

2. Caroline Gordon and Allen Tate, *The House of Fiction: An Anthology of the Short Story with Commentary* (New York, 1950), vii.

3. Caroline Gordon, *The Strange Children* (New York, 1951), 105–6. Gordon points out several times in the course of the novel that the maintenance of the house and the happiness of its many visitors are specifically Sarah Lewis's responsibility. When the cook, Jenny, is not around to do the cooking, Lucy explains, "Mama has to do it, and it makes her awful mad. One time there was an Englishman visiting here and Jenny was off, . . . and he left a three-dollar tip on the dresser. Mama told Jenny she was a good mind to take it herself!" (117).

4. Caroline Gordon, *The Malefactors* (New York, 1956), 50.

5. Gordon to Tate, November 9, 1955 (Princeton University Library).

6. In the winter of 1933, Tate briefly abandoned Gordon for her cousin, Marion Henry—an event that would seem to be behind this part of the plot of *The Malefactors*. Makowsky, in her discussion of this and similiar episodes in Tate and Gordon's marriage, points out the link Gordon saw between Tate's writer's block and his infidelity (Makowsky, *Caroline Gordon*, 119–21).

7. The novel was initially dedicated to Day, who objected when she read its accounts of Catherine Pollard's preconversion Black Masses (Makowsky, *Caroline Gordon*, 208–9; Waldron, *Close Connections*, 333).

8. Sally Fitzgerald lamented to Gordon's protégé, Flannery O'Connor, that in *The Malefactors* "the Faith is unintentionally made to seem too much like chiefly a refuge for the losers in the battle between the sexes." O'Connor responded sagely that "some kind of loss is usually necessary to turn the mind toward faith." But Fitzgerald's point is well-taken: Vera has not suffered just any loss, but the loss of her husband. (Catherine Pollard also found faith when she lost a man, we learn.) I would suggest that Vera's Catholicism, like Gordon's, is not a refuge for the losers in the battle between the sexes so much as a superior site, from the woman's point of view, on which to continue the fight. See Flannery O'Connor, *The Habit of Being*, ed. Sally Fitzgerald (New York, 1979), 159.

9. For an overview of Gordon's changing perspective on Crane, see Ashley Brown, "Caroline Gordon and Hart Crane: A Literary Relationship," *Visionary Company* 1–2, nos. 2–1 (1982): 57–63.

10. Makowsky reads the inscription on Gordon's tombstone in this way: "In one sense, this is an admission of defeat and a warning to other women: Eve had no business writing all those novels. In another sense, however, there is a faint glimmer of hope: Eve persists in writing, even to the verge of the grave, although she must use a masculine 'voice' as authority and permission. However grotesque this mimicry appears, it attests to the truth Gordon felt that her life and work revealed: the female voice can be subverted and distorted into that of a freak, the male voice speaking from the female corpse, but it cannot be completely quelled or denied." Veronica A. Makowsky, "Caroline Gordon on Women Writing: A Contradiction in Terms?" *Southern Quarterly* 28 (1990): 52. This number of the *Southern Quarterly* is a special issue on Gordon.

III. *CRANE: MODERNISM IN REVERSE*

FIVE. *A Resurrection of Some Kind*

1. William Blake, *Poetry and Prose of Blake*, 34 and 41.

2. This letter to Tate, the earliest letter preserved, is dated May 16, 1922. On June 4, Crane sent Gorham Munson a draft of the second section of "For the Marriage of Faustus and Helen," which was at this time called "The Springs of Guilty Song," commenting that "it is something entirely new in English poetry, so far as I know. The jazz rhythms in that first verse are something I have been impotently wishing to 'do' for many a day" (Crane, *Letters*, 89).

3. On Crane's relation to "anti-Puritan" culture critics of the 1920s, including Van Wyck Brooks and Waldo Frank, consult Alan Trachtenberg, "Cultural Revisions in the Twenties: Brooklyn Bridge as Usable Past," in *The American Self: Myth, Ideology, and Popular Culture*, ed. Sam B. Girgus (Albuquerque, 1981). See also Warren I. Susman, "Uses of the Puritan Past," in *Culture as History*, 39–49. On the debate about "the problem of youth" and the rise of what Paula S. Fass calls "peer society," see Fass, *The Damned and the Beautiful: American Youth in the 1920s* (New York, 1977), 29–46 and 119–221 passim.

4. John Milton, *Complete Poems and Major Prose*, ed. Merritt Y. Hughes (New York, 1957), 125.

5. A complete transcription of the fragment can be found in Unterecker, *Voyager*, 434–35. A note on the copy of it in the Beinecke Library at Yale reports that the document was found in a book Crane left in Cuba. In Tate's version of events, the quarrel between them began when he overheard Crane complaining to the farm's owner, Mrs. Turner, about the mess Tate had left in the yard after chopping wood that winter, and when he came outside to remind them that Crane, who felt that chopping "constricted his imagination," had not helped chop the wood. Crane's account, since it is close to his complaint that "You expect me to welcome 'failings' that haven't yet appeared in your work," presumably poetry, suggests another reading: "I had been talking to Mrs. Turner around on 'our' side of the house about some plans for cleaning up some rubbish, etc., when suddenly a door opens from the Tates' kitchen and Allen shouts out, 'If you've got a criticism of my work to make, I'd appreciate it if you would speak to me about it first!' " (Crane, *Letters*, 245–46). Crane does not specify what sort of "work"—chopping or writing?—he thought Tate meant.

6. John T. Irwin, "Figurations of the Writer's Death: Freud and Hart Crane," in *Hart Crane: Modern Critical Views*, ed. Bloom, 186. Irwin's emphasis falls on the more optimistic interpretation that, when he chose to control his own death, Crane discovered "a means to join the great dead who, because they sacrificed their lives to their art, have survived in their works."

7. I follow the nuanced dating of Crane's work recently presented by Marc Simon in his edition of Crane's poems (Crane, *The Poems of Hart Crane*) and by Edward Brunner in his *Splendid Failure*. According to Brunner, the period under special consideration here includes the composition of several lyrics and fragments (including "At Melville's Tomb" and "Repose of Rivers") as well as—in whole or in part—the following sections of *The Bridge*: "To Brooklyn Bridge," "Ave Maria," "Cutty Sark," "Three Songs," "Harbor Dawn," "Van Winkle," "The Dance," "The Tunnel," and "Atlantis."

8. Thomas E. Yingling, *Hart Crane and the Homosexual Text: New Thresholds, New Anatomies* (Chicago, 1990), especially 24–44. See also Robert K. Martin, *The Homosexual Tradition in American Poetry* (Austin, 1979), and Gregory Woods, *Articulate Flesh: Male Homoeroticism and Modern Poetry* (New Haven, 1987).

9. Allen Grossman, "Hart Crane and Poetry: A Consideration of Crane's Intense Poetics," in *Hart Crane: Modern Critical Views*, ed. Bloom, 225.

10. *Crane, The Complete Poems and Selected Letters and Prose of Hart Crane*, ed. Brom Weber (New York, 1966), 199–200.

11. For an overview of the legal issues raised by the confiscation of *Ulysses* and the removal of the restriction in 1933, see Felice Flanery Lewis, *Literature, Obscenity, and the Law* (Carbondale, Ill., 1976), 125–33.

12. Tate to Crane, April 9, 1923 (Columbia University Library).

13. See Crane, "Wind-blown Flames: Letters of Hart Crane to Wilbur Underwood," ed. Warren Herendeen and Donald G. Parker, *Southern Review* 16, no. 2 (1980): 339–76. Underwood's letters from Crane were placed in Beinecke Library at Yale "under restriction" until 1978 by Philip Horton, Crane's first biographer, at Horton's own initiative; some of them were printed in censored form in Brom

Weber's edition of Crane's letters (Crane, *The Letters of Hart Crane*). The correspondence with Underwood, which began in 1920 and ended in 1932, was one of the longest Crane sustained; it is also one of the most important and least commented upon. In the introduction to their selection of letters, Herendeen and Parker rightly claim Underwood's early poems as a significant influence on Crane's.

14. These pages can be found with Crane's other correspondence with Underwood in Yale's Beinecke Library. Crane's selection, omitting the sentence-fragment "Church music," starts on page 475 of the 1961 Random House edition of *Ulysses*.

15. Crane to Underwood, October 30, 1922, in Crane, "Wind-blown Flames," 359.

16. The importance for Crane of Wilde's *De Profundis*—another suppressed text—has never been remarked, in part because Crane was himself reluctant to claim it. Although it was not published in its entirety until 1949, Crane could have read much of Wilde's prison letter, gathered from newspaper reports of the courtroom battle for rights to publish it, in Frank Harris, *Oscar Wilde: His Life and Confessions*, 2 vols. (New York, 1916). Published, like "C 33," in New York in 1916, Harris's *Wilde* is a potential source for Crane's title.

17. Tate to Crane, October 15, 1923 (Columbia University Library). One wonders on the basis of this letter if Crane had at some point sent Underwood's Petronius to Tate; Tate's casual reference implies that they had at least discussed it. Crane's letters to Underwood frequently and delightedly mention Madame Cooke and other transvestites. For example: "I should like very much to have seen you, drunk delicious home brew at Mme. C——'s and seen her fly her fanny about in those new empire gowns you mention" (Crane to Underwood, July 4, 1922, in Crane, "Wind-blown Flames," 356). On the uncertain social status of cross-dressing in this period, see George Chauncey, "Christian Brotherhood or Sexual Perversion?"

18. In her introduction to *Between Men*, Eve Kosofsky Sedgwick explains her use of the term "homosocial": " 'Homosocial' is a word occasionally used in history and the social sciences, where it describes social bonds between persons of the same sex; it is a neologism, obviously formed by analogy with 'homosexual,' and just as obviously meant to be distinguished from 'homosexual.' In fact, it is applied to such activities as 'male bonding,' which may, as in our society, be characterized by intense homophobia, fear and hatred of homosexuality" (Sedgwick, *Between Men*, 1). Sedgwick's further claim that male homosocial bonds are homophobic in a way that female homosocial bonds are not, is quite dubious; yet I find her argument useful and important.

19. The poem reworks a letter to Munson that describes Crane's feelings about working for his father in Cleveland: "I contrive to humanize my work to some extent by much camaraderie with the other employees and this is my salvation there. . . . The few people that I can give myself to are out of physical reach, and so I can only write where I would like to talk, gesture, and dine. The most revolting sensation I experience is the feeling of having placed myself in a position of quiescence or momentary surrender to the contact & possession of the insensitive fingers of my neighbors here" (Crane, *Letters*, 35).

20. Sherman Paul, *Hart's Bridge* (Urbana, Ill., 1972), 43. Sherwood Anderson's story "Hands," from *Winesburg, Ohio* (New York, 1960) is an important model for the poem, as Thomas E. Yingling notes (Yingling, *Hart Crane and the Homosexual Text*, 111–12).

21. Reported by Susan Jenkins Brown in *Robber Rocks*, 69.

22. Gorham Munson, *Waldo Frank: A Study* (New York, 1923), 63.

23. James Longenbach, "Hart Crane and T. S. Eliot: Poets in the Sacred Grove," *Denver Quarterly* 23, no. 1 (1988): 103.

24. T. S. Eliot, "Reflections on Contemporary Poetry," *Egoist* 6, no. 3 (July 1919): 39–40.

25. The passage Crane copied for Tate begins: "Admiration leads most often to imitation; we can seldom remain long unconscious of our imitating another, and the awareness of our debt naturally leads us to hatred of the object imitated. If we stand toward a writer in this other relation of which I speak we do not imitate him, and though we are quite as"—at which point Crane comes to the page break, without completing Eliot's sentence: "likely to be accused of it, we are quite unperturbed by the charge." The quotation I have given in the body of the text follows directly.

26. T. S. Eliot, *The Waste Land: A Facsimile and Transcript of the Original Drafts Including the Annotations of Ezra Pound*, ed. Valerie Eliot (New York, 1971), 54–69.

27. T. S. Eliot, *Collected Poems 1909–1962* (New York, 1963), 43–44.

28. Wayne Koestenbaum, *Double Talk: The Erotics of Male Literary Collaboration* (New York, 1989), 113.

29. Perry Meisel, *The Myth of the Modern: A Study in British Literature and Criticism since 1850* (New Haven, 1987), 101. The two alternatives here signify, Meisel argues, a conflict between Arnoldian and Paterian strategies in Eliot's poem.

30. See James E. Miller, Jr., *T. S. Eliot's Personal Waste Land: The Exorcism of the Demons* (University Park, Pa., 1977), 103–12.

31. Maud Ellmann, *The Poetics of Impersonality: T. S. Eliot and Ezra Pound* (Cambridge, Mass., 1987), 64.

SIX. *Dice of Drowned Men's Bones*

1. Melville, *The Writings of Herman Melville*, Vol. 3, *Mardi, and a Voyage Thither*, ed. Harrison Hayford, Alma A. MacDougall, and G. Thomas Tanselle (Evanston and Chicago, 1970), 81.

2. The history of the publication of *White Buildings* is told from the perspective of Crane's publisher by Walker Gilmer, *Horace Liveright: Publisher of the Twenties* (New York, 1970), 129–33. Unterecker mentions, along with the story of Crane's difficulty getting *White Buildings* published, an interesting mix-up: "An article by Allen Tate on the 'Voyages' set that was intended to accompany the poems in *The Guardian*, a Philadelphia magazine, never appeared, although a disastrous advance announcement did," reading " 'Voyages,' four remarkable poems by Allen Tate will appear in the next issue.' " The magazine folded before the error could be corrected. See Unterecker, *Voyager*, 407.

3. *Dial* 80, no. 5 (May 1926): 370.

4. Consider a transitional text such as John Macy's *The Spirit of American Literature* (Garden City, N.Y., 1913). Macy's history includes chapters on figures from

the nineteenth-century canon (Whittier, Longfellow, Irving) and from the twenti-eth-century canon (Whitman, Twain, James), but mentions Melville only once (beside Stowe and Norris).

5. See Merton M. Sealts, Jr., *Pursuing Melville 1940–1980* (Madison, Wis., 1982), especially 232–49. Carl Van Doren's comments on Melville in *The Cambridge History of American Literature* isolate a point at which Melville's reputation as a romancer classed with Cooper begins to give way to his reputation as a novelist classed with Hawthorne.

6. Melville calls himself a man "who lived among the cannibals," describing his fears for his reputation, in a letter to Hawthorne, which is quoted by Raymond Weaver, *Herman Melville: Mariner and Mystic* (New York, 1921), 21. On Crane's "cannibal" costume, see Unterecker, *Voyager*, 404, and Tate's comments mentioned above in Chapter Two.

7. On Crane's response to Melville, see R.W.B. Lewis, *The Poetry of Crane: A Critical Study* (Princeton, 1967), 202–3 and passim, and Joseph Warren Beach, "Hart Crane and Moby-Dick," in Trachtenberg, ed., *Hart Crane: A Collection of Critical Essays*, (Englewood Cliffs, N.J., 1982), 65–79.

8. A copy of the draft Crane sent to Frank, October 26, 1925 (Beinecke Library, Yale University).

9. R.W.B. Lewis and John Hollander both note that Crane's phrase elides the first part of the familiar phrase, "far and wide." See Lewis, *The Poetry of Hart Crane*, 204, and Hollander, *The Figure of Echo*, 92. This characteristic gesture brings out the spatial continuity implied in "wide" and suppresses the temporal discontinuity in "far"; it is part of Crane's effort to disregard his irreversable distance in time from Melville by reimagining it as a traversable distance in space.

10. John T. Irwin, "Naming Names: Hart Crane's 'Logic of Metaphor,'" *Southern Review* 11, no. 2 (1975): 286.

11. Harvey Gross, "Hart Crane and Wallace Stevens," in Bloom, ed., *Hart Crane: Modern Critical Views*, 49. Gross's comments, which concern the pentameter in "To Brooklyn Bridge," come from his study *Sound and Form in Modern Poetry: A Study of Prosody from Thomas Hardy to Robert Lowell* (Ann Arbor, Mich., 1964). Gross continues: "Perhaps, by definition, the apostrophe requires no explicit grammar. . . . But without the binding meter, the omission of verbs and uncertain use of reference would be destructively apparent." Herbert Liebowitz makes a related point with reference to Crane's image of the vortex: "The centrifugal force of Crane's emotions needed to be counteracted by the centripetal force of established verse structures." See Liebowitz, *Hart Crane: An Introduction to the Poetry* (New York, 1968), 164.

12. Sharon Cameron provides this phenomenology of Crane's composition in "The Broken Tower": "In the dawn rung in by the bells during which 'The stars are caught and hived in the sun's ray,' the swarming of fragmentary radiance to a honey-colored whole literalizes on another, natural level the gathering of plenitude to one entity. . . . In fact it is the gathering of the stars to the mass of the sun that overflows the bounds of conceptual fullness and compels the 'breaking' in the next stanza. The release from permanent form, the spilling of plenty back into the world, leads to the dissolution of wholeness, to 'broken intervals.' " Cameron, *Lyric Time: Dickinson and the Limits of Genre* (Baltimore, 1979), 231.

13. John T. Irwin, *American Hieroglyphics: The Symbol of the Egyptian Hieroglyphics in the American Renaissance* (New Haven, 1980), 349.

14. John Hollander charts the literary history of the music of the shell in *Images of Voice: Music and Sound in Romantic Poetry*, Churchill College Overseas Fellowship Lectures No. 5 (Cambridge, 1970). Hollander distinguishes two myths about the meaning of the sound "inside" shells: one, that it is the sound of the sea; two, that it is "the roar of one's own veins." "If the first myth is . . . Romantic, the substituted one is just as certainly Symbolist, in, among other things, re-authenticating the imagined exterior sea-sound in the inner perception of an equivalent blood-tide: a Mallarmean shell, and a metaphoric presence not wholly absent from Hart Crane's image of a shell that 'secretes / Its beating leagues of monotone.' " Hollander, *Images of Voice*, 17.

15. In a postscript to his letter to Munson, composed March 17, 1926, Crane describes with approval the treatment of "the logic of metaphor" and "the dynamics of inferential mention" in the notes he had prepared for O'Neill and passed along to Munson (Crane, *Letters*, 237). "General Aims and Theories," this letter to Munson, and "A Letter to Harriet Monroe" are so closely related as to read like versions of one document.

16. This is the generative insight of Edelman's own study, which proceeds as an anatomy of three figural strategies in Crane's work—anacoluthon, chiasmus, catachresis—identified not only with three thematized actions—breaking, bending, bridging—but with the three phases of Crane's career represented by (again in series) "For the Marriage of Faustus and Helen," "Voyages," and *The Bridge*.

17. Crane's most important statement of that refusal, which links a defense of his homosexuality and a defense of his tastes and practices as a poet, is the letter he wrote to Winters on May 29, 1927, beginning, "You need a good drubbing for all your recent easy talk about 'the complete man,' the poet and his ethical place in society, etc." For a text of the letter and a commentary on the relationship between the two men, see Thomas Parkinson, *Hart Crane and Yvor Winters: Their Literary Correspondence* (Berkeley, 1978), especially 84–93.

18. Barbara Johnson, *The Critical Difference* (Baltimore, 1980), 68.

19. Sharon Cameron describes this strategy in a way useful for thinking about Crane: "Dickinson's lyrics are in fact conceived within a tradition of utterance that imagines redemption itself to rest upon a speaker's ability to fight free of the grip of this world, and to embrace instead that unthinkable space whose time exacts no separations" (Cameron, *Lyric Time*, 259). Mutlu Konuk Blasing persuasively links Crane and Dickinson in her rhetorical study of American poetry. She uses Crane's image of the vortex to explain: "Technically, Crane adopts Dickinson's subversive strategies, pitting the centripetal force of formal and literal limitation against the centrifugal force of semantic expansion. The meaning of such poetry lies precisely in its articulating and disarticulating rhetoric and syntax, which precludes certainties and unequivocal readings." Blasing, *American Poetry: The Rhetoric of Its Forms* (New Haven, 1987), 189.

20. Edelman, *Transmemberment of Song*, especially 210–15; Bloom, "Introduction," in Bloom, ed., *Hart Crane: Modern Critical Views*; and Irwin, "Figurations of the Writer's Death." For a systematic definition and history of the trope, see Hollander, *The Figure of Echo*, 133–49.

21. Edward Brunner presents a strong argument for locating the poem's composition between April 24 and May 1, 1926, as opposed to June 1926, during the weeks of intense depression before Crane renewed his work on *The Bridge*, as has usually been the case (Lewis, *The Poetry of Hart Crane*, 211–15). "Instead of being a product of his early weeks of creative stasis on the Isle of Pines, the poem is a product of his joyful days in New York, after his mother had given permission to visit the family cottage in the Caribbean (a permission asked for previously but always denied); the poem looks ahead with optimism to a period of renewed vigor" (Brunner, "Appendix A: A New Background for 'Repose of Rivers,' " in Brunner, *Splendid Failure*, 246–49).

22. When he arrived in Cuba, Crane wrote to Slater Brown and Susan Jenkins back in Patterson: "To me, the mountains, strange greens, native thatched huts, perfume, etc. brought me straight to Melville. . . . Oleanders and mimosas in full bloom now make the air almost too heavy with perfume, it's another world—and a little like Rimbaud" (Crane, *Letters*, 252).

23. Crane sent this odd poem, with a dedication, to Underwood on November 22, 1928 (Beinecke Library, Yale University). Underwood (to whom Crane only seldom sent his work) might have read himself as one of the underwater men Crane writes about here.

SEVEN. *The Floating Singer of* The Bridge

1. Quoted by Frank Harris, *Oscar Wilde*, vol. 2, 574 As I suggested in Chapter Five, this is a biography—and a text of *De Profundis*—that Crane may have read.

2. For a discussion of Thoreau as simultaneously a gay male author and an exemplary voice of "liberal individualism," see Michael Warner, "Thoreau's Bottom," *Raritan* 11, no. 3 (1992): 53–79.

3. Yvor Winters, "The Progress of Hart Crane," which appeared in *Poetry* 36 (June 1930): 153–65, is reprinted in Trachtenberg, ed., *Hart Crane: Critical Essays*, 27.

4. Tate's review of *The Bridge*, a revised version of which appears in Tate, *Essays of Four Decades*, first appeared in the *Hound and Horn* (July–September 1930). On May 23, 1930, in the last letter of his that Crane kept, Tate perhaps wishfully misrepresented the balance between blame and praise in his review (which Crane had not yet read). "In general," Tate told Crane, "it says that the symbolism is too subjective to sustain any epic intention, but that it is magnificent poetry, a magnificent series of poems on a symbolic idea" (Letter, Columbia University Library).

5. Tate to Crane, June 10, 1930 (Columbia University Library).

6. R. P. Blackmur, "New Thresholds, New Anatomies: Notes on a Text of Hart Crane," in Trachtenberg, ed., *Hart Crane: A Collection of Critical Essays*, 55.

7. Eric J. Sundquist, "Bringing Home the Word: Magic, Lies, and Silence in Hart Crane," *ELH* 44, no. 2 (Summer 1977): 381. Sundquist emphasizes that this "joke" expresses and conceals "a rebellion against . . . authority" and "a liberation from its pressure."

8. See James Hoopes, *Van Wyck Brooks: In Search of American Culture* (Amherst, 1977), 22.

9. For a detailed treatment of the myths of Atlantis that were available to Crane, see Alan Trachtenberg, *Brooklyn Bridge: Fact and Symbol* (Chicago, 1965), 143–65.

I agree with Alfred Corn's proposal that really "only three valences of Atlantis seem to have been adaptable to [Crane's] purposes: its geographical situation in the Atlantic Ocean, the story of its having sunk beneath the waves when it fell from virtue, and its prophesied resurgence at some future time." Alfred Corn, *The Metamorphoses of Metaphor: Essays in Poetry and Fiction* (New York, 1987), 185.

10. Donald Pease, "Blake, Crane, Whitman, and Modernism: A Poetics of Pure Possibility," in Bloom, ed., *Hart Crane: Modern Critical Views*, 208–9.

11. According to the text of "Auguries of Innocence" given in Blake, *The Poetry and Prose of William Blake*, 492–93, Crane's version of this couplet is an emendation of Blake's: "We are led to Believe a Lie / When we see not Thro the Eye / Which was Born in a Night to perish in a Night . . ."

12. About Candee, Crane wrote: "Life was a frightful torture for him after all, though . . . we all end up rather mad" (Crane, "Wind-blown Flames," 365).

13. Trachtenberg connects this fragment with representations of Brooklyn Bridge, particularly the view from its midpoint, in the work of John Marin, Frank Stella, Waldo Frank, and others, and provides ways to account for the common fascination with this cultural topos. See Trachtenberg, "Cultural Revisions in the Twenties: Brooklyn Bridge as Usable Past," in *The American Self: Myth, Ideology, and Popular Culture* (Albuquerque, N. Mex., 1981), 60–62.

14. Walt Whitman, *Leaves of Grass: A Textual Variorum of the Printed Poems*, Vol. 1, *Poems, 1855–56*, ed. Sculley Bradley, Harold W. Blodgett, Arthur Golden, and William White (New York, 1980), 219.

15. Trachtenberg describes some of the images of fascination and horror popularly associated with the bridge in his *Brooklyn Bridge: Fact and Symbol* (Chicago, 1965), 136–39 and note 4.

16. Underwood's poem, "Pierrot Speaks," which is one source for the clown figure in Crane's early poems, concludes: "My soul is like a wind-blown flame / Or the unstable sea." It is quoted by Herendeen and Parker, editors, in Crane, "Wind-blown Flames," 343.

17. Paul Giles, whose scattershot study of punning in *The Bridge* is off target as often as on, is provocative here: "A *sweep* . . . is an old word for whip. And *chrysalis*—ostensibly a pleasant image of new life burgeoning in the spring—carries as its more sinister underside 'cry / salis,' a cry from the whip, 'salis' punning on Latin *salix*, willow." Paul Giles, *Hart Crane: The Contexts of "The Bridge"* (Cambridge, 1986), 179.

CODA. *Unanswered Questions*

1. Burke and Cowley, *The Selected Correspondence of Kenneth Burke and Malcolm Cowley, 1915–1981*, ed. Paul Jay (Berkeley and Los Angeles, 1990), 334. Matthew Josephson attributed the remark to Burke; Burke did not remember making it, and did not want to claim it.

2. Reported by Peggy Baird Cowley in "The Last Days of Hart Crane," a memoir reprinted in Susan Jenkins Brown, *Robber Rocks*, 172. There are several stories about Crane's sexual relations with men during the day and night before his death; it is unclear who beat him or why. Crane was beaten (and jailed) often in the final years of his life. The friends and biographers who discuss those incidents seem to hold Crane responsible for them, if only because they imply that he brought pun-

ishment on himself by making advances. There is an implication, familiar from other cases of gay-bashing, that the victim deserved it.

3. Cowley to Tate, June 28, 1932 (Princeton University Library).

4. Malcolm Cowley, *The Dream of the Golden Mountains: Remembering the 1930s* (New York, 1980), 55. This is an account of Crane's departure for the last time from the Patterson area, during which he distributed his possessions among friends there. "Everything was considerate," Cowley writes, "everything was warm, but still one had a feeling of last things, as if we were Roman soldiers casting dice for his garments" (53).

IV. BEYOND MODERNISM

EIGHT. *Robert Lowell's Breakdown*

1. Philip Rahv, *Essays on Literature and Politics 1932–1972* (Boston, 1978), 4.

2. Robert Lowell, *Collected Prose* (New York, 1987), 58. In addition to memoirs and letters, my account of the relationship between Tate and Lowell makes use of two basic sources: William Doreski, *The Years of Our Friendship: Robert Lowell and Allen Tate* (Jackson, Miss., 1990), and Ian Hamilton, *Robert Lowell: A Biography* (New York, 1982). Makowsky and Waldron touch on the relationship in their biographies of Gordon. Other discussions tend to be anecdotal or to present materials also available in these books.

3. Gordon related Lowell's arrival this way: "Allen and I were standing in the circle admiring the lemon lilies when a car drove up to the gate and a young man got out. He stopped down there by the post box and answered the call of Nature then ascended the slope. We stood there eyeing him sternly and were on the point of shouting 'défense d'uriner' when he came up to Allen, regarded him fixedly and muttered something about Ford" (Gordon and Wood, *Southern Mandarins*, 209). For Gordon's treatment of the visit in *The Strange Children*, see the Coda to Part Two.

4. Although Lowell came to study with Tate and Ransom, and he did become Ransom's student at Kenyon College in 1938, Lowell's first bond was formed with Tate, and it was the more important one in every respect.

5. Ford was not the only mediator in these events; Lowell had met Ford through Merrill Moore. Moore was a Fugitive, said to have written in excess of three thousand sonnets; he may be better remembered in literary history, however, as the Boston psychiatrist to whom Charlotte Lowell, the poet's mother, was devoted. The crisis in which Moore intervened came after Lowell struck his father in an argument over his plans to marry his cousin. Charlotte Lowell believed her son might be mad and asked Moore if it would be advisable to place him under psychiatric care; Moore encouraged Lowell to go to Tennessee instead.

6. For other alternatives to the historical narrative I am describing, see Paul Breslin, *The Psycho-Political Muse: American Poetry Since the Fifties* (Chicago, 1987), and Robert von Hallberg, *American Poetry and Culture, 1945–1980* (Cambridge, Mass., 1985). Despite its revisionary stance, Walter Kaladjian's *Languages of Liberation: The Social Text in American Poetry* (New York, 1989) retains the imagery of repression and liberation central to most accounts of the postwar period since the late 1950s.

7. Lowell's account of a reading trip on the West Coast, during which he encountered Ginsberg and other poets, and experimented with metrical looseness as a result, is customarily referred to when critics seek to explain the formal developments in *Life Studies*. See Lowell, *Collected Prose*, 226–27. Lowell's focus in this account on the formal nature of his interest in the Beats disguises his deeper curiosity about the exhibitionism of their work. (Lowell relates relevant, although similar, anecdotes and opinions in his several interviews, only two of which are preserved in *Collected Prose*.) In some ways, Lowell had more in common with the experimental poets in *The New American Poetry, 1945–1960* (New York, 1960), Donald Allen's famous anthology, than with the formalist poets who appeared with him in the competing volume—*New Poets of England and America*, edited by Donald Hall, Louis Simpson, and Robert Pack.

8. Rahv's "Paleface and Redskin" was published in the *Kenyon Review* in 1939. Also relevant is Rahv's "The Cult of Experience in American Writing," which appeared in the *Daily Worker* in 1934. Both of these essays are collected in Rahv, *Essays in Literature and Politics 1932–1972*, 3–22.

9. Irvin Ehrenpreis, "The Age of Lowell," in *Robert Lowell: A Collection of Critical Essays*, ed. Thomas Parkinson (Englewood Cliffs, N.J., 1968), 89.

10. Randall Jarrell, *Poetry and the Age* (New York, 1953), 213.

11. Tate, "An Open Letter," May 24, 1937, in *Davidson and Tate*, 417–18. Tate's letter was addressed to the Vanderbilt chancellor, James H. Kirkland.

12. Ransom won the Bollingen Prize in 1951 and the National Book Award, for *Selected Poems*, in 1964; Tate was awarded the National Medal for Literature in 1976.

13. David Bromwich, *A Choice of Inheritance: Self and Community from Edmund Burke to Robert Frost* (Cambridge, Mass., 1989), 240.

14. Tate wrote on the telegram Lowell sent him on March 1, 1949: "This was sent immediately after he left Yaddo. I was to 'come' to fight evil" (Princeton University Library).

15. Tate to Elizabeth Hardwick, March 30, 1949 (Houghton Library, Harvard University).

16. Tate to Elizabeth Hardwick, April 4, 1949 (Houghton Library, Harvard University). In his account of the episode, William Doreski fairly stresses the element of sexual jealousy in Tate's warning to Hardwick; in this instance Tate counseled her not to let Lowell back into her house (Doreski, *The Years of Our Friendship*, 89–90).

17. Steven Gould Axelrod, *Robert Lowell: Life and Art* (Princeton, 1978), 95. Here is another, typical generalization: "Robert Lowell's poetry has been a long struggle to remove the mask, to make his speaker unequivocally himself" (M. L. Rosenthal, "Robert Lowell and the Poetry of Confession," in *Lowell: A Collection of Critical Essays*, ed. Thomas Parkinson, 114).

18. James E. B. Breslin, *From Modern to Contemporary: American Poetry, 1945–1965* (Chicago, 1984), xv.

19. A. Alvarez, "Robert Lowell in Conversation," in Mazzaro, ed., *Profile of Robert Lowell* (Columbus, Ohio, 1971), 39. The interview is also collected in Meyers, ed., *Robert Lowell: Interviews and Memoirs* (Ann Arbor, Mich., 1988).

20. Robert Lowell, unpublished manuscript (Houghton Library, Harvard University).

21. Transcript of Yaddo Board of Directors meeting, February 26, 1949 (Robert Fitzgerald Papers, Beinecke Library, Yale University).

22. See Michael Paul Rogin, 'Ronald Reagan,' the Movie, and Other Episodes in Political Demonology (Berkeley and Los Angeles, 1987), 236–71.

23. Robert Fitzgerald to George Santayana, May 26, 1949 (Beinecke Library, Yale University).

24. The recipients of the letter were listed at the end of the letter in this order: T. S. Eliot, Allen Tate, John Crowe Ransom, Robert Penn Warren, William Carlos Williams, J. F. Powers, Randall Jarrell, Peter Taylor, Katherine Anne Porter, Louise Bogan, Leonie Adams, Elizabeth Bishop, Marianne Moore, and Willard Thorp. There is a question mark after Thorp's name on the copy of the letter I examined. Karl Shapiro's name has been crossed out and John Berryman's added. The latter revision is suggestive, since Shapiro dissented after his fellow judges voted to give the Bollingen Prize to Pound. Ian Hamilton, who also quotes from this letter, does not list Thorp or Shapiro as recipients; he adds Berryman and R. P. Blackmur (Hamilton, Robert Lowell, 484, n. 14). Hamilton seems to have examined another, later version of the letter.

25. Not all of the letter's recipients accepted that assumption. Fitzgerald preserved unsympathetic responses from Marianne Moore and Louise Bogan (who believed Lowell had behaved badly) and from Katherine Ann Porter (who believed Lowell was insane). It is suggestive that the dissenting letters were from women, since two women were the particular objects of Lowell's attack.

26. Tate to Robert Lowell, December 3, 1957 (Houghton Library, Harvard University).

27. This is handwritten on Tate's copy of the poem. Tate probably wrote this sometime after the 1950s while reviewing his papers, as is the case with other such comments in the archive at Princeton. The quip retains its force, whenever it was made.

28. Hamilton read the comments by Empson and the lines from Lear at Lowell's memorial service in New York; in his biography, where the Empson and Shakespeare quotations provide epitaphs, Hamilton quotes Christopher Ricks's quotation of the same words. David Bromwich comments: "One cannot help noticing how many times this sentiment had to be mediated before it could reach us from a safe distance: Hamilton on Lowell quotes Ricks quoting Empson on Lear" (Bromwich, A Choice of Inheritance, 244). The others, it seems, are there to support Hamilton in a quasireligious claim (in Bromwich's words, that Lowell was "a great man and heroic artist who endured the worst for the sake of all of us"), which had ceased to be widely tenable even before Hamilton published his book in 1982.

29. The essay I refer to, Ohmann's "The Shaping of a Canon: U.S. Fiction, 1960–1975," deals with the practical mechanisms by which certain novels were selected for high critical valuation and eventually made their way into college curricula. Ohmann's primary examples are Franny and Zooey (J. D. Salinger), One Flew Over the Cuckoo's Nest (Ken Kesey), The Bell Jar (Sylvia Plath), Herzog (Saul Bellow), Portnoy's Complaint (Phillip Roth), and the Rabbit series (John Updike).

30. I owe this observation to Lawrence Kramer, "Freud and the Skunks: Genre and Language in Life Studies," in Steven Gould Axelrod and Helen Deese, eds., Robert Lowell: Essays on the Poetry (Cambridge, 1986), 89–90. Sandra M. Gilbert

suggests that the hermit heiress and her son, who is a bishop, point to another generational link: that between Marianne Moore and Elizabeth Bishop. See Gilbert, "Mephistophilis in Maine: Rereading 'Skunk Hour,' " in Axelrod and Deese, eds., *Robert Lowell: Essays on the Poetry*, 77.

31. Transcript of a talk, ca. 1960 (Houghton Library, Harvard Library).

32. This and other valuable information about Lowell's notebooks can be found in Axelrod, *Robert Lowell: Life and Art*, 32, 245–46.

33. Warner Berthoff, *Hart Crane: A Re-Introduction* (Minneapolis, 1989), 22.

34. Lowell to Pound, March 26, 1954 (Beinecke Library, Yale University).

Works Cited

Abrahams, Edward. *The Lyrical Left: Randolph Bourne, Alfred Stieglitz, and the Origins of Cultural Radicalism in America*. Charlottesville: University Press of Virginia, 1986.

Allen, Donald M., ed. *The New American Poetry, 1945–1960*. New York: Grove, 1960.

Anderson, Elliott, and Mary Kinzie. *The Little Magazine in America: A Modern Documentary History*. New York: Pushcart, 1978.

Anderson, Sherwood. *Winesburg, Ohio*. New York: Viking, 1960.

Arac, Jonathan. "Lyric Poetry and the Bounds of the New Criticism." In Hōsek and Parker, eds., *Lyric Poetry: Beyond the New Criticism*, 38–54.

Arnold, Matthew. *Lectures and Essays in Criticism*, ed. R. H. Super. Ann Arbor: University of Michigan Press, 1962.

Auerbach, Erich. *Mimesis: The Representation of Reality in Western Literature*, trans. Willard R. Trask. Princeton: Princeton University Press, 1968.

Axelrod, Steven Gould. *Robert Lowell: Life and Art*. Princeton: Princeton University Press, 1978.

Axelrod, Steven Gould, and Helen Deese, eds. *Robert Lowell: Essays on the Poetry*. Cambridge: Cambridge University Press, 1986.

Baker, Houston A., Jr. *Modernism and the Harlem Renaissance*. Chicago: University of Chicago Press, 1987.

Baldick, Chris. *The Social Mission of English Criticism 1848–1932*. New York: Oxford University Press, 1983.

Beach, Joseph Warren. "Hart Crane and Moby-Dick." In Trachtenberg, ed. *Crane: Critical Essays*, 65–79.

Benjamin, Walter. *Charles Baudelaire: A Lyric Poet in the Era of High Capitalism*, trans. Harry Zohn. London: Verso, 1983.

Berthoff, Warner. *Hart Crane: A Re-Introduction*. Minneapolis: University of Minnesota Press, 1989.

Blackmur, R. P. "New Thresholds, New Anatomies: Notes on a Text by Hart Crane," in Bloom, ed., *Hart Crane: Modern Critical Views*, 17–30.

Blake, William. *The Poetry and Prose of William Blake*, ed. David V. Erdman; commentary, Harold Bloom. Garden City, N.Y.: Doubleday, 1965.

Blasing, Mutlu Konuk. *American Poetry: The Rhetoric of Its Forms*. New Haven: Yale University Press, 1987.

Bledstein, Burton. *The Culture of Professionalism: The Middle Class and the Development of Higher Education in America*. New York: Norton, 1976.

Block, Fred, and Larry Hirshorn. "New Productive Forces and the Contradictions of Contemporary Capitalism." *Theory and Society* 7, no. 1 (1979): 363–90.

Bloom, Harold, ed. *Hart Crane: Modern Critical Views*. New York: Chelsea House, 1986.

Bourdieu, Pierre. *Distinction: A Social Critique of the Judgment of Taste*, trans. Richard Nice. Cambridge: Harvard University Press, 1984.

Bové, Paul. "Agriculture and Academe: America's Southern Question." *boundary 2*, 14, no. 3 (1986): 169–96.

———. *Intellectuals in Power: A Genealogy of Critical Humanism*. New York: Columbia University Press, 1986.

Bradbury, John M. *The Fugitives: A Critical Account*. Chapel Hill: University of North Carolina Press, 1958.

Breslin, James E. B. *From Modern to Contemporary: American Poetry, 1945–1965*. Chicago: University of Chicago Press, 1984.

Breslin, Paul. *The Pscyho-Political Muse: American Poetry Since the Fifties*. Chicago: University of Chicago Press, 1987.

Brodhead, Richard H. *The School of Hawthorne*. New York: Oxford University Press, 1986.

Bromwich, David. *A Choice of Inheritance: Self and Community from Edmund Burke to Robert Frost*. Cambridge: Harvard University Press, 1989.

———. "Parody, Pastiche, and Allusion." In Hōsek and Parker, eds., *Lyric Poetry: Beyond the New Criticism*, 328–43.

Brooks, Cleanth. "T. S. Eliot and the American South." In Simpson, Olney, and Gulledge, eds., *"The Southern Review" and Modern Literature, 1935–1985*, 197–210.

Brooks, Cleanth, and Robert Penn Warren. *Understanding Poetry*. New York: Henry Holt, 1938.

Brooks, Van Wyck. *America's Coming of Age*. New York: Huebsch, 1915.

———. *Letters and Leadership*. New York: Huebsch, 1917.

———. "On Creating a Usable Past" (1918). In Trachtenberg, ed., *Critics of Culture: Literature and Society in the Early Twentieth Century*.

Brown, Ashley. "Caroline Gordon and Hart Crane: A Literary Relationship." *Visionary Company* 1–2, nos. 2–1 (1982): 57–63.

Brown, Susan Jenkins. *Robber Rocks: Letters and Memoirs of Hart Crane, 1923–1932*. Middletown, Conn.: Wesleyan University Press, 1968.

Brunner, Edward J. *Splendid Failure: Hart Crane and the Making of "The Bridge."* Urbana: University of Illinois Press, 1985.

Burke, Kenneth, and Malcolm Cowley. *The Selected Correspondence of Kenneth Burke and Malcolm Cowley*, ed. Paul Jay. Berkeley and Los Angeles: University of California Press, 1990.

Cameron, Sharon. *Lyric Time: Dickinson and the Limits of Genre*. Baltimore: Johns Hopkins University Press, 1979.

Chauncey, George, Jr. "Christian Brotherhood or Sexual Perversion? Homosexual Identities and the Construction of Sexual Boundaries in the World War I Era." In *Hidden from History: Reclaiming the Gay and Lesbian Past*, ed. Martin Bauml Duberman, Martha Vicinus, and George Chauncey, Jr. New York: NAL, 1989. 294–317.

————. "The Way We Were: Gay Male Society in the Jazz Age." *Village Voice* 31 (1986): 26.

Christ, Carol T. *Victorian and Modernist Poetics*. Chicago: University of Chicago Press, 1984.

Coleridge, Samuel Taylor. *Collected Works of Samuel Taylor Coleridge*, ed. Kathleen Coburn. Vol. 5:1, *Lectures 1808–1819*. Princeton: Princeton University Press, 1980.

Conn, Peter. *The Divided Mind: Ideology and Imagination in America, 1898–1917*. New York: Cambridge University Press, 1983.

Corn, Alfred. *The Metamorphoses of Metaphor: Essays in Poetry and Fiction*. New York: Viking, 1987.

Cowley, Malcolm. *The Dream of the Golden Mountains: Remembering the 1930s*. New York: Viking, 1980.

————. *Exile's Return: A Literary Odyssey of the 1920s*. New York: Viking, 1951.

————. "The Merriwether Connection." *Southern Review* 1 (1965): 46–56.

————. "Two Winters with Hart Crane and Allen Tate." In Squires, ed., *Allen Tate and His Work*, 26–33.

Cowley, Malcolm, and Kenneth Burke. *The Selected Correspondence of Kenneth Burke and Malcolm Cowley*, ed. Paul Jay. Berkeley and Los Angeles: University of California Press, 1990.

Cowley, Peggy Baird. "The Last Days of Hart Crane." In Susan Jenkins Brown, *Robber Rocks*, 147–73.

Crane, Hart. *The Bridge*. Paris: Black Sun, 1930.

————. *The Bridge*. New York: Liveright, 1930.

————. *The Complete Poems and Selected Letters and Prose of Hart Crane*, ed. Brom Weber. Garden City, N.Y.: Doubleday, 1966.

————. *The Letters of Hart Crane and His Family*, ed. Thomas S. W. Lewis. New York: Columbia University Press, 1974.

————. *The Letters of Hart Crane, 1916–1932*, ed. Brom Weber. New York: Hermitage House, 1952; repr. Berkeley: University of California Press, 1965.

————. *The Poems of Hart Crane*, ed. Marc Simon. New York: Liveright, 1986.

————. *White Buildings: Poems by Hart Crane*. New York: Boni and Liveright, 1926.

————. "Wind-blown Flames: Letters of Hart Crane to Wilbur Underwood," ed. Warren Herendeen and Donald G. Parker. *Southern Review* 16, no. 2 (1980): 339–76.

Crane, Hart, and Yvor Winters. *Hart Crane and Yvor Winters: Their Literary Correspondence*, ed. Thomas Parkinson. Berkeley: University of California Press, 1978.

Culler, Jonathan. "Changes in the Study of Lyric." In Hošek and Parker, eds., *Lyric Poetry Beyond the New Criticism*, 38–54.

Davidson, Donald. "Certain Fallacies in Modern Poetry." *Fugitive* 3 (1924): 66–68.

————. *Lee in the Mountains and Other Poems*. Boston: Houghton Mifflin, 1938.

————. *The Tall Men*. Boston: Houghton Mifflin, 1926.

Davidson, Donald, and Allen Tate. *The Literary Correspondence of Donald Davidson and Allen Tate*, ed. John Tyree Fain and Thomas Daniel Young. Athens: University of Georgia Press, 1974.

de Man, Paul. *The Rhetoric of Romanticism*. New York: Columbia University Press, 1984.

D'Emilio, John, and Estelle B. Freedman. *Intimate Matters: A History of Sexuality in America*. New York: Harper & Row, 1988.

Doreski, William. *The Years of Our Friendship: Robert Lowell and Allen Tate*. Jackson: University of Mississippi Press, 1990.

Edelman, Lee. *Transmemberment of Song: Hart Crane's Anatomies of Rhetoric and Desire*. Stanford: Stanford University Press, 1987.

Ehrenpreis, Irvin. "The Age of Lowell." In Parkinson, ed., *Robert Lowell: Critical Views*, 74–98.

Eliot, T. S. *After Strange Gods: A Primer of Modern Heresy*. New York: Harcourt, Brace, 1934.

———. *Collected Poems 1909–1962*. New York, Harcourt Brace, 1963.

———. *The Letters of T. S. Eliot*, ed. Valerie Eliot. Vol. 1, *1898–1922*. New York: Harcourt Brace Jovanovich, 1988.

———. *Poems: 1909–1925*. London: Faber and Gwyer, 1925.

———. "Reflections on Contemporary Poetry." *Egoist* 6, no. 3 (1919): 39–41.

———. *The Sacred Wood: Essays on Poetry and Criticism*. 2nd ed. London: Methuen, 1928.

———. *Selected Prose of T. S. Eliot*, ed. Frank Kermode. London: Faber and Faber, 1975.

———. *The Waste Land: A Facsimile and Transcript of the Original Drafts Including the Annotations of Ezra Pound*, ed. Valerie Eliot. New York: Harcourt Brace Jovanovich, 1971.

Ellmann, Maud. *The Poetics of Impersonality: T. S. Eliot and Ezra Pound*. Cambridge: Harvard University Press, 1987.

Erenberg, Lewis A. *Steppin' Out: New York Nightlife and the Transformation of American Culture, 1890–1930*. Westport, Conn.: Greenwood, 1981.

Ewen, Stuart. *Captains of Consciousness: Advertising and the Social Roots of Consumer Culture*. New York: McGraw-Hill, 1976.

Fass, Paula S. *The Damned and the Beautiful: American Youth in the 1920s*. New York: Oxford University Press, 1977.

Fekete, John. *The Critical Twilight: Explorations in the Ideology of Anglo-American Literary Theory from Eliot to McLuhan*. London: Routledge and Kegan Paul, 1977.

Fowler, Alastair. *Kinds of Literature: An Introduction to the Theory of Genres and Modes*. Cambridge: Harvard University Press, 1982.

Frank, Waldo. *In the American Jungle (1925–1936)*. New York: Farrar and Rinehart, 1937.

———. *Our America*. New York: Boni and Liveright, 1919.

———. *The Re-discovery of America: An Introduction to a Philosophy of American Life*. New York: Scribner's, 1929.

———. *Virgin Spain: Scenes from the Spiritual Drama of a Great People*. New York: Boni and Liveright, 1926.

Freedman, Jonathan. *Professions of Taste: Henry James, British Aestheticism, and Commodity Culture*. Stanford: Stanford University Press, 1990.

Fry, Paul H. *The Poet's Calling in the English Ode*. New Haven: Yale University Press, 1980.

Gilbert, Sandra M. "Mephistophilis in Maine: Rereading 'Skunk Hour.' " In Axelrod and Dease, eds., *Robert Lowell: Essays on the Poetry*, 77.

Gilbert, Sandra, and Susan Gubar. *No Man's Land: The Place of the Woman Writer in the Twentieth Century*. Vol. 1, *The War of the Words*. Vol. 2, *Sexchanges*. New Haven: Yale University Press, 1987, 1988.

Giles, Paul. *Hart Crane: The Contexts of "The Bridge."* New York: Cambridge University Press, 1986.

Gilmer, Walker. *Horace Liveright: Publisher of the Twenties*. New York: Lewis, 1970.

Golding, Alan. "Poet-Critics and Professionalism in the 1930s." *Sagetrieb* (forthcoming).

Gordon, Caroline. *The Malefactors*. New York: Harcourt Brace, 1956.

———. *The Strange Children*. New York: Scribner's, 1951.

Gordon, Caroline, and Sally Wood. *The Southern Mandarins: Letters of Caroline Gordon to Sally Wood, 1924–1937*, ed. Sally Wood. Baton Rouge: Louisiana State University Press, 1984.

Gordon, Caroline, and Allen Tate, eds. *The House of Fiction: An Anthology of the Short Story with Commentary*. New York: Scribner's, 1950.

Gouldner, Alvin W. *The Future of Intellectuals and the Rise of the New Class*. New York: Seabury Press, 1979.

Graff, Gerald. *Professing Literature: An Institutional History*. Chicago: University of Chicago Press, 1987.

Gray, Richard J. *Writing the American South: Ideas of an American Region*. Cambridge: Cambridge University Press, 1986.

Gross, Harvey. "Hart Crane and Wallace Stevens." In Bloom, ed., *Hart Crane: Modern Critical Views*, 43–52.

Grossman, Allen. "Hart Crane and Poetry: A Consideration of Crane's Intense Poetics." In Bloom, ed., *Hart Crane: Modern Critical Views*, 221–54.

Guillory, John. "Canonical and Non-Canonical: A Critique of the Current Debate." *ELH* 54, no. 3 (Autumn 1987): 483–527.

———. "The Ideology of Canon Formation: T. S. Eliot and Cleanth Brooks." *Critical Inquiry* 10, no. 3 (1983): 173–98.

Hall, Donald, Louis Simpson, and Robert Pack, eds. *New Poets of England and America*. New York: Meridian, 1960.

Hamilton, Ian. *Robert Lowell: A Biography*. New York: Random House, 1982.

Harris, Frank. *Oscar Wilde: His Life and Confessions*. 2 vols. New York: Frank Harris (private printing), 1916.

Hobsbawm, Eric, and Terence Kanger, eds. *The Invention of Tradition*. Cambridge: Cambridge University Press, 1983.

Hocquenghem, Guy. *Homosexual Desire*, trans. Daniella Dangoor. London: Allison and Busby, 1978.

Hoffman, Frederick J., Charles Allen, and Carolyn F. Ulrich. *The Little Magazine: A History and a Bibliography*. Princeton: Princeton University Press, 1947.

Hollander, John. *The Figure of Echo: A Mode of Allusion in Milton and After*. Berkeley and Los Angeles: University of California Press, 1981.

————. *Images of Voice: Music and Sound in Romantic Poetry.* Churchill College Overseas Fellowship Lectures No. 5. Cambridge: W. Heffer, 1970.

Hoopes, James. *Van Wyck Brooks: In Search of American Culture.* Amherst: University of Massachusetts Press, 1977.

Horton, Philip. *Hart Crane: The Life of an American Poet.* New York: Norton, 1937.

Hōsek, Chaviva, and Patricia Parker, eds. *Lyric Poetry: Beyond the New Criticism.* Ithaca: Cornell University Press, 1985.

Hubbell, Jay B. *Who Are the Major American Writers? A Study of the Changing Literary Canon.* Durham: Duke University Press, 1972.

Hulme, T. E. *Speculations: Essays on Humanism and the Philosophy of Art,* ed. Herbert Read. London: Routledge and Kegan Paul, 1924.

Humphries, Jefferson. "The Cemeteries of Paul Valéry and Allen Tate: The Ghosts of Aeneas and Narcissus." *Southern Review* 20, no. 1 (1984): 54–67.

Huyssen, Andreas. *After the Great Divide: Modernism, Mass Culture, Postmodernism.* Bloomington: Indiana University Press, 1986.

Irwin, John T. *American Hieroglyphics: The Symbol of the Egyptian Hieroglyphics in the American Renaissance.* New Haven: Yale University Press, 1980.

————. "Figurations of the Writer's Death: Freud and Hart Crane." In Bloom, ed., *Hart Crane: Modern Critical Views,* 155–88.

————. "Foreshadowing and Foreshortening: The Prophetic Vision of Origins in Hart Crane's *The Bridge.*" *Word and Image* 1 (1985): 288–312.

————. "Hart Crane's *The Bridge* (I–II)." *Raritan* 8, no. 4; 9, no. 1 (1989): 70–88, 99–113.

————. "Naming Names: Hart Crane's 'Logic of Metaphor.' " *Southern Review* 11, no. 2 (1975): 284–99.

James, Henry. *The American Scene,* ed. Leon Edel. Bloomington: Indiana University Press, 1968.

Jarrell, Randall. *Poetry and the Age.* New York: Knopf, 1953.

Johnson, Barbara. *The Critical Difference.* Baltimore: Johns Hopkins University Press, 1980.

Joyce, James. *A Portrait of the Artist as a Young Man.* New York: Viking, 1964.

————. *Ulysses.* New York: Random House, 1961.

Kaladjian, Walter. *Languages of Liberation: The Social Text in American Poetry.* New York: Columbia University Press, 1989.

Keats, John. *The Poems of John Keats,* ed. Jack Stillinger. Cambridge: Harvard University Press, 1978.

Kermode, Frank. *Romantic Image.* London: Routledge and Kegan Paul, 1957.

Klein, Marcus. *Foreigners: The Making of American Literature, 1900–1940.* Chicago: University of Chicago Press, 1981.

Koestenbaum, Wayne. *Double Talk: The Erotics of Male Literary Collaboration.* New York: Routledge, 1989.

Kramer, Lawrence. "Freud and the Skunks: Genre and Language in *Life Studies.*" In Axelrod and Deese, eds., *Robert Lowell: Essays on the Poetry,* 89–90.

Larson, Magali Sarfatti. *The Rise of Professionalism: A Sociological Analysis.* Berkeley: University of California Press, 1977.

Lawrence, D. H. *Studies in Classic American Literature.* New York: Viking, 1964.

Lentricchia, Frank. *Ariel and the Police: Michel Foucault, William James, Wallace Stevens*. Madison: University of Wisconsin Press, 1988.

———. "Lyric in the Culture of Capitalism." *American Literary History* 1, no. 1 (1989): 63–89.

Levenson, Michael H. *A Genealogy of Modernism: A Study of English Literary Doctrine 1908–1922*. Cambridge: Cambridge University Press, 1984.

Lewis, Felice Flanery. *Literature, Obscenity, and Law*. Carbondale: Southern Illinois University Press, 1976.

Lewis, R.W.B. *The Poetry of Hart Crane: A Critical Study*. Princeton: Princeton University Press, 1967.

Lewis, Wyndham. *Blasting and Bombardiering*. London: Calder, 1967.

Liebowitz, Herbert A. *Hart Crane: An Introduction to the Poetry*. New York: Columbia University Press, 1968.

Longenbach, James. "Hart Crane and T. S. Eliot: Poets in the Sacred Grove." *Denver Quarterly* 23, no. 1 (1988): 82–103.

Lowell, Robert. *Collected Prose*, ed. Robert Giroux. New York: Farrar, Straus and Giroux, 1987.

———. *Land of Unlikeness*. Cummington, Mass.: Cummington Press, 1946.

———. *Selected Poems*. New York: Farrar, Straus and Giroux, rev. ed., 1977.

———. *Life Studies*. New York: Farrar, Straus and Cudahy, 1959.

Macy, John. *The Spirit of American Literature*. Garden City, N.Y.: Doubleday, Page, 1913.

Makowsky, Veronica A. *Caroline Gordon: A Biography*. New York: Oxford University Press, 1989.

———. "Caroline Gordon on Women Writing: A Contradiction in Terms?" *Southern Quarterly* 28 (1990): 52.

Marchand, Roland. *Advertising the American Dream: Making Way for Modernity, 1920–1945*. Berkeley: University of California Press, 1985.

Maritain, Jacques. *"'Art and Scholasticism" and "The Frontiers of Poetry,"* trans. Joseph W. Evans. New York: Scribner's, 1962.

Martin, Robert K. *The Homosexual Tradition in American Poetry*. Austin: University of Texas Press, 1979.

Mazzaro, Jerome, ed. *Profile of Robert Lowell*. Columbus: University of Ohio Press, 1971.

Meiners, R. K. *The Last Alternatives: A Study of the Works of Allen Tate*. Denver: Swallow, 1963.

Meisel, Perry. *The Myth of the Modern: A Study in British Literature and Criticism Since 1850*. New Haven: Yale University Press, 1987.

Melville, Herman. *The Writings of Herman Melville*, ed. Harrison Hayford, Alma A. MacDougall, and G. Thomas Tanselle. Vol. 3, *Mardi, and a Voyage Thither*. Vol. 6, *Moby-Dick, or the Whale*. Vol. 9, *Piazza Tales and Other Prose Pieces*. Evanston and Chicago: Northwestern University Press and the Newberry Library, 1970, 1988, and 1987.

Menand, Louis. *Discovering Modernism: T. S. Eliot and His Context*. New York: Oxford University Press, 1987.

Meyers, Jeffrey, ed. *Robert Lowell: Interviews and Memoirs*. Ann Arbor: University of Michigan Press, 1988.

Miller, James E., Jr. *T. S. Eliot's Personal Waste Land: The Exorcism of the Demons.* University Park: Pennsylvania State University Press, 1977.

Milton, John. *Complete Poems and Major Prose*, ed. Merritt Y. Hughes. New York: Odyssey, 1957.

Mumford, Lewis. *The Golden Day.* New York: Boni and Liveright, 1926.

Munson, Gorham. *The Awakening Twenties: A Memoir-History of a Literary Period.* Baton Rouge: Louisiana State University Press, 1985.

————. *Destinations: A Canvass of American Literature Since 1900.* New York: Sears, 1928.

————. *Waldo Frank: A Study.* New York: Boni and Liveright, 1923.

Nunokawa, Jeff. " 'All the Sad Young Men': AIDS and the Work of Mourning." *Yale Journal of Criticism* 4, no. 2 (1991): 1–12.

————. "*In Memoriam* and the Extinction of the Homosexual." *ELH* 58, no. 2 (1991): 427–38.

O'Brien, Michael. *The Idea of the American South, 1920–1941.* Baltimore: Johns Hopkins University Press, 1979.

O'Connor, Flannery. *The Habit of Being*, ed. Sally Fitzgerald. New York: Farrar, Straus and Giroux, 1979.

Ohmann, Richard. *Politics of Letters.* Middletown, Conn.: Wesleyan University Press, 1987.

Ouspensky, P. D. *Tertium Organum: The Third Canon of Thought, a Key to the Enigmas of the World*, trans. Nicholas Bessaraboff and Claude Bragdon; rev. trans. E. Kadloubovsky and P. D. Ouspensky. New York: Knopf, 1981.

Parkinson, Thomas, ed. *Hart Crane and Yvor Winters: Their Literary Correspondence.* Berkeley: University of California Press, 1978.

————. *Robert Lowell: A Collection of Critical Views.* Englewood Cliffs, N.J.: Prentice-Hall, 1968.

Pater, Walter. *The Renaissance: Studies in Art and Poetry*, ed. Donald L. Hill. Berkeley and Los Angeles: University of California Press, 1980.

Paul, Sherman. *Hart's Bridge.* Urbana: University of Illinois Press, 1972.

Pearce, Roy Harvey. *The Continuity of American Poetry.* Princeton: Princeton University Press, 1961.

Pease, Donald. "Blake, Crane, Whitman, and Modernism: A Poetics of Pure Possibility." In Bloom, ed., *Hart Crane: Modern Critical Views*, 189–220.

Perkins, David. *A History of Modern Poetry.* Vols. 1–2. Cambridge, Mass.: Harvard University Press, 1976–1987.

Poirier, Richard. *Robert Frost: The Work of Knowing.* New York: Oxford University Press, 1977.

Pound, Ezra. "The Audience." *Poetry* 5 (1914–1915): 30.

————. *The Literary Essays of Ezra Pound*, ed. T. S. Eliot. New York: New Directions, 1954.

Rahv, Philip. *Essays on Literature and Politics 1932–1972.* Boston: Houghton Mifflin, 1978.

Ransom, John Crowe. "A Doctrine of Relativity." *Fugitive* 4 (1925): 93–95.

————. *God Without Thunder: An Unorthodox Defense of Orthodoxy.* Hamden, Conn.: Archon, repr. 1965.

————. "Mr. Ransom Replies" (letter). *Literary Review* of the *New York Evening Post* (August 11, 1923): 902.

————. *The New Criticism.* Norfolk, Conn.: New Directions, 1941.

————. *Selected Poems.* New York: Knopf, 3rd ed., 1978.

————. "Thoughts on the Poetic Discontent" (essay). *Fugitive* 4 (1925): 62–64.

————. "Waste Lands." *Literary Review* of the *New York Evening Post* (July 14, 1923): 825–26.

————. *The World's Body.* Baton Rouge: Louisiana State University Press, 1968.

Robinson, Edwin Arlington. *Collected Poems of Edwin Arlington Robinson.* New York: Macmillan, 1965.

Rogin, Michael Paul. *"Ronald Reagan," The Movie, and Other Episodes in Political Demonology.* Berkeley and Los Angeles: University of California Press, 1987.

Rosenthal, M. L. "Robert Lowell and the Poetry of Confession." In Parkinson, ed., *Robert Lowell: Critical Views*, 113–23.

Rowe, John Carlos. "The 'Supra-Historical' Sense of Hart Crane's *The Bridge.*" *Genre* 11, no. 4 (1978): 597–625.

Rubin, Louis D., Jr. *A Gallery of Southerners.* Baton Rouge: Louisiana State University Press, 1982.

————. *The Wary Fugitives: Four Poets and the South.* Baton Rouge: Louisiana State University Press, 1978.

Sayre, Robert, and Michel Löwy. "Figures of Romantic Anti-Capitalism." *New German Critique* 32 (Spring/Summer 1984): 42–92.

Sealts, Merton M., Jr. *Pursuing Melville 1940–1980.* Madison: University of Wisconsin Press, 1982.

Sedgwick, Eve Kosofsky. *Between Men: English Literature and Male Homosocial Desire.* New York: Columbia University Press, 1985.

————. *Epistemology of the Closet.* Berkeley and Los Angeles: University of California Press, 1990.

Shelley, Percy Bysshe. *Shelley's Poetry and Prose*, ed. Donald H. Rieman and Sharon B. Powers. New York: Norton, 1977.

Simpson, Lewis P. *The Man of Letters in New England and the South: Essays on the History of the Literary Vocation in America.* Baton Rouge: Louisiana State University Press, 1973.

Simpson, Lewis P., James Olney, and Jo Gulledge, eds. *The "Southern Review" and Modern Literature, 1935–1985.* Baton Rouge: Louisiana State University Press, 1988.

Singal, Daniel Joseph. *The War Within: From Victorian to Modernist Thought in the South, 1919–1945.* Chapel Hill: University of North Carolina Press, 1982.

Sklar, Martin J. "On the Proletarian Revolution and the End of Political Economic Society." *Radical America* 3 (1969): 1–42.

Smith, Barbara Herrnstein. *Poetic Closure: A Study of How Poems End.* Chicago: University of Chicago Press, 1968.

Squires, Radcliffe. *Allen Tate: A Literary Biography.* New York: Bobbs-Merrill, 1971.

Squires, Radcliffe, ed. *Allen Tate and His Work: Critical Evaluations.* Minneapolis: University of Minnesota Press, 1972.

Stevens, Wallace. *Collected Poems.* New York: Knopf, 1954.

————. *Opus Posthumous: Poems, Plays, Prose*, ed. Samuel French Morse. New York: Knopf, 1957.

Stewart, John L. *The Burden of Time: The Fugitives and Agrarians*. Princeton: Princeton University Press, 1965.

Sundquist, Eric J. "Bringing Home the Word: Magic, Lies, and Silence in Hart Crane." *ELH* 44, no. 2 (Summer 1977): 376–99.

Susman, Warren I. *Culture as History: The Transformation of American Society in the Twentieth Century*. New York: Pantheon, 1984.

Tate, Allen. *Collected Poems, 1919–1976*. New York: Farrar, Straus and Giroux, 1977.

————. *Essays of Four Decades*. Chicago: Swallow, 1968.

————. "The Fallacy of Humanism." *Criterion* 8 (July 1929): 661–81.

————. *The Fathers*. New York: G. P. Putnam's, 1938.

————. "Fundamentalism" (review). *Nation* 122 (May 1926): 532–34.

————. *Jefferson Davis, His Rise and Fall: A Biographical Narrative*. New York: Minton, Balch, 1929.

————. *Memoirs and Opinions, 1926–1974*. Chicago: Swallow, 1975.

————. *Mr. Pope and Other Poems*. New York: Minton, Balch, 1928.

————. "One Escape from the Dilemma" (essay). *Fugitive* 3 (1924): 34–36.

————. *The Poetry Reviews of Allen Tate, 1922–1944*, ed. Ashley Brown and Frances Neel Cheney. Baton Rouge: Louisiana State University Press, 1983.

————. "Sonnet: To a Portrait of Hart Crane" (poem). *Double Dealer* 5 (March–April 1923): 123.

————. *Stonewall Jackson, the Good Soldier: A Narrative*. New York: Minton, Balch, 1928.

————. "Waste Lands" (correspondence). *Literary Review* of the *New York Evening Post* 3 (August 4, 1923): 886.

————. "Introduction." *White Buildings: Poems by Hart Crane*. New York: Liveright, 1926.

————. "Whose Ox" (essay). *Fugitive* 1 (December 1922): 99–100.

Tate, Allen, ed. *A Southern Vanguard: The John Peale Bishop Memorial Volume*. New York: Prentice-Hall, 1947.

Tate, Allen, and Donald Davidson. *The Literary Correspondence of Donald Davidson and Allen Tate*, ed. John Tyree Fain and Thomas Daniel Young. Athens: University of Georgia Press, 1974.

Tate, Allen, and Herbert Agar, eds. *Who Owns America?: A New Declaration of Independence*. Boston: Houghton Mifflin, 1936.

Tate, Allen, and John Peale Bishop. *The Republic of Letters in America: The Correspondence of John Peale Bishop and Allen Tate*, ed. Thomas Daniel Young and John J. Hindle. Lexington: University Press of Kentucky, 1981.

Tichi, Cecilia. *Shifting Gears: Technology, Literature, Culture in Modernist America*. Chapel Hill: University of North Carolina Press, 1987.

Trachtenberg, Alan. *Brooklyn Bridge: Fact and Symbol*. Chicago: University of Chicago Press, 1965.

————. "Cultural Revisions in the Twenties: Brooklyn Bridge as Usable Past." In *The American Self: Myth, Ideology, and Popular Culture*, ed. Sam B. Girgus. Alburquerque: University of New Mexico Press, 1981.

Trachtenberg, Alan, ed. *Critics of Culture: Literature and Society in the Early Twentieth Century*. New York: Wiley, 1976.

———. *Hart Crane: A Collection of Critical Essays*. Englewood Cliffs, N.J.: Prentice-Hall, 1982.

Trilling, Lionel. *Beyond Culture: Essays on Literature and Learning*. New York: Horizon, 1967.

Twelve Southerners. *I'll Take My Stand: The South and the Agrarian Tradition*, intro. and ed., Louis D. Rubin, Jr. Baton Rouge: Louisiana State University Press, 1977.

Unterecker, John. *Voyager: A Life of Hart Crane*. New York: Liveright, 1969.

von Hallberg, Robert. "American Poet-Critics Since 1945." In *Reconstructing American Literary History*, ed. Sacvan Bercovitch, 280–99. Cambridge: Harvard University Press, 1986.

———. *American Poetry and Culture, 1945–1980*. Cambridge: Harvard University Press, 1985.

Wald, Alan M. *The New York Intellectuals: The Rise and Decline of the Anti-Stalinist Left from the 1930s to the 1980s*. Chapel Hill: University of North Carolina Press, 1987.

Waldron, Ann. *Close Connections: Caroline Gordon and the Southern Renaissance*. New York: Putnam, 1987.

Walker, Pat, ed. *Between Labor and Capital*. Boston: South End, 1979.

Ware, Caroline F. *Greenwich Village, 1920–1930: A Comment on American Civilization in the Post-war Years*. Boston: Houghton Mifflin, 1935.

Warner, Michael. "Thoreau's Bottom." *Raritan* 11, no. 3 (1992): 53–79.

Weaver, Raymond. *Herman Melville: Mariner and Mystic*. New York: Doran, 1921.

Weber, Brom. *Hart Crane: A Biographical and Critical Study*. New York: Bodley, 1948.

Wertheim, Arthur Frank. *The New York Little Renaissance: Iconoclasm, Modernism, and Nationalism in American Culture, 1908–1917*. New York: New York University Press, 1976.

Whitman, Walt. *Leaves of Grass: A Textual Variorum of the Printed Poems*. Vol. 1, *Poems, 1855–56*, ed. Sculley Bradley, Harold W. Blodgett, Arthur Golden, and William White. New York: New York University Press, 1980.

Wicke, Jennifer A. *Advertising Fictions: Literature, Advertisement, and Social Reading*. New York: Columbia University Press, 1988.

Wilde, Oscar. *De Profundis and Other Writings*. New York: Penguin, 1954.

Williams, Raymond. *Culture and Society 1780–1950*. New York: Columbia University Press, 1950.

———. *The Politics of Modernism: Against the New Conformists*, ed. Tony Pinkney. London: Verso, 1989.

Williams, William Carlos. *Paterson*. New York: New Directions, 1958.

Wimsatt, William K., Jr. *The Verbal Icon: Studies in the Meaning of Poetry*. Lexington: University of Kentucky Press, 1954.

Winters, Yvor. *The Collected Poems of Yvor Winters*. Manchester (England): Carcanet, 1978.

———. *In Defense of Reason*. Chicago: Swallow, 1947.

————. "Poets and Others." *Hound and Horn* 5 (July–September 1932): 675–86.
————. "The Progress of Hart Crane." In Trachtenberg, ed., *Crane: Critical Essays*, 23–31.
————. "In Vindication of Poetry." *New Republic* 56 (October 17, 1928): 255–56.
Woods, Gregory. *Articulate Flesh: Male Homo-Eroticism and Modern Poetry*. New Haven: Yale University Press, 1987.
Yingling, Thomas E. *Hart Crane and the Homosexual Text: New Thresholds, New Anatomies*. Chicago: University of Chicago Press, 1990.
Young, Thomas Daniel. *Gentleman in a Dustcoat: A Biography of John Crowe Ransom*. Baton Rouge: Louisiana State University Press, 1976.

Index